PROBABLE CAUSE

By 9:30 or 9:45, Carol and Mark became anxious. What was going on? Finally Carol called the police station since it was getting late and the girls needed to be put to bed. The receptionist said the interviews were just about finished.

A short time later, three uniformed officers came to the Doggett ____ Mark met them on the front ____ hardly a word, a co____ ____ on him, grabbed ____ ____ ____cular of police ____ ____ ____ruiser. At the ____ ____ what happened. ____ ____ later, there was another ____ ____ door.

"Officer ____ has probable cause to arrest you on rape of a child in the first."

"What!" gasped Carol, flabbergasted. She felt the metallic snap of the handcuffs at her wrists.

———

WITCH HUNT

A True Story of Social Hysteria and Abused Justice

KATHRYN LYON

AVON BOOKS  NEW YORK

WITCH HUNT is an investigative account of the 1992–1997 child abuse scandal that took place in Wenatchee, Washington. The events recounted in this book are true. The scenes and dialogue have been reconstructed based on recorded formal interviews, police department and other official records, and published news stories. Quoted testimony has been taken verbatim from trial and pretrial transcripts and other sworn statements.

AVON BOOKS
A division of
The Hearst Corporation
1350 Avenue of the Americas
New York, New York 10019

Copyright © 1998 by Kathryn Lyon
Published by arrangement with the author
Visit our website at **http://www.AvonBooks.com**
Library of Congress Catalog Card Number: 97-94318
ISBN: 0-380-79066-1

First Avon Books Printing: March 1998

AVON TRADEMARK REG. U.S. PAT. OFF. AND IN OTHER COUNTRIES, MARCA REGISTRADA, HECHO EN U.S.A.

Printed in the U.S.A.

WCD   10 9 8 7 6 5 4 3 2 1

*To Adrian, Kris, Jeff, Mom, Peter, and the
many wronged families of Wenatchee*

AUTHOR'S NOTE AND ACKNOWLEDGMENTS

In writing this book, I have had to balance the concerns of historical accuracy against the privacy of children. Whether they were abused by a broad network of family, friends, or neighbors (as some authorities claim), or by the intervention of the authorities who are sworn to protect them (as I believe), these children have suffered enormously and I have no desire to subject them to needless embarrassment. On the other hand, it is my opinion that family identities must be recognized in order to remedy the significant wrongs they and their parents have endured. Accountability in such cases has long been compromised, in part because family court proceedings are secret and other state interventions hidden from public scrutiny. Recognizing there is no perfect solution, I have arrived at an awkward one. In circumstances where one or more parents of a child now under the age of eighteen were charged in court proceedings and identified in the public record, I have changed the first names of the children. In cases where parents were uncharged, I have changed both the first and last names of the children. In no other way is this book a work of fiction.

I am grateful to all those who helped make legal and

government documents available to me, and who must remain nameless in the face of ongoing government reprisals. I wholeheartedly thank the many Wenatchee citizens who opened their hearts and minds to make this book possible at a time when speaking out carried dangerous consequences. I wish to thank my friends—many of them strangers when this project began—who offered insight, support, and consolation, among them Cynthia, Dominic, Matt, Jack, and Martha; and the distinguished social scientists, jurists, and journalists who generously contributed to the pages of this book, among them Dr. Steven Ceci, Dr. Richard Gardner, Richard Wexler, Dr. John Yuille, Professor John E. B. Myers, Dr. Roland Summit, Dr. Elizabeth Loftus, Luci Berliner, Dr. Lee Coleman, Dr. Richard Soderstrom, William Claiborne of the *Washington Post*, John Carlin of the *Independent*, Trevor Armbrister of *Reader's Digest*, and Siegesmund Von Ilsemann of *Der Spiegel*. I will be forever grateful to those who stuck with me when I threw conventional wisdom to the winds, especially my family who showed me the purest form of unconditional love in the face of the enormous sacrifices my work in Wenatchee entailed: my husband, Adrian, my sons Jeff and Kris, my mother Ethel.

Finally, I am fortunate in my enthusiastic and supportive editor, Coates Bateman, who has shaped this into a better book, and in my energetic agent, Peter Rubie, who inspired me with his vision, his humanity, and his unswerving belief that I was something more than myself.

Contents

x   **Contents**

Contents

Friends and Neighbors

THE EVERETT FAMILY

Idella and Harold Everett are profoundly limited (Idella has an IQ tested between 58 and 68; Harold is illiterate) and very poor. For years their children **Ann, Matthew, Mary,** and twins **Robert** and **Steven** were questioned by state officials and therapists but denied they were incest victims. In October 1993 Ann was placed in foster care with Robert Devereaux. In March 1994, she was removed and placed in foster care with Wenatchee police detective Robert Perez and his wife Luci; in June 1994, her sister Mary joined her. After years of therapy and months of questioning by Perez, the girls came to name approximately one hundred former family friends, neighbors, and relatives as their molesters, including their parents. Idella and Harold Everett ''confessed'' after Perez interrogated them, then pled guilty. They remain in prison, their children in foster care, group homes, and mental health facilities.

THE HOLT FAMILY

Laura and Selid "Sid" Holt lived in the Everett neighborhood with their children, **Pam, Donald**, and **Michael Holt**. The family was poor. Laura named her husband as Pam's molester after an argument. Shortly after Detective Perez became head of the sex crimes unit, he became suspicious of Laura as well. State officials took the Holt children into custody and Perez questioned them and eventually they named their parents. After interrogation by Perez, Laura and Sid Holt "confessed" and were later convicted and sent to prison. Their children remain in foster care.

THE TOWN FAMILY

Cherie and Meridith "Gene" Town also lived in the Everett neighborhood. Cherie has an IQ of 77 and the family was poor. Cherie reported Gene for molesting his sons, including **Jeff** and **Walter**, after an argument. State officials took the children into custody. Perez interrogated Cherie and she "confessed" and later the children named their parents. Both parents pled guilty and were sent to prison. The children remain in foster care and mental health facilities.

THE RODRIGUEZ FAMILY

Donna Rodriguez and her daughter **Kelly Allbee** once lived down the street from the Everetts. Kelly was a good friend of Ann and Mary Everett. After Ann named Donna among her molesters, Perez interrogated Kelly at her school for several hours. After a time she named several molesters, but she immediately recanted once she was released. Donna was arrested, refused to confess, and her case was later dismissed. Kelly resides with her mother.

THE FILBECK FAMILY

Gary and Scharlann Filbeck were neighbors of the Everetts. Both Gary and Scharlann are profoundly limited (Scharlann has an IQ in the 70s; Gary is totally illiterate) and were very poor and unable to work. Gary was formerly convicted of molesting the couple's daughter, **Caroline**, and for years the girl had been a foster child in the home of Robert Devereaux. After Ann Everett named the Filbecks as molesters, Perez interrogated the Filbecks, who "confessed." Both pled guilty and were released pending sentencing as part of a "deal" to testify against others. Scharlann recanted to the author; Gary testified against Pastor Robert and Connie Roberson and Honnah Sims. The couple received the benefit of the plea bargain: no further jail, and community treatment.

THE MILLER FAMILY

Linda Miller, divorced from **Larry Steinborn**, lived in the Everett neighborhood with her daughters, **Aubrey** and **Charlene**, and sons, **Mark** and **Allen**. After Linda was named by Ann Everett, Perez interrogated Charlene, who named her mother and others. Linda was taken into custody at the Canadian border and driven back to Wenatchee, where Perez interrogated her for several hours starting at midnight. At last she "confessed" and named several others, including the Robersons and Devereaux. She was convicted after trial and sentenced to thirty-three years, but her conviction was overturned and remanded for a new trial in June 1997. Miller's children remain in foster care.

Larry Steinborn, previously convicted for child molestation and on probation, was offered a "deal" in exchange for his agreement to testify against others. The charges against him were later dismissed based on this agreement.

DONNA HIDALGO

Donna Hidalgo is an adult half-sister of Ann and Mary Everett, and lived for a time in a small outbuilding on the Everett property. Her boyfriend was **Manuel Hidalgo-Rodriguez,** a Mexican field laborer who could speak little English. After Ann named Donna, Perez interrogated her, but she refused to confess. She went to trial, the jury hung, and Donna later accepted a plea bargain to greatly reduced charges. She has now served her time and lives in the community, subject to conditions such as registration as a sex offender.

MANUEL HIDALGO-RODRIGUEZ

Manuel Hidalgo-Rodriguez was named by Ann, but he refused to confess and was convicted after trial and sent to prison. The conviction was upheld in the spring of 1997 by the Washington State Court of Appeals. His appellate attorney failed to raise the issue of Perez's relationship with his foster daughters, Ann and Mary. Nor did he raise the issue that the state had amended the information on the eve of trial, adding Ann Everett, on whose testimony his conviction was based.

THE GARAAS-GAUSVIK FAMILY

Barbara Garaas and **Ralph Gausvik** were an indigent family who lived across the street from the Everetts. Ann Everett named them when she went on a lengthy car excursion, which came to be known as the "parade of homes." Both were questioned by Perez but refused to confess. Their children **Tony, Brandon, Laura**, and **Deborah**, were taken into custody by state officials pursuant to a "voluntary" placement agreement that officials pressed them to sign. The children were questioned by therapists, state officials, and Perez and eventually named their parents. Gausvik was convicted at trial and received a sentence over twenty years; Garaas later pled guilty to reduced charges and remains in prison. Their children remain in foster care.

THE BENDT FAMILY

Jeanie Bendt's son **Josh** was questioned by Perez at school and at a mental health facility. He came to name his mother, her boyfriend, and various others. Some of these charges against others were dismissed in part because of problems with Josh's credibility and mental state. Jeanie was interrogated by Perez, "confessed," and later pleaded guilty on advice of her attorney and was sent to prison. The state has terminated her parental rights to Josh.

THE CUNNINGHAM FAMILY

Connie and Henry Cunningham were arrested and interrogated by Perez. Henry confessed and implicated Connie. Their daughters, **Jenny** and **Susan**, said their father raped them and their mother sometimes watched. Henry pled guilty; Connie went to trial and was convicted, largely based on her husband's written confession, although he didn't testify. She was sentenced to forty-six years in prison, but in May 1997 the Washington State Court of Appeals overturned the conviction and remanded the case for a new trial. She was released from prison on

July 11, 1997; by all indications the state does not intend to refile the charges.

THE DOGGETT FAMILY

Carol and Mark Doggett took in the Cunningham children as foster children after Connie Cunningham's arrest. The Doggetts also lived with their children **Ashley, Melinda, Jeremy,** and **Lisa;** their teenage daughter **Sam** was staying with her godmother in California when the problems with her family began. Carol and Mark reported to authorities (Perez and CPS supervisor Tim Abbey) that their son Jeremy had molested one of their girls, and asked that the state place him in custody for the protection of their girls until he could be stabilized in therapy. Perez declined to charge and Abbey declined to intervene. When the Doggetts sent Jeremy to stay with a relative, Perez became suspicious and interrogated the boy, who eventually named his parents. Perez questioned other Doggett children, then arrested Mark and Carol and interrogated them. Although neither confessed, they were jailed and charged. The children were then subjected to rounds of questioning by Perez, caseworkers and therapists, and at various times most of them variously named their parents and recanted. At trial, although the children described patterns of coercion by Perez, the Doggetts were convicted for molesting one of their daughters and sentenced to eleven years in prison. The children remain in foster care.

THE ROBERSON FAMILY

Pastor Robert and Connie Roberson ran the East Wenatchee Pentecostal House of Prayer and a food bank in its basement, and were raising their young daughter when the problems began. Many of the people who had been accused, including the Everetts and Donna Rodriguez, were members of the Roberson church and Robert began to doubt the children were victims and to forcefully question the official investigation. He gathered records and spoke critically in public. Soon he fell under suspicion. Perez questioned his foster daughters, Ann and Mary Everett, and other children and vulnerable adults, and they named the Robersons. They were arrested, jailed, and charged with multiple counts of child rape in March 1995, a few days after Roberson spoke out at a public forum. At trial in December 1995, the Robersons were acquitted of all charges. The Robersons' daughter **Roberta** was returned to their care by state officials.

THE SIMS FAMILY

Arrested in connection with the Pentecostal church after being named by Ann and Mary Everett and other children and vulnerable adults was Sunday School teacher **Honnah Sims**. She was acquitted at trial in July 1995, after she hired a private attorney. Her child remains at home.

THE DAVIS FAMILY

Bill Davis, Pentecostal church van driver, was arrested and charged after being named by various children, including Ann Everett. He made no admissions, and the charges were dismissed in late 1995, during the Roberson trial.

THE DEVEREAUX FOSTER FAMILY

Robert Devereaux was a divorced foster father who ran a group home for girls. After the divorce, Perez and DCFS officials became suspicious that he might give in to what they perceived as a natural male urge to molest girls. After Devereaux grounded his foster daughter **Theresa Sanchez,** she laced Devereaux's soft drink with iodine. Perez questioned her at juvenile hall and she named Devereaux as her molester. The next day she recanted to her caseworker **Paul Glassen** and said Perez had pressured her to lie. Devereaux was interrogated by Perez and arrested. Perez also interrogated several of Devereaux's former foster daughters, some of whom eventually named him, including Perez's foster daughter Ann Everett, and **Bonnie Rogers,** a girl who admittedly made several false sex abuse allegations in the past. Shortly before trial, prosecutors dismissed all felony charges against Devereaux.

PAUL GLASSEN

Paul Glassen reported **Theresa Sanchez**'s recantation about Devereaux to authorities. The next day he was arrested for witness tampering and later charged with obstructing justice. After a visiting judge dismissed the charges, Glassen's name began to regularly appear as a suspected child molester in Perez's reports of his regular rounds of questioning children and vulnerable adults, including his foster daughter Ann Everett. Glassen was never charged based on these allegations, but state officials placed him on administrative leave and later fired him from his job as a State of Washington Child Welfare Services (CWS) caseworker, as well as two of his supporters, CWS supervisor **Juana Vasquez** and caseworker **Juan Garcia.**

There are many others who were accused, interrogated, and charged. Nearly thirty men and women have been convicted; most remain in prison; some thirty children remain in foster homes, group homes, or mental health facilities.

Criminal Dispositions

CONVICTIONS AT TRIAL

- Abel Foncesco Lopez*
- Sid Holt*
- Connie Cunningham
- Dorris Green*
- Michael Rose*
- Manuel Hidalgo-Rodriguez
- Linda Miller*
- Carol Doggett
- Mark Doggett
- Ralph Gausvik

GUILTY PLEAS TO FELONY CHARGES

- Alan Hughes
- Gordon Page
- Cherie Town*

*Confession

- Meridith Town*
- Timothy Durst*
- Joyce Durst*
- Laura Holt*
- Randall Reed*
- Idella Everett*
- Harold Everett*
- Larry Steinborn* (first case)
- Sadi Hughes*
- Gary Filbeck*
- Scharlann Filbeck*
- Lawrence "Leo" Catcheway*
- Barbara Garaas
- Donna Hidalgo
- Henry Cunningham*

DISMISSALS OF FELONY CHARGES

- Noberto Castanada-Macius
- Kathryn Lancaster
- James Buckley
- Donna Rodriguez
- Pam Kimble
- Robert Devereaux
- Edward Lyle Knowles, Jr.
- Edward Lyle Knowles, Sr.
- Bill Davis
- Kerri Knowles
- Karen Lopez
- Larry Steinborn* (second case)

ACQUITTALS AFTER TRIALS

- •Honnah Sims
- •Robert Roberson
- •Connie Roberson

CONVICTIONS REVERSED

- •Connie Cunningham
- •Linda Miller*

Chronology

2/26/92   **Ann Everett** (age seven) sister of **Matthew** (age eleven), **Mary** (age nine), and twins **Robert** and **Steven** (age six), and daughter of illiterate and mentally disabled **Harold and Idella Everett,** was questioned by school, Child Protective Services, and police officials. Ann said two six-year-olds touched her privates the day before. Over the next few days officials questioned Ann, who repeated her allegations. When police questioned Robert, he remembered the incident and verified Ann's story.

Examination of **Ann Everett** by emergency room doctor: Genitals ''grossly normal.''

3/3/92   Examination of **Ann Everett** by doctor who often testified for the state: Genital irregularities consistent with sexual abuse.

CPS persuaded **Harold and Idella Everett** to sign "voluntary placement agreement." **Ann** placed in foster care and repeatedly questioned.

3/16/92   **Ann Everett** disclosed molestation by "Abel" to authorities.

3/19/92   Arrest, interrogation of **Abel Foncesco-Lopez** by police. (Convicted at trial.)

3/92   **Ann Everett** returned home; placed in therapy focusing on abuse.

7/92   Twins **Robert and Steven Everett** placed in therapy focusing on abuse issues.

3/9/93   After a year of questioning, **Robert, Steven, and Ann Everett** told officials their father, **Harold Everett,** hit them with his belt.

3/10/93   **Harold Everett** ordered by CPS to leave Everett home.

4/1/93   (Approximate.) At CPS urging, Idella Everett again signed "voluntary placement agreement." **Robert and Steven Everett** placed in separate foster homes. (Robert ran back home after a few days and refused to return to foster home.)

4/8/93   **Robert Everett** placed by CPS in Pine Crest mental hospital in Idaho. **Ann** and **Steven Everett** scheduled for stays at Pine Crest.

5/5/93   **Mary Everett** placed in therapy by CPS.

5/10/93   Dependency hearing reports: Although the **Everett family** were extremely "bonded" and obviously suffering from Harold's absence, and although Harold had met all CPS conditions, the family was not reunited.

9/24/93   Arrest, interrogation of **Sid Holt** by Perez after **Laura Holt**, following a domestic dispute, turned him in for molesting their daughter **Pam Holt**. Perez and other police interviewed Pam and her brother **Donald,** who disclosed abuse by their parents. Confession. (Later guilty plea.)

10/93   **Ann Everett** placed in Devereaux foster home.

1/1/94   (Approximate.) **Robert Perez** took over as head of sex crimes unit of Wenatchee Police Department. Brief initial training by CPS and local police.

1/10/94   **Laura Holt** took Pam to Perez to report **Leo Catcheway** as another of Pam's molesters. Perez expressed suspicion of her motives.

1/13/94   **Pam, Donald, Michael Holt** placed in foster care by CPS.

1/24/94   First charges filed against **Larry Steinborn**. Confession. (Later plea and sentencing to suspended sentence on condition of community treatment. **Aubrey Miller** later admitted to Perez and other authorities that she, **Charlene Miller**, and **Bonnie Rogers** lied about Steinborn molesting them.)

2/15/94   DCFS dependency reports: **Everett children** continue to suffer from separation from their family, and to deny abuse. **Steven** regularly harmed himself and had threatened suicide.

3/23/94   **Ann Everett** placed at Perez foster home after Devereaux said he was unable to cope with her, although the Perez home was not then licensed for girls.

4/1/94   Arrest and interview of **Meridith "Gene" Town** by Perez after **Cherie Town,** following domestic dispute, turned him in for molesting their sons. Confession. (Later plea and stipulation to twenty-year exceptional sentence.)

4/5/94   Arrest and interview of **Cherie Town** by Perez. Confession. (Later guilty plea.)

5/94   **Robert Perez** completed fifty hours of training at the Washington State Criminal Justice Training Center.

5/26/94   Arrest and interview of **Timothy and Joyce Durst**. Confession. (Later guilty plea.)

6/6/94   Interview of **Jenny and Susan Cunningham**. No disclosures.

Arrest and interview of father **Henry Cunningham** by Perez. Confession.

6/10/94   Perez reinterviewed **Jenny and Susan Cunningham**. Perez told them their father admitted molesting them and at last they made disclosures. Arrest and interview of **Connie Cunningham** by Perez. No confession. (Later convicted at trial for complicity to incest and sentenced to forty-six years.)

6/94   Perez joked at lunch about **Robert Devereaux** molesting his foster girls. Among those present: **Juan Garcia** and **Paul Glassen,** who later formally complained.

7/7/94   **Pam Holt** disclosed molestations by mother **Laura Holt** in counseling.

Interview and arrest of **Laura Holt** by Perez. Confronted with statement of Pam. Confession. Booked on 1,528 counts. (Later guilty plea.)

7/11/94   Perez interviewed **Pam, Donald Holt.** Both named their parents; Pam named Gene Town.

7/30/94   Interview of **Kate Sanchez,** a foster girl of Devereaux's, by Wenatchee Police Officer T. Adcock. Admitted putting iodine in **Robert Devereaux**'s drink.

8/3/94   Interview of **Kate Sanchez** by Perez in juvenile hall. Statement that **Devereaux** molested her and other foster girls.

Interview of **Bonnie Rogers** and several other Devereaux foster girls by Perez. No disclosure concerning Devereaux.

Interview and arrest of **Robert Devereaux** by Perez. Disputed confession.

Reinterview of **Bonnie Rogers** by Perez after she spent several hours in room at police department with a caseworker. Bonnie disclosed molestations by Devereaux.

8/4/94   CWS caseworker **Paul Glassen** interviewed **Kate Sanchez**, who recanted to him and said she lied under pressure from Perez. Glassen reported the incident.

8/5/94   Arrest of **Paul Glassen** for witness tampering for interviewing/taking down recantation of Kate Sanchez. (Charges later amended to obstructing justice and still later dismissed by pro tem judge, but Glassen was fired following extensive period of forced administrative leave.)

9/14/94   Perez interview/arrest **Dorris Green**. Confession. (Trial conviction: twenty-three years.)

9/20/94   Perez and CPS again questioned **Holt and Town children**, who said their parents were involved in swapping children with other adults.

9/23/94   **Ann Everett** disclosed in Perez home to Bob and Luci Perez that parents **Harold and Idella Everett** molested her.

9/24/94   Interview of **Mary Everett** by Perez and CPS. Disclosed molestations by parents.

9/25/94   Arrest and interview of **Harold and Idella and Everett** by Perez. Probable cause found in each case: 6,422 counts. Confessions. (Later guilty pleas, in Idella's case without resolving issue of competency.)

Pastor Roberson went to courthouse and confronted Chelan County deputy prosecutor about his belief the Everetts were innocent.

9/27/94   Interview of **Robert Everett** by Perez. Disclosure concerning parents.

Foster parents of **Robert, Steven, and Mary Everett** reported that the children were extremely upset because Perez told them they would never be going home and they would never see their parents again.

9/30/94   CPS urged **Jeanie Bendt** to sign ''voluntary placement agreement.'' Interview of son **Josh Bendt** at new foster home by Perez, Katie Carrow. Disclosed molestations by Jeanie Bendt and her boyfriend Noberto Macius.

10/94   **Pastor Robert Roberson** went to dependency court to try to get custody of **Matthew Everett,** eldest Everett son. Perez in attendance.

10/4/94   Interview and arrest of **Jeanie Bendt** by Perez. Confession. (Later guilty plea.)

10/5/94   Interview and arrest of **Noberto Macius** by Perez. (Dismissed March 22, 1995.)

10/7/94   CPS caseworker Connie Saracino told **Pastor Roberson** that Perez said he would arrest him if he contacted the Everett children or went to court.

10/25/94   Perez urged DCFS officials to immediately remove the **Everett children** from counseling at
           Children's Home Society, because the "counselors at CHS wouldn't be strong witnesses in
           court." State authorities complied.

11/6/94   (Approximate). Arrest and interview of **Leo
           Catcheway** by Perez. Confession and plea.

11/10/94   Wenatchee CPS supervisor Tim Abbey wrote
           to DCFS state administrators that Children's
           Home Society staff feared arrest for obstructing justice.

12/12/94   **Carol and Mark Doggett** told CPS their son
           Jeremy molested their daughter, and requested
           help for the family. After determining the acts
           were consensual, police and CPS took no action.

12/21/94   **Lisa Doggett** went to California to visit with
           her sister **Sam Doggett.**

12/28/94   Perez and CPS interviewed **Jeremy, Melinda,
           and Ashley Doggett**, who allegedly made
           some statements, and then placed them in foster care and therapy.

           Arrest and interview of **Carol and Mark Doggett** by Perez. No admission.

1/3/95   (Approximate.) Perez and CPS caseworker
           flew to California to transport **Sam and Lisa
           Doggett** to Wenatchee. Placed in separate foster homes.

1/10/95   **Sam Doggett** taken by ambulance to Pine Crest Hospital and released February 7, 1995.

1/20/95   **Ann Everett** made statements to Perez in his home about several molesters.

1/23/95   Interview of **Mary Everett** by Perez and CPS. Reluctant statements about multiple abusers. Mary told therapist she was part of **"the circle."**

        Interview of **Ann Everett** by Perez at home: named several molesters.

1/30/95   **Pastor Roberson** attended **Idella Everett** sentencing and spoke up on her behalf. Allegedly Perez said to him, "We warned you, Roberson, we warned you."

1/95   (Approximate.) Motion to dismiss filed by attorney for **Paul Glassen.**

2/1/95   Interview of **Ann Everett** by Perez concerning **Devereaux.** Statement: Adults (including Glassen and Devereaux) stood in line to have sex with kids.

2/2/95   Interview of **Kelly Allbee** by Perez and CPS. Statements concerning multiple adults.

        Arrest and interview of **Donna Rodriguez** (mother of Kelly Allbee) by Perez.

2/3/95   **Kelly Allbee** released from state custody to father after mother **Donna Rodriguez** refused to sign "voluntary placement agreement." Family made arrangements for Kelly to be videotaped by a representative of VOCAL.

2/95   **Bob Kinkade,** VOCAL representative, filed complaint with Wenatchee police; submitted **Kelly Allbee** videotape. (Shortly after, Perez obtained warrant for Kelly's arrest.)

2/6/95   Pro tem judge dismissed charges against **Paul Glassen.**

2/7/95   Interview of **Idella Everett** by Perez at jail. Statements concerning multiple abusers who swapped kids or paid money for admission to orgies.

2/8/95   Interview of **Bonnie Rogers** by Perez. After initial denial said she and others were molested by Devereaux, Larry Steinborn, and Paul Glassen.

2/13/95   Arrest and interview of **Donna Hidalgo** by Perez for molestations of Everett children. (While awaiting trail, Hidalgo was offered deals based on willingness to testify against **Glassen, Kinkade, Devereaux,** and others. When she refused, the matter went to trial: Hung jury and later plea to a single count of incest.)

3/3/95   Interview of **Ann Everett** at Perez home. Statements concerning Donna Rodriguez.

            Interview of **Jeff Town** by Perez at mental facility. Statements concerning orgies at several

homes, Pentecostal church where kids sometimes fell into trances.

3/6/95   Psychological evaluation: **Steven Everett's** mental condition worsened in the course of therapy and foster care (suicide threats/attempts, self-mutilation.)

3/13/95   Perez and CPS caseworker took **Ann Everett** for a drive: Ann pointed out many locations where she said she and other children were molested.

3/14/95   Six-hour interview of **Ann Everett** by Perez and CPS: Ann named multiple molesters and victims of orgies in the homes she identified the day before.

3/21/95   VOCAL reps **Bob Kinkade** and **Bob Stewart** attended Wenatchee City Counsel meeting and handed out documents and Allbee videotape.

3/23/95   Interview of **Charlene Miller** by Perez: Group sex at Devereaux home, Roberson home, church, and other locations.

    VOCAL public meeting with tapes of Allbee and Aubrey Miller. **Pastor Roberson** attended and did a television interview.

3/24/95   Perez interview of **Linda Miller** for six hours beginning at midnight. Confession named Paul Glassen, Bob Kinkade, Bob Stewart, and many others.

3/27/95   Interview of **Ann Everett** by police and CPS concerning group molestations at Pentecostal church.

           Broadcast of televised VOCAL meeting where **Roberson** was interviewed.

3/28/95   Douglas County and State Patrol search of **Pentecostal church, Roberson home.**

           Arrest and interview of **Pastor Roberson and Connie Roberson.**

3/30/95   Interview of **Mary Everett** by Douglas County Sheriff and CPS with **Ann Everett** present: Many adults did the "wild thing" to her and other kids in a "big room" at the church. In interview that followed, Ann repeated Mary's statements and named nineteen molesters.

4/2/95   Arrest of **Manuel Hidalgo-Rodriguez.**

4/3/95   **Roberta Roberson** located, arrested on material witness warrant.

4/4/95   Interview and arrest of **Kerri Knowles** by Perez, Carrow, John Kruse. Questioned concerning **Bob Kinkade, Bob Devereaux, Paul Glassen.** No admission. (Later dismissed.)

           VOCAL filed suit in U.S. district court against state, county, and city officials.

4/5/95   Interview of **Bonnie Rogers** by Douglas County. Bonnie showed list of abusers and victims she prepared with help, editing by her foster mother.

4/5/95   **Steven Everett** reported as uncontrollable, self-abusive, "in denial," and "noncompliant." Doctor planned to increase his medication.

4/6/95   **Washington State Patrol crime lab** reported all samples from church negative for semen. (This fact was not revealed to the defense for several months.)

Interview of several children on this and following days by Douglas County concerning abuse at church, without disclosures.

(Approximate.) **Steven Everett** ran from foster care and "tried to stick a metal object through his chest."

4/7/95   Interview and arrest of **Larry Steinborn** by Perez and Kruse. Steinborn agreed to a "deal": to testify against others in exchange for no further charges.

4/10/95   Interview of **Charlene Miller** by Douglas County. Admitted Perez and Laurie Alexander said her mother had confessed and what she said. Described molestation by unidentified people wearing black clothes and sunglasses.

4/13/95   Arrest of Pentecostal church van driver **Bill Davis.**

4/20/95   Interview of **Roberta Roberson** by Jeanne
          Dierickx. No disclosure.

4/24/95   Interview of **Michelle Kimble** and her brother
          concerning their mother **Pam Kimble** by
          Perez and CPS. Statements concerning Pam
          Kimble, Pentecostal church, Robersons, Ever-
          etts. (Note: When reinterviewed later by Doug-
          las County sheriff deputy, Michelle recanted
          and said Perez pressured her to lie. Michelle
          said her brother was handcuffed to Perez's
          desk while she was interviewed.)

          Interview and arrest of **Pam Kimble**. No con-
          fession. (Charges later dismissed.)

          ''Town Meeting'' television show taped. **Rob-
          erson, Kinkade, Honnah Sims** were among
          audience members who commented on the air.

4/25/95   During trial of **Mark and Carol Doggett** their
          children described pressures, threats by Perez.
          (Convicted for abusing Melinda and sentenced
          to eleven years.)

4/26/95   Interview of **Bonnie Rogers** by Mike Mag-
          notti and CPS. Discussed list that foster mother
          helped her prepare. (When later confronted af-
          ter investigation, Bonnie said she lied about
          some of the people on the list because of pres-
          sure of the case.)

5/2/95   Arrest and interview of **Scharlann Filbeck** by
          Perez, Magnotti. Confession naming several
          adults, including Devereaux and Glassen.

Arrest and interview of **Gary Filbeck** by Perez. Named several adults: During services at church Pastor Roberson had sex at the altar with children.

5/10/95   Interview of **Aubrey Miller** by Perez, Alexander, and prosecutor: named many adults, including Robersons, Devereaux.

5/11/95   Interview of **Scharlann Filbeck** by Douglas County sheriff's deputy at jail. Statements concerning molestations by church members.

5/22/95   Arrest of **Honnah Sims,** Pentecostal church Sunday School teacher.

5/30/95   Children of **Barbara Garaas, Ralph Gausvik** taken into custody under ''voluntary placement agreement.'' (After days of questioning and therapy, the children named their parents.)

6/95   **Gary and Scharlann Filbeck** pled guilty and were released pending sentencing based on agreement to testify in exchange for no further jail and suspended sentence. (On June 23, Scharlann recanted to author.)

(Approximate.) **Mary Everett** placed as foster child in Perez home. The Perezes took the girls to Disneyland.

7/7/95   Arrest of **Barbara Garaas and Ralph Gausvik.** No admissions.

7/24/95   Wenatchee grassroots group Concerned Citizens for Legal Accountability presents petition with **two thousand signatures** to Chelan and Douglas County commissioners.

7/28/95   Acquittal at jury trial: **Honnah Sims,** who hired private attorney.

8/3/95   Conviction after jury trial: **Manuel Hidalgo-Rodriguez.**

8/8/95   Dismissal all counts: **Donna Rodriguez**, who retained private attorney.

8/24/95   Arrest and interview of **Susan Everett.** Confession. (Later recanted to author.)

          Interview and detention for questioning of **Karen Lopez.**

9/8/95   Chelan County prosecutor's office dropped all felony counts against **Robert Devereaux** in exchange for his plea to misdemeanors.

9/14/95   **Linda Miller** convicted at jury trial and later sentenced to thirty-three years.

9/22/95   **Ann Everett** arrested: malicious mischief for tantrum in Perez home. Released from juvenile hall after she testified against half-sister **Donna Hidalgo.**

9/25/95   **Manuel Hidalgo-Rodriguez** sentenced on one count child molestation 1.

          Dismissal: all charges against **Larry Steinborn** as part of a ''deal.''

9/29/95   Trial of **Donna Hidalgo**: hung jury. (Later pled guilty to reduced charges.)

10/3/95   Letter from Washington State **Governor Mike Lowry** and **House Speaker Clyde Ballard** sent to U.S. Attorney General **Janet Reno** requesting review.

10/16/95   Trials delayed because **Ann Everett** undergoing mental evaluation: She ran away, and lost control around the times she was expected to testify.

11/2/95   Conviction **Ralph Gausvik** after trial. (Later sentenced to twenty-five years.)

11/6/95   State amended charges against **Robert and Connie Roberson** one week before trial with seventeen new counts (new victims and allegations).

11/7/95   Guilty plea: **Susan Everett** to misdemeanor.

11/8/95   Guilty plea: **Donna Hidalgo** to reduced charge of incest.

11/14/95   Trial of **Robert and Connie Roberson** begins with motions.

11/27/95   Guilty plea to two counts incest: **Barbara Garaas.**

12/5/95   Dismissal of all charges: **Karen Lopez.**

12/5/95   Dismissal of charges: **Bill Davis,** Pentecostal bus driver.

12/7/95   Perez testified at Roberson trial that he bruised the arm of **Mary Everett** the morning before she testified against the Robersons (November 30), and earlier twisted her arm behind her back, threw her to the ground, and sat on her.

12/8/95   State Department of Social and Health Services spokesman announced Perez's action was "reasonable restraint."

12/10/95   Arrest and juvenile detention of **Ann Everett** on charges of assault (for kicking her sister Mary) and malicious mischief (for denting the top of the Perez car.)

12/11/95   Acquittal on all counts: **Pastor Robert and Connie Roberson.**

2/2/96   **U.S. Attorney General Janet Reno** declined Justice Department investigation.

2/96 $80 million lawsuit filed on behalf of **Robersons, Honnah Sims, Donna Rodriguiz, Karen Lopez, and Susan Everett** against government officials.

           Lawsuits against government officials filed on behalf of **Robert Devereaux, Juana Vasquez, Paul Glassen, and Juan Garcia.**

6/2/96   **Mary Everett** ran away and recanted to **Roberson;** his attorney, **Robert Van Siclen**; Wenatchee County Commissioner **Earl Marcellus;** and Spokane TV newsman **Tom Grant.** Mary said she lied under pressure from

Perez. She was quickly contained by officials and placed in a ''secure'' facility.

6/96 **Roberson, Van Siclen, Marcellus, and Grant** investigated by authorities on charges of obstructing justice, harboring a runaway, unlawful imprisonment.

11/96 **Mary Everett**'s therapist reported that after Mary recanted and was returned to state custody, she regularly threatened suicide, cut herself with scissors, ran away, sat in street amidst traffic. Mary was then in mental facility.

2/14/97 **Sam Doggett** filed claims against Perez, state and local officials.

5/97 Washington Court of Appeals overturned the forty-three-year conviction and sentence of **Connie Cunningham** and remanded the case for a new trial.

6/97 Washington Court of Appeals overturned the thirty-three-year conviction and sentence of **Linda Miller** and remanded the case for a new trail.

6/19/97 **Complaint and Request for Investigation** filed at the new Washington State Office of Family and Children's Ombudsman. The complaint was based largely on the investigative report by author, and was supported by thousands of signatures and letters of support from legal and social services organizations.

Prologue

When the phenomenon we have come to know as McCarthyism spread its repressive tendrils over academics, artists, and ordinary citizens in the 1950s, it joined a venerable American tradition of national panic and official inquisition. Inquisitions in America, as elsewhere, are a favored line of attack when unorthodox ideas or faceless monsters threaten the established social order. At the helm are impassioned people in powerful positions, driven by the heady sense that their moral codes and goals are also those of their government . . . and, by simple extrapolation, the rest of us.

Typically the accused is often said to be part of a hideous conspiracy; participants are rumored to engage in plots against democracy, or in such antisocial behaviors as bizarre rituals, cannibalism, the maiming and torture of children, incestuous sex, and other exploitation of women and children—our icons of purity. These myths circulate rampantly, sparking panic and outrage among the public.

Although we are a diverse society, our common response to these official targets is transparently predictable. Once we are fully primed by the shocking allegations, once it is clear that dissenters are themselves suspect, the government can count on our fears in order to gain our acquiescence, whatever the method of the inquisition, even if it abridges certain of our constitutional rights. In the long tradition of inquisitions, the accused is presumed guilty and as a practical matter must prove his or her innocence, even if the law places the burden of proving guilt on the state. The framework is simple: The accused may find refuge from certain social and economic ruin only by confessing to real or imaginary sins, crimes, or affiliations, and by spewing out the names of accomplices.

The inquisition of accused witches or religious deviants was an institution that originated in Spain and swept through Europe, starting in the thirteenth century. After England discontinued its practice of burning heretics and adopted a Bill of Rights, the practice crossed the Atlantic to the Massachusetts Bay Colonies.

In the seventeenth century, the very existence of the civilized societies of Salem Village (now Danvers, Massachusetts) and Salem Town (now Salem) depended on their allegiance to the authorities. Puritan society was rigidly cohesive and homogenous; the values of the controlling authorities set the patterns of acceptable behavior. Deviation from society's norms was considered heresy.

The Puritans believed that only a merciless God—and an inspired preacher—could deliver them from the seductive wiles of Satan. When piety and obedience failed, God reached out through the law and through public reprobation: Sinners were pelted with eggs, placed in stocks, publicly whipped, forced to cower abjectly in public places with signs announcing their crimes. A man was whipped for "slothfulness" when he missed a day of worship because he fell in the water, was unable to dry his only suit of clothes, and stayed in bed to keep warm. Another was put in stocks for "lewd and unseemly" conduct when he kissed his wife in public on the Sabbath. Today, at a time when offenders are demonized in the press, or ordered to take out ads or erect signs announcing their crimes, we've come a long way to remind ourselves of an ancient lesson: Public humiliation is a powerful force for conformity.

Witchcraft was among the few crimes punishable by death. Even the most educated of New England gentry believed that once an otherwise mortal woman had put her mark to the devil's contract she could propel herself through the air, perform feats of superhuman strength, alter her appearance, and bestow frightful calamities on her victims. Of thirty-six "witches" executed in America, twenty died in Salem in 1692 based on the words and inexplicable behaviors of a handful of girls. Alarmed parents and authorities concluded there was only one explanation for the girls' fits of screaming, twitching, and wide-eyed trances: the hand of Satan. Soon a number of girls became "afflicted," and the community reacted in a contagion of panic.

The fanatical Reverend Samuel Parris had recently ascended to the pulpit amid a storm of contention. When his daughter started to show alarming and inexplicable physical symptoms, he showed his leadership and community solidarity in the face of Satan by encouraging the relentless questioning of the girl and her friends: young girls between ages eleven and thirteen who often hung out together within the spare confines of their lives.

City fathers called on witch experts and gathered in awed circles around the girls, hanging on their every word. "Who torments you?" they cried. The girls described frightening visions of specters who pinched, bit, pricked, or threatened them. When it became clear to the girls that the adults wanted names, the girls first named a poor and nagging housewife who went from house to house begging and mumbling to herself, and then a prosperous widow who repeatedly missed church services and was rumored to have lived with her second husband before she married him. Showered with questions and attention, the girls at last described being visited by the spectral selves of family friends, neighbors, and acquaintances and, eventually, some 150 "afflicters."

A key accuser was twelve-year-old Ann Putnam; her father, Thomas Putnam, was an ambitious landowner whose prosperity—the usual yardstick of human worth—was on a downslide. According to historians, Putnam threw himself into a single-minded pursuit of witches as a device for gaining political power. After a time, Ann came to name more than a hundred people who had "afflicted" her.

The Salem witch trials lasted only four and a half months—until the accusations strained official credulity. At trials and hearings, the girls screamed and contorted themselves as the accused were led in and sternly interrogated. Although the girls made most of the accusations, adults caught up in the tide of emotion made the formal charges of witchcraft and provided much of the testimony. Many townsfolk stepped up to the bench and listed their personal woes—dead cattle, failed crops, family illness, the inability to pray—then named suspected "servants of the devil," often quarrelsome neighbors, who had by some look or misdeed brought about these misfortunes. The core of the proof before the tribunals became known as "spectral evidence" because, according to testimony, ghostly visions visited their victims while the specter's human counterpart was far away engaging in seemingly innocent activities—or, as was increasingly the case, locked up in a dungeon.

After preliminary hearings, most of the accused were arrested and many were forcibly searched for "witchmarks" or "witches' teats": small warts, pimples, or blemishes that might be signs that they had suckled the familiars of witches. With or without such evidence, many (except for the lucky few who managed to bribe local jailers and escape) slumped in dark dungeons, chained hand and foot to walls that oozed subterranean moisture, their only options death or deliverance through confession, naming other "witches," and signing a written attestation to their confession. Only the brave or foolhardy resisted; many of them were hanged.

Reason at last overtook Massachusetts' governor. He issued an edict that spectral evidence would no longer be admissible in court, and the cases soon evaporated. All of the survivors who could pay their court and jail costs—the price of their food, shelter, and chains—were freed, often emerging to personal ruin: their property and livestock confiscated, their health and reputations destroyed. Within five years, Salem officials publicly apologized for their zeal at a Day of Fast and Repentance.

Decades later, shining words of freedom and equal opportunity for all were written into America's Bill of Rights. Witches were out of vogue, but the concept of witch hunts was not. Alien and sedition laws grew in response to our fears of foreigners and suspect organizations. In our new country, with the ideals and promises of the Bill of Rights, these laws seldom found expression. Yet many citizens held firm to their belief that alien groups were plotting to destroy our free society.

America embarked on a course of fierce patriotism, which included the notion that "aliens" were actual or potential conspirators against American-style democracy. The term *alien* was loosely applied, since all but true Native Americans could be said to be alien to American soil. But the American Indians were being systematically wiped out, and blacks, who had arrived in America before many whites, had been slaves and were distrusted and considered alien themselves because their indigenous culture and traditions were different from those of the ruling majority.

Other early targets for conspiracy theories were the Illuminati, a label for any of various societies of intellectuals or spiritualists committed to a life of superior enlightenment (achievement of inner light) through purity and devotion. In 1776, an ex-Jesuit professor tried to combine Jesuit means of education and discipline with "enlightenment" theories. A German attempted to attach the movement to the Order of Free Masons. As the movement evolved, its promoters claimed the goals of "enlightenment" would eventually displace Christianity with a religion of reason and would form the cornerstone for a new system of justice.

According to Voltaire and some of his French colleagues, the Illuminati were said to conduct their affairs in secrecy. These clandestine affairs took on such frightening and mythical dimensions as cannibalism and sexual perversions and the infiltration of right-thinking society. Few Americans could lay claim to having crossed paths with an Illuminate. So, relying on myths also circulating out of France, Spain, and Germany, Roman Catholics and Freemasons became feared targets of conspiracy theories.

Alien paranoia reemerged in the twentieth century. The notion of socialism, with community members sharing in the production and distribution of goods, was perceived by powerful government figures as an alien threat to capitalism and, hence, democracy. After a time, the more generic term of socialism was supplanted in our consciousness by communism, as formulated by Marx, Engels, Lenin, and others: the hypothetical state of a classless society, ruled by the people, who shared economic goods along egalitarian lines. The efforts to achieve the ideal of communism in the Soviet Union, China, and other socialist states was an often brutally revolutionary and dictatorial process, with its actual focus on state needs rather than individual liberties. Nevertheless, the abstract doctrines of socialism and communism had an understandable appeal to many thinking Americans. These views were labeled heresy by a number of government figures.

The seeds of the Red scare were sown by political opportunists after World War II, motivated in part by the pragmatics of enhancing the nation's economy by feeding our fear of war and thus justifying continued production in war-related industries. Most Americans acquiesced to the official policies of J. Edgar Hoover's FBI and the House Special Committee on Un-American Activities, even when these policies played fast and loose with Constitutional freedoms. Those who weren't scared into accepting the government propaganda that communism was indeed devouring the very fabric of our country were aware that to resist this notion might bring suspicion upon them as well.

In the 1940s and 1950s, America's official response to "un-American" doctrines had two prongs, as it did in seventeenth century Salem: the law and public reprobation. The law meted out procedures and penalties for the apprehension and punishment of heretics and traitors. The media not only stirred our most primal fears, but dealt the accused their most devastating blows: public condemnation that socially and economically ostracized them from mainstream society. Actual proof of guilt was of little moment once the headlines had done their work—and, in any case, proof in the tribunals took on minimal dimensions after patriotic citizens turned on friends, family, neighbors, and affiliates for government pay.

McCarthyism neither began nor ended with the term of U.S. Senator Joseph McCarthy (1946–1957). Once Mc-

Carthy became chairman of the Senate Committee on Government Operations after the 1952 presidential election, he became the symbol for a practice of random public accusations, many of them unfounded; media-fueled sensationalism; and heavily inquisitorial investigative methods, including congressional hearings, with their primary target the communists and their sympathizers, who were believed to have infiltrated American society. Among McCarthy's favored targets were notable intellectuals, scientists, writers, artists, directors, performers, architects, educators, musicians, and doctors—a class that, according to the prevailing political view, were inherently suspect because of their ability to disseminate seditious ideas among the unsuspecting public. McCarthy spread the word.

Studio heads, publishing houses, and academic heads were alarmed by the message and, after token resistance, many quickly caved to the government's demands, pledging to do what they could to prevent un-American activities. Studios submitted names of actors and directors to the House committee so that artists could be "cleared" before they were hired. Publishing houses purged their lists of questionable literature and authors. Schools and universities compelled employees to swear loyalty oaths; those teachers who refused were fired and often called before a tribunal.

McCarthy's congressional hearings were archetypes of political scandal, aimed at exposing individual moral failings and criminal activities through a humiliating public hearing process (or leaked closed-session testimony). That paranoias will crop up every twenty or so years in America is predictable; what set this one apart was the fact that the inquisition had become institutionalized, administered by a bureaucracy with access to intelligence and to a media that could not, as a practical matter, function independently.

Students, professionals, and the rest of us developed a paralyzing apathy when it came to public affairs because controversy and discourse carried the risk of stigmatization and indictment. Immigrants were deported; citizens were jailed; those more fortunate were restrained from thought by fear. The media played a vital role in this fear, or reduced the safe scope of our thoughts to the platitudes of magazine pages or television screens.

The voices of American dissenters were muted as the media focused exclusively on the views of the ruling majority. After all, those who printed words of dissent ran the risk of being labeled communist sympathizers—something no capitalistic news agency could afford. Lawyers were discouraged from defending communists or their sympathizers; a display of too much zealotry in the courtroom might result in a jail sentence for contempt or an indictment for sedition.

Political leaders were of necessity caught up in the paranoia. To be ''soft on communism'' was as fatal to a political career as to be ''soft on crime'' is now. Communism was likened to a disease more insidious than cancer, starving the mind and the soul and the body alike. The effect of sustained community hysteria and fear of oppression were devastating to American society. Charlie Chaplin, exiled to Europe by the purge, commented on the impact on American life in a 1955 interview with fellow exile Cedric Belfrage: ''Compassion and the old neighborliness have gone, people stand by and do nothing when friends and neighbors are attacked, libeled and ruined. The worst thing is what it has done to the children. They are being taught to admire and emulate stool pigeons, to betray and to hate, and all in a sickening atmosphere of religious hypocrisy."[1]

The communist purge of the 1940s and 1950s ended after many informants recanted their statements, the perceived threat of Russian infiltration declined, and the U.S. Supreme Court abolished the crime of noninforming. The American public could no longer generate enthusiasm for the inquisitions, and smarted under the realization that our country appeared ludicrous to other nations that had routinely assimilated American culture, ideas, and commercialism without reading something more sinister into our "alien" incursions on their soil.

When we are safely removed from a national panic, it isn't difficult to see it for the manner of beast that it is. We can probe it as a historical event, grievously carried out and curiously tolerated by those who seem remote from us through the passage of time. But all too often we forget who we are, forget that we are part of a civilized society that depends for its very existence on our allegiance to the authorities, forget that in our great gregarious need we have regularly fallen prey to fear, political mind control, and inquisition. When a new outbreak of community panic and official inquiry reoccurs, we may be the last to recognize it for what it is. In an attempt to make sense of our government's arbitrary actions, we tell ourselves: "They must have done *something* wrong."

Beginning in the 1970s and 1980s, an outbreak of community hysteria focused on mass prosecutions for the ritualistic abuse of children. The allegations were monstrous: children being raped, tortured, mutilated, even cannibalized by conspiring adults, often employees of day-care centers, such as the McMartin preschool in Cal-

---

[1] Belfrage, Cedric, *The American Inquisition 1945–1960: A Profile of the "McCarthy Era"* (New York: Thunder's Mouth Press, 1989), p. 179.

ifornia. The media fanned the flames of our imagination; trials became political forums; public reprobation ensured the ruin, if not the conviction, of the accused. Our shock and outrage were understandable because, after all, child abuse is a terrible thing and our love for our children is primal in its intensity.

In recent years, many of these verdicts have been overturned and troubling questions have been raised about child suggestibility and about the integrity of these investigations, prosecutions, and trials. Frightening patterns have emerged: children influenced by overzealous interrogators and prosecutors who pursued leading and coercive questioning, prosecutors willing to proceed in the face of wildly improbable and uncorroborated allegations such as the murder and dismemberment of babies; torture of children by people dressed as clowns, robots, or suited businessmen; molestations in "secret" or "magic" rooms, on airplanes, in outer space, among schools of sharks.

Playwright Arthur Miller (author of *The Crucible,* a largely allegorical play about the Salem witch trials that suggested his own experiences as a victim of the McCarthy-era inquisitions) spoke by videotape at the three hundredth anniversary of Salem's Day of Fast and Repentance on January 14, 1997. Miller described a prosecutor who pursued a murder case in the face of evidence that proved the defendant's innocence—evidence that he concealed from the defense. The mystery of the prosecutor's reasoning, said Miller, was applicable to Salem as well as to certain child abuse prosecutions. "You can attribute all kinds of motives to it: ambition, bureaucracy, a suspension of the moral beliefs of the person," said Miller, but the fact remains that "there are indeed people, for whatever reasons, or for no reason, who will perpetrate evil, who will proceed with a case even if they know that the thing is cooked up, that it is empty, and will persist to the end, and put people in jail for long years. . . . If that didn't exist you wouldn't have the other problems connected with false confessions.''

Ironically, outrageous prosecutions are made possible because of laws unique to cases of child abuse. The Constitution has been eroded as a refuge for child molesters, much as the common-law protections that we inherited from England (such as rules limiting self-incrimination) were eroded in seventeenth century America because they were believed to impede the punishment of witches. Today, hearsay statements of children and testimony about ''repressed'' memories ''recovered'' in extended therapy sessions have replaced the spectral evidence of 1692 Salem.

In one of the most recent and horrible of modern American inquisitions, prejudice has merged seamlessly with prosecution in the rural community of Wenatchee, Washington. In 1995 I watched the phenomenon unfold, but being an ordinary person indifferently schooled (in immediately post-McCarthy days) in the patterns of repressive American history, I didn't recognize at the time what I was seeing.

I went to Wenatchee to observe and investigate the development of a mass child abuse prosecution, having grown professionally cynical about the failings of the criminal justice system in emotionally charged cases. What I found bore all the classic earmarks of an inquisition. Poor, mentally disabled, and otherwise vulnerable parents were aggressively questioned by government agents who flatly refused to accept information contrary to their expectations. Most of these parents at last yielded, ''confessed'' and named friends, neighbors, and relatives as their accomplices to bizarre and ritualistic sex orgies. Only by confessing and naming others could an accused person assure himself or herself a measure of relief.

According to government documents and child interviews, children who failed to cooperate with the inquisition were threatened with arrest; removed from schools, neighborhoods, churches, and all extended family; medicated; placed in "recovered memory" therapy; or locked for extended periods in mental facilities where for twenty-four hours a day they were surrounded by professionals who unconditionally believed that they were victims. Not surprisingly, "confessions" proliferated and the circle of "abusers" grew as children and vulnerable adults were encouraged to name others in order to save themselves. Those who dared to speak out on behalf of the accused were suspected, sometimes charged.

I was dumbfounded. I didn't understand how it could be that so clear an injustice could be perpetrated in this benign setting, by an ordinary group of largely well-meaning professionals. I was astonished by the enormity of the government's collective if misguided righteousness, and by the power of official animosity when its benevolence was called into question. I was stunned by the equanimity with which courts and citizens accepted the abridgement of fundamental human rights. Although I have gained greater understanding of how these things came to be, I remain amazed by them.

In short order I myself feared arrest for obstructing justice if not child molestation, a scenario with precedent in Wenatchee for those who criticized the government's activities. A Wenatchee government lawyer unsuccessfully moved in court to have me put under oath so that I could be probed about my affiliations and my role in the conspiracy of child abusers. To my astonishment, I had found myself in the midst of a modern inquisition.

1:

Spring 1995

=====

Paradox

=====

In the spring of 1995, I surrendered to transient things: library books, rented movies, flowers that bloomed in a day. My cat disappeared, my kids planned to move out, my husband's thoughts were inscrutable. The professional part of my life didn't bear thinking about; it was something I discarded with my suit, minutes after closing my door at the end of the day.

I was a public defender and had been for over ten years. My practice was top-heavy with the most dismal, the most abstract, the most pointlessly emotional of cases. Worst of all were those of child sexual abuse. Child abuse is awful, but a false accusation is no less devastating. Sometimes I'd sit in my office, listening to fierce denials or tales of destruction, and think of nothing so much as escaping the room and the responsibilities staring at me from across my desk.

Now, as I read newspaper clippings and listened to the May rain fall on my roof, I felt the impulse again . . . but this time it was vicarious. How were the lawyers and public officials making out just across the Cascade mountains in the small central Washington communities of Wenatchee and East Wenatchee? Did these people know what they were doing?

These questions had first been put to me by my boss who considered me the office expert in child abuse cases. "You should go there," he had urged, his voice thick with persuasion and professional concern. "You should find out." It was a wildly impractical suggestion, the kind of thing he would never do himself, a challenge that left me breathless, a promise of escape. I started with the library.

The fifty-thousand-some Wenatchee Valley residents are a diverse economic blend of wealthy orchardists, middle-class businesspeople, and impoverished orchard workers. They share the gorgeous terrain where the mountains meet the desert, the anonymity of being three hours from a major city, and a view of their world filtered through the conservative pages of the local newspaper. Over the years I had driven through once or twice, past sprawling elms and well-kept flower beds and men going to work in their shirtsleeves. At those times I wondered what it was like to live there. But I never imagined anything like this.

Spread out on the ottoman, some neatly scissored, some torn and curling raggedly at their edges, were dark words from grim headlines: WENATCHEE SEX ABUSE PROBE WIDENS . . . A RING OF MOLESTERS OR POLICE CONSPIRACY? . . . SEX-ABUSE ARRESTS BRING CRY OF WITCH HUNT IN WENATCHEE. The articles described the prosecutor's allegations, some with startling imagery. "A collection of incestuous pedophiles lurked among the orchards and brown ridge tops here [in Wenatchee] and across the Columbia River in East Wenatchee, sexually assaulting as many as 48 children," read the *Seattle Post-Intelligencer*.

The reporters spoke of confessions too lurid for family newspapers, although the allegations they revealed were disturbing enough: married couples accused of swapping their children for sex with other parents. According to the Associated Press, defendants signed police statements that related "in crude, graphic terms a shocking pattern of incest between parents and children and between siblings that began when some of their youngsters were preschoolers and continued for years."

The rings served the voracious sexual appetites of fifty-some Wenatchee residents for upward of five years, according to the prosecutors. The case was so complicated by the amount of participants and the swirl of controversy surrounding them that Wenatchee police and prosecutors resorted to a flow chart. Yet, astonishingly, the events had only come to light in the past year, and I first read about them only days before. Either the Wenatchee government was deliberately taciturn or the news had finally reached a level of controversy sufficient to briefly erode the politics and apathy of the major newspapers in Seattle and Tacoma.

The papers told me the official statistics. Between January 1994, when Wenatchee Police Detective Robert Perez rotated into the position as head of what the papers described as the sex crimes unit of the Wenatchee Police Department, and early May 1995, twenty-one people were charged; twelve of these charges resulted in guilty pleas or convictions. (By the end of 1995, forty-six were charged and around thirty convicted.) Some defendants were charged with more than five thousand counts.

The cases early in Perez's tenure followed a simple but unusual pattern. In the first case, police arrested a man for the molestation of his two boys when his wife reported him after an intense argument. A few months later, Perez arrested the wife for molesting the boys, a fact that was in itself strange—I'd never had a female sex abuse client. Even before this woman's arrest the same pattern came up with another couple, the allegations also coming to light after a domestic dispute. First the husband was arrested, then a couple of days later the wife—and booked on 1,528 counts of first-degree child rape.

Chelan County Prosecutor Gary Riesen explained to the *New York Times* that the number of counts represented a rough mathematical formula based on the frequency of sex acts against multiple victims. "Some of these people we've charged are not parents like you or I understand parents to be," Riesen said. "They are people who lived in a house with no rules. There was alcohol, no food for the children, cockroaches in the cupboards. One thing followed another." Had the complicated psychology of sexual expression been reduced to yet another simple equation: Poverty breeds molestation?

Things bounded along in this pattern for a few months: a husband here, a wife to follow, incest on incest, the suggestions of group activity. Then the numbers of victims and offenders mushroomed after Detective Perez's foster daughter came to live with him. First she named her parents and then, several weeks later, all hell broke loose. There followed a string of arrests, confessions, and convictions unprecedented in Wenatchee and, by early indications, elsewhere in the nation.

By all accounts the most incongruous and most disturbing of the allegations involved Pastor Robert and Connie Roberson. By now the papers had picked up on the fact that Roberson was a former Harley-Davidson motorcycle repair shop owner who had begun his duties at the Pentecostal church about five years before, without virtue of officially being ordained. Within the pages of some of the papers rumors became fact, such as the claim that Roberson belonged to a motorcycle gang.

Police did what they could to hint that an aura of weirdness blanketed the East Wenatchee Pentecostal Church.

Said Douglas County Sheriff Dan LaRoche to *USA Today,* "People are shocked that this was at a church, but it's not like churches I'm used to dealing with. The newspapers make it seem like we busted Notre Dame. This guy was a former biker. This is not someone who went to seminary." LaRoche expanded on the theme with the Associated Press: "The church itself is a very messy, grungy place," he said, describing the Pentecostal church as a fringe fundamentalist Christian church.

I studied the Associated Press photos of the Robersons. The pastor's hair fell in tousled bangs across his forehead. He had an amiable smile and a lively expression. Connie Roberson had the kind of attractive, wholesome face you would expect of a pastor's wife or a presidential first lady. They looked like people you could like. Appearances, however, can be deceiving.

The Robersons' lawyer at the time, Eric Christianson, claimed that police targeted Wenatchee residents, including his clients, only after they criticized police methodology. "It's scary, it's extremely scary," Christianson told the *New York Times.* "Anyone who speaks out is being charged. It's the new McCarthyism—call someone a child abuser and destroy their life."

Still, most of the early defendants confessed; judges found their statements admissible against them; most pled guilty. All received substantial sentences according to no particular scheme: A man was sentenced to fourteen years in prison, his wife received a sentence of over forty years—twice as long as one of my clients' recent sentence for child murder. With the arrival of the media for a brief but voracious feeding frenzy, Wenatchee government officials alternately boasted about their prosecutions and downplayed their impact on the community.

"The constant attention has been very wearing," Wenatchee Police Chief Ken Badgley said to the local newspaper, the *Wenatchee World*. "We're like everyone else. We like this valley and the last thing we want to see is something that paints us all with the same brush, because only a very small percentage of the people are on the ugly side. All we want when this is over is for people to recognize what a fantastic job was done," said Badgley. "The bottom line is, we're all willing to take the heat for these kids. That's what keeps everyone going—we've gotten one more kid safe."

Douglas County Sheriff Dan LaRoche complained of different problems. "I haven't returned the phone call to Oprah Winfrey," LaRoche told a local reporter. "I'm getting pretty bogged down with this stuff." The apparent chief critic, Bob Kinkade, a former Wenatchee cop turned commercial fisherman, had similar concerns. "I'm on the phone to *Dateline* right now, so I'll have to call you back," he told the same reporter. When she tried again, Kinkade again declined an interview. "I'm sorry but I'm on the line with *48 Hours*."

"What's wrong with Wenatchee?" asked the *Seattle Times,* a question that, according to the *Wenatchee World,* "left local officials bristling." Wenatchee Finance Commissioner Chuck Johnson responded with ire, "How about if we reverse that and ask, 'What's wrong with Seattle?' Who are *they* to talk?"

The city was clearly worried about its financial backers and tourist dollars. In mid-April 1995, the mayor and the City Council asked the police and prosecutors to brief them on the cases. In response, on April 24, Mayor Earl Tilly issued a letter to the children of Wenatchee, likening the Wenatchee child sex abuses to the Oklahoma City bombings.

Tilly wrote that he had spent considerable time with "the law enforcement men and women who protect us," and concluded, "there is some 'police-bashing' going on by some individuals who have questionable motives. . . . The crimes by adults against children are the most sickening and *cowardly*. . . . Child abuse must be stopped. It will not be tolerated. Safety for the Wenatchee community,'' Tilly concluded, ''is not only a goal . . . this is a mandate!''

Some reporters raised the critical claim that Perez was a rogue cop—that he pursued some aberrant crusade of his own. But, according to police sources, Perez had not been alone when he interviewed the children and adults. ''The idea that there is a conspiracy that would allow all of the authorities in two counties and two different systems to go along with serving someone's crackpot agenda is impossible,'' psychiatrist Roland Summit of Harbor-UCLA Medical Center in Torrance, California, told the Associated Press on May 15. I recognized the name: Summit was one of the bright lights in the child advocacy arena and had been since at least the early 1980s—the man said to coin the phrase ''Kids don't lie,'' a saying that left many of us defense attorneys and parents scratching our heads.

But what of the alternative? *Newsweek* reporter Jon Meacham wrote: ''It is also difficult to believe that a score of adults and children could have rowdy, frequent sex together for so long without being noticed.'' Meacham added, ''taking either side requires equally large leaps of imagination.''

The answer was probably somewhere in between, mired in some treacherous swamp of good intentions. Already I felt drawn to the cases by curiosity and by a stirring of obligation. I had the uneasy feeling that soon I would be wading into the morass of the Wenatchee legal system myself.

*   *   *

Beyond the Cascade mountains, past foothills fragrant with pine and sagebrush, just beyond the orderly rows of mature apple trees, downtown Wenatchee is unremarkable: a stretch of strip malls and fast-food restaurants and signs announcing a tough new anticruising ordinance. On the day that I arrived, it needed one. Cars were bumper to bumper. Shirtless guys perched on the seat backs of their cars and waved to their shirtless pals who were milling around on the sidewalk. What kind of mess was I driving into?

At that moment I could well believe either side of the allegations. The town appeared out of control, lawless, gangland USA. On the other hand, cops were everywhere and that didn't bode well, either. I couldn't remember when I'd seen such a proliferation of police cruisers in such a brief stretch of miles. "God!" I gasped. "This place is terrible!"

I tooled endlessly through town and then came upon a hastily erected carnival and a clump of straggling band members, their hats tucked under their arms. Booths sprawled across a municipal park, a sign proclaimed AP-PLE BLOSSOM FESTIVAL, and I discovered that I had stumbled onto the chaotic tail end of the Apple Blossom parade, an event that was a very big deal to this small town.

It took me three cruises of Wenatchee Avenue, the city's main drag, and two violations of the city's new ordinance to find the office of Jeff Barker, partner in the Wenatchee law firm that was successful bidder for the public defender contract. Just down the block was the squat building housing the offices of the Wenatchee Police Department.

Barker kept me waiting only a minute and then emerged with a warm grin and a shock of red hair. He shook my hand, then took me into an office that was remarkably uncluttered for a man overseeing the defense of so many chaotic cases. Once we dispensed with the preliminaries, Barker drew me a rough diagram of what, he said, were "the rings" and "the circle." The rings, as I understood it, were the first tier of the accused, a ragtag band of poor, mentally compromised, or minority parents. Many of them had confessed to Detective Perez.

"The circle, though, that's where they've gone too far," said Barker, as I stared in confusion at his drawing. He told me about a caseworker charged with something or other, and about Bob Devereaux, who was a divorced foster parent, and about the pastor and his wife and some other church members, while I struggled to keep my facts straight. I hoped that Detective Perez, with his flow charts, had fared better. A few of the circle members were out of the public defender loop, with the mental and financial wherewithal to hire private attorneys, Barker explained. Those with public defenders had to wait awhile to get a lawyer, so that he could sort out the numerous conflicts, said Barker.

But as to the rings, "these people confessed, but then most of them turned around and recanted," said Barker, his tone perplexed. At first it was just the defendant's word against that of Perez, although it was no surprise who the court believed. But in later cases, other cops and caseworkers were present when Perez interviewed defendants and children.

Barker scratched his head. "Looks like they might be guilty." We both knew the truth: No one lies more convincingly than a child molester. And, of course, many had confessed. Yet I could tell the cases bothered him. "I've never seen anything like it," Barker said, "but at least they tell us they're winding down."

Barker leaned back in his chair and regarded me. "You know," he said, "a probation officer called me up when

he was doing his presentence report. He told me he had
to report to me that one of my lawyers committed mal-
practice when he encouraged this guy to plead guilty. He
believed he was innocent.''

Barker chuckled and I chuckled politely in return. We
were the insiders: We knew the realities. The probation
officer was inexperienced or naive, failing to appreciate
that plea bargains are not a measure of truth but of prac-
ticality—the exchange of uncertain trials for staggering
compromises. Plea bargains create serious dilemmas for
innocent defendants, but they deliver courts from con-
gested dockets, and lawyers from the exhausting prospect
of defending their views of justice. This is the system, in
all its corruption and majesty.

In the days and weeks and months to come, I borrowed
money and time and rented a boxy apartment with a view
of orderly streets and massive shade trees and the remarkable hills west of Wenatchee. I stood at the window
in the morning and watched the peculiar golden brightness
creep across the sensuous folds of the hills. How could
things be so wrong under the benign gaze of these foothills?

Perhaps the answer lay in the mind of a child.

2:

1992

═══════

Ann Everett—The Convergence

═══════

According to tourist literature, *Wenatchee* means "robe of the rainbow." The poetic description almost fits. Wenatchee, population twenty-eight thousand, in Chelan County, and East Wenatchee, population five thousand, just across the convergence of the Columbia and Wenatchee Rivers in Douglas County, sprawl beneath treeless foothills remarkable for their robelike creases and folds. But Wenatchee's natural colors are the muted gray-greens of sagebrush, greasewood, and Russian olive trees, the seasonal pastels of the mature orchards at the sunny eastern flank of the Cascade Range.

Sheltered from the western coastal rain, the worst of the prevailing winds of the eastern plain, and the urgency of urban life, Wenatchee is vulnerable to its dueling appetites: the hunger for tourist and investment dollars, the thirst to be simply left alone. If there is one trait that many Wenatchee residents share, it is a fierce autonomy, a pride and defensiveness and brittle independence, a sense of community unique to towns isolated by their geographical and philosophical boundaries.

There is a major one-way street going south and another going north, crossed by side streets with perplexing signs like NO LEFT TURN that tell you that Wenatchee is a town of rules to be reckoned with. Wenatchee officials feel that they know best what is in the interest of their citizens. But, as any child will tell you, paternalism has its price.

The wind tossed Ann Everett's fine hair and raised a flurry of pebbles and cigarette butts from the crevices of the sidewalk. Her house rose high above her, only because it stood on a hillock of ground: It was a drafty, cramped seven-hundred-square-foot featureless bungalow that she shared with her parents, her sister, and her three brothers. She dropped her eyes to watch the rise and fall of the scuffed shoes she had inherited from her older sister. Ann was seven today, February 26, 1992. Her sister Mary was nine. Hand-me-downs were a way of life for the kids in this neighborhood. As she trudged toward school, the streets of awful houses with mossy roofs and jerry-built porches soon gave way to streets of green lawns and shade trees and picket fences.

Something was eating at Ann Everett. School counselor Dennis Bailey, who alternated between his duties at Lewis and Clark and Lincoln schools, read the signs: The girl was withdrawn and preoccupied, she'd acted out today in her class at Lincoln School, and had drawn a picture that her teacher thought resembled gaping genitals. From the day Ann started school in the fall, Bailey and other school officials had formulated the theory that she was a sex abuse victim and he had questioned her four or five times over the months, but up to now she hadn't disclosed anything. Still, the signs were there, and she was one of the poor kids from that run-down neighborhood.

Today was different: Ann told him her privates hurt.

* * *

Wenatchee Police Officer Kevin Dresker took the call. Immediately he heard the note of concern and conviction in Dennis Bailey's voice. He clamped the phone to his ear and listened to the man go on and on about his suspicions over the last several months and about Ann's disclosure today that confirmed these suspicions. *Her privates hurt.* It wasn't much to go on, but if he ignored it there would be hell to pay. Bailey announced that he would now be calling Child Protective Services (CPS), the investigative arm of Washington State's Division of Children and Family Services (DCFS), itself a division of the state's Department of Social and Health Services (DSHS). Should abuse be determined and the child made a ward of the court, the DCFS's other arm, Child Welfare Services (CWS), might eventually provide long-term care. For now Bailey couldn't be sure what, if anything, had happened, but he was confident that the trained caseworkers at CPS would sort it out.

Shortly after Bailey called the CPS office, caseworker Katie Carrow sat across from Ann at a low child's table at Lincoln School. Carrow had been a social worker for Wenatchee CPS for a couple of years. She held a bachelor's degree in resource management, supplemented by several hours of training in child abuse, and was confident of her ability to spot an abused child.

Now, looking at the child, Carrow imagined she saw the signs of poor nutrition and hygiene. Carrow knew about Ann, about her mentally disabled parents and the rumored squalor of her home and neighborhood. Ann's father, Harold Everett, was totally illiterate; her mother, Idella Everett, was mentally disabled.[1] The Everetts had

---

[1] According to a psychological evaluation dated May 5, 1993, Idella Everett's IQ score is 68. More recent psychological testing was done at the Washington Correctional Center for Women and, according to prison staff, her IQ was then 58.

a number of children, which suggested they had no notion of birth control. According to the prevailing, dangerous, perhaps *inescapable* logic within Carrow's office, many of the kids from Ann's neighborhood would be better off in one of Wenatchee's many middle-class foster homes.

"Do you know about good touches and bad touches and secret touches?"

Ann squirmed and said nothing. Carrow smiled to reassure her and settled her elbows on the table. She was an attractive woman, small in stature but with a direct blue-eyed gaze that announced she was not to be underestimated. She took a breath and explained about touches, encouraging the child to join in the discussion.

For a long time, Ann dropped her eyes and fiddled with her toy and scrubbed at her arms with her unkempt fingernails. Carrow was patient, drawing her out, coaxing an occasional smile or sideways glance. At last Ann said two six-year-old boys, first-graders, touched her. After more squirming and stalling, she said their names were Pancho and Julio, and they touched her yesterday in an alley on the way home from school. Her words were, perhaps, ambiguous, communicated with nods and head shakes and terse acknowledgments, but Carrow reported that the boys put their fingers in Ann's vagina.

Serious stuff. But, with kids this age, Ann's story barely rated a point on the obligatory scoring matrix for CPS intervention. Carrow turned the discussion to the girl's parents. "What about your father?" she asked pointedly. "Did he ever do anything that made you uncomfortable?"

Ann shook her head. Carrow persisted. After all, it was her obligation to assist the child in overcoming the complex network of loyalty, embarrassment, trauma, and resistance that was known in industry shorthand as "denial." Ann stubbornly refused to say her father molested her, but after a time tears welled in her eyes and ran down her cheeks until she wiped them away with a grubby hand.

Carrow immediately jumped to one of her insider conclusions: Ann wasn't supposed to talk about something. Family secrets were tough to break, especially if they were backed up by threats.

Carrow said good-bye to Ann, got in the car, and drove through narrow streets crowded with older model cars and clumps of Hispanics who turned and glanced at the state vehicle, their expressions mocking or hostile. The Everett house huddled dismally behind a sparse and weedy lawn in a shabby neighborhood five minutes from the CPS office. Dank curtains hung from the windows; the paint was peeling from the door.

Idella Everett answered Carrow's knock, a large woman in a spreading dress. "Hello?" she said in a tremulous childlike voice. Carrow's eyes slid past her. Inside, the house was cluttered with laundry, dishes, toys, and the detritus of poverty. Everett's smile was timid and, perhaps, defensive. Of course Carrow couldn't discern the intangibles: the question of whether the family loved each other and accommodated each other's needs.

She explained she was a social worker with CPS. The woman nodded her recognition of the words—CPS had helped the family before. Carrow smiled, but her questions had a purposeful edge. She made determined eye contact, but Everett's eyes quickly darted away in the disconcerting manner of the walleyed.

"Ann said something happened in an alley," said Everett. "I think she said Mary was there, too." Everett summoned the girl, but she was withdrawn and largely unresponsive and said she didn't remember.

Carrow knew a thing or two about dysfunctional families from experience, training, and the rumor mill. She told Everett to sit across from her at the wobbly kitchen table, and then she bluntly dissected the family tree. Everett dropped her head like a child would, and said in an almost-whisper that her father had molested her for years when she was a kid.

Carrow put the woman on the spot: What about your kids? The woman shook her head but said Ann went to her grandfather's house around a month before. It was the early formulation of a *theory*, one that was altogether more acceptable to Carrow than Ann's allegations. Carrow told Everett that Ann was off to the doctor.

Ann clamped her thighs together and Central Washington Hospital emergency room doctor Thomas B. Ettinger had to use mild force to pry them apart. At seven, the girl had acquired adult values about modesty. She whimpered in distress: The procedure was sometimes uncomfortable, maybe painful for a child this age, Dr. Ettinger knew. Regrettably, he had a job to do. While he worked, as was his custom, Dr. Ettinger asked Ann why she'd come to his office. She haltingly told him two boys from school touched her in the "groin area." She gave few details.

Dr. Ettinger completed his exam, snapped off his rubber gloves, and smiled at Ann. "Go ahead and get dressed," he said. The girl's face was flushed with embarrassment or discomfort.

For many emergency room doctors, vaginal examinations of young children are among the most unpleasant of the tasks they are called upon to perform, yet not nearly as onerous as testifying about their findings. This time court wasn't indicated: Dr. Ettinger had found nothing amiss. Dr. Ettinger told Carrow that Ann's examination result was "grossly normal." Carrow was unsatisfied.

The next day she called Officer Dresker and they sat down with Ann at Lincoln School. Ann hugged a small stuffed animal, one of those cheap, well-worn toys that had gone beyond the stage of recognition. "What's his name?" asked Dresker.

"Brownie," said Ann in a tiny voice. She was a cute little thing, shy and apprehensive about answering questions, or maybe merely traumatized. Officer Dresker and Carrow chatted with her about Brownie and then went on to easy stuff about her name and address and phone number. After a time, the girl relaxed a little.

"Katie and I are kid safety persons. Do you know what that means?"

Ann shook her head.

Dresker explained that it was his job to talk to kids to figure out if they had problems. "Do you have some problems?" he asked. Again she shook her head. Knowing that children are often reticent when it comes to matters of abuse, Dresker pressed on.

"I hear that you've already talked to Katie about touching?" Ann nodded almost imperceptibly. "Can you tell me about the different kinds of touching?" he asked gently.

Ann buried her face in Brownie. Dresker repeated his question and her shoulders lifted in a shrug. "I don't know," she almost whispered. Clearly he'd have to educate the child.

Officer Dresker explained the concepts of *good touching,* in which "someone may kiss or hug you," and *bad touching,* "like when someone hits or kicks you." *Secret touching,* he explained, was "when someone touches your 'private part.' " He asked Ann to define what a private part was. She was embarrassed or defensive, but at last she recited the rudiments of her anatomical knowledge in the sanitized slang of children and child advocates: "pee-pee," "private," "boobies," and "bottom."

Dresker ran her through the different kinds of touching again for good measure and then asked her if she had touching troubles. Ann scrunched Brownie to her chest, twined one ankle around the other, and dropped her chin to her chest. "I've had troubles with bad touching," she said softly.

Bad touching? "Tell me about it," Dresker said.

In the tiny voice and mechanical, stilted manner that announced she'd been over this territory before, Ann said she was walking down an alley on her way home from school when two boys touched her.

"Where did they touch you?"

Ann squirmed and spoke from within the furry confines of Brownie. "My peepee," she said.

Dresker wanted something more tangible. He drew six boxes on a sheet of paper and labeled the first one "hug," the next, "pinch," the next "tickle," and the final box "secret or private part touch." The child untwined her legs, leaned across the table, and pointed to the last box. Dresker fumbled with his papers and drew out an anatomical drawing of a female child. Ann pointed to the groin.

She had cooperated and yet he was dissatisfied. He had all the evidence he needed but the wrong perpetrator: What could he do to a six-year-old? To a law enforcement officer, a crime demanded a *consequence*.

Ann wasn't being forthright, Dresker concluded. Her versions of what she had been touched with (a hand or a stick) and who was with her (her sister Mary or her brother Robert or maybe both) were inconsistent. In his report he wrote: "Carrow and I both felt that Ann had been molested, but that she was afraid to tell us who had molested her, so she was making up a story about Julio and Pancho. Julio and Pancho are both in the first grade at Lincoln School. Some of the statements and the apparent amount of physical damage to Ann didn't match what we were told."

When he wrote these words in his incident report, he

did so mindful of the fact that Ann's medical exam *had not* left him with the smoking gun of physical damage to her "privates." In keeping with his opinions, Dresker considered and rejected talking to Pancho and Julio.

Instead, he mulled things over for a few days and then went to see the Everetts. He sank into a sagging overstuffed chair across a drift of dust motes from Harold and Idella, and analyzed their dirt-poor, defeated, guarded faces—faces like those worn by people who were guilty of something. "So," he said in a confrontational tone, "what's going on with Ann?"

The Everetts had it down cold: Ann came home from school and said two boys had kicked her in an alley. The version was somewhat different from the one Carrow had told him, but then it evolved still further: The day after Ann told them this, Katie Carrow from CPS told them two boys had touched Ann in an alley; the next day the Everetts questioned Ann, who said two boys "put their hands inside her."

Dresker urged the Everetts to help him sort out the clues. He clarified the consequences of evasion and reminded them their daughter's privates hurt. It didn't sound like kid stuff to him. Now how could they explain that?

The Everetts looked at each other, shrugged, muttered, and rambled until Idella at last recalled that three weeks ago Ann had to see a doctor for a kidney infection. Dresker wondered if the results of her pelvic examination would be different if the doctor knew about the kidney infection. Dresker decided to give Carrow a call.

First thing the next morning, March 3, Carrow picked up Ann and told her she was going to see another doctor. Ann protested, but she was reminded it was for her own good. This time Carrow drove her to the office of Dr. Douglas A. Eisert, pediatrician at the Wenatchee Valley Clinic. In addition to his specialty in pediatrics, Dr. Eisert was a graduate of a three-day course in sexual assault. Frequently state officials called him to testify in these cases; this time promised to be no exception if his examination confirmed the suspicions and "history" of sexual abuse that Carrow had described.

Ann was extremely shy with Dr. Eisert, burying her face in her hands and refusing to answer the most simple questions. He didn't bother to take a history from her parents. According to his training, parents may be unreliable informants at this stage of the game. Instead, he positioned the girl with her knees flexed against her chest and got on with his examination. The girl was pale with anxiety, but Eisert noted in his report that she was compliant.

While Ann got dressed, Dr. Eisert told Carrow that although there was no visible evidence of tearing or scarring, the amount of her hymenal tissue was less than that found in some nonabused children—she might have been penetrated by someone's finger.

Armed with this new information, Dresker and Carrow sat down and questioned Mary yet again, but she stuck to her story. She hadn't been with Ann in the alley, she said; she hadn't had any "touching troubles" of her own.

At last, Dresker and Carrow tracked down Robert, one of Ann's six-year-old twin brothers. Ann had said Robert was in the alley when everything happened, but then she'd said the same thing about Mary, Dresker reminded himself. Dresker asked a couple questions and Robert said he remembered the incident: on February 25 he was walking a little ways behind Ann in the alley when two boys started to pick on her, he said.

"I saw Julio hit Ann in the privates with a stick," he said. His sister had her clothes on. Robert's story paralleled Ann's, but it diverged markedly from Dresker's expectations. By now the girl's words were little more than tiresome "denial" to him, Carrow, and school authorities. The family appeared to be banding together, preserving its secrets. Clearly, some more intensive intervention was needed to shake Ann out of her pattern of denial.

At the end of a long and only partially rewarding day, Carrow returned to the Everett home. She explained that Ann had to go into foster care "for her own good." It would be a "voluntary placement agreement,"[2] and Ann could go home once the investigation was complete. The Everetts had to *voluntarily* sign a consent form, that was all: a simple form conceding the girl was better off in foster care . . . for now. Harold and Idella looked at each other anxiously, and Idella started to cry, sputtering something about her daughter being better off at home. But they came around, as Carrow no doubt expected them to.

In fact, CPS had no legal authority to do an *involuntary* placement of Ann, since she had described only "third-party" abuse.[3] But the Everetts were mentally disabled, illiterate, ignorant of the law. What they *knew,* what they *feared,* were the consequences of resisting CPS.

As soon as Harold and Idella signed the papers, Carrow gathered Ann's meager belongings and hustled the girl to the car. The child dragged her feet and looked over her shoulder, but by now she recognized the futility of resis-

---

[2] Children may be placed in foster care when there is probable cause to believe that the child is abused or neglected by a parent or caretaker or that the child would be injured if not taken into custody. In cases not rising to this level, the child and parent(s) may agree to a voluntary shelter care placement and give written consent, or the child's parent or guardian can voluntarily request the placement with the agreement of the department. In terms of foster care placement, DCFS is required to give due concern to several factors, including the child's individual needs, and ethnic and religious background. (Revised Code of Washington 13.34.050; RCW 26.44.050; Washington Administrative Code 388-70-013.)

[3] According to the Child Protective Services manual, "[a] referral shall be assigned for investigation and the provision of services only when the alleged perpetrator is the child's parent or caretaker . . . or a third party and the parent is negligent in protecting the child from further abuse and neglect." (CPS Manual, Ch. 26, 26-21, Rev. 41 09/93.)

tance. Soon they were on their way to the home of Pete and Debi Cawdery. Cawdery was a foster parent with deep convictions about abuse victims and a close affiliation with CPS, a woman known as a helpful aid to disclosures. Time was short: A voluntary placement agreement was only good for a couple of weeks.

The next day, March 4, Cawdery began the exhaustive process of probing Ann for the truth; she said simply that Pancho and Julio hurt her. Cawdery was no more satisfied with this information than Dresker and Carrow. She told Ann she would be there anytime she wanted to talk about the truth.

"I want my mommy," cried Ann. She missed her parents and her big sister and her brothers and her friends and her toys, and became increasingly miserable and withdrawn. The CPS records said in typically sparse fashion that Ann "did not adjust well during her foster care placement." Worse, in the eyes of the authorities, she wasn't responding to the rounds of gentle questioning by her foster mother and the professionals. She now clammed up when Cawdery or Carrow asked or suggested who touched her. After a time it had become clear to Ann that no one wanted to hear about Pancho and Julio.

A week later, on March 11, Cawdery called Carrow to say Ann still "wasn't ready to say who hurt her," according to the language of Dresker's police report. Cawdery was worried because she was running out of time. By her words and manner, she suggested to Ann that she would have to disclose if she wanted to go home to her family.

The next day the girl came around. Cawdery reported excitedly to Officer Dresker that she and her husband Pete had sat down with Ann in their well-kept home among Ann's new toys and she told the truth at last. "She said she was walking down the alley to her friend Valerie's house when a man who was best friends with her [half] sister Karen grabbed her and put his hand in as far as it would go,'' said Cawdery. Cawdery thought Ann said the man's name was Abel. She told her foster daughter she was proud of her and Ann said, ''I'm proud of me, too.''

Bingo! Dresker swung by Carrow's office and they drove to Lincoln School. They'd just wrap this up and then nail the guilty party.

They sat on the floor with Ann and made small talk about her new dress, one of the more tangible benefits of foster care. The floor was hard and Dresker was uncomfortable. But what did it matter? They were finally cutting to the chase. He tried to break the ice, but after all this time the girl still hadn't warmed to him. He reminded Ann of their other talk about touching, ''touching troubles'' in particular.

''Shall we talk about your touching troubles?'' he asked. Ann looked wary, dropped her eyes, and wrapped her arms so tightly around her toy seal that he could barely make out what it was. At last she barely nodded. Beyond her bare nod, they could get nothing out of her. He would back off and work up to it slowly, but every time he tried to talk about ''touching troubles'' Ann's eyes welled and she averted her face or buried her head in her arms.

Dresker interpreted the child's behaviors as symptoms of abuse and the related coping mechanism of denial, rather than as signals that he was pushing too hard. At last he got out his pile of materials and drew some stick figures on a piece of paper—varying them to represent sizes and sexes. When Ann pointed to the taller of the several stick figures, the one without a dress, Dresker concluded that she was touched by an adult male.

But who was he? Ann wasn't saying. She huddled miserably, clutching the seal, rocking a little, trying to ignore him. Whisper the name to the seal, urged Dresker. It took time and considerable urging, but at last she faintly whispered the name "Abel." Dresker propped some anatomical drawings in front of her and she pointed obediently, at last satisfying him that Abel had touched her vagina with his hand.

She said Abel was a man who "used to live with my [half] sister." After nailing down a few more details about where things had happened and the fact that a kid named Valerie was there and very likely saw everything, Dresker was satisfied and told her she was brave for telling.

It was long past lunchtime. Dresker and Carrow drove the girl to McDonald's. Ann sat mutely, barely touching her food. From there they went to the Maid O'Clover convenience store near the alley, where they asked her to show where the things had happened. Ann cried most of the time she was questioned, a fact that Dresker and Carrow attributed to the trauma of the molestation.

In the next few days, Dresker did some more investigating. Mary said she couldn't remember an incident between Ann and Abel, although Ann said she had been there. Another lead dried up. Although Ann said Valerie had been with her in the alley that afternoon and probably saw what happened and she had definitely told her about Abel touching her, Valerie couldn't remember seeing any touching incident involving Ann and couldn't remember talking with her about it, either. Dresker needed a confession.

On March 19, Dresker got hold of Abel Lopez. It took a while, through contacts with Hispanic relatives, but at last Lopez came to the station. It turned out that the man could barely speak a word of English, but Wenatchee Police Officer Homer Ramirez agreed to translate. Ramirez advised Lopez of his Miranda rights. Lopez marked the portion of the form saying that no, he did not want to talk to the police.

The officers put their own spin on his response, interpreting it as a language problem rather than an actual assertion of a right. Surely the man didn't want it to appear that he had something to hide. After they explained things to him, Lopez agreed to talk to the officers and initialed the form to negate his response.

Dresker told him he knew Lopez had touched Ann. Lopez denied it. Dresker said he had medical proof. Still Lopez held his ground. The only touching was when Ann touched his arm, asking for candy in the Everett home. Dresker drew a diagram of the site of the touching. He reminded Lopez that a doctor's report proved the incident. According to Dresker's report, "I told Abel that Ann said that the touching occurred and the doctor's report confirmed that touching had occurred and I just wanted him to be honest with me so I could hear his side."

He told Lopez if he wasn't honest with him, it could hurt him later on. He made it crystal clear that so far he hadn't been honest. He suggested mildly that maybe Ann *wanted* Lopez to touch her. Maybe she touched *him* first. Maybe she *made* him touch her.

Officer Ramirez appealed to Lopez's machismo. He urged him to be a man and come clean. It would go better for him in court if he told the truth as he and Dresker perceived it.

"I guess if you say it happened then I'll take the blame for it," said Lopez dubiously, some hours after the questioning began. With prompting from Dresker, he said Ann grabbed his hand and put it to her crotch and he snatched it back.

The words the officers wanted were there, but the man was clearly confused. Lopez asked if he could go to court about this. "Yes," said Dresker. He typed up the man's statement in English, and when it was finished, Ramirez read it to Lopez in Spanish, and Lopez signed obediently. Then he asked if he could be arrested because of his statement. Dresker said he'd have to put him in jail for the night.

Lopez began to gesticulate emotionally and talk in rapid-fire Spanish. He wanted a lawyer, he ranted. Because the man was blurting out things, Dresker concluded there was no need to comply with his request. It was a lie, Lopez raved. Ann's parents were mad because he had a new girlfriend. He'd lied because Dresker and Ramirez promised he wouldn't get in trouble if he cooperated.

After Lopez was put away, the talk around the police station and the CPS office was that Ann was holding something back. Because this was third-party abuse, CPS was forced to return the girl to her family. Among the professionals who considered this fact with stirrings of speculation and regret was Wenatchee Police Officer Robert Perez.

3:

1992–1994

====

The Everetts: A Family Unraveled

====

Once Ann Everett made her "disclosure" about Abel Lopez, CPS directed its singular brand of beneficence toward her family. First, Katie Carrow packed Ann into her car and took her home. Then Carrow sat down and explained the ground rules to the Everetts. The catch, which was really a *bonus,* as she explained it to Idella, was that Ann must be immediately enrolled in therapy. Idella smiled abstractly and agreed, her eyes trained on her daughter. Except for some new clothes, Ann appeared unchanged.

In fact, the changes in the girl were profound. In foster care, and now in therapy, she experienced regular confusing reminders that she was a victim. After a time, victimization defined her relationship to many professionals—a relationship with relentless prosecution at its core. Whatever her problems were before, she had been above all else a child. Now she was simply a victim—manipulated, cajoled, pushed this way and that, until she came to accept her spot at the losing end of the spectrum of self-esteem.

Worse, she learned a hard lesson about the fragility of family bonds: Someone could come at any time and take her away. She loved Harold and Idella, and the thought of losing them filled her with terror. Every night she crawled under the covers with her mother—the only way she could sleep.

Her teachers dutifully reported her behaviors to CPS: She sometimes cried when things got to her; she had problems concentrating; even when she wasn't actually crying, her face was sad. Her therapist, Norma Priebe, wrote in her report that Ann was "showing symptoms of a child who continues to experience abuse in the family home." Priebe vowed to get to the bottom of it, to test her theories. She probed the girl, and at last Ann said there was "a lot of yelling," and she didn't like it. After a parade of questions, she said her dad sometimes spanked her and the other kids. Priebe concluded the discipline was "abusive."

When Ann said she spent a weekend alone with her father, the therapist repeatedly asked her what had happened. Ann wasn't telling but said, "It's too late"— words that signaled abuse to Priebe. She said Ann "uses many avoidance behaviors to not answer questions." And then there were her persistent urinary tract infections. Maybe her parents weren't giving her the medicine— maybe it was something else.

The specter of incest was debated in the halls of CPS, but nonetheless Carrow wasn't convinced it was true. Idella, a simple woman with a childlike morality, staunchly denied it and Carrow apparently believed her. Although she held fast to her beliefs at staff meetings, many of her colleagues found her naive.

But no one found her naive when it came to allegations of physical abuse. In the face of Ann's resistance to therapeutic disclosure, Carrow energetically urged Ann's twin brothers, Steven and Robert, to talk about family problems. If there were any, she couldn't pry it out of the boys. Undeterred, she set out to pursue her theory that Harold Everett had battered his children. Maybe Pastor Roby would help her out.

Pastor Robert Roberson, known to his congregation as Pastor Roby, was gregarious, boyish, and unconventional. In his mid-forties, he had an animated face, a mop of brown hair, and a strong chin that quivered with laughter or sadness when he emoted. Roberson had been a Boeing employee for nine years, then he worked in a shop repairing tractors, motorcycles, and gill-net boats and doing fiberglass work. When he moved to East Wenatchee in the fall of 1978, he continued to do repair services, even opening his own repair shop, where he did diesel work, repaired motorcycles and snowmobiles, and drove a wrecker truck.

For seventeen years Roberson was a member of the East Wenatchee Pentecostal Church. The church's pastors came and went. When they went, he filled in. At last, church elders told him they would officially turn the job over to him if he wanted it, although he wasn't ordained. Due to the church's erratic ministry, there were almost no active members left. The first service, it was just Roberson and his wife Connie. Roberson preached a sermon on obedience and Connie grinned and said, "Amen."

Pastor Roby's enthusiasm for the ministry was infectious and soon his church was accumulating parishioners. Outspoken and insightful, he cared a great deal about his small congregation. Many of them were terribly poor, a fact that in 1991 inspired Roberson to open the East Wenatchee Food Bank.

The food bank was a sweat-of-the-brow, seat-of-the-pants operation. With no discernible budget, Roberson cajoled contributions of food and sometimes money from citizens and grocers and such agencies as Northwest Har-

vest and the Community Action Council. Anyone qualified; no one was turned away. Hundreds of people lined
up for food on Tuesdays, Thursdays, and Fridays. On
Mondays in the wintertime, the Robersons gave boxes of
groceries to Hispanic families.

As if the Robersons weren't busy enough, they were
trying to raise their infant daughter, Roberta. Then the
problems with Ann began.

In 1992, Thursday night at the church was affectionately known as "kids' night," but officially known as
"Christian Pathfinders." There were many activities—
arts and crafts, singing, games, food, and Bible verses. On
a kids' night, Carrow showed up at the Pentecostal
church. She directed her no-nonsense blue eyes at Pastor
Roberson. "We're concerned about the Everett family,"
she said.

The Robersons knew the Everetts well. They were
members of the congregation, and Matthew, the oldest
Everett boy, helped Roberson at church and was like a
son to him. The boy was at his house almost every night,
when he wasn't helping out around the food bank. Roberson also kept an eye on the Everett twins and Ann and
Mary, and found the kids well-adjusted.

"We think something's up," Carrow said, according to
Roberson. "I've just been over at the Everett house and
I'm here to take pictures of Steven. We believe," she said,
lowering her voice, "that Harold's been hitting the kids
with a belt."

"Oh?" said Pastor Roby mildly. Harold, as he saw it,
was a lazy guy, more inclined to give an offhand slap
while sprawled on the couch than something deliberate
and intense. "Why do you think that?"

But Carrow was noncommittal. "Would you help us
out?" she asked. "We want to photograph the injuries.
I'd like you to be my witness."

Roberson thought about this awhile. What she suggested made him uncomfortable. It seemed somehow wrong or out of place. Were there some rules about confidentiality that applied to nonordained ministers? Still, if the kids were being abused, maybe it was the right thing.

"We can do it here at the church," she suggested hopefully. "Or," she added wistfully, "I could get an officer to help me out."

"No problem," said Roberson. "Let's do it here."

In the small church office, amid the clutter of church and food bank literature and half-completed sermons, Steven reluctantly pulled down his pants. According to Roberson, Carrow snapped a couple of pictures, then moved closer to peer at his buttocks. Nothing. If there were welts, if there were bruises, they had healed. In the face of the child's denial, it would take some injury that was more than transient, something that left a mark, to instigate criminal charges. If the kids weren't telling, she needed something more than theory for any CPS intervention with teeth.

In this way, Pastor Roby became involved in the CPS investigation of the Everett family. Carrow regularly called him or left messages, checking up on the Everett kids. She urged him to report any problems to her and reminded him that Harold was suspected of belting his children.

"No problem," he said. After all, reporting suspected abuse was the morally responsible thing to do, and is a legal requirement in Washington State for doctors, social workers, law enforcement officers, teachers, and other professionals, who are also subject to criminal charges for failure to report. But Roberson didn't see a thing.

Thwarted again, Carrow turned to the mode of therapy to explore her theory. In the summer of 1992, she enrolled Robert and Steven in what proved to be a lengthy course of therapy at Children's Home Society, an agency holding a contract with the state Department of Social and Health Services (DSHS), which is the huge state agency encompassing CPS. Mary and Matthew held firm that they weren't abused and they weren't going to therapy, either. Carrow questioned them many times, but otherwise she left them alone. For now, they were lost causes.

Not so Ann and the twins. Abuse therapy merged with investigation and the kind of therapeutic tough love reserved for victims: Their disclosures were the first step in getting Mom and Dad the intervention—and help, of course—that they needed. The expectations of the professionals were clear and the children were consistently disbelieved.

The children resisted and therapy moved to another level. After Ann was in therapy for nearly a year, her counselor wrote that she was "dissociating"—a clinical term meaning she was mentally distancing herself from the reality of her victimization.

The theory of dissociation originated with mentors of Sigmund Freud—Jean-Martin Charcot and Pierre Janet, who theorized that when a person suffers an unbearable trauma, the event may be driven into another, separate level of consciousness. The theory of dissociation has been widely adopted in a number of controversial therapy programs in which therapists suggest to clients that their problems might stem from "repressed" memories, use such techniques as drugs and hypnosis to retrieve "repressed" memories, and then confront these memories as part of the recovery process.

Repressed memory therapy is considered unreliable by leading experts on child memory. But it is widely practiced in Washington State, in part because the state was the first in the nation to allow recovered memory claims under the Crime Victim Compensation Program. Between

1990 and 1995, Washington State paid $2.5 million for repressed memory therapy for better than 325 people. But a 1996 state-sponsored report found the therapy appeared to be harming patients rather than helping them.[1] The subjects of the report were adults, and experts theorize that the therapy technique is far more confusing and destructive to children. Yet the therapy was vigorously pressed on many of the children in the Wenatchee child abuse prosecutions.

The therapists scrutinized the children's behavior and their bodies for clues to support their expectations. Steven was "self-abusive": He had a small purplish bruise that he attributed to a time he bit his arm; his therapist saw what she took to be a "rope burn" at the back of his neck. After a time in therapy, Robert became aggressive in school, started fires, stole, tried to jump from a moving car, and, perhaps most telling of all, became enraged in therapy to the point that he "needed to be physically restrained." Indeed, the children Pastor Roberson had per-

---

[1] The author of the report, nurse Lori Parr, found most repressed memory claims were for multiple personality disorders and satanic ritual abuse. Out of 30 cases she reviewed, 168 recollections of murders were reported; other recollections were of sexual mutilations and sacrificial ceremonies. No matter how implausible the "recollection," it was pursued in therapy, said Parr. Not only did Parr have concerns about the validity of the abuse, but the therapy appeared to be ineffective, even harmful. Although most participants were married before therapy, most were separated or divorced within five years. Most lost their jobs and their level of functioning consistent with employability did not improve. Of twenty-five patients who were employed when the therapy began, only three remained employed after therapy; twenty-one were found to be of "low income." All thirty patients remained in therapy after three years and eighteen were in therapy five years later. The report recommended that patients be warned of the fact that such therapy is controversial and could have harmful side effects. Wrote Parr, "It appears that the longer the patient is in treatment, the more disabled (s)he will become."

Labor and Industries Director Mark Brown, whose agency oversees the Crime Victim Compensation Program, found the results "very troubling" and sent a letter to lawmakers that indicated that his staff will work to develop a standard-of-care guideline for anyone seeking mental health coverage. Recently the department agreed to provide compensation only where the allegations of recovered memories have been substantiated.

ceived as well-adjusted in the days before therapy were now undeniably troubled.

Several times the boys passed CPS scrutiny without signs of physical injury. At last, Carrow sent the twins to Dr. Eisert, who was more discerning: He found a tiny "well-healed" opening at the mouth of Robert's urethral passage. Dr. Eisert asked the boy a series of pointed questions, and Robert at last said a seven-year-old bit his genitals one day on the playground while he was fully dressed. No one was convinced.

At last, after months of therapy designed to help the children overcome their resistance and reconstruct their memories, the shackles of denial were broken. By coincidence or an energetic congruence of effort, Robert, Steven, and Ann "disclosed" on the same day, March 9, 1993, almost exactly a year after the state first trained its watchful eyes on Ann. Carrow, the therapists, and the police converged on the children, and although they were reluctant and in Ann's case used "avoidance behaviors," in separate interviews each said Harold smacked them with a leather belt. Robert said his dad squeezed or bit his genitals. The "whoopings" left marks, the kids said, but, if so, nothing was visible to Carrow's discerning eye . . . not now . . . not earlier.

The disclosures were a major event in terms of CPS intervention. Although no criminal charges were filed, the allegations of physical and possible sexual abuse by the children elevated the situation beyond mere third-party abuse and would have permitted the filing of a dependency action. Instead, Carrow persuaded the Everetts to sign a Voluntary Service Agreement, which permitted the state some hard-hitting interaction with the family without any need for scrutiny by defense lawyers and court commissioners.

The next day, Carrow ordered Harold Everett to get out

and live on his own, and warned him he'd have to get counseling for domestic violence and anger management if he ever hoped to return. But, on reflection, she decided that perhaps she was too hasty. She had underestimated Idella's need for Harold's support; now the woman's limitations became glaringly obvious, and the family fell into disarray.

Matthew, who was twelve, stayed away from school most days to help his confused and despondent mother. Mary, ten, a girl Carrow called a "parentified homemaker type," stood by her parents, but admitted to being scared and sad, facts that were themselves ominous to CPS. Ann, nine, regularly flew into tantrums; by summertime the authorities pondered placing her in a mental hospital. All in all, state officials admitted the children had been harmed by their separation from their father.

But no one fared worse than the twins, Robert and Steven, seven, who, Idella admitted, were handfuls themselves. She reluctantly told Carrow she hit Steven for taking a bath with his clothes on. Alarmed, Carrow talked to the twins. Later she said the boys begged her to be placed in foster care. She was quick to oblige. She pressed the idea on Idella, who in turn called Pastor Roberson.

"Don't do it," said Roberson firmly. "It's too hard to get your kids back again."

But Idella was afraid to resist. She'd have to go to court otherwise, Carrow told her. The court might force her to give up her children. Besides, the caseworker said a voluntary agreement was best.

On that very day, March 25, Carrow pressed Idella to authorize the state to remove her children from her home by signing a Voluntary Placement Agreement, valid until April 10. Then Carrow packed up Robert and Steven and a few needed belongings, and drove them to separate foster homes. She explained in her report that she obliged the boys by separating them from each other.

If so, the experience failed to live up to the twins' expectations. Although Carrow reported that Steven was doing fine in foster care, and in fact he wanted to remain there for "two months," perhaps "forever," the foster parents said he was withdrawn and depressed. Within six days, Robert ran back home and stubbornly refused to return to his foster home, although Carrow, Robert's therapists, and his teachers leaned on him. Instead he daily grew more defiant and out of authoritarian control.

On April 8, Carrow bundled him into a state vehicle and drove him to Pine Crest Hospital in Coeur d'Alene, Idaho. Pine Crest is a locked private mental hospital and treatment facility with units for adults, children, and adolescents. At Pine Crest, private inpatient residency for abused kids was a simple matter: not tangled up in the complicated legal maneuverings of lawyers and court commissioners; not impeded by the burden of proving "grave disability"; not subject to legal scrutiny over the course of medication or length of stay or other legal technicalities that were requirements of Washington's civil mental health commitment process in state-run mental health facilities.[2] Under an inexplicable provision of Washington state law, Pine Crest enjoyed a specific exemption from the usual state bid requirement for provision of care services.

Because the facility drew considerable revenues from Wenatchee cases, it shared a successful symbiotic relationship with the Wenatchee state officials. Wenatchee's

[2] Revised Code of Washington Chapter 71.34 balances the mental heath care and treatment needs of minors with parents' rights to participate in treatment decisions for their children, and "to protect minors against needless hospitalizations and deprivations of liberty." At an initial commitment hearing to be held within seventy-two hours, the child has the right to an attorney, to present evidence, and to question witnesses.

Department of Social and Health Services (DSHS), the greater administrative body for a number of more specialized divisions, including the DCFS, contracted with Pine Crest for a variety of reasons, but, according to former DSHS employees, it contracted almost exclusively with the hospital for inpatient treatment in sex abuse cases because the facility's staff reliably extracted information from recalcitrant kids and reported back to caseworkers and the court. Yet the hospital was nearly four hours away and across the state line, and outpatient evaluation and treatment was locally available, many times less expensive, and licensed for this purpose.

Robert was hospitalized at Pine Crest for two months, until June 3, without any type of legal intervention. During that time, Carrow decided she would file a dependency petition effective on the boy's release because he was stubbornly opposed to voluntary foster care. The court would force his hand. There was also the worrisome fact that instead of opening up at Pine Crest, Robert now said Harold *hadn't* bit or squeezed his penis. The marks were made when his father "whipped his bare butt" with a belt, according to the language of Carrow's report. It was important to separate the boy from his siblings and the pressures to recant or deny in his home environment. Carrow made arrangements for Ann and Steven to go to Pine Crest as well.

Meanwhile, the Everett home environment was working hard to repair itself. Every Tuesday, Harold and Idella made the long trek to Idaho to visit Robert. According to DSHS records, Harold "complied fully with everything CPS asked/encouraged him to do," and visited regularly with the rest of his family at the DSHS office. "The visits indicated a strong bond and attachment despite the 'dysfunctional family behaviors,' " the records say.

"Things will be different," he told Carrow. He promised he wouldn't physically discipline his kids, he had an appointment to enter another level of counseling, and he seemed to genuinely care about his family. Carrow decided that the family should be reunited "for the issues within the family to be rectified fully." On May 10, she filed the dependency petition but recommended that Harold come home as a first step to reunification. It was not to be. Although she recommended that Steven and Robert stay in foster homes, she admitted, "There are concerns that separation of the children will cause feelings of abandonment."

When Robert was again placed in foster care, he came for weekly visits displaying his new possessions. "It's not fair!" Ann told Pastor Roberson. "Look at his stuff!"

In the face of her mounting stress and such frustrations as the possibility of reunification that was offered and then ripped away, Idella become overwhelmed, and ill with congestive heart failure and depression. Carrow reacted predictably to the family, which was suffering mightily from its separation—she removed yet another child. She gathered up Ann, who had returned from a lengthy stay at Pine Crest, grabbed her belongings, and drove her to the large colonial-style home of Robert Devereaux, to stay with several other girls who were Devereaux's long-term foster daughters. Matthew, who promised to stay in school, and Mary, who remained "parentified" and protective of Idella, refused to go.

Weekly hour-and-a-half visits between the Everetts and their children in the CPS office were chaotic. According to DCFS records, the kids bounced off the walls, "fighting, insulting and belittling each other and themselves." Everyone left overwhelmed, depressed, and emotionally drained, especially Idella. It took hours, even days for the kids to settle down in foster care.

Carrow changed the visiting schedule so the Everetts

could visit individually. Observing these visits, Cliff Snyder, DSHS home support services specialist, concluded: "The Everett family demonstrate an extreme emotional bond for one another which I believe has grown out of a strong interdependency, and a need to survive. The intensity of this bond has made the separation very difficult and confusing for all involved."

The kids became increasingly conflicted and distressed in the course of therapy, which evidently focused on issues of physical and sexual abuse. In February 1994, Robert's therapist, Donna Anderson, reported that at times he "verbalized" molestations and at other times said, "It's a lie." Mary was placed in weekly therapy in April 1993; by February 1994 she remained "very guarded about reveiling [sic] what was happening at home." Steven's therapist said that the boy "continues to shut himself off" from disclosures and that he had become "periodically" self-abusive: "hitting himself in the face, punching and kicking hard objects." Worse, Steven had recently threatened suicide. "This may be a reaction to the holidays and the anniversary of his being placed in care," wrote Steven's therapist in a letter to his caseworker.

State officials conceded that Ann also had a hard time adjusting to foster home placement. In therapy she begged to go home. She refused to follow household rules and told Bob Devereaux that she didn't have to because she was going home soon. Nevertheless, her counselor was satisfied that she should stay in foster care despite her wishes and the undisputed fact that her parents had complied with all of the department's demands, because such tangibles as her appearance and hygiene, school performance and overall attitude improved in the Devereaux home.

Bob Devereaux wasn't so sure. Recently divorced and

running the home alone, he found Ann an extremely needy child. She flew into rages and screamed so loudly she permanently damaged her vocal chords. He saw to it that his foster daughter bathed, brushed her teeth, combed her hair, and went to school. But, in the face of her unhappiness, her oppositional behavior, and her increasing demands, Devereaux decided he simply couldn't cope with Ann and do justice to his other foster girls.

Sometimes she was defiant because she wanted to go to programs at the Pentecostal church on weeknights or when she had homework or when Devereaux didn't want her to stay out late. Ann wasn't alone; another of his foster girls, Bonnie Rogers, was always begging him to go to the church. Once when he had to say no, Ann was so angry and out of control that she bit him, Devereaux later testified.

In the face of his request to remove Ann, foster care licenser Connie Saracino immediately thought of Detective Perez and his wife Luci. The Perezes had no children and she knew that Luci wanted a child. Also, the girl was a problem and needed some straightening out, and she probably knew a thing or two she wasn't telling. Perez was adept at straightening out kids and facts. Saracino called Luci and asked her if she would work on Bob and convince him to take in Ann. The Perezes weren't licensed for a female foster child, but that could be handled internally. It was really only a matter of adjusting the paperwork.

Over the weeks, Luci worked on Bob Perez repeatedly and at last he broke down. The girl was a cute little thing despite the limitations of her parents. On March 23, 1994, state officials placed Ann in the home of Bob and Luci Perez. Neither the fact that she was removed from her parents' home amid rumors and speculation of incest, nor the fact that Perez headed the sex crimes unit of the Wenatchee Police Department, troubled Wenatchee DSHS or law enforcement.

At first Ann was withdrawn around Bob Perez. Later, in court testimony and in his infrequent confidences to the media, he described her early days in his home as chaotic. ''She was like a wild creature,'' he told a reporter from the *Seattle Times*. ''She was terrified by every movement.'' Later he imagined he understood why. ''She had been beaten and abused so often, she trusted no one. Imagine your child goes to bed every night . . . and when the lights go out, that child lays there expecting to be molested or even raped. Can you imagine?''

For several months, Perez could do little more than imagine. Ann didn't relate to him and he treated her with equal reserve.

4:

Spring–Summer 1995

═══════════

Reality Check

═══════════

As I read the reports of the state actions toward the Everett family, I could see that Perez had a conflicted and often strained relationship with his foster daughter that spun off from his affiliations with DSHS officials and the great common ground of expectations and investigative powers that they shared. Had this fact affected the reliability of his investigation of sex abuse cases, as some newspaper reports had implied? Even if it had, couldn't the prosecutor or the court system sort it out? As a lawyer I had an ingrained loyalty to the judicial process. Like most people, I assumed that with a case of this magnitude there had to be something to it. Some disagreed, but they were far from unbiased themselves.

In the spring of 1995, I sat in on a community meeting in Wenatchee's town hall. Someone passed around a petition calling for a governmental investigation of the sex ring prosecutions; the petition was eventually signed by nearly two thousand Wenatchee-area residents. The level of concerted anxiety and despair in the room was almost palpable, and speakers described what was happening as a "witch hunt," and Perez as a crusader turned monster.

I shrugged away the tired and inflammatory words, but something definitely was amiss. By now I had a library table, a chair with a sagging rush bottom and original green paint, and an aged word processor, and I could begin the process of figuring out what it was.

Answerable to no one, probing a mystery with the tools of my profession, from the first I found the process invigorating. I discovered some things about myself: that I was disciplined and comfortable working alone; that the great solitude of my Wenatchee apartment nicely balanced the noisy family life I came home to three or four days a week. I often sat at my kitchen table thumbing through documents, glancing up now and then to watch the play of light on the craggy foothills or the spare clumps of furniture in my apartment. At these times I felt a burst of pure exhilaration: a feeling that never quite left me in the time I spent in Wenatchee.

Yet as the days passed in a morass of paperwork, at times my well-being all but evaporated. I gathered documents, sorted them, summarized them, charted them, stored them in the tiny dim memory of my word processor, tried to make sense of them. I reviewed countless police reports, witness statements, and confessions that sickened me with their long-winded, graphic detail. I was tempted to accept the words at face value; when confronted with shocking, explicit, and unequivocal official documents, it's very difficult to be skeptical or even objective. But I reminded myself that pedophiles and their victims are notoriously reticent in describing sexual events, and I had never read anything less reticent than these statements.

Many of the events were so extraordinary that it was surprising the word hadn't gotten out for years. Others were simply odd, such as the persistent claim that Wenatchee molesters were all the time sticking their entire hands inside somebody, or forcing someone's hands inside themselves. Surely such a thing is unusual . . . and difficult to accomplish? Like everyone else, I contemplated it silently but was too embarrassed to talk about it. When at last I did, Dr. Richard M. Soderstrom, a gynecologist practicing since 1963 and on the staff of the Children's Hospital in Seattle since 1972, told me the insertion of a hand in a child's vagina is "physically impossible" because the bony pelvis is too small, and nearly impossible in the case of an adult female except in the late stages of childbirth. So why was it possible in Wenatchee? And if it wasn't, what did this say about the other "facts"?

When I sat down and compared the statements, their style, vocabulary, and detailed content were remarkably similar, and written almost entirely in the form of direct quotations, although notes, if they had ever existed, existed no more. Among the mass of repetitive reports only two things were clear: None of the statements were spontaneous and almost all of them were filtered through the mind and onto the computer keyboard of one man: Detective Bob Perez.

I talked to various Wenatchee defense lawyers and I learned a thing or two from their perspective: Every person who was convicted of a felony was represented by a public defender on contract as part of a bid system. Those who shared in the contract had private practices of their own that competed for the attorneys' time; there was no budget within the contract for investigators or expert witnesses. Every time they needed expert help, the public defenders had to go to court and plead (often unsuccessfully) for expert witness or investigator fees from state funds—with the prosecutor strenuously objecting. Hearings and trials were astonishingly brief considering the consequences. There were only a handful of prose-

cutors and three judges in town, all of them elected officials. Because everybody knew each other and had to get
along, many professional relationships became, in a word,
incestuous.

The office of Wenatchee CPS Supervisor Tim Abbey
was in "the building with the rock," Abbey told me.
Later I saw what he meant. His window had an unob-
structed view of a giant boulder left by some long-ago
glacier, too big or too ornamental to move. As views go,
the rock was astonishing: an implacable curvaceous mon-
olith. I wondered how many anxious parents had sat in
this very spot and stared at the rock while Abbey broke
the news that their children wouldn't be coming home. I
suspected that, like the rock, he couldn't be budged.

Abbey had kindly blue eyes, a nicely trimmed beard,
and an intelligent appraising manner that might have put
me at ease if I wasn't concentrating on the task of staying
in his office. He made it clear to me that he would terminate the interview if my questions crossed into privileged or otherwise taboo territory. For all his easy manner,
it was clear that he was wary as well.

"You must be pretty overwhelmed with the number of
kids you've got in foster care now," I suggested.

"Not really," he said blandly, explaining that only the
distribution and not the *number* of his clients had
changed. "The kids were all on our caseloads anyway."
Whatever his words implied, fifty-some children had by
now been removed from their homes as part of the investigation and many of them had not been former CPS
clients.

Abbey was stung by recent criticism, some of which
was directed at him. He resented the claim that his two-
to three-hour child interviews were "unusually long."
Anyway, he growled, the defense attorneys weren't enti-

tled to complain. "How come *they* can get by with lead-ing questions?" he asked, looking at me closely in recognition of the fact that I was a "they" myself.

I looked uneasily at the rock. "They were doing *that*?" I waited a minute, then asked blandly, "What's wrong with leading questions anyway?"

He looked at me guardedly. I was either stupid or fish-ing. "The law says to avoid leading questions."

"Why is that?"

His response was immediate. "Because the defense can *skewer* us if we do." Among Abbey's gripes was the le-gitimate concern that the defense attorneys were subject-ing the children to multiple interviews. "I can understand they have the right to discovery," he said, "but there should be some way to make it humane."

But what of the scores of interviews of the same kids by the police and CPS? Surely the process was equally painful for the children? Abbey's expression told me he didn't agree. "It's a unique situation because of the group sex rings," he said.

"All—" he said, "no, the *vast majority* of our office's cases—are joint interviews between CPS and law enforce-ment." He explained this was a matter of policy devised by Chelan County Prosecutor Gary Riesen, in accordance with the language of the law. He went on to explain that the police are "primarily responsible" for these inter-views because "they have a much higher burden of proof," and therefore take the lead in the questioning pro-cess.

I asked about notes, the absence of which was a sore point with critics. Abbey politely described the joint po-lice/CPS policy. He said that both the police and CPS caseworker take notes. Because the police officer has to prepare a report (and CPS caseworkers apparently do not), the cop and the caseworker get together after the interview, but not necessarily on the same day as the interview, and share and compare notes before the report is written to see if they "drastically disagree." What if they drastically disagree? "The notes must be conformed," said Abbey. The policy of changing notes "to make sure they're accurate" was described as a "rule."

"You can't write down everything, not both your questions and answers," he said of interview notes. He pointed out that I wasn't writing down my questions. True. I thought I had been doing well in managing to surreptitiously scribble down his answers before he decided to throw me out.

"So why not tape the interview?" I asked, mindful of the fact that he had declined my invitation to tape this one.

Abbey bristled. "In the McMartin case," he said (referring to the disastrous California prosecution that had cost the state millions and led to no convictions), "the interviewer bore the brunt of the criticism." He said the interviewer's techniques had been dissected by the defense, which was "unfair" and led to "all of the tapes being thrown out on *technicalities.*" (These "technicalities," as I well knew, were a barrage of suggestive questions by a social worker, Kathleen "Kee" MacFarlane, who was employed by prosecutors to interview alleged victims of child sex abuse at the McMartin family preschool.) As a consequence, the state attorney general's office had discouraged his department from videotaping interviews, he said, although the Wenatchee DSHS offices had a room set up for this purpose.

I asked Abbey how therapy ties in to the equation and he explained that the state DSHS contracts with counselors, most of them through Mental Health (part of the state DSHS Regional Support Network) to provide services for children. Therapists are "encouraged to call [CPS] right away'' when children make ''disclosures,'' he said, and added that ''there are usually ongoing dialogues between therapists and CPS.''

''Foster parents are part of the team,'' said Abbey, although he denied that foster parents are given ''any particular message'' about interviewing children about abuse. The practice certainly wasn't discouraged. ''They can let the kids talk or not talk,'' he said.

He implied that the children's statements had been spontaneous and the disclosures credible. He cited experts who supported his belief that ''the vast majority of children don't lie about sex abuse. . . . In our role we believe kids unless it's otherwise proven.''[2] Of course, believing kids is a selective process. Abbey admitted that many kids were interviewed who said the abuse alleged in their case hadn't happened. Yet in such cases the question wouldn't end with the child's denial. Even if a child makes a false allegation, he said, ''it must mean that something else is going on.'' The solution was intensive intervention: foster care, therapy, and containment from the more obvious risks of contamination and influence.

Much of this risk came from family members. As a matter of law, children are removed from their homes where there is a risk of imminent harm, he said, but as to separation of siblings, ''it depends.'' Certain brothers and sisters are separated if they are ''abusing each other,'' but they are also separated when one's statements might ''contaminate'' another's.

Clearly separation of siblings was tied in to prosecution, and it was just as clear that the practice played havoc with other DSHS goals. ''No one wants to have a child's statements contaminated, but after a time there is a need for permanency planning,'' said Abbey. As to lengthy separations, ''no one wants to wait two years before matters go to trial.'' He shrugged. ''Where there are longer delays, does this mean kids shouldn't be together?'' he mused. ''The decision to place kids together may hurt either the prosecution or the defense.''

Surely the decision about where to place kids must rest on something other than trial strategy, I suggested. Because separation from family members is painful or even harmful to children, shouldn't the practice be disfavored by those entrusted to protect children?

''I'm not sure my role is to protect,'' he said, then quickly corrected himself. ''Don't get me wrong, my role is to protect children. But we want to protect their statements as well.''

''Is the separation done to protect kids' statements?'' I asked.

Abbey at first refused to comment, eyeing me warily. ''Yes and no,'' he said at last. Then he took me quickly to the safer ground of state law requiring consideration of such factors as safety, availability of resources, and maintenance of family ties. Proximity to parents and schools and extended family members must also be considered, he said, but ''that is a function of resources.'' Resources in Wenatchee are limited, he said.

Abbey said that the prosecutions had been unusual. As recently as two years ago, Douglas County, which is also served by his office, had the lowest number of child abuse referrals in the state, around four times lower than any other county in Washington. But he left no doubt that, in his opinion, the present investigations were reliable, although much of the abuse was alleged to have happened at least two years previously.

''The defense community wants to skewer Perez because of his level of activity in these cases,'' he said. ''Perez is fairly new, but he only did one interview alone.'' The statement was significant but entirely inaccurate according to witnesses and Perez's own police reports.

"Nobody can second-guess these cases as much as we do ourselves," said Abbey. "I've lost sleep." It was quickly apparent that his fears were more of critical scrutiny than of the harm to children. He said he was concerned about an outside investigation and about an internal audit, since "the office has been scrutinized tremendously. . . . They might start from the position of assuming guilt. Someone may be *scapegoated*!" The *someone*, he acknowledged, might be him.

Abbey said that his critics (and the occasional friend) "think we've gone too far. I need to listen to my opponents," he said generously. Yet, in his opinion, the children's "disclosures" over the last year were reliable because the children had no opportunity to conform their stories. He said that he was unaware of any situations in which children were confronted with the statements of others. "I would have to be concerned if an interviewer said, 'This is what someone else said,'" he said coolly, adding that this would be a significant form of leading question that would contaminate the subsequent statements.

I emerged from the chill of the rambling brick building to be blasted in the face by summer—hot sun, birdsong merging with the Muzak that is piped through the heart of town, an aromatic whiff of sagebrush and cottonwood trees down by the river. It was altogether intoxicating to me that day: I had just taken out a loan to finance my unpaid leave of absence, invested two hundred dollars in battered Wenatchee thrift shop furniture, and signed a six-month lease on an apartment that rose modestly from the hill across the river. I felt good . . . virtuous . . . far removed from compromise, but I reminded myself that an excess of crusader zeal was a factor at work in these prosecutions.

I wasn't yet sure where Abbey fit into this equation. Either the man was smooth and not much concerned with the truth, or he was in the dark. After reviewing scores of police reports and talking to children, former Wenatchee DSHS employees, and the accused, I became satisfied it was not the latter. For one thing, Abbey was in large part responsible for Perez's initial training.

Although Perez showed early signs of success in rounding up Wenatchee pedophiles, he had next to no experience in these cases and his only initial training concerning child abuse cases was in January 1994 after he began his nearly solo job of Wenatchee police sex crimes investigator: approximately twenty-one hours of in-house training by Wenatchee employees including Abbey, a coroner and a prosecutor. The instructors did not provide written materials, and Perez did not take any notes of their lectures. Perez later said, as part of a sworn deposition, that he could not recall that there was any training on how to interview children.

It was not until May 1994 that he attended an officially recognized training course in child physical and sexual abuse at the Washington State Criminal Justice Training Center in Burien, Washington. By then, Perez, who had no previous experience as a child abuse investigator, had been heading the sex crimes unit for four months and was already well on his way to uncovering the sex rings. Official accounts of the length of his training varied, but he later testified that it met minimal state requirements of just over fifty hours. The training included some sessions on how to recognize and investigate child sexual abuse. A few of those hours involved techniques and cautions on interviewing children.

The instructors gave him two reference guides: He skimmed them briefly during training, read them through over the next few months, referred to them occasionally thereafter, and then put them aside. Over two years later, Perez testified that he hadn't read anything else on the subject since his training—no books, no articles, no CPS interview guidelines, no studies, nothing. Still, he picked up the basics of conventional child abuse training.

Much of the conventional training of child protection workers, prosecutors, and police since the 1980s has been strongly reactive to a lengthy period in American history when the statements of women and child victims were largely discredited or ignored—and to laws set up to address this problem. In response to public pressure for reforms better geared to protect children, in the 1970s Congress enacted the Child Abuse Prevention and Treatment Act (CAPTA), which provided federal matching funds to states that adopted its provisions. Not surprisingly, all fifty states adopted CAPTA, which combined major financial incentives with coercive reporting requirements and led to a rash of overreporting.[1]

Several categories of professionals (teachers, physicians, psychologists and other mental health professionals, law enforcement personnel, social workers, pharmacists, and many others) are required to report suspected abuse at risk of criminal and civil penalties. The rest of us are largely granted immunity from liability for reporting and can do so anonymously.

Enticed by the lure of federal dollars, a variety of state and private agencies concerned themselves with identi-

---

[1] According to a recent study, less than one-third of cases that were reported and then investigated in 1994 were found to be substantiated. U.S. Department of Health and Human Services, National Center on Child Abuse and Neglect, Child Maltreatment 1994, *Reports from the States to the National Center on Child Abuse and Neglect* (Washington, DC: U.S. Government Printing Office, 1996).

fying, investigating, and validating abuse allegations, and treating or sheltering perceived victims. The industries successfully fed each other and derived financial windfalls from long-term care, regular referrals, and the systematic sharing of information. Agencies and individuals (including therapists and foster parents) serving special-needs kids like reported sex abuse victims received extraordinary federal and state money.

At a time when national adoption of CAPTA led to rapid expansion of child welfare programs, a network of industries were hungry for easy road maps to direct them through the morass of child abuse allegations. Perhaps the most influential of the theories seized on by child advocates were those of adult psychiatrist Dr. Roland Summit, who for thirty years has been employed as a consultant on a community mental health program at the Harbor-UCLA Medical Center in Torrance, California.

In a widely circulated but then-unpublished paper written in 1979, "The Child Sexual Abuse Accommodation Syndrome," Dr. Summit, who is not a child psychiatrist and who does not work directly with children, explained away the issues that made it hard to prove abuse (such as denial or recantation) by redefining them as "coping mechanisms." As he put it to me when I interviewed him, "The very things kids did to cope with being abused were the very things people used to disbelieve them." He described five categories of coping mechanisms—secrecy, denial, delayed disclosure, unconvincing statements, and retraction.

Dr. Summit's doctrine has been grossly oversimplified by its detractors. For example, a member of VOCAL (Victims of Child Abuse Laws) defined Summit's theories to read:

(1) When a child denies abuse, they have been abused.
(2) When a child says they have been abused, they have

been abused. (3) When a child recants an abuse, they have been abused. (4) Therefore, it is logical to conclude that all children have been abused and therefore all who have children have either abused their child or have allowed their child to be abused.

Dr. Summit is offended by this oversimplification. Yet, when I talked to him, he admitted that the Child Sexual Abuse Accommodation Syndrome became a prosecution tool in the early days when courts, prosecutors, therapists, social workers, and child advocates were feeling their way down the slippery slope of child interviews. "There was an enthusiasm to provide credibility to children in those days," he said, admitting some of his followers went too far.

Dr. Summit's theories became thoroughly misused as a primary and nationwide means of detecting child abuse and of giving the status of symptomology to such concepts as "denial," "delayed reporting," or "recantation." Although the syndrome wouldn't appear in published form for another five years, he traveled around the country lecturing on the subject and testifying at trials and hearings. At a hearing as part of an attempt to overturn a conviction in Kern County, California, Dr. Summit explained how to extract "disclosures" from children:

> The investigator must wait to build a trusting relationship and hope to find some way to pry open the window of disclosure. This usually requires multiple interviews, ingratiation, and separation from suspected perpetrators. Direct questioning may be unproductive unless coupled with confrontation, presenting the child with reassurance that the examiner already knows what happened. The investigator provides either a hypothetical based on experience with other cases, or assures the child that another victim has already broken the secret.

Today most knowledgeable child interviewers discourage multiple interviews and avoid such techniques as confronting the child with their expectation about what happened, or providing the child with actual or hypothetical information about the alleged events.[2] But in the 1980s the effects of such techniques were less well understood and, as Summit admits, "We made mistakes." In many communities, like Wenatchee, the learning curve was gradual at best.

Another theory that was laid at his feet was "Children don't lie," or the more cautious theory "Children don't lie about sex abuse," both statements that Dr. Summit now dismisses as "fatuous" and possibly attributed to him as "backlash terms" by those attacking the work of child protection advocates. His words, in fact, were: "It has become a maxim among child sexual abuse intervention counselors that children never fabricate the kinds of explicit sexual manipulations they divulge in complaints or interrogations." The words are complex and no doubt confusing, but Dr. Summit's theories have been embraced (in oversimplified form) by many professionals and have repeatedly justified suggestive and aggressive child interviews.

The process of single-minded pursuit of theories based on little or no reliable evidence has led to some of the most horrific mass criminal prosecutions in our nation's history—many of them in the area of child sexual abuse. Several of these cases had their origins in the fantasies of

---

[2] According to discovery requests made by defense counsel in Wenatchee prosecutions, the Wenatchee DCFS office uses the CPS Child Interview Form Guidelines prepared by the Harborview Sexual Assault Center in Seattle. Among these materials are the "Principles for Legally Sound Interviewing." These include avoiding preconceptions; avoiding coercion, pressure, intimidation, reward; asking open-ended questions; and avoiding suggestive questions that contain an expected answer.

women with emotional disturbances; their claims were taken seriously by investigators who, given the state of their knowledge or biases at the time, were quick to believe them.

Southern California during the 1980s was the site of several alleged cases of ritual abuse. Virginia McMartin, with the assistance of her daughter Peggy McMartin Buckey, ran the McMartin Preschool in Manhattan Beach, California. Peggy's husband Ray Buckey, who was a test engineer at Hughes Aircraft, helped build the school and construct play equipment. One day one of the mothers of preschoolers repeatedly questioned her two-year-old son. After a while the boy said Ray Buckey "took his temperature." The mother surmised that the "thermometer" was Buckey's penis.

Although a medical examination of the boy's anus was inconclusive, police phoned parents, then sent a letter to two hundred families urging them to question their children about unusual goings-on at the day-care center. Parents questioned children; stories of games like "tie up" and "horsey" emerged; ambiguous statements were interpreted as abuse. Repeatedly questioned, children embellished their stories and named other "victims." Confronted with this information, other children "disclosed."

At last the children were referred by prosecutors to Kathleen "Kee" MacFarlane, a social worker who worked at Children's Institute International (CII).[3]

---

[3] In 1976, Kee MacFarlane, who held an undergraduate degree in art and a master's degree in social work, was in her twenties and only recently out of college. She was hired as a sex abuse specialist by the National Center for Child Abuse and Neglect (NCCAN), shortly after the adoption of the Child Abuse Prevention and Treatment Act. MacFarlane's job at NCCAN was to review grant applications and make decisions about the child abuse proposals and research that she felt deserved federal funding; thus MacFarlane played an early and significant role in deciding public policy adopted by all fifty states, which conformed their laws to

MacFarlane used the technique of "therapeutic" interviews with hand puppets, and "anatomically correct" dolls. The sessions, which were audio or videotaped, were an irresistible blend of suggestion, taunts, shame, and praise, and yielded increasingly fantastic stories.

In addition to more commonplace stories, children said Ray killed pets while dressed as a clown, fireman, Santa Claus, and policeman. One of the children talked about a "goatman," people dressed as witches, being buried in a coffin, being on a train where men in suits hurt him, staples in his ears and nipples and tongue, scissors in his eyes, animals being chopped up, being hurt by a lion, a baby being chopped up, having to drink the baby's blood. Another child talked of being forced to drink urine and eat feces with chocolate sauce, a story that was adopted by other children.

Most of the authorities believed what they chose to and discarded the rest. They were apparently unfazed by the fantastic claims; the absence of physical evidence, including corpses or mutilated remains; even the obvious mental instability of the mother who first brought her suspicions to light and had been zealously pursuing them ever since. The woman accused more and more people of molesting her son, called the police and hysterically reported that someone broke into her home while she was gone and raped the family dog, and became reclusive, barricading herself in her home, while clutching a twelve-gauge shotgun. By the time she died of liver deterioration secondary to alcoholism a couple years later, the woman claimed to have divine powers.

The prosecutions went on unabated, but not every pros-

CAPTA requirements. Despite widespread criticism of her methods, MacFarlane continues to receive lucrative grants for her work in the area of child interviews, and continues to lecture widely on the subject.

ecutor was comfortable with this fact. At first, "I myself had a bunker mentality," former McMartin prosecutor Glenn Stevens told me. "There was no doubt in my mind that they were guilty." This had much to do with the number of kids who made the allegations, and his natural assumption that the cases were based on hard evidence.

But when the cases became increasingly fantastic, Stevens sat down and questioned kids and found they adopted improbable scenarios according to any direction he led them with his questions. Testimony at a preliminary hearing "blew such gaping holes in the case" that Stevens felt it was his obligation to act in the interests of justice. First he appealed to his boss, the district attorney, and urged him to dismiss the case. But, according to Stevens, the DA responded, "If the judge denies the motion [to dismiss] we'll look like fools in the press." At last, feeling he had no recourse, he himself went to the press. Stevens was promptly asked to resign from his position with the prosecutor's office.

Peggy and Ray Buckey went to trial in 1987, charged with 218 counts. The prosecutors "just threw shit against the wall to see if the stuff would stick," said Stevens. The trial dragged on for twenty-eight months, which made it the longest and most costly in American history. In 1990, Peggy was acquitted of all charges and Ray was acquitted on some counts and received a hung jury on others. By then Ray Buckey had been in jail for five years. Ray's second trial resulted in another hung jury and ultimate dismissal. The cases cost state taxpayers millions of dollars, and McMartin and the Buckeys seven years of horrendous jeopardy.

Another case arising from a mentally ill woman occurred even earlier. In Kern County in Central California in 1980, Mary Ann Barbour was found brandishing a knife and talking frantically about her six-year-old step-granddaughter being molested. She was taken to a psychiatric ward and diagnosed as delusional and suffering from a form of schizophrenia, and then placed on antipsychotic medication. Barbour had a steel plate in her head as a result of falling from a moving car, and she had suffered physical abuses as a child. She was preoccupied with examining her stepgrandchildren's genitals for signs of abuse. When she believed she detected abnormalities, she took the child to a doctor. Neither the doctor nor a social worker could extract disclosures from the child.

Barbour remained obsessed with proving her theories. She contacted her congressman, the state attorney general, then pulled a knife and a gun on her husband to attract the attention of authorities. Instead she was hospitalized in a mental institution. After her release, Barbour at last contacted the leader of a local chapter of a national victims' rights organization. The matter was ultimately forwarded to child protection authorities, then to a deputy sheriff. Finally two of her stepgrandchildren were taken from their family and booked into a juvenile home. After ongoing "therapeutic" relationships with child advocates, the children eventually made disclosures and were finally placed with Barbour.

The placement was chaotic: The girls' behaviors became highly sexualized; they had nightmares and threw tantrums. And Barbour showed disturbing signs of mental illness. She became obsessed that the family was in danger from the girls' "molester," and called up the child protection office to report that the girls and a growing number of other children were tied up, chained, beaten, filmed and photographed, forced to watch movies of child murder and mutilation, and driven to motels to have sex "with anyone who wanted them."

Despite her obvious mental illness, authorities arrested most or all of the people Barbour named, searched their homes (recovering no pornography or other evidence), and placed their children in juvenile homes. Before trial, one of her stepgrandchildren (who was moved to foster care because of Barbour's claim that her life was in danger) recanted much of her story. She said Barbour questioned her for "a whole day" and she wouldn't believe her when she said no. "She kept on asking me and asking me and I told her that he did not molest me, but she kept on saying, he did, he did, he did, and I said no, he didn't and so I had no choice." Rather than accepting the recantation, authorities contained the girl in a children's home, visited her almost daily, and kept a close eye on her siblings for signs of recantation.

At trial, the children testified in monosyllables about being molested in acts of bizarre group sex. All four defendants were found guilty in May 1984; the judge sentenced each defendant to over 240 years in prison. Although pending charges were dropped against other defendants because the defense attorney was able to show that Barbour was mentally ill, the judge ordered that, as a condition of dismissal of the charges, the documentation of Barbour's mental illness be sealed or destroyed.

In the 1980s about fifty people were charged in connection with eight separate alleged child sex rings in Kern County, California, all stemming in some way from Barbour's claims. Some of the accused were people like Brenda and Scott Kniffen, who agreed to be character witnesses for other defendants. Of the twenty-six defendants who were tried and convicted by juries, at least fourteen have recently had their convictions overturned and been released from prison. Former assistant district attorney Andrew Gindes was reprimanded by the appellate court for "gross misconduct" and "a blind quest to convict."

In the spring of 1984, when a television special *Some-*

thing About Amelia heightened public awareness about incest, and the McMartin case exploded on the media, twenty-four people in Jordan, Minnesota, were arrested on charges of being part of a child pornography and sex ring. Defendants included a deputy sheriff, a police officer, and others who were accused of molesting their own children and swapping them around. Eventually the children accused their parents of murdering babies, making children drink babies' blood, and throwing bodies into the river. The cases included claims that people were charged in retaliation because they spoke out against the prosecutions. But the Jordan case was notable for the fact that prosecutors acted responsibly. In early 1985, only a year after the allegations emerged, the state attorney general's office reported that the cases should be dismissed because of badly flawed investigations, including the lengthy and repeated questioning of children.

Increasingly, the role of investigation guised as therapy was shown to be destructive. At the Little Rascals daycare center in Edenton, North Carolina, four therapists, aware of local rumors, decided that each of the children in the center had been abused. Many of the children subjected to the therapy now show signs of trauma as a result and remain in therapy years later. "This did not meet up to anything that I'm aware of in terms of minimal standards of therapy," a psychiatrist told the PBS series *Frontline*. "I don't think the kids got any treatment. In fact, I think a lot was done to undermine their mental health." Ironically, only those children who were sent to therapists outside of the community or who received no therapy appeared to be doing well.

Some appellate courts have become increasingly sensitive to flawed child interview techniques. In 1985, Kelly Michaels was arrested after she quit her job at the Wee Care day-care center in Maplewood, New Jersey. Investigors questioned kids repeatedly after one made an abstract statement: Ultimately their disclosures included claims that Michaels raped them almost daily for seven months using forks, spoons, twigs, and Legos; put peanut butter on her genitals and had them lick it off; made them eat her feces and drink her urine; forced them to play naked sex games; and threatened to kill them and their parents if they told. Yet no staff members saw, heard, smelled, or suspected anything. Despite the improbabilities of the testimony, Michaels was convicted in 1988 and sentenced to forty-seven years in prison.

In 1993, the New Jersey court of appeals ruled that Michaels hadn't received a fair trial, in part because the judge questioned the children in a less than impartial way. The jury watched on closed-circuit television as the judge sat with children on his lap, whispering in their ears and urging them to whisper back, playing ball with them, "encouraging and complimenting them," according to the appellate court's written opinion. The New Jersey State Supreme Court later upheld the appellate decision and, in an opinion, wrote that the case was rife with "egregious prosecutorial abuses." The court found that all twenty children were threatened, bribed, or led, and none of their statements was spontaneous. Michaels was released after five years in prison, and the case was remanded for possible retrial; prosecutors declined to retry.

According to an article published in early September 1995 in the *Washington Post,* "The days when prosecutors would seek sexual abuse indictments on the basis of fantastic testimony by small children are over." The article implied that across the nation, professionals took to heart the serious lessons of the more notorious cases. In fact, by my observations in Wenatchee, the reality may be something else entirely: destroying notes, refusing to videotape, charging cases selectively and distilling the provable from the impossible—all strategies geared toward courtroom victories and not ultimate justice.

In some ways the Wenatchee cases were typical of notorious child sex abuse prosecutions. The key child witnesses, many of them friends who played at each other's houses, enjoyed a constant stream of attention from authorities and were reminded of their own power over—and vulnerability to—adults. Most of them were sequestered from families, schools, churches, and friends and were involved in a process of long-term investigation guised as ''therapy.''

In other ways the Wenatchee cases were distinguishable. In Wenatchee, children were typically in the nine- to thirteen-year age group. Almost none of their statements was the result of spontaneous offerings. Instead of questioning all named or identifiable victims, in many cases the investigators depended on a handful of dependable informants—some of whom had made false allegations in the past—and then questioned them again and again. The child interviews were, perhaps, more appropriately characterized as coercive than suggestive. The allegations did not have their apparent origin in the minds of emotionally disturbed women, but in the biases, expectations, and crusader zeal of Detective Perez, his supportive colleagues, and like-minded state caseworkers.

5:

Winter 1993–Summer 1994

═══════════

The Hunt Begins

═══════════

Teddy bears spilled from every available surface of Wenatchee Police Detective Bob Perez's office: the floor, the
windowsill, the desk, the top of the filing cabinet,
the upper rim of the bulletin board beside his desk. On
the bulletin board were photos of missing children beside
childish drawings and a couple of *Far Side* cards. You
couldn't be in doubt, upon entering Perez's domain: He
was a man who cared about kids.

Perez's desk was in an optimal location, tucked into the
corner of the large room shared by detectives and cops
from the street crimes and the property units. Two large
windows stood beside his desk, but he often kept the lou-
vered blinds shut, opting for privacy in keeping with the
defensive wisdom or paranoia of his profession. From this
vantage point, he studied the unformed faces of children
and the shopworn faces of the adults he interrogated.

Despite a popular image of being hardened to their profession, most cops hate to investigate cases of child sexual
abuse. The cases are complex, frequently abstract, emotionally wrenching, and involve the embarrassing prospect
of talking to kids about sex. By all indications, Perez held
a different view.

He didn't talk much about his childhood, his emotional and physical estrangement from his parents which left him with feelings of abandonment, his turbulent relationships with women. But these experiences helped to form the complicated terrain of his personality. Perez had a crusader's sense of commitment toward children, a driving ambition to succeed in the evidentiary no-man's-land of child abuse investigation, and the hope of becoming chief one day. In the fervor of his convictions and ambitions, he sometimes embraced the dangerous principle that, where protecting children was concerned, the ends justified the means.

Luci Perez agreed. Her parents once ran a foster home that over the years had included many abused children. A childhood of vicarious victimization left its stamp on Luci, and her resentment fed into Bob's resolve.

The Wenatchee Police Department investigated crimes in the greater metropolitan area of Wenatchee. Under the chief were two captains, a handful of sergeants, a lesser number of corporals, and a couple dozen patrol officers. There were only four detectives, each in charge of a basic unit. Chief Ken Badgley hit on the idea of rotation, to prevent officer burnout and problems of morale. The officers rotated between units and specialties every couple of years. In January 1994, without any previous training or experience in child sex abuse investigations, Bob Perez became official head of the unofficial crimes against persons division of the Wenatchee Police Department, the unit assigned to investigate allegations of such crimes as assault and physical and sexual abuse of children. The position carried with it an automatic, if temporary, elevation to the position of detective.

Of necessity, Perez often worked alone within his department. But he wasn't truly alone. Through the years he'd made some useful connections in the world of child advocacy, so that now he was a familiar figure around the Wenatchee Division of Children and Family Services offices. Most of the social workers liked his jokes and banter. They spoke the same language, shared great commonalities of expectations, values, and beliefs. Like Perez, they felt they could discern the corruption at the heart of so many of Wenatchee's families. Certainly this was true of Tim Abbey, and of CPS caseworkers Dean Reiman and his wife Pat Boggess, Katie Carrow, Laurie Alexander, and other senior social workers who were among those who went to parties at Perez's home and invited him to lunch at least twice a week. Together Perez and these caseworkers now were able to work as a team.

Sometimes Perez took the back way to the offices. Other times he tucked his thumb in the belt of his trousers so that his palm rested lightly on the butt of his revolver, squared his shoulders, and strode purposefully past the lines of Hispanics and poorly dressed Caucasians at the welfare and food stamps counter. He felt an ill-concealed contempt for the welfare system and the people who fueled it.

At these times, Perez skirted the crowd, passed through a side door, nodded at the receptionist and barged on through into the large cluster of cubicles and offices that made up the Wenatchee Child Protective Services (CPS) and Child Welfare Services (CWS), both arms of the greater body of the Washington State Division of Children and Family Services (DCFS), itself a department of the huge, altruistic, and largely out-of-control bureaucracy of the Washington State Department of Social and Health Services (DSHS). Among the cluster of cubicles, Perez regularly scanned client intake sheets, child abuse referral forms and client files.

At morning staffings, the caseworkers, joined by Perez, sat around a table drinking coffee and describing their caseloads of kids and their limited or dysfunctional parents. These staffings were invaluable sources of information for him, as was his unimpeded access to DSHS client files. He came to appreciate the frustrations of the caseworkers, thwarted by caseloads and a mass of legal and bureaucratic mumbo-jumbo from simply doing their jobs as they saw fit.

Perez could intervene where they could not. His transition into the crimes against persons unit was a seamless merger of their mutual goals. Inexperienced and minimally trained in investigating child sexual abuse, within months he seemingly unraveled a case of unprecedented dimension and complexity. But, like many complicated things, the cases had a simple origin.

The Holt family's problems came to a head in September 1993, after Laura and her husband Selid "Sid" Holt had an intense argument. Laura, a round woman in her thirties from the poor part of town, found a hotel receipt in Sid's pants, and one thing led to another. By four in the morning, Sid not only admitted to her that he'd been seeing another woman, but that he'd had sex with their daughter Pam, who would be ten years old in three days, and taunted that the girl was a better lover than her mother. Laura took Pam to the rape crisis center, then reported Sid to the police and, after a time, her husband was put away.

But CPS had lingering concerns about Laura Holt's parenting skills. Assigned as the family's caseworker, Dean Reiman went to the Holt home and found it disheveled. He told Laura she had to enroll in parenting classes and put all three of her kids in counseling. Still dissatisfied, Reiman questioned her children at their school. He asked if Laura had touched them as their father had touched Pam. The kids said no.

Reiman made several return visits to the Holt home. The house was cleaner, but he suspected something was amiss. He gently questioned Laura about drugs and alcohol. She denied she had a problem and he had no solid evidence to the contrary.

On January 10, 1994, only ten days after Detective Perez's rotation began, Laura Holt walked into the Wenatchee police station and asked for Perez. The detective remembered the woman from the time he had talked to her at the rape crisis center after she had turned in her husband for molesting her daughter Pam. He knew there was speculation about her and recalled that CPS suspicions didn't rise to the level that would allow them to intensively intervene. As soon as he saw Laura's doughy, anxious face, Perez eyed the woman with professional curiosity.

She had the little girl with her. He regarded the child's solemn eyes and round face and remembered she was around ten. The woman sat heavily in one chair in front of his desk and her daughter perched uneasily on the other.

Laura Holt launched into an explanation about Sid, but Perez waved her words away. "I know all about your husband," he said. She then began a rambling dialogue about Pam telling her a man named Leo Catcheway once molested her and now her daughter was afraid because she heard he was coming back to town. Perez narrowed his eyes, leaned back in his chair, and nursed his growing speculation that the woman was playing games, trying to get her husband off. "He's a figment of your imagination," he said.

Pam started talking about Catcheway, but Perez leaned forward and interrupted the girl by directing an observation at her mother. "You're trying to change your daughter's statement, rehearse her into saying something different,'' he said, according to Laura.

Over the next few days, Laura tried to report Leo Catcheway. She left messages with Pam's school counselor, left two or three messages for Reiman at CPS, then tried to explain the situation to his receptionist. No one returned her calls. Instead, Perez's theory took hold.

On Thursday, January 13, Reiman talked to the Holt children at school. The next day, the kids begged her to let them stay home from school, said Laura. Pam and six-year-old Michael clung to her, and twelve-year-old Donald looked at her with anxious eyes. At last Pam said she had a feeling they wouldn't be coming home.

Laura hugged her two oldest children and watched as they trudged dejectedly toward the bus. Somehow she got through the morning, mostly by consciously pushing her worries away. As Michael left for afternoon kindergarten, he again clung to her and begged her to let him stay home.

They were due home at 2:45. At around 2:20, the phone rang. It was Reiman, his voice resolute: ''I have your children. I'm putting them in a safety house.'' Enraged and terrified, Holt threw the phone across the room. When Reiman at last came to her door, she imagined her fist connecting with his chin. Instead she counted to ten and listened while he explained that the state had filed a dependency petition and her kids would be placed in foster homes. It was temporary, he assured her, until Sid pleaded guilty or was convicted at trial. Convinced she was aligned with her husband, the authorities doubted Holt would protect her children.

She protested that she'd turned her husband in, and now he was safely locked in jail. She cried and pleaded, but Reiman was unshakable. He handed her the paperwork. ''You'll need to get an attorney,'' he told her. Laura asked him to explain the dependency hearing to her, but his reply confused her. All she understood was that it was her first chance to regain her family.

Perez later told a Seattle reporter that he started to wonder what Sid Holt's wife was doing not long after the man was arrested. The fact that women abusers are universally recognized as rare reflected badly on more conventional interview methods, he said.

"Nobody ever asked the question about mothers; it was too horrible. Mothers are supposed to protect their children," he said. Perez had no similar reservations. "I'm no better than any other investigator," he said of his first successful investigation of a female suspect. "I just asked the next question."

State authorities placed Pam Holt in therapy focusing on abuse. Her therapist, foster mother Deborah Gambill, and Reiman repeatedly urged her to disclose abuse by her father . . . and her mother. After more than six months of the process, Pam said her mother molested her. Reiman placed the call.

Perez drove to the Holt home on July 7 at 9:30. It was the morning of a fine summer day, but inside the curtains were drawn and the room was dim. Laura invited him in and made feeble attempts to be hospitable, but he dispensed with the small talk. He bluntly told her that Pam had accused her and now Laura was coming to the station. According to his report, she started to cry. "Am I going to jail?" she sobbed. Perez assured her he just wanted to question her.

At the station, he read the Miranda rights form to her and urged her to initial it. According to Laura, Perez threatened her with lengthy prison time if she refused to initial and then sign the form. Said Perez: "Holt began to cry and said, 'I didn't want to do it but he made me.' I told her that I didn't believe her husband had made her do anything. Holt continued to cry and I gave her a box of Kleenex. I then asked her again what, if anything, she had done to [Pam] or her son [Donald].''

According to Perez, Laura gave a long and graphic statement. Although he didn't record her statement, in his typed report Perez purportedly quoted her copiously: all of the stark minutiae about orgiastic family sex gatherings. She described having sex with her kids alone or together at least once a week, including such acts as intercourse and the children putting their entire hands inside her vagina. Her husband Sid joined in. Once she signed the statement, Perez booked her into the Chelan County Regional Jail on 1,528 counts of rape of a child in the first degree.

When I interviewed her, Laura Holt described the interrogation differently. She said Perez questioned her at the station between 9:45 A.M and 1:30 P.M. ''He told me that I was under arrest and that I could have an attorney appointed, but there was no need to have an attorney,'' she said. She told him the name of her dependency lawyer, but Perez repeated she didn't need one.

He launched into a string of detailed accusations, she said, things Perez claimed he knew to be true. He said he'd talked to her kids and they said it happened (although, in fact, this was not yet the case). ''He said that I was making my kids into liars,'' she said. When she denied it, he told her she was lying. Perez clarified the consequences of lying. ''He said I was looking at forty to fifty years if I didn't say anything, for lying to him.'' He promised the court would give her a minimal sentence if she confessed.

For hours Perez persisted, she said. He threatened her with an eternity of prison and with the words, ''You'll never see your kids again.'' And then he threatened to take her artificial leg.

''You won't need *that* where you're going,'' he said,

pointing to the prosthesis awkwardly concealed under the leg of her trousers. Holt had lost her leg in a childhood accident and now imagined herself powerless, disfigured, and isolated in a population of hardened criminals. She cried hopelessly and shook with fear. At last she yielded just as she had when Perez threatened her with forty to fifty years if she didn't sign away her rights. According to Holt, she didn't give a statement but told Perez to write whatever he wanted.

He wrote, first in longhand and then on the computer, then threw his longhand notes away. When he read her "confession" to her, Laura called him a liar but Perez said, "Well, it's too late now. You're going to jail." He told her if she didn't sign at the bottom of the statement she was going to get more time, said Laura. Defeated, she signed.

At the jail, in court the next day, at every opportunity, Holt denied the statement. But Perez was right—it was too late.

Four days later, Deborah Gambill brought Pam to Perez's office, where he interviewed the child alone and, presumably, handed her a teddy bear, as was his custom. Fully primed by six months of therapy and foster care and the apparent knowledge that her parents had confessed, Pam told him her mother and father had had sex with her and made her have sex with her brother Donald.

Perez asked the next question—one that suggests that he already had a theory that something far more menacing than incest was going on. He asked her about Gene Town, neighbor of the Holts who, along with his wife, had recently come to his official attention. Pam said Town made her sit on his lap and she could feel his penis on her bottom, and he had rubbed her back under her shirt. Perez urged her to talk about Donald and wrote that she said Gene had had anal and oral sex with him.

Gambill brought Donald to Perez's office at 11:45 A.M. and he interviewed him alone. He tried to build up the boy's trust and Donald soon asked him to be his Big Brother. "I told him that I would be his friend even if I wasn't a 'Big Brother' and I would listen to anything he had to say," Perez reported.

He asked the boy if he had any "touching problems" and Donald hung his head. Whatever happened, it wasn't your fault, Perez reassured him. At last Donald said his mother had made him have intercourse with Pam. " 'Did you know my dad made [Pam] suck the dog's dick?' I told him that I didn't and he said, 'He's really sick; my dad,' " reads Perez's report. Donald said his mother "used me as a playtoy and made me do different things"—things that included intercourse.

But he wouldn't talk about the Towns. At this point, he became "somewhat withdrawn," and Perez excused him. Perez gave Gambill his home and office number and urged her to call if the kids made any other disclosures.

In many ways the statements of the Holt children bore little resemblance to their mother's. But this fact had no effect on the prosecution of her case. Judge John E. Bridges found that Laura's statements were voluntarily and knowingly made and thus admissible against her at trial. However, if it were *true* what she had said—that she had repeatedly denied her abuse and only confessed because Perez threatened her with forty to fifty years in prison and promised things would go easier on her if she confessed—it would be a different story, Judge Bridges wrote in his findings of fact. The weight of the evidence was tipped by "the credibility of Detective Perez's testimony" supported by two other officers who were in the shared squad room at times, too far away to hear what was said, but able to hear when Perez raised his voice, wrote the judge.

On the advice of her public defender, faced with the now-recanted but hopelessly inflammatory confession that would be admissible against her at trial, Laura agreed to enter an Alford plea (a designation of guilty plea whereby a defendant agrees to plead guilty and accept the consequences of a conviction without acknowledging criminal responsibility) to the original charges of eight counts of child rape in the first degree. She soon came to regret her decision because she received an exceptional sentence of forty years in prison.

Judge Bridges said that her cooperation in pleading guilty had spared her children the indignity of testifying, which "is a factor in Ms. Holt's favor, although she perhaps does and has minimized her involvement. And the court believes there are and always should be value to plea bargains." But not this time.

Meanwhile, Perez had zeroed in on the Holt's friends the Towns. Cherie Town, whose IQ was tested as 77, lived with her husband Meridith "Gene" Town and their two sons, ages fourteen and eleven, both diagnosed as mentally retarded and hyperactive. As had happened with the Holts, Cherie, after the couple had argued, accused Gene of abusing her sons. On Laura Holt's advice, she reported the abuse of her sons to a rape crisis counselor.

Soon Perez questioned her sons and in short order they were placed in foster care, and subjected to more questioning until they finally implicated their parents. The difference between the Holt and Town cases was basic: in the case of Gene and Cherie Town, Perez was chief investigative officer from the beginning and both went down within a few days of each other. After a lengthy and confrontational session, Gene confessed, and Perez asked the tough question about Cherie, reminding Gene that she got him in this mess in the first place. He cooperated: His wife often molested the boys and had intercourse with them, he said.

Around 9 A.M. on April 5, CPS caseworkers Juan Garcia and Dean Reiman met Perez at the Towns' weather-beaten wood-frame home.[1] According to Garcia, Reiman looked at the diminutive cottage and said, "The place'll smell. I'm staying outside."

Once inside, Perez confronted Cherie with his suspicions that she was involved in drugs and alcohol—a theory that accorded with conventional training that drugs and alcohol lowered the inhibitions. When she denied it, he urged her to step out to the cramped backyard.

Town later told me that once they were outside, Perez blandly announced he was on the verge of arresting her for molestation. He leaned his face next to hers and locked her in his unwavering blue-eyed gaze, she said. "I've heard the stories, and I know they're true. If you don't confess to it, I'll make sure you spend the rest of your life in prison." She said he stepped back a pace or two, yelled at her, accused her of having sex of every description with her children, and claimed there were witnesses.

Cherie said when she cried and denied it, Perez snapped, "Well, you're lying to me. I have the information and it's from more than one person, so I know you're a liar. If you don't tell me what happened, what I know is true, I'll make sure you spend the rest of your life in

[1] Findings of Fact and Conclusions of Law re: CrR 3.5 Hearing, *State of Washington v. Cherie Town*, 94–1–00139–7, filed 6/27/94. As an "Undisputed Fact," Judge T. W. Small found that "On April 5, 1994, Detective Bob Perez of the Wenatchee Police Department went to the residence of Cherie Town at 610 South Mission Street, Wenatchee, in the company of Juan Garcia and Dean Reiman, both CPS caseworkers for the Department of Social and Health Services." This finding was based on live testimony, including that of Detective Perez and Cherie Town. But note: At the trial of Linda Miller in September 1995, Detective Perez testified that to his recollection he had never "worked with" Juan Garcia; and Dean Reiman testified that Garcia was not present at the Town residence with him on that occasion.

jail!'' His voice softening, he promised her if she confessed he'd get her into a drug or alcohol treatment program to shorten her sentence . . . or wipe it out altogether. In fact, he said he'd personally speak to the judge on her behalf, said Town.

Juan Garcia told me he took the Town children outside. They were confused and distraught. While Reiman chatted with them near the car, Garcia strolled into the backyard in time to see Perez interrogating Cherie Town. They had already been at her house thirty to forty-five minutes, he said.

''I didn't do nothing,'' he heard Cherie say.

''Well, I don't fucking believe you!'' Perez yelled at her, according to Garcia.

Garcia had known the woman for years. She had all the earmarks of extreme vulnerability: mental impairment, abject poverty, a history of losing encounters with authority, an obvious and anxious need to please. Because of her missing teeth and her mental impairment, she was hard to understand at the best of times. This was not the best of times: Town cried and was virtually incoherent and clearly afraid.

The woman's distress seemed to infuriate Perez. He paced back and forth and waved his finger at her. ''I don't fucking believe you!'' he yelled at her several times, said Garcia. He said he heard Perez accuse her of a crazy quilt of perversities, and claimed he had witnesses and knew these facts were true. According to Garcia, when Cherie tearfully denied it, Perez called her a ''fucking liar.'' She slumped miserably before him.

After a time, Perez arrested and cuffed her, then took her directly to his office in the Wenatchee police station, where, according to Cherie, he questioned her from 11:15 A.M. until 5 P.M.,[2] at which time she was booked

---

[2] But note: Findings of Fact and Conclusions of Law re: CrR 3.5 Hearing, *State*

into the Chelan County Jail. Perez didn't record the interview. As he has many times testified, he routinely destroyed what notes he took as soon as his report was typed. He had discovered that notes could get him in trouble if they fell into the hands of the defense. According to Cherie, he started typing about ten minutes into the interrogation.

"I know you did it," he said, according to her. "I've got witnesses. Tell me when it happened. Tell me how long it went on. I know it happened. You might as well cough up to the whole thing." He started to tell her the specifics about what he believed, shooting her pointed glances while his fingers busily worked at the keyboard. She said she was crushed by the possibility that she would go to prison for the rest of her life; that, from that moment on, she might never see her children again. She remembered that Perez promised to help her with the judge if she cooperated with him. At last she started to talk. Mostly, she said, she nodded or said yes to things he said.

"You're gonna feel a lot better now," he reassured her.

Cherie felt sick. Within days she recanted her statement.

Cherie Town's statement was a masterpiece of graphic lurid detail, written in language far beyond her mental capacity. Conviction was a virtual certainty unless she could keep her confession from the jury. At a motion to suppress the use of her statement against her at trial, her attorney argued that Cherie's statement was outside her level of intellectual functioning, especially in light of its detail and specific dates and happenings over time.

---

of Washington v. Cherie Town, included the finding, based on Perez's testimony, that questioning lasted approximately two and a half hours. Also note that, according to the Wenatchee Police Department statement form witnessed by Detective Perez, the time of Town's statement was recorded as 12:22 pm.

The report began with the language: "My name is Cherie Lee Town and I am giving this statement to Detective Perez in reference to committing sexual acts with my two sons. . . . I have been advised of my constitutional rights by Det. Perez and I understand my rights. The first time I had sex with [Jeffrey] was in January of 1990. He was sick and wanted to get in bed with me. We were both naked. He started touching my breasts and my vagina. . . . Then he put his whole hand up inside me. . . . I was really excited about what was happening."

The confession went on with increasingly evocative quotations for another six pages.

Judge T. W. "Chip" Small didn't agree with the lawyer's assessment of the woman's limitations, although an unchallenged psychological report stared him in the face and set out Town's IQ. Ignoring this and her tenth-grade education in special education classes, he concluded that she understood and voluntarily waived her constitutional rights because "Cherie Town is a person of at least average intelligence."

Town reluctantly entered an Alford plea to reduced charges, although she had long since recanted her confession.

Gene Town was offered a plea agreement to reduced charges with a standard range between twelve and sixteen years. His options were limited by his lengthy confession and, not surprisingly, he agreed. Surprisingly, on the advice of his public defender he stipulated to an exceptional sentence of twenty years' confinement. When I asked him about it, Gene's attorney explained that an exceptional sentence might raise an issue on appeal.

Among the Wenatchee residents who next fell under official scrutiny were Joyce and Timothy Durst, and Henry and Connie Cunningham. Like Sid Holt and Gene

Town, Henry Cunningham was first charged with incest. Then, according to the police reports, Perez and CPS officials repeatedly questioned the Cunningham girls. At last, on June 10, 1994, they told Perez that not only had their father molested them, often first tying them with ropes and spread-eagling them across his desk, but sometimes their mother stood and watched. Typical of many early court documents of Perez's sex abuse arrests, the Affidavit of Probable Cause, a public record filed in open court, was rich with the kind of graphic, lurid, and evocative detail that inflamed the courts and the media at great expense to the privacy of the children.

The disposition of Connie Cunningham's case proved to be an instructive lesson to the ranks of the recently charged. She was charged with twelve counts of complicity to incest in the first degree, a charge that did not require proof that she molested her children. She denied the charges and went to trial. Upon her conviction—a conviction based largely on her husband's confession—Judge Small imposed an exceptional sentence of 560 months (46 years), roughly twice the high end of the standard sentencing range, although Connie was not alleged to have herself molested her children. Judge Small based his ruling, in part, on Cunningham's refusal to "accept responsibility for the offenses" by pleading guilty.[3]

While the cases ground away, Dean Reiman asked Pastor Roberson to allow the Holt children (who were members of the Apple Valley Baptist Church) to attend his church unescorted. Roberson was at the time considered a valuable resource for CPS; Reiman urged him to keep

---

[3] In May 1997, the Washington State Court of Appeals overturned Connie Cunningham's conviction and remanded the matter for a new trial, based on the violation of her right to confront her accuser when her husband's confession was used against her at trial.

an eye on the kids in case family members tried to contact them.

One day their foster mother Deborah Gambill approached Roberson after bringing the children to the church. "They were brought to me because of a heinous tragedy," she said, according to Roberson. Her voice was soft, but her words were heavy with meaning.

He looked at her. "You're kidding!" he said. The Holt kids had seemed perfectly normal to him.

"Well," she said enigmatically, "you would have to understand what they've been through."

"Maybe," he said, "but I don't see anything traumatized about how they act." But he was moved by her words and started to watch the children closely.

Then, in the early months of 1994, Reiman called him. "We have some more children from the Apple Valley Baptist Church that we'd like to become part of your congregation," he said, explaining only that, "there have been some problems." He told Roberson what he already knew: that his church was small, that he got involved with the people in his church, and that he'd be in the position to protect them and to notify CPS if there were problems.

What was he referring to? Roberson wondered. Reiman wasn't saying and Roberson knew and respected the limits of caseworker confidentiality. He hung up the phone, puzzled. He couldn't say no to these kids coming to his church, but on the other hand, why should he assume responsibility for a bunch of unsupervised children? It sounded like there was going to be a batch of them.

According to Roberson, there was among them the Holt kids and the Town kids—all of them removed from the Apple Valley Baptist Church.

One day, at the food bank, he pumped Deborah Gambill for information. "What's this all about?" he asked.

Gambill was standing beside him, handing out food to

the needy. She pushed back a strand of hair, looked to see if anyone could overhear, and then took him aside.

"Dean Reiman told me that there's a possibility of . . . well, of sexual misconduct, maybe group sex, at the Apple Valley Baptist Church," she said, according to Roberson.

He was stunned. "Group sex!" he gasped. "Where did you get this?"

"Dean Reiman," she said, according to Roberson. "He . . . well, *we* believe that some of the congregation, or the staff, or the administrators of the church might be up to something, some sexual activities with the kids."

"But who did you hear this from?"

Gambill pulled herself up defensively. "Well, talking to some of the workers at CPS, we put two and two together and realized that all the Towns, the Holts, the Everetts, Donna Rodriguez's daughter, all belonged. It's the one common thread. Besides, one of my relatives lives across the street from the pastor there on Miller Street. I know he beats his kids and he and his wife are very abusive to their children," she said, according to Roberson.

He pulled his fingers through his hair. "Well," he said slowly, "I don't know anything about the pastor down there, but I know sometimes people give pastors kind of a rough deal. Do you really know this to be true?"

She leaned close and lowered her voice, said Roberson. "All I can say," she breathed, "is I talked with Dean Reiman, and the caseworkers down there really are out doing an investigation. They really believe that the one thing these kids have in common is the Apple Valley Baptist Church. So we just feel the best bet at this point is to keep the children separated from that church." Roberson then went to the tiny cluttered church office to call Reiman in order to confirm this information. According to him, Reiman wasn't in; the call was referred to Tim Abbey.

"I can't really comment on that," said Abbey after the pastor confronted him.

"Well, I need to know," said Roberson. "If there's really a problem around here and I have some of the people in my church now, then I need to know what to be looking for."

"We'll get back to you," Abbey replied tersely.

The return call, when it came, was from Reiman. "We just have some concerns we're looking into," he said, noncommittally, according to Roberson. Reiman confirmed that these concerns were regarding possible sexual abuse in the church, but he refused to provide details. "We appreciate your concern," he added, before hanging up.

In fact, Reiman, Abbey, and other Division of Children and Family Services caseworkers, working closely with the police, struggled to weave their suspicions and disparate clues about affiliations into a fabric that would hold together. Investigations increasingly focused on children, many of them made accessible to the authorities because their parents were induced to sign "voluntary" agreements for their placement or treatment. When I talked to him, Abbey said many of the ongoing disclosures were an outgrowth of foster care and therapy. Kids came forward "because of children feeling safer in counseling and foster care." The Perez foster home was a case in point, he said, as opposed to Ann Everett's previous placement with Bob Devereaux, where the usual correlation between foster care, trust, and disclosure had been reversed . . . all the way up the line to her caseworker.

6:

Summer 1994

═══════

Single Male—Unheeded Warnings

═══════

Robert Devereaux recalls that it was 1987 and he was approaching fifty and working as an insurance company executive when he and his wife Maxine took in their first foster child. The boy lived across the street; his mother had recently committed suicide. Bob felt bad for the boy, but still Maxine had to talk him into it. With their kids only recently grown, he had rosy notions of loafing and travel and hobbies and similar self-indulgences. But the idea soon took hold.

Over the course of the next five years, the Devereauxs took in over two hundred foster kids. Most came and went; a few became permanent residents. In time, their roomy colonial-style home became a bustling foster group home for children, many of them the troubled hard-to-place kids who needed long-term foster care.

Maxine Devereaux had no interest in maintaining a foster home after the marriage fell apart in 1991. The prospect of going it alone was formidable. Bob, a soft-spoken, diplomatic man, talked it over with the kids. They wanted to stay. Four of the girls had been with Bob for years: Bonnie Rogers, Theresa and Lois Sanchez, Caroline Filbeck. He was their "dad" and he loved them as daughters. The decision was inevitable. First, he had some culling to do. For troubled kids, coed group homes were an invitation to teenage sex. Since all but one of his foster children were girls, choosing the gender was easy.

Bob insisted on standards and discipline above and beyond the excruciating minutiae of state requirements. He was strict, there was no getting around it, grounding the girls for running around in their underwear or violating other rules about modesty, for skipping out on chores, for breaking mundane household rules. He rigidly adhered to foster care requirements, contacting the authorities when the circumstances warranted it. Some of the girls had problems based on their histories of abuse—acting out sexually toward Devereaux or other foster kids. He reported it each time. When the kids groused about his rules, Devereaux reminded himself that these kids *needed* structure and consistency.

"I was *always* being grounded," wailed Nikki Simpson when I talked to her. "The only way I could get off groundation faster was to do extra chores. There used to be this whole row of trees along the street on the side of the house. I had to cut them all down by myself. By the time I got done, I was off groundation anyway."

Bob Devereaux was tough. But, above all, he was kind: a warm and loving teddy bear of a man. He was the kind of dad most of these kids had missed.

"This is a man who cared about discipline and modesty and about us," Nikki told Dorothy Rabinowitz of the *Wall Street Journal.* "This is a man who went without all year and bought nothing for himself so he could give us . . . a proper Christmas."

In the years before their divorce, Bob and Maxine Devereaux were well-respected, described by Perez and by some state social workers as model foster parents. But with the divorce, the honeymoon with the child care officials was over. Immediately, rumor, speculation, and recrimination settled over the orderly two-story home. The reason was simple: Devereaux was a man, the children were girls. Or, according to the prevailing theory of various Wenatchee officials, *a man with an opportunity is a molester.*

Ugly words about Devereaux bounced along the halls of DCFS, the police department, other foster homes. Many caseworkers, particularly Abbey, Reiman, and Boggess, were suspicious of the man from the moment of his divorce. DCFS officials told him that, now that he was single, he would be unable to resist a natural male urge to have sexual contact with adolescent females. Based on "anonymous" complaints, state officials investigated the Devereaux household a couple of times, even removed the girls briefly for questioning. All the girls were wholeheartedly supportive of their foster father; nothing could be substantiated and all appeared to be well.

Abbey was unsatisfied. He complained, frequently and often, about Devereaux's likely propensities. His concerns spread at meetings of foster parents attended by a large crowd, including Bob and Luci Perez and Janet Rutherford. To Rutherford, a tiny woman with huge brown eyes, a ready smile, and childlike energy, the possibility that Bob Devereaux was a molester seemed unlikely. At a panel discussion to recruit future foster parents, Bob Devereaux was one of the featured speakers. "He was the role model of foster parents," she said. "He was like a Greek god." As she came to know him better, her respect for him grew. "I saw how he handled the girls, how he took care of them. He went over and aboveboard doing the right thing for the girls. I never questioned that he loved what he did."

It was the *reason* Devereaux loved foster parenting that worried Abbey.

"It doesn't look right," he told Devereaux. "You, a single guy, around all those girls." Men in that position can give in to their impulses, he announced flatly. Devereaux protested that he had strict rules about modesty, that he knocked on the girls' doors to wake them in the morning but he wouldn't go inside, that he had neither the inclination nor the lack of self-control to be a molester. Abbey was unmoved. But he was prepared to compromise.

"I'll tell you what," he said. "If you sign a contract to hire a live-in housekeeper as a respite care worker, you can continue to be a foster parent." Devereaux would have to pay for the housekeeper out of his own pocket. Thinking of the girls, he felt he had no choice. He signed a contract.

The first housekeeper was a deputy sheriff. That ought to satisfy them, he thought. But one day she worked a double shift in her job as deputy. Devereaux was left alone with the girls and the echo of Abbey's warning: *A man with an opportunity is a molester.* Ridiculous, but he'd agreed to have a housekeeper. Shrugging, he called the DSHS office.

Abbey reacted predictably: Cops worked cops' hours, so the lady had to go. The second housekeeper didn't work out, nor the third. Devereaux asked himself why he was going through this process. He already had ten kids in the house, and he was paying for respite care.

In early 1993, caseworker Juana Vasquez was Devereaux's supervisor at the Wenatchee office of the state Child Welfare Services. Vasquez was the child of migratory workers from the Wenatchee area. She studied hard, struggled for grants and scholarships, and worked her way through university. She worked in a variety of social service jobs, and for a time was a well-liked dean of admissions and director of minority affairs at Gonzaga University in Spokane. She returned to Wenatchee to take the less prestigious position of caseworker mainly because she wanted to give something back to her community and to her people. She soon found she was regarded as merely another Hispanic troublemaker at the Wenatchee DSHS office.

Vasquez heard all of the complaints about Bob Devereaux from Boggess, Abbey, and, above all, Reiman. Without exception, the complaints came down to the fact that Devereaux was a single male. She knew that the home had survived several departmental referrals calling for the investigation of Devereaux as a possible child molester on the strength of rumors and speculation—nothing concrete, nothing that could be substantiated, nothing any of Bob's kids would validate. And nothing to it, most likely, nothing but discrimination, she told herself. Who should recognize the ugly spreading stain of discrimination better than Juana Vasquez?

"If you feel this way," she said to Abbey and other caseworkers, "why don't you just shut the foster home down?" Abbey explained that the speculations were unproven.

Other caseworkers agreed with Vasquez. One of them was Paul Glassen, a scholarly social worker with the Wenatchee Child Welfare Services office. Glassen held a BA degree in rehabilitation counseling and a master's in clinical sociology. He had worked as a social worker or mental health counselor for twenty-eight years, including a stint in residential treatment facilities for children. For the last three years he worked out of the Wenatchee office as a caseworker. He was known for choosing his words carefully, then speaking his mind; and also for analyzing the official written policies and procedures of the Child Welfare Services and its parent division, the Division of Children and Family Services, and then religiously applying these policies. Glassen was, in short, the kind of man unlikely to survive the slippery politics of the Wenatchee DCFS office.

Glassen knew the stories about Devereaux, and how they changed upon his divorce. The stories didn't reflect his own observations. "I found him a very, very dedicated foster parent," Glassen told me. "In fact he was very determined to be in compliance with the policies. He worked very closely with the juvenile authorities and with the police." The rumors were groundless, in Glassen's opinion, groundless and stupid, and they were coming from the usual crowd: Reiman, Boggess, and Abbey. "I began to associate them with the kind of ethnic bias I had seen on their part. Now it was a matter of gender bias against the foster parent because he happened to be a male who had female foster children."

"Do you think I should have to put up with this?" Devereaux asked Vasquez in early 1993.

To his relief, she said no. "There are lots of single women foster parents," she told him, "and they don't have to have a housekeeper." She suggested he take his complaint to the administrators at the regional level of DCFS.

Devereaux placed a phone call to DCFS Regional Administrator Roy Harrington in Spokane. According to Devereaux, Harrington confirmed it: There was nothing to justify this practice in the law or DSHS policies. Devereaux tore up the contract.

To hell with Devereaux, stormed Abbey and others. "I knew there was a great deal of resentment by some of the staff," said Glassen. The rumors and speculations spread quickly, causing the Devereaux home to be continually scrutinized.

For some, the equation between Devereaux's opportunity and his propensity to molest was absolute. "A lot of people wondered," Abbey said. In fact, the DSHS caseworkers weren't alone in their thoughts. Bob Perez, good friends with Tim Abbey, thought the speculations had that *ring* about them—that solid reverberation in the gut that grounded them in reality.

And then one day Bob Devereaux came into his office, one of his foster girls in tow.

Theresa Sanchez was one of Devereaux's long-term foster girls, long ago diagnosed with fetal alcohol syndrome, which left her mentally impaired. She was a pretty girl of fifteen, with straight brown hair, oval eyes, and a shy smile. As she matured, she grew more attractive— and more vulnerable. Her sister had been a gang member, but Devereaux was determined that Theresa would be different.

One day, the girl sneaked out and came home late: vague, disheveled, and largely incoherent. She trudged upstairs and slumped on a bed. Devereaux's initial anger turned to alarm as he took in her appearance. He questioned her insistently, but Theresa said she couldn't remember much about what happened after she met five or six guys in their twenties. She said the men gave her something to drink and she passed out and woke up with no panties on. To Devereaux, all the signs were there: Theresa had been raped.

He bundled the girl up and took her to the emergency room at the hospital. He sat in a chair too small for his bulk, thumbed through magazines too trivial for the circumstances, stared at framed posters too bland to be art. When Theresa came out, he patted her hand and waited with her for the results of the vaginal culture. At last,

Devereaux was called into an examining room, where he stared at posters, expanses of chrome instruments, and, at last, the face of the doctor as he told him the vaginal culture confirmed the presence of semen.

Damn it, Deveraux told himself, those bastards weren't getting away with this. He took Theresa straight to the Wenatchee police station. The officer who greeted him was Detective Perez.

When Perez looked at Devereaux, he saw a tall, clean-cut man in a short-sleeved knit shirt that bulged with the paunch of middle age; a strong face with lines of accumulated laughter around his eyes; and, on this occasion, an angry intense gaze. Perez's eyes dropped to Theresa, her face sullen, her skin flawless, her eyes lowered in embarrassment or shame.

Perez narrowed his eyes and pointed to the chairs that stood before his desk. "Sit down," he said.

Devereaux repeated what Theresa told him of her recollections. He described her condition and the results of the rape test. "She doesn't remember what happened, exactly," he said. He noted with dismay that not once had the detective reached for his notepad.

Perez leaned back in his chair and regarded the pair appraisingly. "Well," he said at last, according to Devereaux, "if she doesn't remember, I can't do anything."

Devereaux was taken aback. "But we've got their description. We know some of their names. Can't we match them up with the DNA from the semen?"

"There's nothing we can do," Perez repeated icily. For him this particular case was closed. But the case against Devereaux had begun.

"My suspicion started with a gut feeling," Perez said of this incident to the *Seattle Times*. "Devereaux brought a girl into the police station. He wanted me to tell this child she shouldn't have sex with her boyfriend. But the way this came across, it wasn't so much that he was doing it as a concerned foster parent, but that he was jealous.'' Perez's suspicions grew. ''Then I would see him out driving in his car and it would appear more as a social relationship than a parent-child relationship. . . . Then a child said he'd allow them to sit on his lap and drive the car. And that didn't sound right either.''

The image of Devereaux driving with a child on his lap evolved in Perez's mind. One day at lunch at a popular Wenatchee restaurant, Perez cracked jokes born of the popular local speculation. He was surrounded by potted plants and plates of half-eaten food and cops and caseworkers from the DCFS office. Warmed by the food and the audience, he became expansive. Glassen hadn't had many social dealings with Perez and found himself surprised that he not only dominated the conversation, but dominated it with ribald humor and stories. Many of the jokes and stories targeted Bob Devereaux.

''Well,'' said Perez, his words heavy with sarcasm, according to Glassen, ''some of these children are old enough to drive. I'll *bet* he teaches them to drive.'' He raised his voice in a mocking imitation of Devereaux. ''Come on, honey, sit here on my lap and grab this stick shift.'' Perez half clenched a fist in midair inches from his crotch.

Glassen turned away in embarrassment. He found himself shocked, not because he believed the detective, but because the story was told in this public place in the presence of various professionals who, to his profound disgust, were *laughing*.

''Well, that's just Perez,'' a caseworker said later with a shrug. ''That's the way he talks all the time.''

Glassen wasn't willing to simply shrug it off. He filed a formal complaint.

Perez first swore he'd never made the joke.[1] Then he offhandedly acknowledged it. "When you have your lunch breaks, your off time, you blow steam off. . . . You say things that in regular circles would make people's hair curl or turn grey. But it doesn't mean anything," Perez said to the *Seattle Times*. "All I said was I hope I'm still working in detectives when and if a child discloses and says something happened."

Two months later he had the opportunity.

On the balmy evening of July 30, 1994, Devereaux let the girls camp out in a tent in the backyard. It was fun for them but tedious for him: He set his alarm so he could check on them every couple of hours. One time he awoke to find most of his girls running around with some kids from across the street, and Theresa in the tent with her boyfriend. The party was over.

The boy called the next morning and talked to another foster child. He bragged to her that he'd had sex with Theresa. The girl promptly told her foster father. Devereaux's response was immediate. Theresa was vulnerable and he was obligated to protect her. First he grounded her, then he broke the bad news. "No more boyfriend!" he announced with an unwavering expression that told her the discussion was over.

Theresa was furious. Later that day she lightly laced Devereaux's and Bonnie Rogers's soft drinks with iodine. She put the most in Bonnie's drink because she thought she was the one who told on her. Devereaux immediately detected the smell of iodine and didn't drink more than a sip. He looked at Bonnie, who was grimacing, and went to find Theresa. "What's going on?"

---

[1] Perez allegedly admitted the remark to tort investigator Fred Baker, per communication from Patty Baron, DSHS Torts Claims Division.

The girl confessed, her face flushed, her eyes defiant. Devereaux glowered at her. He'd have to report the incident according to DSHS procedure. He called the Child Welfare Services office, spoke to Glassen, and was referred to Linda Woods, the caseworker on duty. Devereaux hoped that Woods would merely come out to take down a report. Instead she called the police.

By 6:15 P.M. dinner would usually be simmering on the stove. Instead, Officer T. Adcock of the Wenatchee Police Department was at the door. Devereaux led him into the living room, where Linda Woods, Theresa, Bonnie, and another woman were sitting. Adcock listened to Devereaux's explanation as he gathered up the iodine bottle, one of the used glasses, and some of the remaining liquid and placed them in evidence containers. Then he turned to Theresa.

Adcock advised her of her Miranda rights and she promptly confessed. The girl's words were halting and slow and she showed the same bland disregard for consequences that so often mystified him about teenagers. She'd been angry, she said. A seven-year-old neighbor child also drank from the laced soft drink, Adcock learned.

He took Theresa to the Wenatchee police station and introduced her to Detective John Kruse. Then Adcock phoned the poison control center, determined that the few swallows of diluted iodine that the children had ingested wouldn't be lethal, and called Devereaux with the good news.

Kruse took down Theresa's statement, typed it up, and had her sign it after he read it to her. In part, she said:

Today, 7/30, I found a bottle of iodine that said it was poisonous. I found it in [Bonnie's] little jewelry box. I knew she had stolen it. [Bonnie] and Bob had bought

some 32 oz cups of pop and brought them home to 500
Ramona. I took the iodine and poured it in their cups. I
poured most of it in [Bonnie's] because I was maddest at
her and poured the rest in Dad's. I did this because I
wanted to get rid of them. I knew they could die from this.

Theresa was booked into juvenile hall, then charged
with two counts of assault in the first degree and one
count of assault in the second degree. The case, but for
its final disposition, appeared to be closed.

When word of the events found their way to Perez, he
concluded the crime portended a greater evil. Perez announced around the DSHS offices that Theresa had found
a way to get back at Devereaux for molesting her. On
August 3, he questioned her by herself at the juvenile
center.

"Hi, how're you doing?" he said.

"Fine," Theresa murmured automatically.

Then he went right to the heart of the matter, according
to Theresa. "What goes on in the Devereaux house?" he
asked.

"Just the normal family stuff," she said.

"Does Devereaux tuck you in at night?" asked Perez,
according to Theresa.

"Yeah," she said, suspecting where this was leading,
"but he doesn't touch us."

Perez questioned her for a couple of hours. His questions "made me feel low about myself," she said. Perez
"was putting words in my mouth, mixing things up." He
said Devereaux abused her and his other foster kids, she
said. For a long time, she said no. He leaned over the
table, his eyes locked on hers. She wished he would simply go away. Tears fell from her eyes and ran down her
face and she wiped them away.

Theresa started to talk, to say what he wanted, hoping

to put an end to it, hoping he'd leave her alone. Yes, she said, Bob had touched her.

Perez leaned closer. "Do the other girls do it, too?" he asked.

"Yes," she lied. "They jack him off."

Theresa later remembered that day with regret. "It didn't feel right in my heart," she said.

From juvenile hall, Perez went straight to the Devereaux home. As he strode from his car, chin thrust high with purpose, he took in the well-kept lawn, the stand of roses by the path to the door. From the outside, you'd never know. Perez rapped forcefully and, after a moment, Devereaux stood before him, his face drawn with wariness or anxiety or some expression meant to mask his guilt.

"You've gotta come to the police station."

"I can't right now," said Devereaux in confusion. "The kids will be all by themselves."

"It's gotta be right now," Perez said.

"What's this about?" asked Devereaux. The detective stood mute, his eyes scanning the expansive living room. Devereaux tried again. "Can't we talk here?"

Perez drummed his fingers impatiently on the butt of his revolver. "We're going to the station," he said.

At the station, Devereaux sat uneasily across the desk from Perez. His eyes drifted to a bank of teddy bears that huddled incongruously above the bulletin board. He was in a large room with several desks scattered about. A few cops drifted in, glanced his way curiously, drifted out. He started at the sound of Perez's voice.

"Theresa says you've been raping her for years."

Devereaux gaped at him in astonishment. Perez stroked his mustache, the gesture so ordinary that perhaps Devereaux had imagined the words. But then, according to Devereaux, Perez leaned forward and said, "I know it's true, so you might as well admit it."

"No!" he protested. "I didn't do anything!" He could hear the tremor in his voice, the inadequacy of his words. He struggled to gather his wits. What was he supposed to do in this situation? "I want an attorney," he managed at last.

"If you want an attorney," said Perez flatly, according to Devereaux, "you're in jail." He took out his handcuffs and slapped them meaningfully against his palm. Heart fluttering in fear, Devereaux backed off. But, as the approximately four hours of interrogation continued, he renewed his request for an attorney over and over, he said. Each time Perez reminded him that the consequence of demanding a lawyer was jail. Devereaux didn't know whether Perez would jail him as a suspect as an alternative to yielding to his request, but under the circumstances he was afraid to challenge him.

For Devereaux, the experience was humiliating and often bewildering. But one thing was obvious: Perez believed he abused Theresa and other foster children and he wouldn't accept any information to the contrary. Perez accused him of having intercourse with Theresa. He accused him of making one of the girls sit on his lap, causing him an erection, and then, as Perez put it, "you got your jollies." The words careened around the room, deadly as ricocheting bullets. It went on for hours: Perez hurled astonishing accusations at him; he responded with feeble and doomed denials.

"You'll go to prison for the rest of your life," said Perez. "You know what they'll do to you in there! You're not gonna like it." Devereaux looked away, sickened with his own imaginings. Although he'd never before been arrested, he'd heard the stories, like everyone else. He tried not to listen as the detective reminded him of what happens to sex offenders in prison, the least of which were regular beatings.

Perez's voice softened. "You might as well confess. If you do, I'll see you get treatment." Could that be so bad? Chatting with a shrink about his problem for an hour or so each week and then getting in his car and driving back home? Think about it, said Perez. Devereaux could live free, safe behind his own walls. He stared at Perez. Considering the alternatives, the possibility of treatment—lying to a psychologist to stay free—was hugely seductive.

"But I didn't *do* anything," he protested in that doomed shaky voice.

"Children don't lie. Are you calling your kids liars?" snapped Perez, according to Devereaux.

After a time, Perez left the room. "I'm gonna talk to Bonnie," he announced. Bonnie Rogers had been waiting at the station for hours. Devereaux himself waited in the room for a seeming eternity: one hour and fifteen minutes. When the detective at last returned, he appeared disgruntled.

"Bonnie Rogers is still defending you," he growled. "But I know you did her."

Now Perez was clearly running out of patience. He again reminded Devereaux of his options: unthinkable time in prison for the rest of his life, or becoming a pariah in the community. Devereaux looked at him numbly. Perez glanced around the room and, seeing they were alone, got up.

"You fucked your kids!" he yelled, according to Devereaux. "You *fucked* your *kids*!"

Devereaux gasped. At that moment he could foresee his fate in Perez's reddened face, his bulging eyes, the veins standing out on his neck. He had never been arrested, jailed, or had any dealings with interrogation. The terrible choices confounded him; his imaginings raised nightmarish primal fears. What chance would a mild fifty-eight-year-old man have in a world of hardened criminals? He was shaking and tears stood in his eyes. He wanted this awful day to end. At that moment he started to believe that it would indeed be better for him to "confess."

So, after hours of ruthless interrogation, he made a statement that he now describes as sarcastic. The words reflected his desperate ambivalence: a confusing blend of confession and denial.

"Okay I did it," he snapped. "But I can't give you any fucking details because it didn't happen!"

Perez started to type: It was confession enough for him. When Devereaux read the typed statement later attributed to him, he was shocked. Perez claimed that he had admitted to specific sexual acts, including making Bonnie touch his penis two or three times. Devereaux denied he said this and refused to sign the confession that Perez had prepared for him. It was, he now says, a "flat-out lie."

Perez's handwritten notes dated August 3, 1994, support Devereaux's claim. Perez quotes Devereaux as saying some of his foster girls acted out sexually, but nowhere do the notes say he admitted molesting them.[2]

Bob Devereaux was arrested and booked, but he quickly made bail.

But Perez was on a desperate mission. First he questioned his own foster daughter, Ann Everett,[3] who had

---

[2] In all criminal discovery attempts, Perez said that he had retained none of the notes of his interviews. Perez's attorney Patrick McMahon produced Perez's notes, dated 5 P.M. August 3, 1994, in 1996, as part of a civil discovery action by Devereaux's attorney, Steve Lacy.

[3] Ann was again interviewed by CPS caseworker Katie Carrow and by Wenatchee Police Detective Terry Pippin on August 10, 1994, according to Carrow's CPS Service Episode Record dated August 10, 1994. Ann said that Devereaux treated her well. She said she never had any problems with Devereaux and never witnessed any sexual abuse in his foster home. This interview was withheld from the defense during Devereaux's criminal prosecution, and was either not recorded, destroyed, or unreported by Detective Terry Pippin, although Devereaux's attorney, Steve

lived with Devereaux before moving in with Perez; she denied that Devereaux had touched her.

Then he interviewed Terri Hockett, another of Devereaux's foster girls. "You're not leaving this room until you tell me that something happened between you and Devereaux," Perez allegedly told her. Terri resisted.

He questioned Bonnie Rogers again. By now she had been waiting in a room at the Wenatchee police station for hours. While she waited for Perez to come back to talk to her, caseworker Linda Woods encouraged her to make disclosures with the assistance of a drawing of a human figure. When Perez finally arrived, according to his report, the girl was "ready to talk" and, according to a defense interview, Woods said she left the room so Perez could be alone with Bonnie.[4]

According to Perez's report, Bonnie said Bob Devereaux first sexually touched her when she was eight years old, "just after I moved in with him." Her description was similar to Perez's joking speculations about Devereaux at the restaurant. Bonnie said twice a week or more, she sat on Devereaux's lap facing away from him, while he unfastened her pants, rubbed her buttocks, and put his hand under her blouse and fondled her breasts. Another time, "Bob put his finger inside me. . . . But," she added, "I hit him." When no one was home, Devereaux raped her on the couch, but she "tried to sleep and block out what he was doing." She said Devereaux raped her about five times a month and tried to force her to perform oral sex. He warned he would "stab me or kill me if I told

Lacy, had requested all relevant police and CPS documents and the production of exculpatory information as required by the rules of criminal discovery.
[4] Whether Woods was present during the interview is a subject of debate. Although Perez wrote in his report that Woods was present when he interviewed Bonnie, Woods later told a defense attorney she had left the room and Perez acknowledged this claim. More recently, as part of civil discovery pending lawsuits, both Perez and Woods alleged she was present.

anyone what he was doing." Everything happened while Bonnie was alone with him.

Within two to three hours of making bail, Devereaux was rearrested.

That night Paul Glassen of CWS got a phone call from a seventeen-year-old girl who was one of Devereaux's foster kids. "Perez arrested Dad and left us alone," said the girl. Glassen was astonished by this breach of established procedure.

He left a phone message for Perez to confirm the arrest and to find out if it was necessary to arrange alternate emergency placement for the girls. Next he drove to the Devereaux home to stay with the girls, while he and other caseworkers tried to line up temporary places for them to spend the night. "They needed a great deal of counseling," he said. "They were very upset." All agreed that they didn't want to be moved. "They didn't want to go anywhere else. This was their home."

Glassen waited with the girls at the Devereaux home from 3:30 P.M. until around 5, when the first of them were transported to the police station for questioning. Nobody had dinner. By 7 P.M. all of the kids were gone, and none of them would return.

The next morning, August 4, Glassen went to the Chelan County juvenile detention facility to see Theresa, who was a child on his caseload. The facility was a cheerless place, a jail for kids, whatever the authorities say about rehabilitation. But the kids rarely stayed long. This particular visit came at the request of juvenile probation officer Katie Hershey, who wanted him to help Theresa complete some medical paperwork. He also wanted to talk to her about her future plans. She wouldn't stay locked up forever.

"We spoke for a long time," Glassen said, "just about

the issue of placement. And at this time I didn't know if she'd been interviewed or not.''

Finally, according to Glassen, Theresa blurted, ''I told a whole bunch of lies yesterday about Dad.''

She shot him an anxious look and then went on. Perez came to talk to her the day before, and what he said had confused and pressured her, she said. After a while she told a lot of lies, she repeated. ''The cop was out to get Dad,'' said Theresa. ''He said Dad touches us under our clothes, and things like that, like when we're in bed.'' Perez told her other girls said Devereaux molested them. However, Perez's police report clearly reveals that none of Devereaux's foster girls were even interviewed before he went to see Theresa.

''He said Bonnie told him she goes on Bob's bed and screws around,'' said Theresa. ''He was, like, trying to set Dad up or something. But it's not true. We might sit by his bed when he's lying down, but the cop tried to say Bonnie got on him''—she hesitated, flushed—''you know, like, on his penis.

''I told him another lie about Bonnie going into Dad's room and jacking him off.'' Theresa looked up at Glassen, her eyes sad. ''I feel really bad. I did as soon as the attorney came and told me Dad had been arrested.'' But if, as Perez had said, Devereaux molested the other girls, maybe it wasn't so bad that she lied about him, she said.

Glassen thought about what Theresa's words implied. Given her incarceration and her mental disability, he thought an attorney should have been with her. The questioning sounded highly coercive. ''What training I had was very specific to not ask leading questions, not directing the children in any way, and what she described . . . seemed to go way beyond simply asking leading questions,'' he told me. ''She was very, very troubled by the whole business.''

He scribbled down notes as he spoke to Theresa, then encouraged her to talk to her therapist and disclose what happened. From there, he went directly into the office of the juvenile detention officer, Katie Hershey, and repeated the girl's words. Hershey, who was married to a Chelan County deputy prosecuting attorney, was not very responsive, but she took notes and heard him out. Glassen walked away, his face grim.

Next, he called his supervisor, Juana Vasquez, who assured him he'd done the right thing. Finally, he filed an official complaint against Perez for "emotional neglect/abuse" and "violation of legal and civil and constitutional rights."[5]

Once Detective Kruse got the word, he went to the juvenile facility, talked to Theresa, and prepared a written statement for her signature. She had recanted, all right. In the statement Theresa confirmed the recantation and the fact that she had lied to Perez when she said Devereaux molested her and Bonnie. "I only told the police officer this because he made me nervous," the statement read. But the statement included some additional information. She said that Glassen had asked her "if I thought it was fair that I could get bailed out of jail and Bob would not. . . . I said no, it wasn't fair. . . . I told Mr. Glassen that

---

[5] According to Glassen's Child Abuse Referral: "The nature of the concerns related to Wen. Police Det. Robert Perez' interrogation of child under duress of incarceration possibly in absence of her attorney, CPS worker or other person. . . . Risk persists due to failure of appropriate authorities to investigate suspected abuse while alleged perpetrator [Perez] has continued access to and authority over alleged victim(s)." Glassen said that Theresa was "extremely vulnerable, emotionally scarred, developmentally impaired." In describing Devereaux on the form, Glassen said he "has many years experience specializing in long term care and guardianship of special needs, medically fragile, emotionally and sexually abused children." As to additional facts, Glassen said that the "child is particularly vulnerable at this time due to incarceration on assault charge/relationship to authority of police officer. An additional "risk factor" was "continued access of alleged perpetrator," Robert Perez.

I wanted to go back to Bob's house because that was home for me. . . . Mr. Glassen told me he was mad at the police officer after I told him this [about Perez's interview]." She said his words made her feel guilty.

Glassen checked in again with Vasquez. She told him that rumors were flying about him at the DCFS office. "Well, it sounds like you're doing your job to me," she said, but warned him that Katie Hershey implied that he had inappropriately interviewed Theresa, maybe even influenced her to recant. Glassen was stunned.

On August 8, 1994, Chelan County Prosecuting Attorney Gary Riesen filed an information charging Bob Devereaux with four counts of rape of a child in the second degree involving Bonnie Rogers, and two counts of rape of a child in the third degree and one count of child molestation in the third degree involving Theresa Sanchez. The fact that Theresa had unequivocally recanted her statement made no difference at all.

7:

Summer 1994

═══════

Culling the Caseworkers

═══════

On the afternoon of August 4, 1994, Detective Perez called Wenatchee Police Sergeant Doug Tangen. He was irate. He'd been inundated with calls from caseworkers and Chelan County authorities eager to tell him that Paul Glassen was doing a number on him. Glassen was spreading the word that he "had it in for Bob Devereaux and that Perez had set Bob Devereaux up and the investigation was not appropriate," wrote Tangen in his police report.

Tangen went to Perez's shared office and sat at a desk near the detective. He listened as Perez placed a call to CPS area manager Carol Billesbach. Perez told her that Glassen was "slandering" his investigation and "questioning his integrity." He growled that the man was going around telling other law enforcement professionals that he'd "fabricated" or "used questionable tactics" in the Devereaux investigation, and that she had better persuade him to back off. When Billesbach said she couldn't force a caseworker into silence, he snapped that he'd consider suing if the "personal slander" didn't stop. Although Perez wasn't sure of the basis of a lawsuit at the time he made the threat, he later said of his words, "Anybody can sue anybody for anything these days."

In the face of Perez's frustration, Tangen offered to lend a hand. Perez accepted, saying he hadn't "had much luck with Carol." At 4:30 P.M. on August 4, Tangen spoke to Wenatchee Police Captain Jim Boles. They agreed to talk to Glassen's supervisor and silence him, or, in the words of Tangen's police report, "put a stop to his actions."

At 5 P.M., Perez called Tangen on the car phone. According to Tangen's report, Perez claimed he had just learned that Glassen had talked to Theresa, although this interview took place that morning between 11 A.M. and noon, and he had already received a flood of related phone calls. Tangen then called Katie Hershey at the juvenile facility.

Hershey apologized profusely. She felt very bad, she said, because she was the one who had asked Paul Glassen to come to juvenile court to sign medical release papers for Theresa. When she thought it over, Glassen seemed concerned about the investigation of the Devereaux case even before he went in to see Theresa.

Hershey said when Glassen returned after seeing the girl, he had some notes on a yellow piece of paper. He shoved them in her face as if they were proof of something or other. He told her Theresa had recanted and claimed that Perez asked her leading questions. As if this weren't bad enough, she saw Glassen consorting with Bob Devereaux "off and on all day," after Devereaux had posted bail. Hershey explained that his actions so upset her that she decided to contact the prosecutor's office.

It was a short walk across the street to the office complex her husband shared with the other deputy prosecutors. In fact, Hershey was in talking to Chelan County Prosecutor Gary Riesen when Perez called Riesen to complain about Glassen.

Glassen's actions were upsetting to other Wenatchee

officials: He had committed an unpardonable breach of the political social order by diverting suspicion from Devereaux, a suspect, to Perez, a cop and integral part of the Wenatchee legal structure. This sin of diversion would be attempted again and again in the months and years to come. When it happened, the sin would be flung in the face of its source—the criminal suspect or his lawyer, the critics, the media. After all, those who questioned the authorities were themselves suspect.

Worse, Glassen had contributed to the process of recantation, a dangerous practice that, if unleashed, might undo Perez's investigation and the delicate balance of Wenatchee's criminal justice system. According to long-standing theories embraced by many child welfare officials, recantations were in fact coping mechanisms or even symptoms of abuse victims, but this was a hard thing to prove to a jury. For the most part, Wenatchee police and prosecutors found recantations to be legally meaningless except when they fell into the hands of the defense and fouled up cases. The authorities knew how to separate kids from the obvious risks of recantation. But when the risk came from one of their own, it presented a greater dilemma.

At 6 P.M., Tangen called Riesen at home and told him he wanted to interview Glassen "to stop Mr. Glassen from any further tampering." According to Tangen's report, Riesen agreed that the police should convince him to stay away from the Devereaux witnesses.

Tangen and Perez left several messages with Juana Vasquez. When she returned Tangen's calls, he told her the police were investigating Glassen for witness tampering. The call was a frustrating experience for him. "She immediately began to defend Mr. Glassen's actions," he reported. "She said the reason Paul was at the Devereaux home this afternoon was to get clothes for the girls." It was an unsatisfactory excuse, in the apparent opinion of Tangen and his colleagues, even though it was true. Police and DCFS officials were also apparently disturbed by the facts that Glassen had watched Devereaux's arraignment, driven him to his home, and read through his notes in Devereaux's presence. Glassen's motives were unfathomable to the officials, but what was clear was the man was getting in the way.

Tangen reminded Vasquez that Glassen was a suspect in witness tampering, according to Riesen, and she should warn him to stay away from any of his clients that might be witnesses because even contacting them would be viewed as a crime.

She said she could arrange a police interview with Glassen, but she wanted to be present. Then she shifted to the offensive, complaining that Perez had left the Devereaux foster children unattended, an action she called dangerous and an exception to established procedure. Tangen made a mental note of the woman's insubordinate attitude. "That's a separate issue," he said, something he'd bring up at the meeting.

Although Vasquez agreed to set up a meeting by 7 P.M. on the fourth, she called Tangen back at that time to say she'd talked to Carol Billesbach and they decided to contact Assistant Attorney General Leslie Allen for legal advice, since this was also a departmental matter. She said she'd get back to him once Allen returned her call.

Despite the delays, the case against Glassen was heating up. Officer Gordon, Sergeant Sherie Smith, and Detective Kruse obtained signed statements from two of Devereux's foster girls: Glassen had told them he was worried that Perez was making up the case against Devereaux.

A whole day passed and still Tangen hadn't confronted Glassen. On Friday, August 5, under the admittedly mistaken impression that Vasquez failed to return his call, he contacted Wenatchee Police Captain Rick Murray. He said he doubted the woman "understood the gravity of the situation" because she was always defending Glassen. Tangen then called Gary Riesen, who said he understood that a meeting had been set up for 4 P.M. that day.

Returning to his office, Tangen called Vasquez and demanded Glassen's identification information for his report. She said she didn't think she could give him the information. Incensed, he called Riesen to report Vasquez's defiance and was told to address the issue at the meeting.

At 4 P.M. Tangen showed up at the meeting site full of righteous indignation and learned that Vasquez had left a message to say she didn't know where Paul Glassen was, as he was out in the field. Seething, Tangen announced to a woman at the attorney general's office that not only was Vasquez openly defying him and failing to "realize the gravity of the situation," but the Child Welfare Services office was not cooperating, either.

At approximately 4:30 P.M., Vasquez called him back to give some identification information about Glassen. Her words appeared to be a halfhearted capitulation delivered in a guilty stammer, followed by a feeble explanation. She said that she hadn't actually seen Glassen since around 3 P.M. and wasn't sure he'd found out about the meeting. She said he wasn't in the office, to her knowledge, and that he was often out in the field. Tangen reprimanded her for failing to cooperate and said he would go out and look for the man and bring him to the station for questioning.

As Tangen hung up the phone, Dean Reiman of CPS walked into the office to see him. According to his report, Reiman had come on another matter. But, inevitably, the talk turned to Glassen—Reiman said he'd just seen the caseworker at the office. Vasquez was lying, covering up, and hindering his investigation, Tangen concluded.

Tangen and Kruse raced to the DCFS offices. They walked straight up to Glassen and demanded to talk to him. Glassen set his jaw but agreed to cooperate. Then Vasquez strode up and suggested that the interview take place in her office.

As soon as they were in her office, Kruse advised Glassen of his Miranda rights. "What's this all about?" Glassen asked. Tangen explained they'd come to talk with him about his conversations with the witnesses in the Devereaux case.

Glassen drew himself up, his eyes wary behind his wire-rimmed glasses. "This appears to not be a case between the police department and my agency but between the police department and me," he said.

"That's correct," said Tangen.

"In that case, I'd better have an attorney."

"In that case," replied Tangen, "you're under arrest for witness tampering."

Tangen cuffed the man's slightly trembling hands behind his back. Glassen held his head high in the face of his humiliation as Kruse marched him past the state employees and clients, who turned to look at him with curious stares or outright smiles of derision. Glassen thought of his wife, Suzanne, and his little son.

Tangen stayed behind for a moment to talk to Vasquez. "You're coming very close to obstructing a police investigation," he warned.

Having just observed a blatant display of police power, Juana Vasquez should have been cowed. Instead, she politely but defiantly told him that she was busy herself and didn't keep track of her subordinates' comings and goings. "Would you always know if Detective Perez was at his desk if I were to call to talk to him?" she queried.

The woman's impertinence stung Tangen. He assured her that he was in control of his department, unlike her.

He turned on his heel and walked away. Maybe they'd arrest her later.

Paul Glassen endured the indignities of the booking process. He was fingerprinted and his mug shots were taken. Then, to his great relief, he was released with a warning that he could expect to be formally charged and arraigned later.

"I had made the decision to charge him at this time because I could not seem to convince him or his boss of the seriousness of his action," wrote Tangen. "I felt with him at least being charged I could convince CWS administrators to relieve him of his duties involving the witnesses to the Devereaux case."

Glassen later said that although he had some phone contact from the attorney general's office about a possible 4 P.M. meeting on Friday, August 5, nothing was ever confirmed with him. Assistant Attorney General Leslie Allen later gave the same information to Tangen. Glassen was appalled by his arrest, astonished that his actions had even come under fire. He felt that he had been doing his job and that to do anything less would represent professional negligence.

Although he was not immediately prosecuted, he was placed on home assignment on August 10. Home assignment turned out to be paid administrative leave, except he was required to be at home between normal working hours, to avoid any contact with DSHS clients or the media, and to stay away from the office and any official business. His assignments served no useful purpose except to shut him up; keep him out of official hair; deny his access to documents, clients, and the flow of information; humiliate and intimidate him; and provide an instructive lesson to those who might thwart the official investigation. Because he was an active professional, he found the process painful and degrading. He remained on home assignment for approximately eleven months. The official reasons given for his suspension were based on allegations that he had acted insubordinately, obstructed a police investigation, and failed to report cases of child abuse.

"For weeks and months I was just taken aback," he later said. He was convinced that the official actions represented retaliation not only for his role in taking down Theresa's recantation, but for his other actions that bucked the Wenatchee DCFS mainstream. He had frequently complained about unchecked and systematic discriminatory actions against Hispanics and people of poverty that he had observed among some of his colleagues at the Wenatchee DCFS offices. He once worked to reunite a child with his father, who was a convicted felon and a Mexican citizen. Glassen acted by the book and the court saw it his way, but he had incurred the ire of the child's foster family, Reiman, and other DCFS caseworkers.

At Glassen's arrest, Detective Kruse said to him, "You're the caseworker who . . . sent that kid back to that Mexican drug dealer, aren't you?"

Glassen later said, "I was just astounded to think he'd say anything like that to me under the circumstances."

He wasn't formally charged by the Chelan County Prosecutor's Office until approximately two months after his arrest. Because Theresa wouldn't retract her recantation or say he pressured her, the state couldn't support a felony charge of witness tampering. Instead, he was charged with the misdemeanor offense of obstructing an officer. Ultimately, the charge was thrown out by a Wenatchee pro tem judge. But, as with so many Wenatchee residents who thought their troubles had abated, Glassen's were about to begin in earnest.

Juana Vasquez was troubled not only by the Wenatchee Police Department's response to her and Glassen, but by their investigation of the Devereaux case. Once Devereaux was charged with sexual abuse, she asked for the documentation of the routine CPS investigations into his conduct that normally would be generated by an arrest on these kinds of charges. To her surprise, she learned that no caseworker had been assigned to the case. No one could produce so much as a referral. Her astonishment was noted by her co-workers.

On August 6, the day after Glassen's arrest, she was called into a meeting between Carol Billesbach and Dee Wilson, acting DCFS regional administrator. Wilson told her that he was going to give her a personal conduct report for misconduct, because she failed to cooperate with the police investigation. The report was already completed, she saw, filled out by Reiman. She tried to explain her concerns about the way Perez and caseworkers including Reiman had acted in the Devereaux case.

"Shut up about that, Juana," said Wilson, according to Vasquez. "You're not to talk to anybody about that and you're not to talk to me."

She felt uneasy about the whole series of events. She'd felt that way many times since she filed a racial discrimination suit against the Washington DSHS, Abbey, Boggess, and Reiman in June 1992. On June 24, 1994, only about a month before Devereaux's arrest, she had been awarded $60,000 in damages in Chelan County Superior Court, after a unanimous jury verdict.

She had sued out of concern for her clients. She was appointed Wenatchee Child Welfare Services supervisor in 1989 in part because the job was under an affirmative action program favoring people bilingual in Spanish and English. According to her testimony and that of four other caseworkers, senior Wenatchee DSHS employees were highly resentful that she had even applied. Reiman came to her and said his wife, Boggess, was much more qualified than she. "He told me he would never allow himself to be supervised by a Mexican," she said.

Vasquez was also upset by the discriminatory attitudes within the DSHS office. "I'll tell you the attitude that I . . . saw in the office was just, let's just get these kids out of this home, place them in foster care, and basically let's see how fast we can terminate parental rights," she said to me. According to Vasquez, the practice was generally limited to Hispanic families, low-income families, and families of parents disadvantaged by low IQ or other disabilities.

"Their general attitude was that the white community could provide better for these [Hispanic] children. As far as the disadvantaged, low-IQ people, they would make reference to them as 'well, these retarded individuals . . . if these kids stayed with them, that's how these kids are going to be, too.' " She said that she disagreed because the kids would be exposed to school and other normal environments. Besides, services are available within DCFS to assist parents with limitations to care for their children within their homes.

"My understanding is that we had the highest termination rate statewide," said Vasquez. "People all over the state would be amazed at how many terminations we did. Termination for minority parents went very quickly, within a matter of six months, six to nine months. As far as low-IQ people, I would see the same pattern," she said.

"If they had someone to adopt the children then or they wanted to help a foster parent or an adoptive family get the kids, then their attitudes would change toward the clients and the termination. And I mean that these clients would never be able to do anything to satisfy the social worker so they could reunify the family. This was just a fast, one-track route," she said.

So, in August 1994, Vasquez was disheartened by the

events, but not really surprised. She was assured that, unlike Glassen, she wouldn't be placed on administrative leave. Meanwhile, she kept busy.

One of the things she did in the weeks after the Devereaux arrest was schedule his alleged victims for genital examinations as a matter of DSHS policy. She approved the exams with the department and Wenatchee Police Sergeant Doug Taggart. Then, on the date scheduled to take the girls to the doctor, Perez intervened, she said. "You're not doing that," he announced through a CPS official, according to Vasquez. He gave her no explanations.

On September 15, Carol Billesbach met with her and told her she would be placed on administrative leave, effective immediately. Her only responsibility was to sit by her phone during working hours. She was barred from speaking to DSHS clients, approaching the DSHS offices, or speaking to the media. Vasquez remained on administrative leave for more than a year, between September 15, 1994, and late October 1995. She found the experience untenable.

"You feel like you're a prisoner," she told me. "I don't know if I should be attentive to my kids because they're right there in front of me or if I'm supposed to be sitting by the phone. I don't know when I'm gonna get a call about another allegation or if I'm gonna be fired. It's just horrible and you don't know what's gonna get done to you next."

Her fears were justified. On September 30, City Attorney Patrick McMahon told the *Wenatchee World* that he was considering filing obstruction charges against her. She was fired more than a year later, in October 1995, following an extensive Office of Special Investigations report written by a DCFS worker from a nearby town who was said to be a friend of Abbey's. The report listed her cumulative alleged failings, including her insubordinate attitude and her obstruction of the police investigation of Devereaux. By this time, the action was anticlimactic, almost a relief.

For two years, CPS caseworker Juan Garcia was a vocal advocate for reforms within the Wenatchee DCFS office—specially trained Spanish-speaking court interpreters, Hispanic or multilingual foster homes, greater sensitivity to the linguistic and cultural needs of Hispanic families. He was better known around his office for making waves.

He was upset by Devereaux's arrest because he greatly respected the man. Not only had he been shocked, like Glassen, by Perez's jokes about Devereaux at the restaurant, but he heard Perez speculate openly about Devereaux a day or two before he arrested him, he said. On the days after Devereaux's arrest he loudly complained within the DCFS office that Perez had set Devereaux up. He reminded his colleagues of Perez's jokes about Devereaux at the restaurant. By August 5, Garcia was placed on administrative leave.

State officials claimed there was a more sinister reason for their actions—that Garcia had had inappropriate sexual contact with a minor while on vacation with her and her foster family, the Campbells. Not so, said Garcia, he was set up like Devereaux before him. In fact, the Campbells' allegations of misconduct occurred only after Devereaux was arrested, only after Garcia was outspoken in Devereaux's defense; and then, in response to DCFS questions, the girl denied it. No criminal charges were filed.

In another twist, while Garcia was on vacation with the foster family, a state offical removed a twelve-year-old boy on his caseload from foster care and returned him to his mother, who was nearly totally incapacitated by an inoperable brain tumor—expressly against Garcia's recommendation. Unsupervised and wild, the boy required foster care, but the department was reluctant to accommodate the child's needs at state expense. Although the boy's mother was admittedly incapable of parenting, she was neither abusive nor, in a strict sense, neglectful. Shortly after Garcia was placed on leave, he learned the boy murdered a Hispanic field worker—an avoidable tragedy and a serious state misstep.

A day or two after the murder, Abbey came over with the boy's file and told Garcia he wanted him to "work on the files to make it appear that I'd justified" the boy's removal from foster care, Garcia said. According to Garcia, Abbey asked him to remove the previously filed Service Episode Record, the handwritten contemporaneous documentation of caseworker activity, and substitute a newly completed but backdated substitute.

Garcia refused. Abbey insisted. Garcia held his ground. Abbey explained that the concerns about the Wenatchee CPS activities in the matter came from the top. He showed Garcia a memo from DCFS Regional Administrator Roy Harrington.

The memo read:

Why did I have no clue that at least one of these kids were ours until I see the Wenatchee World? This murder is getting statewide attention—If you don't think I and Oly (Olympia, the state capital) have an immediate need to know then something is truly, truly wrong over there. I want some info ASAP—immediately—summarizing our involvement. Why in the hell you all didn't get me info as soon as you knew we had a history with this (these) kids is beyond me. Read the Goddamn media policy which Carol referenced to all of you two weeks ago. Get me some info in writing now! Fernandez, Glassen, Garcia and now this. The two of you better get a hold of things over there. I don't want to see or hear finger pointing, I want results. Get me some info.

Garcia read the memo with interest, but refused to budge. At last Abbey reminded him that he was being investigated by the DSHS Office of Special Investigations (OSI). "This can be very difficult for you, if we don't get the cooperation," said Abbey, according to Garcia. On the other hand, said Abbey, "We can work this out. It's real simple . . . to do this."

To Garcia, Abbey's meaning was clear: He was being blackmailed.

"Hell, no," he said. "Get out of here."

Abbey warned him that unless he cooperated, "it's gonna be . . . much more difficult," according to Garcia. "I can't help you if you don't help me."

He said that he was "stunned" by Abbey's words.

Abbey returned two or three times to his home. Each time, the talk turned to Garcia's OSI investigation.

"You can investigate me, Tim, till the cows come home," he said.

Still Abbey persisted. "I can't promise what is going to happen, but I can tell you that this can be . . . a one-month investigation or it could be ten months or a year," he said, according to Garcia.

It was nearly a year later, on June 21, 1995, that Garcia was fired, months after a damning OSI report was released, concluding that he had committed a variety of wrongdoings. The report was based on interviews with such Wenatchee DCFS employees as Abbey, but Garcia said that he was never interviewed.

The Devereaux case and the Wenatchee government's official response to its detractors chilled other Wenatchee professionals. In communications to DCFS staff, including Abbey and CPS caseworker Steve Warman, staff members of Children's Home Society, a Wenatchee counseling agency holding a DSHS contract, said they were afraid of the police. In a memorandum to Harrington and Billesbach, Abbey wrote on November 10, 1994, "Recently Children's Home Society has made comments to DCFS staff, Steve Warman and myself, that they are afraid that the police will arrest them for obstructing justice. They also made this comment to the deputy prosecutor, Alicia Nakata. This was in reference to the Devereaux case."

Also in late 1994, Perez asked CPS caseworkers to replace certain Children's Home Society therapists with new or more reliable therapists. He said that the current therapists weren't sufficiently accepting his methods and might not make good witnesses. Although many counselors objected because their patients were high-risk children with whom they had developed therapeutic relationships, Billesbach agreed to his demand. Her objective was to support the police, she said.

With the troublemakers out of the way, Wenatchee DCFS officials had no problem with the goal of supporting the police. Vasquez, Glassen, and Garcia told me in separate interviews of a long-standing pattern of internal bias and discriminatory practices among many of their former colleagues, which now appeared to spill over into Perez's investigation. The relationship between the Wenatchee DCFS and the police was complicated by the kind of police demands for full cooperation and complicity that Glassen and Vasquez had recently experienced. But most of the caseworkers apparently welcomed Perez's methods, which dovetailed nicely with their own methods and expectations.

Most of the suspected child molesters were marginal people Perez and his DCFS supporters openly suspected were part of an abusive population: Hispanics, the poor, the mentally and emotionally impaired, and other vulnerable people. Many of the families lived in impoverished neighborhoods in what the Wenatchee Valley authorities perceived as squalor, again confirming popular theories.

"Most of them had nothing to do but collect monthly welfare checks and try to figure out ways to entertain themselves. Unfortunately they decided to entertain themselves by having sex with their children and other people's children," Perez said to a reporter for the *Seattle Times*.

This statement mirrored the sentiments that Vasquez had heard many times around her office, she said. "I know the attitude of the social workers . . . the comments to describe clients of poverty or physical or mental limitations: 'scumbags,' 'sleazeballs,' 'mentally retarded,' 'God, those people stink!' . . . And then they've followed through [on] their comments with actions."

Glassen said the "extremely vulnerable" parents that had been his clients were now subjects of the investigation. "It's a very ugly business when that's the kind of person the police go out and pick up and tell they're going to accuse them of additional offenses and then work out some sort of plea bargain, where they get that person to testify against someone else."

According to my investigation, Perez often worked in close association with a select clique of CPS caseworkers.[1] Among those who willingly embarked on the crusade

---

[1] The DCFS Manual, Chapter 26, Child Protective Services, Rev. 41. 09/93 states that the CPS worker may request the assistance of law enforcement to assist with an investigation. The caseworker is authorized to interview children "outside the presence of the parents where the child is found." Such locations may include school premises, day-care facilities, or the child's home. "The social worker shall gather information for risk assessment, family evaluation, and case planning rather than gather evidence for criminal prosecution. The social worker is not a law enforcement agent but shall work cooperatively with law enforcement."

was Katie Carrow, who often went with Perez while he interviewed children. Later, she reflected to a reporter, "I know without our intervention these children would be leading lives of abuse and mental illness. I've had some time to think about it, and I'm real comfortable with what we did—all of it."

Other caseworkers were long ago tried and rejected by Perez. One of them was Juan Garcia. He watched Perez question an eleven-year-old girl about allegations of physical abuse. "When I arrived," said Garcia, "Detective Perez was already halfway through his interview, standing up, using his obvious techniques that he uses for adults . . . having the girl sit instead of standing and facing him."

He recalled that Perez picked up his cell phone and said, "I'm gonna make a phone call." He told the girl that he was going to put in a call to juvenile hall if she didn't cooperate, said Garcia. The girl was "very, very scared." Perez refused to let her go to the bathroom. "Not until we're done," said Perez, according to Garcia. Garcia disapproved and Perez knew it.

Another time Garcia said he heard Perez threaten that CPS would step in if a woman didn't cooperate. "He pointed right at me and said, 'Juan is gonna take your children if you don't tell me who abused your child,'" Garcia said. When the woman denied abuse, Perez said, according to Garcia, "I don't fucking believe you and you better tell me the damn truth or Juan's gonna take your children." Perez's claims were false: There was insufficient basis for family intervention. "And I stepped in there and I said, 'I'm not taking nobody's child without evidence.' And I left the room." Garcia said that he made a complaint and after that Perez avoided him whenever possible.

By the usual yardsticks, the joint investigations by Perez and CPS personnel were successful, leading to a

string of confessions, plea bargains, and trial convictions—
and to widespread complacency among the officers of the
court. After all, deception to extract confessions is a long-
standing, perfectly legal, and even desirable police tactic,
according to accepted law enforcement tradition and training. Perez was not obligated to imagine the costs of such
betrayals on the bonds of families and neighborhoods and
friendships.

8:

Looking Back

═══════════

Crusader—Robert Perez

═══════════

The Wenatchee Chamber of Commerce boasts that each year the Wenatchee Valley has three hundred sunny days, which are reflected in the sunny dispositions of its fifty thousand residents. To those who live, as I do, under the brooding skies of western Washington, the concept has a powerful appeal. In any case, the area's official population fluctuates drastically, due to a harvest-time influx of seasonal labor. At such times, nearly two-thirds of Wenatchee-area residents are said to be Hispanic.

Reticent about his history in his most talkative moods, Wenatchee Police Officer Ricardo Robert Perez, Jr., doesn't admit to being of Hispanic heritage. Born on October 17, 1953, he has told friends that he is a *"true Spaniard,"* and his blue eyes and blond hair are a visible reminder of what, to him, is his cultural superiority. Because of his ambivalence toward his roots, he has habitually avoided acknowledging them.

Perez values his nearly Nordic appearance, and it shows. His hair and mustache are always neatly groomed; he polishes his boots as often as his revolver. He carries himself with the time-honored arrogance of policedom:

chest thrust forward, shirt stuffed deep into his trousers to emphasize the width of his shoulders, hand resting lightly on the butt of his revolver. At six feet, he cuts an imposing figure, an image of order in a chaotic world.

February 1992 was a transitional month in Wenatchee, with entire days of balmy springlike weather, followed by numbing cold and sudden gusty winds. Perez made the best of it, sitting at his typewriter hunkered over the hefty packet of foster care application forms. It was his wife Luci's idea to apply for foster care, one of the many accommodations that comprise a marriage. The Perezes were childless as a matter of choice: his, not hers. He'd had a vasectomy years ago. Who would have known, three marriages later, that having kids would still be an issue?

Both of my children are raised and no longer live at home, he typed. Raised and gone and no longer his concern, alienated as they were by his ex-wife Rebecca and her onslaught of lawyers and therapists.

My wife and I have a rich, full life and want to share it with a child who may never have known or been in a home where he or she was loved and cared for.

Luci was a legal secretary, tall and slender and brunette and intense. She shared his deep concerns about the kids from the families who made up the low end of the city's economic scale.

As a police officer, I see these children every day and I here [sic] all the people who say, 'Something should be done for these children,' and that's where it ends—talking about it. My wife and I decided that we wanted to do more than just talk about the problem and want to become part of the solution.

Bob and Luci Perez were prepared to care for thirteen-year-old Daniel Sutter, a boy who'd gotten in enough trouble to come to his official attention. There was something about the boy, some stirring of humanity in Perez himself, that told him that Daniel was worth saving. Perez had a generosity about him, a willingness to share his time, even venture across treacherous emotional boundaries, when it came to children.

After twelve years with the Wenatchee Police Department, he appreciated the intricacies and pitfalls of the paper trail. He was treating the application with characteristic thoroughness, although in some ways it was bureaucratic nonsense. Daniel was unofficially placed with him anyway; official placement appeared to be a foregone conclusion. Perez came well-connected at the Wenatchee Department of Social and Health Services office.

I may become upset or angry if a child continually breaks the rules.

I will not deal with a child or adult when I am upset or angry. I will wait until I have calmed down, thought the problem over and come to a conclusion on how the matter should be handled before the matter is discussed. I have found after raising two children that nothing is accomplished when you act out of anger or when you are upset.

The questions were in that slippery, emotionally charged territory of adult responsibilities and discipline. With his own kids Perez rarely had to do more than take off his belt and their fear and apologies followed. Still, who could tell what foster care officials considered reasonable discipline? He wouldn't mention physical discipline and the problem would be avoided.

A greater problem was presented by his own documented behavior: the official complaints, the letter of reprimand by Chief Badgley, the personnel performance evaluations regarding his employment by the Wenatchee Police Department, the lawsuit for unlawful imprisonment and intentional infliction of emotional distress, the claims of excessive force, the dissolution and custody pleadings. These things—this accumulation of *words,* some profoundly negative, some merely ambiguous—were the inevitable wake of a cop who did his job according to the dictates of his convictions.

Back in 1986 an African-American woman complained that he yelled at her son, "Little black boy, you get back in the house." She reported that he said of her house, "That place is nothing but a slime bag house, those people are garbage. I wouldn't let my dog stay there." *Preposterous*, Perez said, and the other officer backed him up, as fellow police officers predictably do. Also predictably, Chief Badgley found the complaint to be unfounded. There were only about a hundred blacks in Chelan County, out of a population of fifty-eight thousand. The statistics spoke for themselves.

The personnel reports were part of his confidential interdepartmental file and, perhaps, outside the scrutiny of the child welfare people. Which was just as well. The 1989 performance evaluation claimed he was *"pompous"* and *"arrogant"* and that he appeared to *"pick out people and target them."* To Perez, the report was a stunning and personal frontal attack.

Phrase after phrase marched down the page: *"When dealing with adults feels challenged and is defensive." "Causes problems by crossing arms, puffing up his chest." "Presents an image of looking down on people, badgering them." "Gives the impression of wanting to trip triggers, likes confrontation and likes having power over people." "Is like a wound up wire, ready to spring." "Has the idea that people always have to do what he tells them all of the time." "Is developing a reputation of being a hothead in the community." "Drawing the side-arm—'the getting of the upper edge'—a power over the people, drawing the gun because police carry guns."*

The evaluation criticized his "mental acuity," referring to an accidental discharge of his firearm. There were scathing criticisms that his Spanish interpretations had become interrogations,[1] that he had to be reminded to write reports, that he appeared "egotistical." In one breath they said he lacked self-confidence and in the next they said he was overbearing.

In the end he signed it: "Robert R. Perez Jr." (having long ago relegated his first name to a middle initial), along with his supervisor, his division commander, Chief Badgley, and five other evaluators. He kept his cool, but inside he was seething. Afterward, he put it into perspective as professional jealousy: He was *a man who got results*. You only had to look at his arrest record to see that.

In April 1990 the chief and other evaluators still harped on Perez's interpretations and his reluctance to document things. "When interprets for other, Perez still tends to be the interrogator, rather than the interpreter. He needs to remember that most assignments require a report to document [them]." But in April 1991, there was a mere paragraph in the personnel conduct report referring to areas of improvement. It talked about "foul language," but added, "we all slip from time to time." Bob Perez was famous for his profanities. The evaluation also suggested, "Don't let personal feelings cloud your decisions." But, bottom line, "Your work on public relations this year has been very good, keep up the good work."

---

[1] The 1989 performance evaluation contains language that helps to explain certain of Perez's habits as relevant to his later actions: "Shouldn't have to be asked to write a report when an interpretation has been performed. When asked to interpret just interpret, don't test their English skills. If we can't understand them we can't understand them. When told to ask a question ask the question and give the answer back. During an interrogation don't become the interrogator, interpret for the interrogator." (Wenatchee Police Department Annual Performance Evaluation: Robert R. Perez, 2/24/89)

Perez had accomplished much in the way of good work over the years. He overcame a rough stretch in his twenties when he was convicted for writing a string of bad checks and for reckless driving. There was another difficult time in his thirties when he was officially reprimanded for illegally claiming unemployment benefits and living expenses while he went to the police training academy. But then he completed his GED and landed the job with the Wenatchee Police Department and connected with what was, in many ways, his destiny.

He took particular pride in his ability to relate to children. Even in the hated performance evaluation of 1989, the evaluators recognized this when they said in regard to public relations: "Kids a 5 [the highest potential score] everybody else a 1."

I enjoy children when I can share new experiences and ideas with them. The memories that come immediately to mind in regards to my own children are teaching them to ride a bike for the first time, taking them on camping trips, watching my son catch his first fish, seeing the wonderment on their faces when they went to Disneyland for the first time.

They had been good years, those early years with Michelle and Christopher, the children of Perez's first ex-wife, Rebecca. In fact, he adopted them in 1979 when they were around three and five years old. The act was generous, an act of love. But, above all, it was audacious.

Bob Perez met Rebecca and her then-husband Lenny Williams in the early 1970s when Becky and Lenny were in their mid-twenties and he was in his mid-teens. Lenny ran a bicycle repair shop at the time, and Perez and his best friend John Gustafson, a kid his own age who was the Williamses' foster son, sometimes hung out around the shop.

According to Williams, Perez was fed up with school and angry with his parents. He looked with envy at his friend and his cozy foster child relationship with Williams and his attractive wife and their two-year-old son Christopher. When Perez asked if he could stay with his family, Williams agreed. Perez came to live with the Williamses in 1971 at the age of seventeen.

It wasn't long before Williams became convinced that his wife was having an affair with their unofficial teenage foster son, Bob Perez. He got up at night and saw them together, she in her nightgown. Williams told me Bob and Becky spent a lot of time openly enjoying each other's company; in his view they were far too intimate. Most damning of all, he found used prophylactics in the wastebasket. A year after he took him in, Lenny threw Perez out of the house, accusing him of sleeping with Becky. At the time, she was pregnant with her second child, Michelle. There was speculation and rumor about the baby's parentage.

As Williams recalls it, he and Rebecca divorced in September 1976 and within a few days Rebecca and Bob Perez were married. Lenny fought for custody of Christopher and Michelle, but Rebecca prevailed. When Bob and Rebecca Perez decided to move to Texas, Lenny resisted; again Rebecca prevailed. After the move, Lenny tried without success to locate his children.

Then, in another move of bitter irony, Perez decided he would adopt the children. Once the idea took hold, he was unstoppable. The adoption took place without a hitch—and without any actual notice to him, said Williams.

When the couple returned to Wenatchee, Williams again tried to regain custody of his children, but this time

Perez shoved the adoption papers in his face. He was astonished.

"There's nothing I can do," Williams said the judge told him. "You'll have to go to Texas and move to have the adoption vacated." Williams, who lacked the necessary substantial finances to do such a thing, was consumed with bitterness at his legal impotence. They can't do this to me, he told himself, while knowing in his heart that they had.

In this curious and quasi-legal manner, Perez succeeded in acquiring half-interest in Rebecca's children. But then the marriage fell apart.

Rebecca submitted a sworn affidavit for a restraining order on June 21, 1982, a few days after their separation, claiming that Perez "physically and verbally accosted" her in order to get money from her. She claimed he was "very volatile." She said the neighbors had urged her to call the police a couple of times before because of some confrontations, and the police responded. He threatened to confront her at work so she would lose her job, and she feared he might break into the home, she said.

After Perez's divorce from Rebecca, his relationship with the kids went sour. They squabbled, shut him out, refused to appreciate him. Their court-ordered psychiatrist, Douglas J. Shadle, wrote to the court in 1985 and revealed that Michelle was "adamantly opposed to further visitation with her father." Dr. Shadle added that Chris had "difficulties" when he returned to his mother's home after briefly staying with Perez. Dr. Shadle recommended that Chris and Michelle be seen in counseling with Bob Perez, but after a time or two, Perez dispensed with that suggestion.

To him, the children's attitudes may have represented a rejection of him, much as he had felt himself rejected when his parents had abandoned him to the vagaries of schools and the households of others. He decided to handle these rejections as he had handled the ones before them, by wiping the slate clean.

Resolutely, he went to juvenile court and asked the court commissioner to terminate his parent-child relationship with Christopher and Michelle, according to his exwife, Jeanette Burch, who was married to him at the time. Said Burch, the commissioner regarded him with surprise and, in the interests of the children, denied Perez's motion, but allowed him to be relieved of his obligation of child support for Michelle.

His second marriage fared no better.

Perez paid his own way to go to the police academy between March 7 and May 20, 1983. Although since 1981 (on off-hours from his job as a long-haul truck driver) he had been working as a reserve officer for the Douglas County sheriff, and although he had applied at several police agencies, Perez had been unsuccessful in finding a paying police job. Police departments typically pay for employee training, but Perez hoped taking the course on his own initiative would give him a competitive edge in the marketplace.

Then he had to pull a few strings: there was, after all, the matter of the theft charges for writing bad checks. One of his superiors at his reserve officer job for the Douglas County sheriff wrote a letter to the municipal court judge requesting that Perez's criminal record be expunged. Perez hand-carried the letter to the municipal court and handed it to the judge's clerk. Jeanette was her name: she was slim and pretty and she immediately took a shine to him. She smiled at him and dug out his records and then whisked them away to the judge.

She didn't say anything about it to Perez, but later said she never saw a record expunged in this way before. Usually it was a matter handled in open court by lawyers pleading for a break for their clients. No matter; it only took a minute for his record to be sealed as far as law enforcement was concerned.

This act of closure signaled the beginning of his relationship with Jeanette. She soon found herself swept off her feet by Bob. He, in turn, was impressed with her connections within the court system. Not three months later they were married.

From the beginning, the marriage was stormy. Jeanette came to believe she was a stepping-stone for Perez in his ambitious professional drive. Her ties with the courts and the police department impressed him in the days before their marriage. But after the wedding things abruptly changed.

"When you married me, you divorced them," he said petulantly, according to Jeanette. "They're no longer your friends, they're *my* friends now."

She said he discouraged her relationships, not out of jealousy but out of an apparent conviction that people were plotting against him. When he entered a room and found Jeanette talking to someone, he demanded to know what they were talking about. After a time, she found it easier to simply keep to herself.

Her husband also kept to himself, polishing his guns, watching black and white movies on television, listening to rock classics or to the Eagles, standing on the well-tended lawn and watching the sprinkler. And then Jeanette insisted she wanted another child, besides her son from a previous marriage.

"You just want a kid because you want a plaything," he yelled at her, according to Jeanette. "Just like all the other people in this town." Perez, who had long ago had a vasectomy, started staying out at night, claiming he was on stakeout duty, she said. She suspected he was seeing a woman named Luci.

Bob and Jeanette Perez divorced in 1986. She swore in an affidavit for a restraining order that Perez watched her house, broke in and took things, broke into her car, had a cop pull her over without cause. Perez filed his own affidavit claiming he hauled out thirteen garbage sacks of the stuff she had left behind. She sewed together his pants legs and sleeves and the zippers on his coats, he said. In the end, when they divided up their property, Jeanette placed their marriage certificate beneath the cockatiel at the bottom of the birdcage.

Bob and Luci Perez were married in June 1989. By the spring of 1992, the marriage had hit some rough spots—and the worst of these may have stemmed from Luci's wish for children.

In April 1992, in recommending that Bob and Luci Perez be approved for foster care, the social worker stated Bob Perez's philosophy about Daniel: "If they work with him now, Bob won't have to deal with him [as a policeman] when the boy is an adult." Because the Perezes were aware of the boy's "criminal symptoms," she concluded, they "are in a good position to guide and shepherd the boy in some more useful behavior. They will work long and hard on the project and I can only wish them well."

Thirteen-year-old Daniel's "criminal symptoms" appeared while he was living in the Perez home, long before the licensing was approved. On February 27, 1992, Perez went to light a cigarette and his lighter was gone. Immediately his thoughts turned to the boy.

He saw to it that Daniel was arrested and placed in juvenile detention. Eventually Daniel entered a guilty plea to theft in the third degree. The court ordered him to serve a total of eleven days, to be on a 7 P.M. curfew, and to "follow all rules." Within weeks Perez hauled the boy in for lying to him, getting bad grades, and otherwise failing to follow the rules. In all, Daniel spent forty-one days in juvenile detention for the theft of Perez's cigarette lighter.

But, far from improving because of Perez's attentions, Daniel's "criminal symptoms" again got the better of him on July 30, 1992. First Perez became convinced that Daniel had turned down the oxygen on the fish tank. When he confronted him, Daniel denied it and said Perez had falsely accused him. Daniel flew off in a rage and the next thing Perez knew, he scratched Perez's favorite chair with a knife. Perez immediately pressed charges.

The court convicted the boy of malicious mischief and, because of his mystifying behavior in the face of Perez's generosity, ordered him to do a stint of evaluation or treatment at Pine Crest Mental Hospital in Idaho. Perez told the judge he was through with him, and the court recommended a group home when Daniel was released. No doubt Perez believed he'd be dealing with him as an adult. But, by 1994, Daniel was small potatoes.

During a six-month period ending in December 1994, Perez arrested more than fifteen alleged sex offenders, most at least loosely associated with each other. The arrests were a matter of pride to the Wenatchee Police Department and to the Chelan County Prosecutor's Office—arrests backed by a solid conviction rate. All were based on word of mouth and none of these words were spontaneous. But they snowballed. A rumor or ambiguous comment or stray thought formed a theory—the theory led to the process of interrogation—the interrogation yielded a confession—the confession implicated others in conformity with the theory—a score of confessions followed.

9:

Autumn 1994

====

Fragile Bonds—Harold and Idella Everett

====

In the fall of 1994, dozens of adults and children were sucked into the yawning maw of the interrogation process. Sometimes Perez stood in the waning sunlight with his feet on the spreading lawn of his new acreage, his eyes on his duck pond bordered by evergreen trees, and his mind on his remarkable accomplishments. He was tireless; he was courageous; he was a force for social betterment; he was on the side of the angels.

One of them lived in his home: Ann Everett, ten-year-old daughter of impoverished and illiterate Harold and Idella Everett. The Everett children had a turbulent history under two years of intensive state intervention—foster care, therapy, mental hospitalizations, regular rounds of official interrogation—and Ann and her four siblings yearned for the family to be together. It was a reasonable dream. After all, the Everetts weren't charged with any crime, met all of the DCFS conditions for reunification, and officials conceded the family was exceptionally close. Yet from the start Bob and Luci Perez treated Ann as a member of the family because they viewed her as in "long-term" care, which, roughly translated, meant she would be a foster child until she turned eighteen.

Although Perez testified that he didn't recall whether he and his wife were licensed as foster parents when Ann came to live in their home on March 23, 1994, the fact is they were not. This was not to present a problem for them or for DSHS foster care licenser Connie Saracino, who begged Luci to talk Bob into it in the first place. Later, Saracino urged the Perezes to adopt the girl.

When Ann arrived at the Perez home she was afraid of Bob Perez. He was, after all, a big man with a sometimes brusque manner. Although she slowly bonded with Luci, Bob had almost no contact with the child for the first two or three months. Dealing with the girl took patience and time, of which he had little to spare, preoccupied as he was with his investigations. To him, Ann was almost a nonentity, a silent enigma, except when she played up, and then she was quite a handful. As he described it, she threw "fits," and acted "like a wild animal." When something frustrated her, like the fact she couldn't go home, her small face reddened and distorted into ugly lines and she screamed herself hoarse and heaved things around the house.

Bob and Luci Perez were forced to cope with Ann's nightmares, bed-wetting, guilt, and behavior problems, and speculate about what was behind these things. She was surely "disturbed" when she came to his home directly from the Devereaux home, said Perez. He later testified that the girl lived at his home for close to nine months before their family relationship became even "tolerable."

Nevertheless, the Perezes showered her with gifts: clothes, an electric train, a bicycle. Perez said he was "taken by her plight" and he had "a lot of feelings of sympathy for her." Slowly she worked her way into his consciousness as something more than a target for speculation. They sat on the couch together and watched television, and made strained small talk at the dinner table. In the summer of 1994, Ann, Bob, and Luci went camping.

Perez bantered with his foster daughter and tried to put her at ease and at last she warmed to him. He said he came to love Ann but "not as a real father. . . . She still loves her parents and expresses that." She had her own room for the first time, and the large house, yard, and swimming pool, the ducks and turkeys and dogs offered so much more than her family's seven-hundred-square-foot cottage. Still she wanted to go home.

Ann lived in his home for around six months and was in therapy for a couple of years before Perez got around to questioning her about her problem behaviors, he said. It was nine months into his investigation of the spreading epidemic of molestation in his community before she came through.

It was September 24: Ann let slip a few words that forewarned Perez that important news was imminent. He reassured her she was safe, it wasn't her fault, it was okay to tell, and whatever she said would help her folks, who had a problem. Despite the obvious risk that someone would come along and claim his relationship influenced her statement, he didn't get out his tape recorder or call for backup. Instead he and Luci sat the girl down in their comfortable living room and hung on her every word. Ann's words were tragic: Her parents both molested her and Harold had had intercourse with her from the time she was around six years old.

The detective sat rigid and watched her talk and writhe with discomfort, and as he did, he visualized the unkempt old man repeatedly thrusting himself inside the little girl—a girl who was not some statistic on an incident report but, for all intents and purposes, Perez's own child. The shock was somewhat lessened because he had been contemplating Harold's potential misdeeds for some time. Once she told her story, Ann cried and asked him if he had to tell her parents what she had said. Perez reassured her and urged her to go on. She said her brother Robert said Harold had molested him, too.

The next day at around 10 A.M., Perez and CPS caseworker Laurie Alexander drove to Foothills Middle School to interview Mary Everett. Over the years, police and CPS officials had questioned Mary many times, and each time she denied she was abused. Since May 5, 1993, when she was forced to go into therapy, she was treated as a victim with terrible memories pushed far into her subconscious, but she firmly denied it. Something about the sessions always made her cry.

This time Perez sat down, locked the girl in his intense gaze, and told her a story—a tale of victimization and responsibility and sickness and its cure. Ann was worried about her, he said, and about her brothers. The family was Mary's responsibility, he said. He told her what Ann had said about problems at home. He reminded her he expected the truth from her, and that her parents needed her help to deal with their problems. He made it clear he wasn't leaving until Mary accepted her responsibility to help her parents confront these problems and that he wouldn't accept her denials. Perez claims he was patient but firm, questioning the girl for hours. Finally the tears that had been welling in her eyes overflowed and she sobbed.

"I want it to stop."

This ambiguous statement was taken as a disclosure. Perez persisted: Mary cried harder.

Neither her tears nor the length of the interview affected Perez. At a defense interview, he said he wasn't trained in the appropriate length of an interview because this was a "nonissue." Tears and stubborn denial were ways of coping with abuse and the first step to a child's recovery was to pull down these barriers—no matter how painful the process became. In a sworn deposition, Perez said that he regularly challenged children's answers, even telling them they were liars when they denied that they were abused. His interviews continued until the child fully disclosed the things he knew. Still, he conceded when interviewed by a defense investigator, at the point when a child "hides under the desk or becomes hysterical," it would be "a pretty good sign" to end an interview.

But on this day and many other occasions, tears were no impediment. At last Mary mopped her eyes and asked if she had to go to a foster home if she told Perez what he believed. She wouldn't say anything if it meant she'd be taken from her parents. Alexander broke the brutal news to her: She had to go into foster care whatever she might say. But Alexander reminded her of the upside: By telling, she was actually *helping* her parents, ensuring them the treatment they needed. Maybe, once the treatment took hold, the family could reunite. Exhausted and sobbing, at last Mary said or acknowledged that her mother and father had molested her for several years, most recently the previous week.

Perez, Alexander, and another cop drove to the Everett home and crowded into the tiny living room with Harold and Idella Everett and some other individuals who had the good sense to keep their mouths shut. The Everetts shrank back like people with something to hide. Actually they were almost paralyzed by the balance of power. Except for a brief time when the family lived in California, Idella, forty, had lived in Wenatchee in a neighborhood such as this and had been pushed around all her life. She dropped out of special education classes when she was at the age equivalent of eighth grade. Like Harold, who was in his sixties with grown kids almost her age, Idella was totally illiterate, ignorant, and inept at standing up to the authorities.

Perez again dispensed with the small talk and launched into the Miranda rights, although, according to his report, he put them in "easy to understand words." Then he bluntly spelled out what the girls had said. Perez told the Everetts they were under arrest, although Harold immediately stammered he was innocent.

"What for?" Harold protested. "I didn't do anything to my kids."

The sight of the man evoked the powerful image brought by Ann's words. Perez pulled his handcuffs from the back of his belt, slapped them against his palm, and restrained Harold. Harold's grown daughter Donna Hidalgo watched the arrest. Her stepmother was close to her own age but was mentally more like a four- or five-year-old child. "You're a sick perverted bastard," she heard Perez say to her father. Then, to Idella, "You're a sick perverted bitch, lower than scum on earth."

Idella began to cry. She had never been to jail, never been in trouble. She watched in wonder as Perez forced her husband's arms behind his back, locked the handcuffs around his wrists, handed him over to the other cop. The cop clutched Harold's elbow, so that he had no choice but to stumble beside him out the door, down the uneven concrete steps, across the sidewalk to the police car. After the car drove away, Perez came up to her. "I'll try to keep you out of jail if you tell me what I want to hear," he said, according to Idella.

Perez tells it differently: After the other officer hustled Harold off to jail, Idella "hung her head and started to say something but stopped."

"Now that Harold's gone, do you want to talk to me?" he asked. She nodded her head yes, according to his report. "Harold makes me do it." Once he was satisfied that the woman was referring to abusing her children, Perez drove her to the station, questioned her, and prepared a typed statement for her signature.

Idella said she didn't admit to anything at her home. She sat with Perez and CPS caseworker Laurie Alexander at the Wenatchee police station for what she believed was four and a half hours. "He was telling what they was doing to the kids," she told me. Every time she denied something happened, Perez called her a liar, she said. He also swore at her, she said, although the strongest of his words that she could bring herself to repeat were "shit" and "damn."

As he questioned her, she several times asked for her attorney Rebecca Shaw, who had represented her in the dependency proceeding. According to Everett, Perez replied, "You don't need Rebecca Shaw. You don't need a lawyer."[1]

"If you say what I want you to say, you won't have to go to jail," he told her, according to Idella. Otherwise she'd go to jail for the rest of her life.

"Then I made up a story," she explained. It was a story along the lines of the one Perez told her. She believed she had no choice if she wanted to see her children again, if she wanted to avoid a life sentence. "I didn't know what was going on and he was just somebody to be afraid of." She said she finally signed the statement because she believed she had no choice, although she couldn't read it or understand its implications.

Although her "confession" was detailed and graphic, it was far outside her vocabulary and the limits of her IQ.

---

[1] At this time Idella was clearly in custody, a criminal suspect, and under interrogation. If her statement is true, all questioning should have ceased. If Perez viewed her request for counsel as equivocal, under Washington state law, his questions should have been limited to those that would clarify her request.

According to her statement, Idella said she saw Harold have weekly sex with their children from the time Mary and Matthew were five, and the twins were four. Harold had forced her to watch and to penetrate her daughters with her fingers.

The interview wasn't recorded; Perez made no notes, or he destroyed them. Almost immediately, Idella recanted.

A couple days later Perez and Alexander talked to the three Everett boys, but only Robert was helpful, although he sometimes spoke in a curiously tentative way—which Perez did his best to rehabilitate. According to Perez's report, after repeated questioning, a briefing on the fact that his sisters had told, and a reminder that he needed to help his parents overcome their problem, Robert said, "Dad touch[sic] my penis with his hand and pulled on it. He made me take a hold of his penis with my hand; *he probably made me put it in my mouth.*" [italics added] When Perez urged him to explain, Robert said, "He would pee in my mouth."

Perez questioned the boy about what had happened to his brothers and sisters. Although, in describing oral sex, Robert first said "he did it to [Steven], too," he later said, "I never saw him do it to [Steven]."

The detective pushed on. *"I probably might have seen him do something to [Mary],"* said Robert. [italics added] Perez pushed for clarification. "He had his penis in her mouth." Although Perez heavily laced his report with quotations, the interview was not recorded and he either made no notes or he destroyed them.

Although he reported the boy as cooperative in the interview, the events that surrounded it suggest otherwise. A few days later, according to DCFS records, Robert and Mary's foster mother Mary Wawers called the children's caseworker and said she wanted the children moved out of her home because she and her family felt they were "on call" to Bob and Luci Perez, and that the Perezes had "control over them," to the point that the Wawers had "no say in what happens." After all, Perez's visits were highly disturbing to her family.

Wawers said that Mary and Robert were very upset after Perez visited them that week because he told them they were never going home. After he broke the bitter news, both children cried "a lot" and clung to her, and Mary severely regressed, several times urinating and defecating in her pants. "Bob is the reason my parents are in jail," she had sobbed.

Steven Everett had a visit from Perez on a similar brutal mission. His foster parents reported he was quiet and withdrawn after Perez told him he'd never see his parents again.

Upon hearing of Harold's arrest, Pastor Roby Roberson raced to the Chelan County Courthouse. "I headed right up to the courthouse the day of his arrest, met with Roy Fore, the deputy prosecutor for Chelan County," he told me. He explained to Fore that he knew the Everett family and thought there was some kind of mistake because he'd never seen anything in his years of knowing the Everetts that would have given him a clue to this.

"Mr. Roberson," said Fore, "we have a full complete written confession from Mr. Everett. He's confessed . . . to the sexual abuse of the kids."

"How could he do that?" Roberson snapped in exasperation.

"What d'you mean?" asked Fore.

"Harold doesn't read or write," said Roberson dryly. "He's illiterate."

"Well, we have his written confession."

"No," growled Roberson. "You *don't* have his written

confession, because he can't read and write.'' Fore appeared taken aback.

Roberson persisted stubbornly, his anger growing. ''Well, this is sure strange, because I don't see how I could be so conned. . . . I mean nobody's spent more time in their household than me. I've never seen anything like that.''

On September 26, 1994, the Chelan County Superior Court found probable cause against Harold Everett for 6,422 counts of rape of a child in the first degree. The court found probable cause against Idella Everett for 1,586 counts of rape of a child in the first degree and 4,836 counts of aiding and abetting rape of a child in the first degree. The astonishingly precise array of counts was based on the usual mathematical formula of multiplying the frequency of sex acts by multiple victims.

Idella's mental limitations were obvious and clearly raised issues of her competency and her ability to make a free and voluntary confession. Her attorney, Rebecca Shaw, moved for an order to appoint an expert at public expense to assess her client's mental competency at the time she confessed. Although the prosecutor made his usual strenuous objection, Judge Bridges granted the motion. Shaw retained psychologist Dennis R. Shephard.

Surprisingly, Shaw and Judge Bridges later ignored the need to consider the results of Shephard's assessment, which resolved the question of competency.[2] Shaw ad-

---

[2] A confession is inadmissible unless it is freely made and without compulsion or inducement. The confession must be the result of rational intellect and of free will (*State v. Ortiz,* 104 Wn. 2d 479, 706 P. 2d 1069 (1985); *State v. Rupe,* 101 Wn. 2d 664, 683 P.2d 571 (1984). In Washington, the court must determine the totality of circumstances under which a statement is made, by considering such factors as the defendant's mental ability. Among factors a court must consider is mental retardation, although that factor alone is not determinative. The mental condition of a defendant may preclude a defendant from making a knowing and intelligent waiver of his rights because of the defendant's susceptibility to suggestion or real or perceived intimidation. Under these circumstances, the defendant's statements

vised Idella to enter into a plea agreement forfeiting her right to trial. She explained to her client that she had little choice, given the fact of her confession—although its admissibility had never been determined and Idella might have been incompetent at the time. Harold had already agreed to plead guilty to lesser charges, Shaw reminded her.

"She said I didn't have a chance any other way," said Idella, who now regrets her decision. "I never done nothing."

Judge Bridges accepted Idella's plea agreement without first satisfying himself that Idella was able to understand the proceedings or the plea agreement. Everett was returned to the Chelan County jail to await sentencing.

It was only with difficulty that I was able to interview Idella Everett months later at the women's prison. According to a prison official, she spent most of her time huddled in a fetal position on her cot, too overwhelmed to speak. Having read abstract police reports, I wasn't prepared for the stark reality of the woman's mental disabilities. According to prison officials, she was tested at the prison: her IQ was in the high 50s.

Idella's smile was tremulous, her eyes frightened, her speech halting, and her comprehension of why she was in prison almost nil. "I told some lies," she said of her encounter with Perez. "He said if I said something he wouldn't put me in jail." Everett had only the barest understanding of what had happened in the courtroom. She had entered a plea she called a "yeah and no," which translated, I assumed, to an Alford plea. Had she been charged with a crime? "I guess," she said, blinking her eyes in confusion.

---

must be excluded as involuntary (*State v. Cushing,* 68 Wn. App 338 [1983]; *State v. Sergent,* 27 Wn App 947, [1990]; *State v. Davis,* 34 Wn. App. 546, [1983]).

10:

Autumn 1994

Credibility Contest

Perez busied himself with cases that fell in line precisely in accordance with his theories. The prosecutors waved the banners of their magnificent conviction record based primarily on guilty pleas, and made self-important statements to the local paper about protecting kids and rousting out the bad element in their community. In my experience the process of plea bargaining wasn't something to brag about. The procedure was logically tied to the dynamics of the judicial system . . . which in Wenatchee was a sight to behold.

Every time someone came before them on sex charges, the three judges validated Perez's actions, and took his word that he didn't threaten limited people with horrendous sentences to get them to confess. As elected officials, judges can rarely afford to rattle the power structure of prosecutors and police unions on big cases. What was surprising was that Wenatchee judges refused to accept that the defendants were particularly vulnerable, even when retardation stared them in the face. The fact may have had much to do with the human emotions of the judges after they waded through the graphic confessions.

But emotions have their consequences. The judges apparently resented and disbelieved the claims of coercion brought by local defense lawyers who doted on judicial appreciation and trust. In view of the lawyers' professional affiliations, the problematic confessions, and the massive sentences imposed on those defendants who went on trial, many public defenders became fainthearted, or merely realistic about their clients' chances in the courtroom and urged them to plead guilty, even to testify against others. Under the right circumstances, I might have done the same myself.

For many defendants, the offers were difficult to resist—reduced charges and sentences, sometimes the possibility of community-based treatment. Yet some public defenders advised their clients to plead guilty even when the prosecutor's sentencing recommendation was severe or charges were not reduced. The reasons for the lawyers' advice eluded me then as they do now, but no doubt the lawyers and their clients were discouraged by the absence of minimal checks and balances in the Wenatchee legal system—a system that logically led to a pronounced police arrogance and a lack of concern for constitutional "technicalities."

On September 14, tipped off by a landlord that Dorris Green allowed the Holts to babysit her children—an action that signified negligence if not complicity in the case of Green and opportunity in the case of the Holts—Perez urged Green to come to the station. Because Green was expected in court on a welfare fair hearing matter, she asked him to call her attorney, Ray Grimm, to let the court know she might be late. Later Grimm testifed that when Perez phoned him with Green by his side, the detective assured him that Green wasn't a suspect and said he'd call a halt to his questioning and give Grimm a ring if this fact changed or if he felt the need to advise Grimm's client of her Miranda rights.

Yet as soon as he hung up the phone, Perez advised Green of her Miranda rights using a standard form and had her initial each line because judges place great stock in such things. Now, if she confessed, he was covered.[1] Perez questioned her for nearly four hours, ignoring her repeated requests to have Grimm there, she said. At last she "confessed" and the detective prepared a typed statement that Green had had sex with her children and the Holt children, and that she saw Laura Holt have sex with a child. Once, one of the Holt boys came in while Green was taking a shower, threw a rope around her neck, and forced her to the floor, where they had intercourse. Green later said she confessed to lies under pressure.

Perez disagreed. The interview was "relatively calm," he said in testimony. "She cried occasionally, you know, real softly. But other than that, it was a quiet and easy-going interview. . . . As a matter of fact, I treated Ms. Green very gently throughout this. I mean, there wasn't any need to be—I don't know what the word is—I guess to raise my voice at all to make a point. She was very cooperative."

---

[1] The defendant's right to counsel under U.S. Constitution's Sixth and Fourteenth Amendments, and Washington State Constitution Article 1, Sec. 9, attaches where adversarial judicial proceedings have been initiated by formal charges, preliminary hearing, indictment, information, or arraignment. This right is distinct from the Fifth Amendment right to have counsel present during custodial interrogation. By invoking the Sixth Amendment right to counsel at the time formal proceedings are initiated against a defendant, the defendant does not also invoke the Fifth Amendment right to have counsel present during a later interrogation regarding a different charge. Under *Miranda v. Arizona* et. al., once a person has become suspect and is in custody, she must be advised of her rights including the right to counsel. A request for an attorney must be scrupulously honored, but may be subsequently waived. The police may not resume questioning until counsel has been provided to the defendant or the defendant has initiated the questioning. Where a suspect makes an equivocal request for counsel, police questioning is limited to questions designed to clarify the request.

Perez called Grimm once Green's confession was typed. ''She's beating around the bush, and she's asking to talk to her lawyer,'' Perez said to Grimm before handing the phone to Green. Not surprisingly, when she hung up she told Perez she couldn't answer any more questions. He told her to sign the statement and she meekly complied.

Green recanted her statement and moved to suppress it as involuntary. Judge Bridges disagreed: She had initialed each right and voluntarily waived her privilege against self-incrimination and her right to counsel—until she asked for an attorney. Accepting Perez's testimony and rejecting Grimm's, he ruled that this point was reached only after Green's statement was complete. Judge Bridges made the curious ruling that her statement was admissible, but not her signature.

With her recanted, detailed, but unsigned statement used against her, supported by Perez's testimony about his version of the facts, Green was convicted at trial on January 25, 1995, on three counts of rape of a child in the first degree and one of child molestation in the first degree. Judge Carol Wardell sentenced her to twenty-three years, the high end of the standard sentencing range for the charges, because her graphic confession defied any possibility that she was innocent. ''It is very detailed, very bizarre,'' said Judge Wardell of the confession. ''There is no way Detective Perez could have made it up and then had in confirmed in two separate interviews with the children later.'' Yet the children's statements were in many ways inconsistent with Green's.

Several community members sent letters to the court in support of Green. Judge Carol Wardell said in open court she found it ''reprehensible'' that so many people who hadn't heard the evidence presented to the jury could believe the woman was innocent.

*   *   *

Hot on the heels of the Green arrest came the arrest of Randall Reed on September 15, for the molestation of the Town children. The theory with Reed was that he shared space in the Town home and had the opportunity to molest their children. Reed, forty-three, entered a guilty plea to reduced charges on November 9. In a statement prepared by his attorney, he said, "Because of liver damage that has affected my brain and memory I have no recollection. I want to make sure it doesn't happen again and I believe the State could convict me at trial."

On September 30, Jeanie Bendt called Katie Carrow, caseworker for her six-year-old son Joshua, who had severe mental and emotional problems. Carrow's department had recently sent Josh to Pine Crest, where he was diagnosed with major depressive disorder, attention deficit hyperactivity disorder, and oppositional defiant disorder, and at last released him on medication. In the course of the conversation, Bendt, who has mental limitations of her own, said something that Carrow took to be an admission that she'd abused Josh.

Carrow went to Bendt's home and induced the woman to sign a Voluntary Placement Agreement authorizing removal of her children from her home. In short order, a caseworker packed up Josh and some of his possessions and drove him to his new foster home. Within hours, Carrow and caseworker Linda Woods went to see Josh. "I did not intend to do an actual sexual abuse interview," Carrow wrote. "Yet, as it turned out, Joshua was ready to talk."

She asked Josh if he felt safe at his new home and if he even knew what safe was. He responded quickly said that *safe* means "you don't let anyone touch you." According to Carrow's report, the people who had touched him were his mommy and "daddy" (Bendt's live-in boy-friend, Noberto Castaneda-Macias). He said his dad put his penis in his bottom every day, and his mom had intercourse with him. Said Josh, "Daddy is not going to be a cop anymore because he's in jail and he's not coming out." Although Carrow was quick to point out in her report that Noberto Castaneda-Macias had never been a cop, she had no similar skepticism about the rest of the boy's statements.

Jeanie Bendt agreed to meet with Carrow and Perez at Carrow's office at 10 A.M. on October 3. According to Bendt, she was chatting with Carrow when Perez burst in, rattled through the Miranda warnings, and announced she'd molested Josh. Bendt protested; Perez called her a liar. Worse, he said, she was calling Josh a liar. "You're going to jail nonstop for a long time unless you tell us something," he said, according to Bendt. She claims he asked her to name friends who had had sex with kids. He told her what he "knew." He said she could go home if she told, she said. At last Perez took his handcuffs out of his pocket. "He told me I was going to prison for twenty years or more unless I said to him what he wanted to hear," Bendt told me.

She shot to her feet and tried to walk away, but the door was locked. Perez slapped the cuffs against his palms. "Okay, that's it, I'm through fooling around with you. You're under arrest and you're going to prison for a long, long time." Hours after the interview began, Bendt "confessed." "I just told him I was giving him what he wanted to hear because he said I could go home if I did. . . . Perez also wrote down what he wanted me to say and not what I said," she said. She was booked into the Chelan County Regional Jail on 1,860 counts of rape of a child in the first degree, and 840 counts of child molestation in the first degree. She immediately recanted, but a judge found her statement was knowing and voluntary and admissible against her at trial.

While she waited in jail, the prosecutor's office plied Bendt with plea offers, all hinging on her willingness to testify against others. Every time she refused, the amount of potential prison time went up, she said. When she declined all offers, the prosecuting attorney and her lawyer wrote to her saying that if she didn't accept a plea bargain, additional charges would be added. Under the circumstances she felt she had no choice but to plead guilty, but she wouldn't agree to testify to lies about anyone else.

On January 6, 1995, Bendt entered into an Alford plea (not the caliber of the one she would have been offered if she'd agreed to testify against others) to greatly reduced charges. Bendt's lengthy plea statement, prepared by her attorney, detailed the risks presented by trial and the potential consequences of a guilty plea, most notably that over the last few months some defendants who had gone to trial (such as Connie Cunningham) got sentences as high as forty to fifty years. Bendt's statement got her lawyer off the hook: She acknowledged that a dependency court was likely to terminate her parental rights to her son Josh. She would have no chance to see him again, at least until he turned eighteen. Although she received a sentence of 198 months on each count, to run concurrently, for Bendt the termination of her parent-child relationship was the deepest cut of all.

The children of more than a dozen jailed defendants, including the Holts, the Towns, and Jeanie Bendt, became ready sources of information, useful to test governmental theories of friendship, proximity, opportunity, and complicity. Under state authority, which again proved to be virtually unchecked by the courts, the kids were tightly isolated; contained in cooperative foster homes experienced at creating an atmosphere ripe for disclosure; placed in therapy dealing with issues of abuse, memory, victimization, and denial; and often carted off to Pine Crest Mental Hospital in Idaho, where they were surrounded twenty-four hours a day by authorities who believed unconditionally that they were victims. Not surprisingly, stories proliferated. Yet none of Perez's interviews with the children were recorded; nearly all notes (if taken) were destroyed.

One of these interviews was an instructive lesson to the authorities: Notes were sure to trip you up if they fell into the hands of the defense. Perez was careful to avoid anything but the fleeting existence of contemporaneous notes, but he overlooked the danger of CPS recordkeeping.

On October 12, Carrow and Perez again questioned Josh Bendt.

"Is my mother in jail?" asked the boy, according to Perez's report.

"Yes, she is," said Perez. "How do you feel about that?"

"Happy," said Josh, launching into a whole new version of events—without prompting, according to Perez's report. "She touched me in a privacy way in the bathroom." He said his "dad" came in and touched him with his hands and a stick or a ruler. "My mom touches my privates with her knee, hands, arms, body and hurts it." Josh described other bizarre incidents. "She puts water in my butt after I go poop." He described multiple sexual acts involving his "dad" and mom. He said his "father" put a ruler in his bottom. "I was two years old, I think," he said, when the incidents happened.

Josh said Jeanette and Shorty visited with him and his family. Jeanette was a Mexican woman who lived in a trailer and she'd had sexual intercourse with him, he said.

"They have animals and they abuse them and stuff. . . . They touch them on the front private."

Armed with this information, Perez went to the Chelan County Jail to question Jeanie Bendt about Jeanette and Shorty. Although, according to Washington's interpretation of Constitutional right to counsel, Perez could no longer question Bendt without her attorney present, he justified it to himself because he was questioning her about a case other than her own. If there were to be additional consequences to her, he couldn't be blamed.

Bendt stared at him in puzzlement, then offered up what she could. She didn't know a "Jeanette," but she knew a woman named Kathy who was Caucasian and lived in a house, not a trailer. But she had kids with the names Josh gave.

Perez tracked down Kathryn Lancaster, but she wouldn't admit a thing. He arrested her anyway. Despite the detail of his police incident report, Perez left out other details: that Jeanette was Mexican and Kathryn was not, that Jeanette lived in a trailer and Kathryn in a house. Nor did these significant details crop up in the prosecutor's Affidavit of Probable Cause. But there these details were, in Katie Carrow's notes, and the defense attorney made an issue of it.

Months later, in March 1995, on the prosecutor's motion Judge Carol Wardell dismissed the charges against Lancaster and Castaneda-Macias because the parties stipulated that Josh was incompetent to testify due to his mental instability and personality disorder.[2] The parties "agreed there was no corroborative evidence of tearing

---

[2] Jeanie Bendt pleaded guilty without knowledge that her son might have been incompetent to testify against her. The court later denied a motion to vacate her plea based on these grounds.

or scarring." Shorty was apparently never identified or charged.

The case against Kathryn Lancaster was *not* dismissed based on the serious discrepancies between the facts and Josh's statement, and perhaps these facts weren't known to the court.[3] Still, for Perez the lesson was clear: *Notes must be destroyed.* Perez now threw away CPS notes at the end of interviews, knowing that there would be no way for the caseworker to make copies for his or her own records.

Other stories led to the arrest of Lawrence "Leo" Catcheway, the so-called figment of Laura Holt's imagination. By now, Perez's theories had evolved. He discovered that Catcheway was or had been the boyfriend of Dorris Green and was living with Green when her alleged crimes took place.

On September 20, Perez and Carrow questioned the Holt and Town children, who first described sex with Catcheway in a tent and their homes. But then the statements took on a new dimension: After lengthy questioning, Donald Holt said parents trooped their kids to houses and swapped them around for sex. The next day, Walter Town talked about sex between kids and adults at the Holt

---

[3] In order to meet the requirements of due process of law, the prosecutor is obligated to disclose material exculpatory evidence to the defense and to preserve such evidence for use by the defense. Under the standard adopted by Washington courts, criminal charges must be dismissed if the state has failed to preserve "material exculpatory evidence." This standard does not require police to preserve and retain everything of conceivable significance or that the evidence might have exonerated the defendant. The evidence must have exculpatory value that was apparent before the destruction and be something the defendant could not otherwise reasonably obtain. Under the Fourteenth Amendment, the state's failure to preserve "potentially useful" evidence does not represent a denial of due process unless a defendant can show bad faith on the part of the state (*State v. Wittenbarger,* 124 Wn. 2d 467 (1994); *California v. Trombetta,* 467 U.S. 479, 81 L.Ed. 2d 413, 104 S.Ct. 2528 (1984).

home. The statements of the boys bore little or no resemblance to what they had said before.

On September 29 and 30, Perez and Carrow interviewed children described in court documents only as J. A. and E. A. Once again, the children described multiple sexual acts involving numerous adults and children. But most interesting of all, "Leo took pictures with a big camera. Leo liked to take pictures and he told us what to do in the movies and who should go in next."

With the theory of a cameraman, the Wenatchee sex cases had all the earmarks of a conspiracy involving pornography and the nationwide exploitation of children. The sex ring theories had emerged full-blown. Yet no films, slides, photographs, or other pornographic materials were ever recovered to support this theory. This fact didn't stop Perez and prosecutors and other officials from alluding to the existence of videotapes to the media and the courts.

Despite the increasing complexity of the cases, the prosecution of sex rings seemed entirely achievable, especially as such defensive police strategies as destroying notes and not recording interviews was unchecked, defense tactics were disfavored, and the defendants disbelieved. Police and proscutors experienced no serious challenges at the court level, and Judge Wardell's admonition about speaking up for the guilty was dutifully reported in the *Wenatchee World* as a clear message to Wenatchee residents.

And then came trouble: people who refused to confess, and community members—even outsiders—who supported them.

11:

Winter 1994

════════

The Doggetts—Child Protective *Services?*

════════

Once high school sweethearts, Carol and Mark Doggett long ago moved to Wenatchee from Sacramento in hopes of providing a better life for their kids: Sarah (age fifteen), Jeremy (thirteen), Lisa (twelve), Ashley (ten) and Melinda (nine). In 1994, Sarah—everybody called her "Sam"—returned to Ukiah, California, to stay for a year with her godmother, Kathi Hansen, who had been her mother's close friend since high school.

Carol and Mark completed courses at Wenatchee Valley College on June 10, 1994, and Carol quickly found a job. Most days, after the sun dropped low, she strolled down to River Front Park and jogged along the concrete path by the river, breathing in the aromatic scent of sagebrush and cottonwood trees. When she could, she brought someone with her because so many strange things were going on in Wenatchee these days. She replaced the vinyl on the dining room chairs, worked on her journal on the family's new computer, and helped her sister Terrie plan for her wedding at the end of August.

Ashley and Melinda were going to Columbia Elementary School in the fall; Jeremy and Lisa would be in middle school. Mark was continuing his education at Central Washington University, majoring in psychology while he worked at a computer lab. The family had hopes of buying the house they were renting if they could talk their landlord into a break on the down payment.

Only two things marred the Doggetts' happiness that summer: Their family friends, Connie and Henry Cunningham were arrested on unspeakable child abuse charges; and the family missed Sam.

On July 18, Carol wrote to Sam: "Speaking of Cunningham's [sic], it's not good for them at all. Connie had started divorce proceedings and we all thought everything was going to be okay and the family could start healing, but then they arrested Connie too and now she's in jail on charges of aiding and abetting child rape because they said if it had been going on for so many years, she must have known about it." Carol went to see Connie in jail and found the conditions harsh: "Inmates can't eat with anything but a spoon, the toilet is right out in the open, and she is in a room with about 20 other women. They all sleep on a cement floor on thin pads."

Carol tried to imagine living under these conditions but quickly pushed the thoughts away into the safe, distant, foreign territory populated by *someone else*. She wasn't sure what to believe about her friend's guilt. "I am taking a non-judgmental position," she wrote. Like most Wenatchee residents, she found the allegations of sex rings so monstrous and, in their vastness, so confusing that she preferred not to consider them. She was confident that the court system would sort things out.

But she couldn't mentally disconnect from the Cunningham children, Jenny (fifteen) and Susan (seventeen), who were friends of Sam. After a time, the Doggetts agreed to take in the Cunningham girls as foster children.

After Jenny and Susan were interviewed by a defense

attorney, caseworker Dean Reiman called Carol. "Get after those girls," he said. "They aren't cute anymore. They think they're the center of attention. We don't want to hear their giggling. We don't want to hear about Henry's favorite positions. This is serious business. *It's time to put their mother away.*"

By fall, Carol wrote to friends about their summer. Referring to her expanded household, she said, "Everyone is healthy and hopefully happy. I have adopted a new goal: To provide a safe haven where children can explore their creative and intellectual talents. Sounds idealistic! Good!"

Mark and Carol Doggett's optimism ended abruptly in December 1994.

First, on Saturday, December 10, they received the news that Sam had made a serious suicide attempt by taking an overdose of pills. The images were horrifying—two hundred pills, a cryptic suicide note, tubes and machines in a hospital. Sam's crisis counselor at Vallejo Hospital helped the Doggetts to unravel their daughter's motive, which was in itself stupefying: Lisa had confided to Sam that Jeremy had molested her. Sam felt responsible: She failed to protect her sister after she had so many times promised herself she would.

After they hung up the phone, Mark and Carol woke Lisa and told her what happened and why. Lisa was too sleepy for artifice: She wiped away her tears and confirmed it. Carol and Mark grappled with serious questions. Sam was going to be all right . . . but for how long? And what about Lisa? What should they do with Jeremy?

In a voice both consoling and firm, Sam's crisis counselor in California urged the Doggetts to enroll Jeremy and Lisa in counseling right away. On Monday, Mark took Lisa to a mental health center and made an appointment for Jeremy. Lisa's counselor, Cindy Andrews, told Mark she'd make a referral to CPS.

The Doggetts welcomed the news because when it came to questioning their kids about these things, they were out of their depth. Carol left a message for Dean Reiman at CPS. She wanted the matter investigated: How long had it been going on? What was the extent of the sexual involvement? Were other of her children involved?

On December 14, Perez and Abbey drove to Orchard Middle School to interview twelve-year-old Lisa and fourteen-year-old Jeremy. Both flushed, dropped their eyes, and admitted they had intercourse a few times. According to Perez, Lisa "didn't seem overly upset." By all accounts, it was consensual. But where had the boy gotten the idea? Jeremy had the answer: The summer before, he'd been molested by a camp counselor, and another time by a neighborhood boy.

Mark Doggett greeted Perez and Abbey on the porch of his home, while Jeremy went inside. The porch could use a paint job, Doggett had long hair and an untamed beard, and the Doggetts had taken in the children of their friends the Cunninghams. Perez made a mental note of these things. He leaned a shoulder against the doorjamb, locked Doggett in his blue-eyed penetrating gaze, and dropped the bombshell that Lisa and Jeremy had had sex for four years. Doggett was silent for a long moment; Perez took him for a man who wasn't surprised. Abbey said as a precaution he'd have to remove the Cunningham children.

"What about Jeremy?" asked Doggett. "What about your investigation of him?"

"It's all over," said Perez, explaining the sex had been "mutual."

"It's a family matter," said Abbey.

When she got home, Carol was upset. Surely there was

a risk that Jeremy, as a previous sex abuse victim and, now, an untreated sex offender, might molest one or more of the girls. She left a message for Reiman. "Why aren't you taking Jeremy?" she said on his voice mail. He never returned her call, according to Carol.

Mark and Carol helped Jenny and Susan pack, handed them over to caseworker Linda Woods, said their good-byes, talked late into the evening. Part of the problem was their schedules: Carol worked until 5 P.M. and, once college resumed, Mark wouldn't be home from Ellensburg until 4 P.M. or later. Maybe they could find a place for Jeremy to stay, at least until he was firmly involved in counseling.

On December 15, Carol called Abbey. "Where can we put Jeremy?" she said.

Immediately Abbey sounded suspicious. She tried to explain that she and Mark wanted to place their son in a treatment center. "It'd be easier to place all of the girls than to find a place for Jeremy," Abbey snapped, his voice rising in anger, according to Carol. "Why do you want to *do* this?"

Carol was astonished at the suggestion. Abbey reminded her that he and Perez had determined Jeremy and Lisa had had consensual sex, something that isn't criminal in Washington if the kids are within two years of each other's age.

She understood these things. It wasn't about a crime, she explained, but about her fear that her other girls were at risk. Then, summoning up her courage, she added that Susan Cunningham had told her, just before Abbey took her from the Doggett home, that Ashley had disclosed sexual contact with Jeremy as well.

Still Abbey was unimpressed. In exasperation, Carol told him that therapist Cindy Andrews had once told her that perpetrators were usually sexual molestation victims themselves. She reminded him that Jeremy was molested by a neighbor boy years ago and by an adult at scout camp. Surely this simple equation, this blatantly obvious, well-known theory could not be ignored.

To her dismay, Abbey repeated it would be easier to place the girls. Grudgingly he told her to bring Mark and come to his office on Monday to discuss the matter.

On December 16, Carol left a message on Abbey's answering machine that she'd be moving Jeremy to her sister Terrie's house at Moses Lake on the coming weekend. During the business week of December 19 to 23, she left several messages at CPS, mainly asking that Susan and Jenny be allowed to come home to them now that Jeremy was no longer in the home.

On Tuesday, December 20, Mark took Lisa to her appointment with Cindy Andrews at Mental Health. On Wednesday he took her to the airport to catch a flight to California to stay with her sister Sam for Christmas. On Friday, December 23, he drove Ashley to an appointment with the family doctor as a prerequisite for placement with the mental health program.

With Sam and Lisa in California and Jeremy at Terrie's home, it was a bittersweet Christmas, but Mark and Carol sat beside the tree they had hauled home from the woods outside Wenatchee and told themselves that they'd handled the situation responsibly. Now their family could heal with the help of their faith in the Mormon religion and their own strong bonds.

On December 28, the world as the Doggetts knew it exploded.

Carol was at work when she got the call from her sister Terrie, who was clearly upset. "They came and took Jeremy!" she said, explaining that Perez and Tim Abbey came to her house. "Who *is* that man Perez?" Terrie asked. "He bullied his way into my house without any paperwork! They took Jeremy against my will! They said they were taking him in to the CPS office for questioning!''

Jeremy had answered the door, she said. Her son Ted had asked Perez who he was. The detective ignored the question.

Perez approached Terrie, who was sitting on the living room couch. ''We're here to question Jeremy,'' he announced. ''Why is he *here* anyway?''

''You'll have to ask Mark and Carol that,'' she said coldly. She asked the men to leave her home.

According to Terrie, Perez leaned over her, his manner threatening. ''We don't play the game this way.'' She recognized that it was futile to resist, and watched as he and Abbey took Jeremy away.

Carol was quick to reassure her sister. ''It's okay,'' she soothed. ''I half expected them to question Jeremy again now that they heard Ashley has disclosed something.'' Then, in words that she now finds hugely ironic, she added, ''CPS stands for Child *Protective* Services. They're there to help families.''

Later in the day, Terrie called Carol back. ''They called to tell me that they've taken Jeremy into custody and they won't be bringing him back.''

''That's okay,'' reassured Carol, ''it's probably just because they decided he's a perpetrator.'' Despite her words, she felt a stab of fear for Jeremy. But at least the officials were finally taking her concerns seriously.

Detective Perez's police report describes the official version of his interrogation of Jeremy. Perez learned on December 17 that the boy was sent to Moses Lake to live with his aunt. It seemed ''odd'' that the Doggetts would send him away ''so that foster children could remain in the home,'' he said. Such a circumstance accorded with a popular Wenatchee theory—the Doggetts had created an opportunity for themselves. Perez and Abbey arranged to visit Jeremy in Moses Lake on December 28.

They picked up Jeremy from his aunt's home, and drove him to the Moses Lake CPS office. After they extensively questioned him, the boy said that he had sexual contact several times "with others, including his two sisters." Then he described molestations by his parents that began when he was three or four years old, according to Perez.

In a defense interview, Jeremy said the interrogation lasted for approximately five hours. Perez's manner was immediately threatening. Jeremy haltingly told him he molested his sister Lisa a few times.

"We know it's been going on for five years," Perez said flatly, according to Jeremy, and then added, "We think you're a victim, too."

"He said my parents were abusing us," Jeremy said. "I said no." He asked Perez, "What did they do anyway?" Perez was happy to oblige with his speculations and convictions. Jeremy, at first, denied it all.

According to Jeremy, Perez told him several times he was a liar. He asked the same questions over and over. "He kept saying he knew the truth, but then he would say things I knew were not the truth, so I knew he didn't know the truth." Jeremy said he was "overpowering. He didn't believe anything I said." He became increasingly coercive, said Jeremy. "He threatened that I'd go to juvie if I didn't start telling the truth. . . . He threatened me about making a statement. I thought he was pretty mean. He'd get mad at me."

At last Jeremy broke down and told Perez what he had so clearly indicated he wanted to hear.

According to Perez's report, Jeremy's parents called him and Sam into their bedroom and made them have sex. "They made us take our pants off and get on the bed. My dad and Sam had sex; it was straight sex where he would be on top of her. My mom got on top of me and had sex with me. She made me rub her breasts. I had a hard-on; it just happened.'' These things happened one to five times a week, according to Perez's report. Jeremy said his other sisters were involved as well and sometimes his parents made the children ''do it together while they watched.'' Ashley and Melinda were included once they reached about four years of age, he said.

''I don't think Dad ever had four girls at once,'' Jeremy purportedly said. ''One would be with Dad and the others watching. Dad would change off. Mom would tell me to shut up and hold still.'' The most recent episode was December 8 or 9. His father told Jeremy, Lisa, and Melinda to go into his bedroom, where Carol was waiting. ''Okay, you know the routine,'' said Mark.

Abbey wrote his own report of the interview, one that in many ways diverges from Perez's report. According to Abbey, Jeremy said Sam was mean to him and once made him eat dog feces. She made him have sex with her, made Lisa molest her with a coat hanger, made him watch while she molested Lisa.

Jeremy said his parents often had sex with him, wrote Abbey. It was an ''ongoing occurrence . . . day or night. . . . When they got tired they made us go back to bed,'' Abbey quoted Jeremy as saying. It happened since he was three or four and Sam was five or six. The family switched partners, but Jeremy ''never had to wait a turn since he was the only boy,'' wrote Abbey.

When Carol got home from work that day, she and Mark went upstairs to talk to Melinda and Ashley. She explained to the girls that some men would probably be coming to talk to them about what had been going on with Jeremy. She urged them to be honest and tell the truth.

At around 6:30 or 7 in the evening, Perez, Abbey, and another Wenatchee police officer knocked on the door. Mark answered the door and Carol soon joined him, Abbey, and the officers on the porch.

"Hi, Carol," said Perez.

Carol smiled at them pleasantly. She told the men she'd expected them to interview the girls and she told Melinda and Ashley to cooperate and tell the truth.

Perez and Abbey said they'd be taking the girls to the police station for interviews. "We'll bring them back in a couple of hours," said Perez mildly.

Carol went to get the girls. She gathered up their coats and they went out to the porch. The girls were afraid. "You're going to bring us back, right?" asked Ashley nervously.

"Oh, yes," said Perez, according to Carol. "We'll bring you right back home."

Expected and long overdue as the actions might be, Carol immediately felt a rush of anxiety. She took Abbey aside. "He's not lying, is he?"

He looked at her. "He *never* lies." Reassured by Abbey's words and her trust in the fair workings of the system, Mark and Carol waved good-bye to the children. Unfortunately, many parts of their statements were taken as admissions of guilt, including the benign words, "We've been expecting you."

Abbey sat in on the interviews in Perez's office at the station. On the ledge behind Perez an assortment of teddy bears grinned their comfortless idiot's grins.

"Your brother said there were some problems at home," said Perez. Ashley "hung her head and nodded," wrote Perez in his report. He asked her how old she was when the problems started.

"I think I was around four. I know I felt scared." The detective reported that Ashley said her dad came into her room and sat by her on the bed. "I don't remember what he did that time, but it hurt. I had bad dreams about it." Twice a week or more, according to the report, "he would come in . . . and make it sound like a game. Dad said we were playing house. I remember at the end, I put my clothes back on." Sometimes her brother and sisters were involved. Once her father "rubbed her privates" and her mother sat and watched. According to Abbey's report, Ashley said Mark touched her over her pajamas. Both her mother and her father came up to her room during summer nights and touched her.

According to Perez's report, sometimes her parents played house with her. "Mom had to pretend to be the maid and clean. I was the wife and dad was the husband. Mom was dusting. My dad said we just got married and he wanted a kid. He made me undress and then practiced making a baby with me. He got on top of me and he was kissing me and then he kept doing it. Then the door opened downstairs and he put his clothes on and told me to put my clothes on. This happened in my brother's room in the summer."

Sometimes Carol got undressed and went "up and down" on her. "Sometimes, my mom would put her hand down there and put her finger inside me," said Ashley, according to Perez.

According to Abbey, when asked where she wanted to live, Ashley said, "I would feel safer in foster care. I would miss my parents but I would feel safer in foster care."

After an hour, Abbey beckoned nine-year-old Melinda into the room. It was 8:30, around her usual bedtime, but her eyes were wide. Perez asked her if she knew the difference between good touch, bad touch, and secret touch. In a tiny, stilted voice the girl told him. He asked her if she had problems like that. According to his report, Melinda hung her head and nodded yes, just as her sister had done. She cried and said a problem happened with her parents twice a week, but she didn't explain. Melinda "was unable to continue with the interview from this point and due to her emotional condition, the interview was stopped."

In the months to come, the Doggett children told a far different story about the interviews—a story of confrontation and disbelief and coercion—but the interviews weren't recorded and the truth remains mired in debate.

By 9:30 or 9:45 P.M., Carol and Mark became anxious. What was going on? Finally Carol called the police station to say that it was getting late and the girls needed to be put to bed. The receptionist said the interviews were just about finished.

A short time later, three uniformed officers came to the Doggett home. Mark met them on the front porch. With hardly a word, a cop slapped the cuffs on him, grabbed his arm, and, in the vernacular of police reports, escorted him to their cruiser. At the time, Carol didn't know what happened. Then, a few minutes later, there was another knock at the door. Carol opened it. Three uniformed officers stood on the porch.

"Officer Perez has probable cause to arrest you on rape of a child in the first degree."

"What?" she gasped, flabbergasted. "You've got to be kidding!"

Clearly the officers weren't kidding. They told her she had to go to the station. The next thing she knew, one of the officers forced her hands behind her back and she felt the metallic snap of the handcuffs at her wrists. The cop took her elbow and she stumbled clumsily beside him to the door. She asked for her coat and to tell her sister-in-law, who was visiting for a few days, where she was going. "Sorry, ma'am," said the cop tersely.

"I was totally in shock," Carol said.

The officers walked her down the darkened sidewalk, where she felt suddenly, embarrassingly exposed. One of them opened the door of the police cruiser; another shoved down on the top of her head as she awkwardly lurched through the door. Carol heard the crazed static of the police radio. Familiar streets slid past.

At the Wenatchee police station, an officer took her to a room where Perez and Tim Abbey were sitting at a desk flanked by teddy bears. "Bob," she gasped to Perez, "what is this all about?"

"You know perfectly well what's going on here. Your children have told us everything," Perez said, according to Carol.

"Told you *what*? I've been open and up-front with you from the beginning!"

"No," snapped Perez, according to Carol. "You *haven't* been honest and up-front from the beginning, Carol. What about playing house and practicing making babies while you played maid?"

"I never did that!" Carol gasped in astonishment.

Perez read the Miranda rights from a printed form. Carol, who had never been in trouble with the law, could scarcely believe she was hearing the words directed at herself. As instructed, she initialed each right. She also signed a statement saying she refused to talk.

During the course of the interview, she asked for an attorney three times; each time Perez ignored her, she said. "You don't need an attorney."

"You know what will happen if you don't talk, don't you?" Perez growled, his face close to hers, according to Carol. "If you drag this out, it will make it harder on your children. The courts don't like that." He raised his eyebrows meaningfully. "You'll go to prison for the rest of your life. That's a long long time." According to Carol, he told her what her kids said she did and she reeled with astonishment.

"You'll never see the light of day again," said Perez, according to Carol. "If you don't cooperate, you'll never see your kids again." From that moment forward, she might never see her children again. Tears came to her eyes.

"I never did those things!"

"Are you calling your children liars?" he said, according to Carol. "We know all about you and Jeremy."

"I never molested my children!"

"Connie [Cunningham] sat right there and said the same thing!"

"Don't you compare me with Connie or any of your other cases," she protested.

"Are you saying you don't *remember* molesting your children?" Perez asked mildly, according to Carol. She felt he was trying to trick her.

"Of course I don't remember molesting my children, because it never happened!"

She was right, the words were a trap. Later, Perez and Abbey interpreted her statement as if she had indeed said she couldn't recall molesting her children: a close second to an admission of guilt. From Carol Doggett's interview onward, the theory of lost or faulty memory was a recurrent theme in Perez's reports.[1]

He tried a different tack. "Do you do drugs?" he asked softly. Lack of inhibition because of dependence on drugs or alcohol had long been another of his favorite theories.

"I haven't since I was a teenager."

---

[1] It is logical to conclude that Perez had by now become educated in popular theories on repressed memory, since many of the Wenatchee "victims" were in "recovered memory therapy," possibly including his foster daughter.

"What about your husband?" he asked. "Does Mark do drugs?"

"He's been clean and sober for three years."

"What would you say if I told you I had reliable sources that say your husband is doing drugs?"

"I think I would know."

"Well," said Perez sarcastically, "you should."

Desperately Carol tried to seize control. "Were the interviews taped?" she asked.

Perez scowled at her. "I never tape interviews," he said.

"Was anyone else there when you did the interviews?" she persisted.

"Yes," said Perez. "Tim Abbey was present. Do you trust Tim Abbey?"

"I *did*," said Carol.

She stood up as Abbey approached her. "Tim, were you there?" she asked him.

"Yes," said Abbey.

"And do you believe this stuff?"

Abbey looked at her coldly. "From the bottom of my heart, yes, I do."

She threw her hands into the air. "Well, where was *I* when all this was going on?" she cried. Perez and Abbey just stared at her.

She was going to jail, there was no doubt in her mind. But surely, it would just be for the night. "Abbey swooped in on me and had me sign voluntary placement paperwork for the kids to go into foster care." With no other place for them to go that night, she felt she had no choice.

She was booked into the Chelan County Regional Jail. At the jail, one of guards said in her presence, "We sure are getting a lot of these cases."

"Yeah," said another. "It's that new guy. He's bringing 'em in like crazy."

Perez describes his interview briefly. According to the Affidavit of Probable Cause, which reflects his report in the brevity of thwarted officialdom: "After being advised of her rights and the allegations, Carol Doggett refused to talk and stated that she wanted an attorney. At this time, Perez ended the interview and informed the defendant that she would be permitted to contact an attorney from the jail. Perez asked the defendant no further questions; however, while preparing the form necessary to book Carol Doggett into jail, the defendant stated 'I don't *remember* molesting my kids.'" (italics added)

After waiting a seeming eternity, Mark Doggett was escorted into Perez's office. Perez sat behind his desk, stroking his mustache.

"Your wife is in denial so she is being booked into jail as we speak," said Perez coldly, according to Mark. "Are you willing to cooperate with me?"

"I am," said Mark. "Because there's something terribly wrong here."

"What's wrong is you and Carol have been molesting your children."

"That's not true!" protested Mark. "We rarely even spank our kids, let alone abuse them." He said he couldn't remember any sort of behavior in their home that could even be termed inappropriate.

"Wouldn't you agree that prison isn't a very good place for child molesters?" queried Perez with narrowed eyes.

"Prison is a *very* good place for child molesters," said Mark. "When they're in prison at least you know they're not molesting children."

"Don't you think that treatment is a better option?" Perez persisted.

"As far as I know, there's no evidence to suggest that treatment is effective for child molesters."

The calculated intellectualism, the feigned superiority of the man's answer no doubt infuriated the detective. According to Mark, Perez's face reddened, his eyes bulged, his mouth pursed, and he spit out the words: "If you don't start cooperating and tell me what I want to hear, you'll never see your family again!"

Mark struggled to control his anger. "Your idea of cooperation seems to be for me to tell you that I did something that I didn't do. I'm simply not going to do that!"

"Fine," snapped Perez, according to Mark. "You can rot in prison! The interview's over."

Having said that, Perez questioned him about his past drug and alcohol use. He told Mark he knew he had molested his kids while he was blacked out.

"I told him that I did a lot of things I'm not proud of while I was using, but that hurting my kids—in any way—was not one of them."

Abbey urged Doggett to confess, and told him in graphic and shocking terms what he could expect in jail if he didn't. "He also told me that he and Bob [Perez] would sleep with their wives that night and that I couldn't see my wife for a long, long time."

Within the Affidavit of Probable Cause against Mark Doggett, the theme of not remembering was fully explored. "After being advised of the charges and his rights, the defendant stated 'I *don't think* I ever molested my children.' When asked what he meant by that, the defendant said 'he *didn't remember*' and 'I *don't remember* ever doing it.' According to Perez, the defendant never denied sexually abusing his children but continued to say, 'I *don't remember* doing it.' Mark Doggett went on to indicate that his children were truthful and that [Melinda] was 'always truthful.' When told that all three children had indicated sexual contact by him and his wife, Perez asked the defendant if his children were lying and the defendant said, 'no, there [sic] are not lying, but I *don't remember* molesting them.' '' (italics added)

A study in brevity and redundancy, the affidavit resoundingly made its point.

Mark and Carol Doggett were booked into jail on over a thousand counts each. Carol was formally charged with five counts of rape of a child in the first degree; two counts of rape of a child in the second degree; two counts of rape of a child in the third degree and two counts of complicity to rape of a child in the first degree. Mark was similarly charged.

When I talked to her, Carol theorized that the actions of the state might have been motivated by its concerns about state liability because Jeremy had molested her children while foster children were in her home. Indeed, Abbey started a frantic round of correspondence with DCFS administrators Billesbach and Harrington, explaining the actions of the Wenatchee DCFS, the gist of which was to show that the Doggetts had "lied through their teeth" in order to be licensed for foster care.

12:

Winter 1994–Spring 1995

════════

Sam Doggett—Uncivil Commitment

════════

In the days before Christmas, Sam Doggett tried to put the suicide attempt out of her mind. She greeted Lisa at the airport, talked excitedly with her, made plans for the holidays. She and Lisa were inseparable.

A couple days after Christmas, Kathi Hansen approached Sam and gently told her that her parents had been arrested for molesting her and the other girls. She stared at Hansen in astonishment, but the woman insisted it was true. Then Sam went to tell her sister. The girls hugged each other and cried.

"If it happened to you," Sam assured Lisa, "you can tell me. It isn't your fault."

"Nothing happened!" Lisa cried. "I wanta go home."

Perez told her the girls had to return to Wenatchee to testify, said Kathi. He assured her it would be over in a couple of weeks.

"You can both come back here to stay with me," she reassured them.

Kathi and Paul Hansen frantically considered what they should do. They called the girls' uncle Jim, who told them of an organization called VOCAL, an acronym for Victims of Child Abuse Laws. The organization had national roots and was made up of people concerned about what they considered to be the growing hysteria about child abuse, many of them purportedly falsely accused.

A couple of days later, the girls met their uncle Jim in Williams, California. He drove them to his home in Folsom to spend the night, and the next morning took them to a meeting with George Wemberly of VOCAL. Wemberly, a large man with an effusive manner, chatted with the girls for a while and then videotaped their statements. According to Sam, who could hear her sister's interview, Wemberly asked the girls if they had seen their parents naked or if they had touched them "in the wrong way." Lisa said no and, when it was her turn, so did Sam.

A day or two after their return to Ukiah, Kathi approached Sam and Lisa. "Detective Perez just called," she said. "He said your parents' trial will be in two weeks. You'll have to go down and testify. He said that after you testify you'll be able to come back to California," she said. Neither Sam nor Kathi had sufficient legal experience to recognize that the trial date suggested by Perez was unrealistic and misleading.

"I insisted that while you're down there, you and Lisa be allowed to stay in a foster home together," said Kathi.

"Are you sure?" asked Sam.

"He practically promised me that you girls can stay together. He said he knew where you'll be staying and that it's a good foster home."

Kathi told Sam that she and Lisa had to meet Perez and CPS caseworker Pat Boggess the next day at their hotel in Sacramento. There were a lot of things to be done first. Sam and Lisa packed their clothes. Kathi drove Sam to the high school, where she picked up her missing assignments from the few days she'd missed because she was in the hospital. They went to the office and got a home study course for a two-week period. Then they drove to the home of Sam's grandmother to spend the night.

The next morning, Kathi and the girls walked uncertainly into the hotel lobby. Kathi clasped a manila folder jammed with legal guardianship and other papers; the girls lugged their suitcases. Perez and Pat Boggess watched them approach. Perez strode forward, his chest thrust out with authority, his footfalls muffled in the plush carpet; Boggess trotted to keep up.

Kathi introduced herself and fumbled with the folder. "Here," she said, thrusting it forward. "I have legal guardianship records on Sam. Her school enrollment paperwork is in there as well."

"We're not interested in that," said Perez, according to Sam. "I'm in authority here. What we have to do will overrule anything in that." He glanced scornfully at the folder.

"My parents didn't molest me!" Sam announced to Perez. "I don't know why you're doing this." He ignored her, she said.

"It's really important that the girls stay together," said Kathi. "They need to be placed together in foster care. Are you sure they'll be together?"

"Yeah," said Perez smoothly, according to Sam. "We already have a foster home where they'll both be." Boggess smiled and agreed.

During the fifteen minutes or so that Sam, Lisa, and Kathi were at the hotel, they remained together. According to Sam, there was never any discussion about legal paperwork, such as the DSHS Interstate Compact paperwork,[1] which is usually a Washington State requirement

---

[1] According to the Interstate Compact on Placement of Children (Revised Code of Washington 26.34.010), a state agency cannot bring a child into another "party state" for placement in foster care unless it complies with specific provisions of the statute and any applicable laws of the receiving state. The requirements include

before a child can be transferred from a state wherein she is under legal guardianship.

From the hotel, Boggess and Perez took the girls to a government office in Sacramento, then took Lisa into a room and closed the door. A woman with a professional nurturing smile gave Sam a tour of the office complex: just another bland office building with cubicles and potted palms—and child abuse posters, frightening reminders of why she was here.

Sam wondered what was taking so long. Lisa, at age twelve, wasn't strong like her, she believed. She lacked self-confidence and felt the need to please people. What were they doing to her?

Three hours later, her sister emerged, her face blotchy with emotion and spent tears. Sam was unnerved at the sight of her. In a pinched voice, Lisa told her what Pat Boggess had said. ''She said Dad's been using drugs and shooting heroin and messing around with other women.''

Lisa said she didn't know what to believe, but she appeared halfway convinced. Sam didn't believe a word of it. She squared her shoulders and watched Perez approach her.

''It won't be necessary to talk to you,'' he said, according to Sam. ''We've got all we need to know.''

Sam tossed back her long light brown hair and leveled her blue eyes at him. ''Why don't you have me go to a doctor? I'm a virgin. That will prove it.''

---

notification to authorities in the receiving state (here Washington) of its intent to bring the child into the state, and the reasons for this action. ''The child shall not be sent, brought, or caused to be sent or brought into the receiving state until the appropriate public authorities in the receiving state shall notify the sending agency, in writing, to the effect that the proposed placement does not appear to be contrary to the interests of the child.'' Penalties for failure to comply might include civil or criminal liability and suspension or revocation of license, permits or other legal authorization held by the sending agency which allows it to place the child. In this case the girls' mother Carol Doggett may have given permission for the transport when she signed the Voluntary Placement Agreement.

Perez's face tightened. "That won't be necessary," he said, according to Sam. "We know what happened." With that, he walked away. Sam looked at Lisa, who hunched her shoulders in misery.

Nobody said much on the way to the airport. Sam's thoughts were in turmoil, but she decided that she couldn't show her fear and confusion. At the airport, Boggess took the girls aside, her face stern. "If you cause any trouble, make a scene or anything, you'll be separated," she warned, according to Sam. "You won't be able to see each other again."

Sam sat beside Lisa on the plane and watched white clouds swirl surrealistically below them. Soon they were making their descent toward the Seattle-Tacoma Airport, where they had a one-hour stopover.

The girls wandered down ramps and walkways and escalators, with Perez and Boggess flanking them. Everywhere Sam looked, people milled about or strode with purpose, their faces animated or stressed or merely bored. At last she and Lisa sat down in molded plastic chairs near the Horizon Airlines boarding area.

Perez sat down heavily beside her. Later she said, "I was kind of curious about why he did that because I think he knew I didn't like him very much." She tried to ignore him and went on chatting with Lisa.

After a minute, according to Sam, he leaned over and whispered, "You know your dad raped you. Why don't you just admit it?"

Sam gasped with surprise and was immediately furious. But she couldn't talk back or they'd take Lisa away from her. A few minutes passed. Out of the corner of her eye, she saw Perez lean toward her. *Ignore him*, she told herself.

"You know your dad raped you," came his whispered voice. "Why don't you just admit it?" Shaking with anger, she dug through her bag and fished out her school-work. She deliberately started doing math.

The third time, she said, Perez made no attempt to lower his voice.

"You know your dad raped you. Why don't you just admit it?"

Sam flushed with embarrassment and rage. Her pen snapped in her shaking hands. Ink spilled on her blouse. "Can I go to the bathroom to wash this off?" she said, daring to look at Perez. He was smiling at her.

"Yeah," he said, grinning.

She hurried to the bathroom past throngs of people. She could tell someone—but what could she say? And who would care anyway if a cop questioned her? Her eyes welled with tears and she lowered her lashes so no one would notice.

Back on the plane, still unnerved by Perez's words, Sam again questioned Lisa.

"Are you absolutely *sure* nothing happened?" she queried.

"Yes," said Lisa firmly, according to Sam. "What about you?"

"Yes," said Sam forcefully. "You know me. I wouldn't *let* it happen.

The small plane tossed in the turbulence from the mountains below them. Sam watched the mountains un-fold into the Wenatchee Valley, saw the distant glint of the Columbia River. She glanced over at Perez. She hoped he'd leave her alone.

The Pangborn Airport in East Wenatchee is a long stretch of tarmac, a single rambling building, and a neat cluster of parking areas. As the girls walked down the ramp, they saw people standing around near the runway. Lisa huddled close to Sam. Sam wondered if their foster parents were waiting for them.

Detective Perez pointed to a man standing a little bit apart from another couple. "That's your caseworker, Dean Reiman," he said to Sam. "You'll be going with him." Then he pointed his finger. "Lisa, you'll be going with that couple. They're your foster parents."

All of the long day's fear and frustration and outrage rose in Sam. They had lied to her! She and Lisa would be separated. Lisa rushed to her and they clutched each other fiercely. "Don't let them take me away!" Lisa sobbed.

"You're liars!" Sam screamed. "You promised we'd be together, and we haven't done anything wrong! You're breaking your promise!"

After a few minutes, someone spoke to her. Sam's face was buried in Lisa's hair, so she couldn't see his face, but she believes the voice was Perez's. "Okay, you girls. Enough of this! It's time to go." The man's voice wasn't concerned; it wasn't angry; it was merely impatient.

Lisa clutched her tighter. *I won't let go*, Sam told herself. *Not ever!* Then someone grabbed the girls' arms and started to tug. The girls clung harder. The tugging grew in strength. Sam ignored the pain, but she could feel Lisa slipping away. Finally, Lisa's sobs became screams, something Sam had rarely heard from her sister.

"You're hurting me!" Lisa screamed. "Let go! You're *hurting* me!"

Through her tears, Sam saw the vivid red marks on Lisa's arms. As the foster parents dragged Lisa away, Sam heard her sister's shoes scraping on the tarmac. "Don't hurt her!" Sam wailed. "Let her go!"

She fought with Perez, Reiman, and Boggess, who were holding her back.

"Sam," Lisa cried out to her, "don't let them take me away!"

And then Reiman took Sam's arm and pulled her to his

car. She tried to struggle with him, but by then she was having a full-scale asthma attack. While she gasped for air, Reiman fished through her bag for her inhaler.

"Don't be mad at us," Reiman cautioned Sam. "Blame your parents. It's *their* fault!"

Reiman dropped her off at the foster home of Mickie Reyes-Vogam. There were lots of other foster kids there, all of them strangers to her, as was Mickie. Everyone gathered around her curiously as she sobbed and puffed at the inhaler.

"If you want to talk, I'm here," Reyes-Vogam said kindly.

Sam told the woman what had happened. "Well," said Reyes-Vogam, "maybe they had a court order to do that." She didn't ask Sam any more questions.

Over the course of the next two weeks, Sam was a virtual prisoner. She wasn't allowed any contact with her sisters or anybody else she knew other than CPS personnel. She wasn't allowed to go to school and she even had to go to work with Reyes-Vogam. She busied herself completing her schoolwork and the new assignments the school had given her—work meant to cover a two-week period.

On January 10, Reyes-Vogam took Sam aside and told her Reiman and some others wanted to meet her at the CPS office. On the way down in the car, Reyes-Vogam said, "You know that whatever else happens . . . I'll always love you and always be there for you."

Sam was immediately suspicious. *Great*, she told herself. *Something's gonna happen!* She tried to prepare herself for the worst, which, she had recently learned, could be bad indeed.

She walked with Reyes-Vogam across the lobby, past the receptionist, and into the DCFS offices. Reiman met her at one of the offices. His face was stern. Her heart thudded dully: She'd seen *that* look before.

"Sam," said Reiman, according to Sam, "we believe that you're suicidal and you have an eating disorder."

She started to protest. She wasn't much of an eater, but she was no longer suicidal. She had learned at the hospital the collateral effects of suicide and she would never do anything to intentionally hurt Lisa.

Reiman cut her off. "We're going to hospitalize you for your own good." He added that she was so violent he had no choice about what was going to happen next.

Despite her curiosity and dread, Sam said nothing. She wasn't going to prove him right. The next moment, a couple of ambulance attendants entered the office, pushing a gurney. "I could tell that Dean was expecting me to make a big fuss," Sam told me. "So of course I didn't." She lay down meekly on the gurney while the attendants strapped her down with leather restraints at her waist and wrists and ankles.

Nobody told her where she was going or even what type of hospital it would be. As they wheeled her out toward a waiting ambulance, Reyes-Vogam came toward her, wiping her eyes. "I asked if I could drive you there and they said no."

Sam hadn't been allowed to pack any clothes or even bring her school bag, which was in her foster mother's car. She just had the clothes she was wearing.

She stared at the roof of the ambulance, at the patches of sky and hills and the occasional treetops visible from the ambulance windows. After about an hour, one of the attendants leaned over the seat back.

"You won't punch me in the nose if I unstrap one of your wrists?" he asked, smiling.

Sam smiled back and said no.

With one arm free, she felt more normal. One of the attendants asked if she wanted something to eat, but she

declined. Instead she passed the time, as prisoners often
do, by dozing.

The drive took about four hours. At last the ambulance
stopped and the attendants unstrapped her and walked
with her into an inauspicious brick building. She saw the
sign, PINE CREST HOSPITAL. Within the day, Sam learned
that Pine Crest was a mental hospital in Coeur d'Alene,
Idaho, with separate units for adults, children, and adolescents.

According to hospital records, officials placed her in a
small observation room with a bed, a closet, a bedside
table, a chair, and a large expanse of glass designed, obviously, for observation. She was introduced to her counselors and learned that she would be placed in group and
individual counseling.

Although she was from the first described in hospital
records as physically healthy, with no obvious signs of
anorexia, bulimia, or suicidal ideation, Sam remained at
Pine Crest for five weeks. Dr. Billy Barclay did a psychiatric evaluation. Sam denied drug or alcohol use and
said she was a virgin and that the allegations were ''preposterous.''

Dr. Christina Zampich also evaluated the girl. According to Dr. Zampich, ''Rationalization, denial and exter-
nalization typically form the core of her defenses. She also
uses intellectualization as a major defensive tactic in situations she perceives as affectively stressful.'' So much
for Sam's efforts to reason with the doctors.

''Sarah [Sam] does not appear to be under an undue
amount of stress at this time,'' wrote Zampich. ''It is
likely that her functioning has been relatively stable and
that her behaviors are usually the result of purposeful
decisions. She is not likely to engage in impulsive acting out at this time and may be more deliberate in her
actions. . . . There were no indications in testing of thought

disorder problems or underlying psychosis.'' Nevertheless, Dr. Zampich recommended that Sam be considered for antidepressant medication.

Despite Sam's physical health and the evidence of emotional stability, she was forced to remain at Pine Crest for another four weeks after the testing was complete. During this time she was not advised of her legal rights or provided with a lawyer, legal paperwork, or any form of legal process. All of these things would be required if Sam were civilly committed to a mental hospital under Washington state law.[2]

According to Sam, her counselors urged her to take mood-altering drugs, which she refused, but didn't approach the issue of suicide, which was the major reason she understood she was hospitalized. It was little wonder. Dr. Barclay completed a discharge summary describing her as ''intelligent and more complex than most persons her age.'' There were no indications of a thought disorder.

Then Dr. Barclay went on to describe Sam's social ''history,'' which he gleaned only from Washington state officials because, of course, neither she nor her parents were considered believable. ''The patient's psychosocial history had to be by way of the authorities in view of the parents' incarceration. A truly amazing collateral history was obtained, one in which there was active sexual activ-

---

[2] Revised Code of Washington 71.34 governs mental health services for minors. According to this law, a minor over thirteen years old can be involuntarily civilly committed when the child ''is brought to an evaluation or treatment facility or hospital emergency room for immediate mental health services.'' If the professional in charge of the facility evaluates the child's mental status and finds she suffers from a mental disorder, and the child doesn't consent to treatment, the minor may be detained for up to twelve hours so that she may be evaluated by a county designated mental health professional. If the professional determines the child is in need of treatment, the child is entitled to such rights as an attorney, a hearing, and the right to present evidence. An evaluation or treatment agency includes a public or private facility certified by DSHS to provide emergency, inpatient, or outpatient care, and a separately designated portion of a state hospital.

ity amongst family members and friends with the patient and her siblings and her parents all involved with each other and with multiple family members in the same area.''

The history was indeed truly amazing, given the fact that it was entirely inconsistent with the facts alleged by Sam's brother and sisters, after separation, therapy, and hours of interrogation by Perez and state officials. No extrafamilial or extended-family group sex was alleged about Mark or Carol Doggett. Yet the strict parameters of truth were no apparent impediment to state officials. This false ''history'' clearly fueled the imaginations of the Pine Crest staff and affected the integrity of Sam's treatment and, perhaps, that of others who followed her to the facility.

In the face of this astonishing information that Sam refused to endorse, the Pine Crest staff subjected Sam to what they called ''reverse room restriction.'' She had to ''earn the privileges of being alone in her room by cooperating.'' The meaning of *cooperating* was made clear to Sam. Her therapist told her many times that she was in ''denial.''

''Are you ready to talk about your sex abuse yet?'' said the therapist. She said Sam didn't want to accept the truth of the abuse, which was understandable because some things are hard to accept. Yet all of her siblings had disclosed abuse by their parents, she said. ''It's okay,'' the therapist added, according to Sam. ''When you come around, I'll be there.''

''Well,'' said Sam, ''you've gotta release me sooner or later.''

It was true. Much to the apparent distress of the Pine Crest staff, she was released to the custody of DSHS without making a disclosure. Dr. Barclay noted in his report, ''I've only seen one other case similar to this, who happened to be a girl of similar age who was the daughter of another family in the neighborhood where this girl came from. It appeared then that there were several families who were conspiring to live in a lifestyle that was considered unacceptable by the society as a whole, and the children were every bit as much a part of this as the parents. I'm not sure that anyone has studied cases such as this enough to know what the outcome might be.''

Clearly, the complicated conspiracy theory of child swapping and extrafamilial orgiastic sex gatherings was embraced without question by yet another core professional affiliate of the Wenatchee government. In the weeks and months to come, Pine Crest Hospital got many more opportunities to study the Wenatchee phenomenon and to work on children with issues of denial and recantation. But not with Sam. On February 6, a staff member came to tell her she'd be leaving the next day.

The next morning, Dean Reiman and Sam's guardian ad litem, Karen Bird, drove her back to Washington. The conversations were superficial: Nobody talked about Sam's family, her parents' cases, or her hospital stay. They drove her to Omak and placed her in a group home. Nobody explained to her why she wasn't returning to Mickie's foster home, or even to Wenatchee.

To her surprise, she found things to like about the group home. ''They actually listened to me,'' she said. ''They listened to what I had to say and they believed me.'' Another thing about the group home pleased her. ''When I told them I wanted to go to school, they put me in school.''

Sam was taking few things for granted these days. But she was relieved to be returning to school. Her first school day at Omak High School was February 13. Affable and outgoing, she soon made friends. She now says that she had no behavioral problems, was a student in good standing with better than a 3.3 grade-point average, and was well-liked at the group home. But these things didn't seem to matter to the Wenatchee authorities. To her profound disappointment, Sam was denied any contact with her sisters.

One day, Reiman came to the school to talk to her. He told her that all of her sisters were examined by doctors. "They're obviously abused," he told her, according to Sam. "They're hurt. They're damaged for life."

"Well, I'm not," she said. She told Reiman she was a virgin, and urged him to take her to a doctor to have her checked out.

"That won't be necessary," said Reiman, according to Sam, in words reminiscent of Perez's in Sacramento. "We already know it's true."

The group home apparently only allowed a one-month stay. When her mouth was up, officials placed Sam in the foster home of Barbara Barr, also in Omak. She was allowed to remain in school. Sam was pleased to learn that Barr also went to the Mormon church. But barely a week later, she was driven to Wenatchee for a defense interview and placed in the Wenatchee home of yet another foster parent, a woman affectionately known as "Grandma." To her dismay, she learned that once again DCFS officials had lied to her when they said she could stay with Barr and work to resume a normal life. She wasn't allowed to return to Omak, return to school, see her siblings.

Sam said she asked to go to school more times than she could count. Each time she received a similarly evasive answer from Dean Reiman, her foster parents, her guardian ad litem, and others: "We'll see." From the day in early April when she returned to Wenatchee to talk to the attorneys, until the end of the school year, she wasn't allowed to go to school or even to do correspondence or home study courses, she said. No one told her why.

On top of everything else, Sam wasn't allowed to see her sisters. She learned that Melinda and Ashley had lived together for a time before trial. But then Ashley recanted and the girls were separated in an apparent attempt to preserve Melinda's statements. Sam learned her sisters were removed from their former school and, after Ashley's recantation, Melinda, too, was taken out of school. Although her younger sisters were allowed to have supervised visits with each other, they weren't allowed to visit Sam, their parents, or any extended family.

One day, Sam learned that Lisa's therapist, Cindy Andrews from Children's Home Society, wanted to talk to her. She agreed in hopes of helping Lisa, but she soon came to regret her decision.

Andrews told Sam her sisters all said their parents had molested them. Not only had Mark and Carol molested her, but she had molested her brother and sisters, said Andrews, according to Sam.

"That's not true!" protested Sam.

Andrews told her she was in denial, that her mind had blocked away the memory. "She really confused me because she said that I had a memory block and I might not be *choosing* to not remember, but I was not remembering things," she said. Andrews said that "there were ways I could remember things if I wanted to," she said. Sometimes hypnosis can restore a memory, the therapist suggested.

Sam quickly became confused. "She was just so convincing. She had me thinking what if I *do* have a memory block?" she later said.

Walking away from the session, Sam reminded herself she'd never had any memory problems in the past. She worried because she understood her sisters had been seeing Andrews since January and they'd be much more vulnerable to the therapy technique than she was. She told herself angrily that the therapist had mixed her words around. Andrews's mind was "definitely made up and she didn't want a lot of information," said Sam.

13:

Spring 1995

═══════

The Doggett Trial

═══════

As the time for the Doggett trial drew near, state officials apparently became consumed by the urgency of winning the trial (and thereby validating their actions) in the face of mounting community criticism. The children's statements had to be developed—and preserved from outside influences. But the state would couch it as *therapy*.

Whenever possible, state agents isolated the children from the dangers of recantation. In a letter written after the trial, Cindy Andrews said the goal of therapy for the Doggett children was to promote recovery. "This goal, thus far, has been difficult to achieve, as during our sessions the children reveal a *network of continual contacts by their former peers and family friends.*" (italics added)

In another letter written around this time, Boggess and Reiman described "unauthorized contacts" with the Doggett children by friends, family members, and others who refused to believe the Doggetts had molested their children and "who continue to support the couple in their efforts to circumvent the judicial process. *Such community behavior represents a subtle, and yet sometimes not-so-subtle psychological warfare in this town in an attempt to enlist the participation and recantation of at least one child witness.''* (italics added)

The two daughters of Mandilee Richerson had been friends of the Doggett children for years. Richerson was a substitute teacher who sometimes taught at the children's school. One day she suggested to Melinda's foster mother that they arrange a get-together between Melinda and Richerson's daughters. She said she'd be happy to drive Melinda to services at the Mormon church. The foster mother smiled politely and thanked Richerson.

A few days later, Deputy Prosecutor Roy Fore told the court that Richerson was ''lurking in the bushes'' across the street from the foster home and finally came up to the door and told Melinda she'd ''better quit her lying or she would go to hell.'' Richerson said this statement was a completely false interpretation of her meeting with Melinda's foster mother.

Within days, the Wenatchee superintendent of schools told Richerson she could no longer work in the district. Officers came to her door, serving her with a restraining order, barring her from the school. At last, Richerson agreed not to contact the Doggett children; in exchange, she was allowed to come and go at her children's school as any parent would—but not work as a substitute teacher.

Carleen Arnold was another longtime friend of the Doggett family. Jeremy Doggett occasionally ran away from foster care to her home. ''He's changed so much,'' Arnold told me. ''He's become so worldly. And he hates Detective Perez. He said he'd like to get a gun and shoot him.'' Jeremy came to hate himself as well; in fact, he became ''self-mutilating,'' said Arnold, adding that she'd seen the boy cut himself with a knife.

In the spring of 1995, Arnold ran into Melinda Doggett at a garage sale. Immediately Melinda threw her arms around her and cried, Arnold said. ''I'll be a good girl,'' she sobbed, according to Arnold. "I'll do all the chores without saying anything. Please take me back to my mother."

It wrenched Arnold, but she told the girl the truth. "I can't do anything about it," she said softly. Arnold drove on to another garage sale. She strolled among the tables and then returned to the car. There in the car sat Melinda, who had followed her.

"I'll be a good girl," she implored. "Will *you* take me?"

She told Arnold she wasn't allowed to go to school. "I have to do all my work at home." Nor was she allowed to go to the Mormon church, she said.

Arnold remembered that Jeremy had told her the same thing. Jeremy said his caseworker had warned him, "as long as he had any control, I would never be allowed to go into an LDS [Latter-Day Saints, or Mormon] foster home or go to church again," said Arnold.

Although the children were isolated from friends and family, CPS caseworkers and law enforcement officials rushed to fill in the breach. Carol Doggett heard that Pat Boggess frequently gave Melinda gifts of toys and books, and visited her nearly every day, and Melinda went on a camping trip with Deputy Prosecutor Roy Fore and his family and Perez.

By February, as the date of the joint trial of Mark and Carol Doggett approached, Chelan County prosecutors had many worries about their case. Jeremy had almost immediately recanted, as part of a psychological evaluation by Drs. Virginia and David Philips of Wenatchee. As the Philipses put it, Jeremy "was feeling discomfort about the disclosures that he had made to investigators on previous occasions regarding the extent of sexual abuse in the family. He stated, for example, that he had only de-

scribed the abuse, including sexual involvement of his
parents with children in the family, because investigators
had not believed his other statements that nothing had
happened. . . . Regarding his parents' incarceration, he
said, 'I don't like it. I know they shouldn't be there.' "

Jeremy also recanted to his guardian ad litem. The state
stepped up his therapy. At a defense interview on February 8, 1995, Jeremy said his parents had molested him,
but said he was threatened and lied to and made allegations to get out of trouble.

Ashley recanted to her counselor Cindy Andrews at the
Chelan County Mental Health Clinic.

Melinda gave only abstract information when Perez interviewed her. At other times, she denied her parents had
molested her. When, after months of therapy, she finally
disclosed, Mark Doggett was charged with four additional
counts of molestation and four counts of child rape with
Melinda as a named victim. In a defense interview that
followed, Melinda said Roy Fore had told her he believed
she was molested by her parents. She said Boggess and
Reiman had told her if she remembered, this would "all
be over with."

Lisa couldn't or wouldn't make any verbal disclosures
about her parents molesting her. Instead, she wrote a note
to Detective Perez describing abuse, after she was interviewed for hours at a second interrogation session. Yet
Lisa recanted as well. A week after she denied that she
was abused, she was reported as vomiting and lethargic.

On February 22, Lisa was examined by Dr. Dougal
Chisholm of the Wenatchee Valley Clinic because of
tiredness, lightheadedness, and vomiting. At the time, Lisa
was a foster child in the home of County Commissioner
Tom Green and his wife Judy. "This has obviously been
an extremely traumatic time for her and she has not had
any physical examination or follow-up for this problem,"

wrote Dr. Chisholm. Nor did the state want one. Because the Doggett trial was pending, Chisholm asked Lisa's caseworker Dean Reiman if he should do a pelvic exam for court. Although both of Lisa's parents were accused of penetrating her, Reiman said that wouldn't be necessary, according to Chisholm's report.

Other troublesome questions were raised by the exam. "Her social workers are Pat Boggess and Dane [sic] Reiman. . . . She is seeing a counselor, Cindy Andrews, who feels that she might be depressed and apparently would like her to be on medication. Apparently Mrs. Green has related to Ms. Andrews that I will be the family physician involved, and Ms. Andrews stated to Mrs. Green that I was not someone who prescribed medication in the way she would like to see them utilized," wrote Dr. Chisholm.

After Lisa denied abuse at a defense interview on March 17, the prosecutor said in the courtroom that she was depressed to the point of "self-mutilation."

Mark and Carol Doggett weren't faring much better. Mark began to keep a journal in jail, twenty-one days after his arrest, on January 13, 1995. "I'm trying very hard to have enough faith in the Lord to not be scared and for the most part I do all right," he wrote. "But sometimes I just feel overwhelmed. I think the scariest, most frustrating thing is knowing that we are so completely innocent and that may not be good enough to set us free. You believe that by simply telling the truth everything will work out, but then you realize that people with the power are simply not telling the truth."

He and Carol were represented by public defenders. After more than three weeks, Mark still hadn't seen his attorney. A couple days later he sent a letter to Judge Small advising him of this situation, as well as a letter to the American Civil Liberties Union. Mark spent the long days sleeping, writing letters, studying the scriptures.

On January 26, Mark, "got to thinking about Harold Everett—he just got 23 years and 4 months for child rape . . . thing is . . . Harold pleaded guilty . . . I wonder how many people Perez has intimidated into pleading guilty . . . and then hung out to dry . . . I really have no reason to feel sorry for myself—it could be much, much worse."

On February 2, Mark saw Carol at a dependency hearing for the first time since their arrest. "We aren't allowed to talk to each other," he later wrote in his diary, "but we were sitting around a table. . . . I actually found it difficult to pay attention to what she was saying because I was wrapped up in the music of her voice. . . . Carol is such a trooper! She had used dampened colored pencils to apply as make-up . . . her use of colored pencils tells me (and I may or may not be reading this right) just how desperately she is concerned about getting the kids back."

The next day with the help of family and friends, the Doggetts at last scraped up the money to make bail, under a court order that they have no contact with each other or any minor children. In his journal Mark wrote, "I've been thinking more and more about the kids and just how traumatic an ordeal this has been for them—the more I think about it the angrier I become and the more determined to see that those responsible will not be allowed to inflict similar damage on other children. I intend to take this case as far as I am legally allowed to in order to see that safe guards are legislated to prevent such blatant and appalling abuses of power."

By February 20, Mark was getting "numb" and "mega-lonely" for Carol and the kids. "Maybe I should just leave off thinking for awhile and see what happens."

By the end of the next day, Mark was outraged. "Got up. Got dressed up. Went to court. Sat around for an hour. Found out the hearing had been postponed. Went to my attorney's office. Sorry we didn't tell you. Sorry but most if not all of the evidence you've collected that shows Perez to be a liar, cheat, and ne'er-do-well is probably not admissible as evidence in court, but everything he says the kids have said is. More upset than I've been to date. Obvious now that the real trial will have to be held in the court of public opinion with the media as the prosecuting attorney and Perez et al., the defendants.''

"I miss Carol so much it hurts," wrote Mark the next day. "Sure I miss her physically, but more than that I miss the companionship and togetherness. And, of course, there's the kids—always the kids. I've always known that they play a big part in my happiness, but I guess I've never really appreciated just how big a part. I'd grown accustomed to [Melinda] running into my arms every time I walk in the door, and the hugs they'd each give me every time I came home, and before they went to bed, and just out of the blue. They say that we're strengthened by our trials—well, doggone it I don't know that I ever wanted to be this strong.''

On February 24, Mark had cause to feel better. Judge Bridges amended the conditions of their release and allowed Carol to come home. "Spent most of the rest of the day just being together—took a nap and, literally, slept in each others arms. What a great thing it is to hear Carol's voice around the house and to wake up along side of her! Praise the Lord!''

The next day they met with Karen Bird, the kids' guardian ad litem who had been appointed by the court to advocate for their best interests. She told them the disturbing news that a strange man had been following the Doggett children and trying to question them. "This man is supposedly a stranger to the kids and is certainly no one Carol and I could think of.''

The man turned out to be a VOCAL representative who approached the children at the bus stop and on the street in order to take their statements. Although the state couldn't establish that the Doggetts had sanctioned his actions, and both denied it, the events proved to be a setback to their credibility.

By the end of February, Mark was still having trouble with his public defender, who committed the last straw by moving his office without telling him. Mark contacted the office of aggressive Wenatchee lawyer Steve Lacy but learned he was on vacation. Then, wrote Doggett, he got a call from John Henry Browne, "a real hot-shot lawyer from Seattle," who said he would take the case and told Doggett he was confident the case would be dismissed once the state found out he was on board. Doggett tried to raise Browne's ten-thousand-dollar retainer but had no luck. Nor would Browne agree to take the case on a staggered payment basis. "Seems like justice costs these days," Mark wrote in his journal. Desperate, he wrote another letter to the court complaining about his problems with his legal representation by Wenatchee public defenders.

On March 6, the Doggetts went to a rally protesting the actions of the police and the DSHS. Mark was heartened by the support from passersby. After he came home, a letter arrived at around 3:45 P.M. announcing that he was required to appear at a hearing at 3 P.M. He raced to the attorney's office, then on to court. "I'm all torqued off at these imbeciles and hurry over to the courthouse, run up the stairs rather than wait for the elevator, find where my hearing's supposed to be, go inside, find Randy, and he tells me that the hearing already happened and that I didn't need to be there anyway," wrote Doggett in his journal. "If it wasn't my life they were playing with I'd probably find some humor in the sordid affair."

On March 13, Mark and Carol Doggett went to court for a child hearsay hearing. But the hearing was delayed for a couple of days because, according to Mark, the prosecutor said that Melinda was "too stressed and traumatized to see me—they want to have a screen put in place around the witness stand that allows us to see her but prevents her from having to see us. . . . When it was over Carol and I waited out in the hallway . . . who should come tripping down the hall but Melinda. Carol said, 'Oh look Mark, it's Melinda,' and Melinda turned toward us, started to run toward us, was somewhat restrained by (we presume) her foster father, and ended up standing less than ten feet away from us, jumping up and down, hugging herself repeatedly, and blowing us kisses."

Mark went on to comment angrily about the state's motion. "Traumatized my patoot! The only reason they want that screen in place is because they know that as soon as she sees us it will be all they can do to keep her from running into our arms . . . which is precisely what I told Randy when the suggestion was first made."

The trial of Mark and Carol Doggett began the last week in April and lasted two weeks.

"Your parents have been given an opportunity to plea-bargain so that they can get counseling," Deputy Prosecutor Fore said to Sam just before the trial. "It would be smart for them to accept this offer."

The offer was generous: no further jail, and community-based treatment in exchange for a guilty plea to seriously reduced charges. As it now stood, the Doggetts faced potential life sentences. The Doggetts turned it down.

Every morning, the Doggetts dressed, walked through the sunshine and occasional gusty winds to their car, and drove to the courthouse, where the scraps of their faith in the criminal justice system were steadily eroded. Worst and best of all were the moments when their children testified on April 25.

Melinda testified first, Pat Boggess at her side. "Why are you here?" asked Fore.

"Because so I can testify because my mom and dad did some bad touching."

Fore asked Melinda some general questions and she said she was no longer going to school. Then he went on to questions about problems at home.

She said her dad had touched her while she was lying on the floor in Jeremy's room. Her father "was just sitting there and touching me . . . He put his finger in the crotch," she said.

"You said your mom touched you," said Fore. "When did she touch you?"

"Like my dad touched me one night, and then my mom touched me the next night." She added, "She put her finger in my crotch." Melinda said her mom and dad were wearing all of their clothes when they touched her, and she couldn't remember if she was undressed.

Fore asked her if she ever told anyone that she couldn't remember.

"Yes," said Melinda.

"Was that true when you told them that?"

"No."

"How come you didn't tell them the truth then?"

"Because I was afraid that—afraid they'd tell that, like, we wouldn't be a family again."

"Do you want to be a family again?"

"Yes."

On cross-examination, Melinda told Carol's defense attorney Keith Howard she started to remember being touched after she moved to her new foster home. Pat Boggess told her she should remember, she said.

"Has someone said that if you say your mom and dad

touched you, they will get help, and then you will be able to go home?''

"Yes," said Melinda.

"Okay. Who said that?"

"Like Pat [Boggess] and Roy [Fore] and Kris [foster mother].''

"So they said the quickest way for you to go home is to say that your mom and dad touched you?'' asked Howard.

Fore objected and the court called a recess to discuss the objection. When court resumed, Melinda modified her answer.

"Okay. You said that someone has said to you that if you say that your parents have touched you, then they can get help and you can go home, right?'' said Fore.

"No. If like I tell the truth," said Melinda.

"Then they can get help, and you can go home?"

"Yes."

"Okay. And the truth not too long ago was that you didn't remember, right?''

"Right."

"Okay. Now the truth is something different?"

"Yes."

"Okay," Howard said, picking up his previous thread. "And have you been told that the quickest way for them to get home is for you to say they touched you?''

"No," said Melinda.

"During our little break, did you talk to Pat?"

"Yes."

"Okay. And she told you to change: 'if they touched you' to 'tell the truth,' right?''

Melinda shook her head.

On redirect, Fore questioned her about his interviews with her when he said her parents needed treatment. "Did we have a meeting, a later meeting after the time that we were talking in the office, and you told me about your mom and dad touching you?'' asked Fore.

''I think so,'' said Melinda.

''And was it in that later meeting that I told you about the treatment thing?''

''Yes.''

''Do you remember what I told you about the treatment thing?''

''Not really.''

''Try and remember real hard. Did I also tell you that if they did these kind of things that they could go to jail, too?''

''I don't think so.''

Melinda testified that Perez only talked to her for a half hour, that she liked him, and that he treated her ''good.''

Both Lisa and Ashley denied their parents had sexually molested them, although both said they had accused their parents before.

''Why did you say that your parents did all those things to you if it wasn't really true?'' queried Fore of Ashley.

''Because at first when I was meeting with Bob Perez, I told him no, that nothing happened; and he—he kept on asking me the same questions over and over and over again but in different words, and—and he—he wouldn't, like, really believe me that nothing happened, so I had to tell him something.''

Fore asked Ashley, ''Have you ever had any trouble sleeping since all this started?''

Ashley said, ''Sometimes I just can't get to sleep. I, like, stay awake all night sometimes. I, like, wake up in the middle of the night and I can't get back to sleep.''

Lisa said her parents hadn't touched her inappropriately. At this point Fore introduced a letter into evidence that Lisa had produced after meeting with Perez and Pat Boggess in a CPS office.

"Did they tell you things that your brother and sisters may have said?" asked Fore.

"Yeah, kind of," said Lisa, adding that they didn't provide details of her siblings' statements. After a while, she asked permission to write things down and they gave her a pad and pencil and left the room.

The letter read: "I love my mom and dad a whole lot, and I want to be able to live with them again. But I do want them to get the help that they need."

The letter went on: "Dad: It started when my mom and dad were separated. Me and my brother and sister would trade off going to my dad's house. While I was there my dad never smoked or did the drug thing in front of me. When he was drunk, though, he would sexually abuse me. He would put me on the hide-a-bed and molest me by either just touching me all over or by actually fucking me."

The letter continued. "Mom. My mom would touch me whenever she felt like it. And when I hugged her good night she would touch me, too. That's mainly all she did, but she watched what my dad did to me and didn't do anything about it.

"Both. It stopped happening when they found out what Jeremy had been doing and sent him away. I still want to live with them again, but I want them to get the help that they need, and I want them to stop doing it. I didn't tell anyone because I was afraid to because they said that something would happen if I told someone. My mom also fucked me when she got really mad or her and my dad got in a fight."

Fore clarified with Lisa that she hadn't understood what the word *fuck* meant and thought it meant "touching all over."

"Did you write the letter because anybody pressured you to?" queried Fore.

"Kind of," said Lisa.

"Who pressured you to write it?"

"Bob."

"You mean Bob Perez?"

"Yeah," said Lisa.

"What did he do to pressure you?"

"It was like just what he said to me, what—"

"What did he say?" Fore interrupted.

"Well, he said like—"

Fore interrupted again. "Did Bob Perez tell you that you needed to tell the truth?"

"Yeah."

"Did he ever tell you that your mom and dad had done bad things to you?"

"Kind of, but no."

"I didn't hear the last part."

"I said, kind of, but no."

"Did he say bad things about your parents?"

"Kind of, but not really."

"What do you mean by kind of, but not really?"

"He kind of said stuff about them, but it wasn't really bad."

Fore didn't ask her to clarify her statements. "Do you remember when you talked to me and I asked you if you were pressured, and you said that about Bob Perez, that you liked him, that he was nice, and you never felt manipulated or forced to say anything?"

"No."

Lisa testified that she wrote a letter to Cindy Andrews about her interview with Bob Perez. In the letter Lisa wrote, "I felt like I had to write stuff 'cause what Bob said and how he said it to me. He said, I have all today and all tonight and most of tomorrow to sit and wait here until you tell me the truth (what he thought was the truth.)

"I knew then that he wasn't going to believe me until he heard what he wanted to hear. So I asked if I could write stuff down instead of say it to their faces. I was going to tell the truth before the lie got too big, but I tried and nobody believed me. So I said it again, and it grew into a bigger lie."

On cross-examination, Carol's attorney Keith Howard asked Lisa, "And when you were talking to Mr. Fore about stuff that happened in California and statements that you made, you were still caught up in that story, right?"

"Yeah."

"Caught up in that lie about your parents?"

"Yeah."

"And you're out of that lie now?"

"Yeah."

"How does that make you feel, good?"

"It makes me feel clean," said Lisa.

Jeremy testified that Perez had pressured him, called him a liar, and asked him the same things over and over. He said Perez had threatened to put him in juvenile hall unless he said his parents molested him. Nevertheless, said Jeremy, the acts occurred and he lied to the detective when he denied it. When Perez repeatedly raised his voice and accused him of lying, he admitted the truth.

"I hate him [Perez]," Jeremy testified. "He raises his voice. He's not very nice, I don't think."

Perez testified that he accused Jeremy of lying, but he denied that he had threatened him with juvenile detention. He acknowledged he told Lisa he had "all today and all tonight and most of tomorrow to wait," but explained that he was merely trying to emphasize his patience.

Cindy Andrews testified that the girls were preoccupied

in therapy with talking about how much they missed their family. Andrews said she had recommended that Ashley and Melinda be separated because she thought the older girl might be influencing the younger to recant. The girls talked incessantly about wanting to go home, back to their family, church, and friends.

A Wenatchee medical doctor testified, with the aid of colposcope slides enlarged on a screen, that he had found "notches" on the hymen of the Doggetts' nine-year-old daughter Melinda, which, he said, were consistent with digital penetration. The defense didn't call an expert to refute these findings.

Gerald McCarty, a psychologist and psychoanalyst from Lake Stevens, Washington, testified that the questioning of the Doggett children by Wenatchee police was akin to the questioning of the enemy in Korean prison camps. When children are isolated, repeatedly questioned, and provided with information about the beliefs of others, they may start to falsely believe what they are told, he said. He testified that, after reading police reports, he believes that this indeed happened to the Doggett children.

But Wenatchee clinical psychologist Dr. Virginia Philips testified in rebuttal that Detective Perez's interview techniques were proper because children often need a certain amount of "pressure" to break through their defenses surrounding sexual abuse.

At the conclusion of the testimony, apparently worried about the upcoming verdict, Fore again offered the Doggetts a plea bargain that would allow them to walk free. They turned it down.

Mark and Carol Doggett were each convicted by the jury of a single count of child rape and a single count of complicity, for acts against Melinda only. Friends and family members gasped as the verdict was read, wept openly, and rushed forward to hug the Doggetts. Outside in the hallway, CPS caseworkers Boggess and Reiman danced and whooped with joy.

Tim Abbey was elated but told the *Wenatchee World* that he was more contained. ''I'm not going to yell or cheer.'' But he said, ''It's like we weren't making all that stuff up.''

''My one regret,'' said Carol at her sentencing, ''is going to CPS for help with family matters. . . . CPS are trained to validate allegations, to convict,'' she said, rather than to protect families and children.

Said Mark, ''My feeling toward this is at no time has the prosecutor been interested in the truth. They had ample opportunity but they were interested in conviction. I don't believe there can be justice without the truth.''

In the end, the Doggetts received a sentence at the highest point of the standard range for the crime of which they were convicted: a little over eleven years in prison.

''I just feel traumatized half the time and fighting mad the other half,'' Carol said in a spartan room in the women's prison. ''I'm like a mother bear. How dare they do this to my kids.''

14:

January–February 1995

═══════

The "Circle" Is Born

═══════

January and February 1995 were months of heavy snow, biting winds, and the bad tempers of enforced confinement. They were months of board games and too much television and few respites from weekend boredom. In the Perez household, January was electric with tension.

Although the Perezes gave Ann Everett the kind of Christmas she previously had only dreamed of—a Lite-Brite set, a farm set complete with tractor and silo, coloring books, and clothes—she soon reverted to the unruly behavior that had gotten her into so much trouble since her removal from the Everett home. The Perezes considered removing the girl from their home as well.

"On numerous occasions we explained to her the need to have her talk to someone or see someone to help her deal with her anger," Perez later testified. In fact, Ann had already done a stint at Pine Crest Hospital in Idaho. Choosing the right therapist for her and the other Everett children was a matter of considerable official concern for Perez.

On October 25, 1994, according to DCFS records, Perez met with DCFS officials and forcefully "requested" that the Everett children be "immediately" removed from their therapy programs with Children's Home Society because of a "conflict of interest" arising from the fact that the agency counsels both parents and children and because the "counselors at CHS wouldn't be strong witnesses in court because not believing seriousness of the sex abuse that was going on." CWS supervisor Steve Warman quickly "directed" caseworker Connie Saracino to terminate the therapy and to advise the Children's Home Society that "we [the department] work co-operatively with the police."

Children's Home Society therapist Donna Anderson was incensed and made a series of angry phone calls to DCFS officials because she said the children would be "devastated" by a change of therapists. On October 26, Anderson "made a lot of accusations toward [the] Department" to Saracino, in the language of Saracino's records. DCFS area supervisor Carol Billesbach reminded Anderson that the department "always cooperated with police Department requests."

But Anderson couldn't put her concerns to rest. On November 8, she and therapist Kathleen Peterson fired off an angry letter to Abbey, Warman, and Saracino, and sent copies to the court commissioner and to the guardian ad litem for the Everett children. The Everett kids had been in therapy for two to three years, explained Anderson and Peterson, and in that time had become "very connected to their therapists. . . . These children have experienced much loss already in their young lives. . . . It is clearly against our professional judgement and we strongly believe this move is anti-therapeutic and damaging to the Everett children." It was no use: The children were removed and Children's Home Society therapists felt themselves to be under fire.[1]

---

[1] Two days later, on November 11, 1994, in a memorandum related to another

With the Everetts' sentencing fast approaching, the children's new therapists were encouraged to write letters by Saracino, who in turn provided this information to the court.[2]

William J. Kauffold, Ann Everett's therapist, said she was referred to him because of difficulties she was experiencing in the Perez foster home. "In fact her parents were about to have her removed," he wrote. Kauffold said her "therapy has gone well. . . . [Ann] takes issues seriously and when she feels you are listening and care about what happens to her, she is willing to respond in a more thoughtful and positive way. I have found that one does not need to apply pressure to [Ann], that she will do that herself. However, a little confrontation and teeth pulling is needed on occasion."

Therapist Cindy Andrews described Mary Everett's repressed memory therapy. "At times," wrote Andrews, Mary was "tearful, crying and sobbing during sessions." Worse, she was not free with her disclosures. "She is reporting symptoms of dissociation and has suppressed (volitional/choice not to recall) most memories of sexual

---

Wenatchee sex abuse prosecution (Bob Devereaux's), CPS supervisor Tim Abbey wrote to DCFS Regional Administrator Roy Harrington and DSHS area supervisor Carol Billesbach that "recently, Children's Home Society has made comments to DCFS staff, Steve Warman and myself, that they are afraid that the police will arrest them for obstructing justice."

[2] It is apparent from these entries that interrogation techniques have fallen under the guise of "therapy." According to many experts, investigation is designed as a means of obtaining maximal information from children and constructing theories about the alleged incidents. The goal of therapy is quite distinct, focusing more on the impact of events. Experts suggest that the goals of therapy and investigation often conflict and these roles should be separated; and that investigation should be complete prior to the beginning of therapy. Otherwise, therapeutic techniques might contaminate a child's recall. (See Lamb, Sternberg, Esplin, "Factors Influencing the Reliability and Validity of Statements Made by Young Victims of Sexual Maltreatment"; Raskin and Yuille, "Problems in Evaluating Interviews of Children in Sex Abuse Cases"; Yuille, Tymofievich, Marxsen, "The Nature of Allegations of Child Sexual Abuse"). It is also apparent that Mary and perhaps other children were in therapy designed to probe "repressed memories."

abuse, although she alludes to sexual assaults by both parents.'' In fact, Andrews wrote that her ''memory seems impaired by volitional suppression of sexual assaults.''

''It is quite obvious that [Mary] attempts to divert any questions or probes regarding history of abuse. . . . At this point, [Mary] demonstrates no insight into the need for treatment. . . . Her disclosures seem somewhat superficial and she tends to minimize the affects of multiple years of chronic sexual abuse.'' Yet there was cause for hope. ''Please note,'' Andrews wrote, ''that the therapist/client rapport building has been increasingly easier as [Mary's] defense mechanisms to guard and protect herself are lowered.

''It will be my goal to reduce [Mary's] suppression stance by assisting her in acknowledging and talking about prior sexual abuse,'' wrote Andrews. ''We will be discussing and working on the reduction of [Mary's] responsibility stance as she feels her parents' incarcerations are faults shared by she and her disclosing siblings. . . . Although I am cautious in my probes and confrontations, I do believe that [Mary] is responding and the therapeutic alliance is positive and moving forward. I feel optimistic that progress with this child will be positive and [Mary] demonstrates this potential.''

Andrews's projections were proven sound only six days later, when the girl demonstrated her potential by her prodigious disclosures. But first came Ann.

On January 20, ten days before her mother's sentencing and three days after the letters by Ann and Mary's therapists were written, Ann's progress improved. It was 7:30 P.M., in that twilight hour before bedtime, when she approached Bob and Luci Perez and asked to talk to them, said Perez. Gone was the little girl who had gone for years without disclosures. Gone were the days of minimization and denial and avoidant behaviors.

"We sat there, we sat and listened and I didn't take notes because I was a parent, not a policeman then," Perez told a reporter from the *Seattle Times*. "Luci and I comforted her, believed her. It was hard for her." Indeed. By the time the interrogation was complete, "she was curled up in a ball under the coffee table."

Although the interview broke Perez's hiding-under-the-desk rule, he concluded that Ann's words and her behavior were therapeutic. "We thought it was great she was getting it out," he later testified.

Ann set things out in geographical fashion, according to his report: the words of a thoroughly "bonded" foster child distilled through the fertile territory of her foster father's mind. First she described the goings-on at the Holt and Town homes, where among those present were Ann's parents, the Holts, the Towns, Dorris Green—and their children. The grown-ups told the kids to undress and to divide into groups, said Ann. Each child lay on the bed and had sex with each of the adults, until it was the turn of the next group of kids, said Ann. Sometimes the adults made the kids "perform sex acts among themselves at the direction of the adults," in the words of Perez's police report. These things happened at least twice a month and usually on weekends.

Then there was Ann's adult half-sister, Donna Hidalgo. "All the time" Donna made her undress and then she "put her finger in my private." It happened in Ann's house and also in the shed behind the house where Donna lived, she said.

Perez listened with interest as Ann talked about the Devereaux home: She walked right in on the sight of Devereaux lying naked on top of Theresa Sanchez. Devereaux yelled at Ann to get out of the room and later fixed her for her indiscretion by coming to her room and doing the same things to her, she said. Then she revealed that yet another of Perez's theories had born fruit. Devereaux made her "sit on his lap and steer the car while he rubbed her vagina," wrote Perez.

Perez assured Ann that she was "very brave for being able to tell me." Then he and Luci coaxed her out from under the coffee table and let her scurry off to bed.

"That first night, when I asked how many were there, and she said, 'There were too many,' it tore up my heart," Perez told a reporter.

But there were some who characterized his relationship with his foster daughter as creating a conflict of interest. Perez didn't want one of his cases dismissed on *that* technicality, either, so he talked to his chief, Kenneth Badgley.

Badgley acknowledged the potential for conflict of interest but didn't reassign the case. As he explained his reasoning, other officers assisted Perez, "and I have complete confidence in their work." Badgley later testified that he had no concerns about Perez's relationship as long as Ann's statements were corroborated. According to his reasoning, CPS workers were present at Perez's interviews with children, corroborating statements could arise from children and adults, and in some cases there was medical evidence.

Perez wholeheartedly supported Badgley's decision to allow him to continue in his dual roles as foster parent and chief sex crimes investigator. "I was very aware that I had to remain objective," he told a reporter.

In the days to come, Ann and her sister Mary disclosed many more events. Perez said he sometimes wrote down the girls' words, other times merely stored them in his memory until he got around to typing their statements in one massive report. None of the interviews were recorded; any notes were destroyed. Yet he was somehow able to pepper sixteen pages of Wenatchee Police Department Incident Report forms with direct quotations from the girls.

Because he didn't date his report, there is no way of knowing when it was actually completed.

At 9:45 A.M. on Monday, January 23, three days after Ann's disclosure at his home, Perez and Carrow were escorted to the counselor's office at Foothills Middle School to interview Mary. Perez was no stranger to the girl; not only did he question her periodically, but she came to his home for social visits. By now she had been in therapy for months, but she had never made a disclosure about anyone but her parents.

Perez told her that Ann was having problems with her half-sister Donna ''Sissy'' Hidalgo, and asked her what she had to say about that.

Mary tried to change the subject. ''I saw my counselor on Saturday and didn't even cry this time.''

What were the sleeping arrangements in the home when Sissy was around? persisted Perez.

''I don't remember anything about Sissy doing any touching to anyone,'' she said, certain of where this was headed.

Mary saw the familiar resolute and disbelieving expressions on the faces of Perez and Carrow and deceived herself that she could stave off the inevitable. The interview took on the timeless rhythm of a police interrogation propelled by an enormous imbalance of power.

Perez pushed for answers. Mary slapped her hands to her face and blotted out the sight of him and Carrow. ''When asked a question, she just burrowed deeper into her hands and huddled in her chair,'' he wrote in his report. Perez probed; the girl retreated further into herself. Rather than discouraging him, Mary's body language told him he was approaching his goal: She did this number before she had come clean about her parents.

Perez and Carrow forcefully persuaded her to drag her hands from her face. Perez looked into Mary's reddened

and fathomless eyes and asked if there were problems
with Sissy and other kids. Her face sagged and she said,
"I don't remember," and started to cry—also a hopeful
sign, something she had done during his last successful
interview. The tears, avoidance behaviors, and statement
"I don't remember" all dovetailed with Perez's theories
about victims of child abuse, some of them grounded in
professional literature.

He was quick to reassure her. There was nothing to be
afraid of; no one would be mad at her for telling. Besides,
Ann told and she was being protected. He reminded Mary
that she was actually helping her family and friends and
neighbors, who could now get help: Her disclosures
would be a massive outpouring of goodwill.

Mary's resistance began to crumble. Perez wanted
names: She reluctantly named people her family had visited. Perez wanted places: She said she had been by the
Holt house, but never inside. Mary "appeared to be protesting too much about never having been inside the Holt
residence and I had information to the contrary, but at this
time, I didn't push the point with [Mary]," according to
Perez. He waited for a couple of minutes before he pushed
the point about the Holts.

"I used to walk on the other side of the street because
I didn't feel safe walking on the Holts' side," she said.
The news was portentous and he urged her on. "I don't
know if [Ann] was in their house or not or my parents,"
she said. Perez noted with interest that she had thrown
her parents into the equation. He asked the next question.

Mary was torn with feelings of betrayal and loss, but
by now resistance had become increasingly difficult. "I
still love my family even though there was bad things that
happened; do you understand that?" Perez assured her
that of course he understood and it was okay to love her
parents, but "they needed some help with their prob-

lems.'' Over the next hours Ann talked about her family and her friends, adding detail as her story spun toward its ultimate conclusion.

She said her brother Matthew molested her, and ''Ann told you the truth about Sissy too,'' a statement that implies that Perez or Carrow told her what Ann had said about Sissy. In the language of her therapy, she said these things weren't Matthew's fault or Sissy's because they ''learned from my dad'' and didn't know any better. Sissy, her friend Kerri Knowles, Mary's parents, and all of the kids had sex together a couple times a week, she said. ''They touched us in a big group-like. . . . They called it 'the wild thing' when they had sex.'' Sometimes her mom and Kerri and Matthew would ''pee'' on her she said.

Perez tested out one of his theories. What about cameras? he asked. Mary didn't know but ''she did say that her parents had purchased a computer right before she was removed from the home.'' That, too, interested Perez, who by now had his theories about affiliations and dissemination of information. And what would people like the Everetts be doing with a computer?

He asked Mary what had happened at Kerri's apartment. She said the place was tiny and it was a tight squeeze with at least ten kids and the Everetts, the Holts, Sissy, Knowles, and other adults, including a man and woman who ''stunk like Walter and Jeff,'' leading Perez to presume she meant Cherie and Gene Town. And Kerri only had a Hide-A-Bed.

But she had other things. ''She had major Star Trek movies everywhere. She had disgusting toys—a dildo and a stuffed animal she made that looked like a penis. She had lots of pretend penises. The adults shoved the dildos up our privates. All of them were telling us what to do. My dad was the main boss.'' Everyone took off all their clothes and piled them up out of the way, then divided themselves into two groups, said Mary. One group of kids watched, while adults and kids took turns having sex on the "icky bed." Contradicting her earlier words, Mary added that the Towns brought a movie camera.

By now Mary appeared tired, the hour was late, and she had missed her lunch. Carrow asked her if she wanted to spend the rest of the afternoon at school or go to her foster home. She said she wanted to stay at school, but she was hungry. It was midafternoon and she had endured the interrogation since 9:45 A.M.

Perez picked Ann up after school and gave her the word on Mary. "There's a lot more," said Ann, "but I don't want to talk about it now." Perez reassured her she could tell him and Luci whenever she was ready—which, as it turned out, was in their living room that night after dinner. Ann said the usual crowd and Larry Steinborn, Linda Miller, Gary and Scharlann Filbeck, Kerri Knowles, and others molested her and a lot of children, so many that Ann couldn't remember all of them. Sometimes it happened at her home, other times at the homes of various families. Parents brought their kids and swapped them around so that each adult had sex with each kid.

After a while, Ann started to show "fatigue" and he told her they'd talk later and hustled her off to bed. By now it was obvious to him, as it would be to anyone: The case was *huge*.

The next day Perez talked to Connie Saracino, who was then caseworker for the Everett children. He told her the news, and Saracino had some news of her own. After Perez had talked to Mary, she told counselor Cindy Andrews she belonged to "the circle," which soon became the official designation for the expanded sex ring. She looked Andrews right in the eye and never cried, a fact that, according to Andrews, was "very significant." Although Perez didn't bother to mention it in his report, Mary was so upset by the day's events that she told her therapist she wanted to kill herself—words that Saracino dismissed as "vaguely suicidal." Mary left the office looking "drained but also relieved." It had indeed been a long day for her.

Perez sat down with Carrow and compiled a list of suspects: twenty-one adults and twenty children, not quite enough children to go around. But, Perez added, "Other possible children victims are pending until interviews can be arranged."

Matthew Everett would not come through. Although he attended counseling sessions with Rodney M. Daut since October 1994, Daut wrote that "he continues to defend his parents and deny that any abuse occurred." Matthew told Daut that "his first preference for a foster home is to be with Pastor 'Robbie.' "

In October 1994, Pastor Roberson was troubled about the Everetts' prosecution, just as he was troubled about other prosecutions, including the Holts'. After watching the Holt kids at his church for a while he concluded they were "respectable, well-behaved children, very gentle, very kind," Roberson told me. In his view their demeanor just didn't fit with what he had been told of their history of victimization; when he reassured them they were free to talk to him, they acted like nothing was wrong. One day he pulled foster parent Deborah Gambill aside and told her he had doubts about the Holt prosecution. "These kids don't show any signs of anything at all," he said.

"I'd be real careful about saying things like that," Gambill warned.

"Well, that's just what I see, Debbie," he said.

Shortly after their arrest in September, Harold and Idella Everett asked Roberson if he and Connie would be

Matthew's foster parents. The Robersons quickly agreed. "Matthew was like a son to me anyway," he told me. "He spent all of his time with me." And the Robersons liked Harold and Idella Everett and wanted to help them. "We were very attached to them," he said. "Harold and Idella were very dysfunctional [but] we really felt that there were many redeeming qualities there for the kids. We felt responsible for them."

As he understood it, Saracino and Matthew's counselor supported Matthew's placement in his home. In October, at the request of the Everetts' attorney, Pastor Roberson was allowed to attend a normally closed dependency hearing about Matthew's placement. The court commissioner also seemed to support the arrangement, but advised Roberson that he and his wife would have to complete foster care paperwork. Detective Perez was at the hearing because of a joint motion by the Everetts' attorneys to have Ann removed from his home due to conflict of interest, but he wasn't invited to respond to the question of Matthew's placement. The commissioner took the question of Ann's placement with Perez under advisement.

Outside the courtroom, Idella's attorney, Rebecca Shaw, told Roberson the officials wouldn't appreciate any presumption on his part that the Everetts were innocent. "They need to know that you're supportive of the kids, that you'll try to encourage the kids to disclose," she said, according to Roberson.

"Hey," he snapped, "I'm not gonna lie. If Matthew says something to me, the court'll be the first to know. I've called CPS every other time they asked me to. I don't have any problem with any of that. But as long as Matthew maintains that they're innocent, I'm gonna promote him in that."

He left the courthouse, went to the DSHS office to pick up the foster care paperwork, then went home to tell Connie what had happened. The Robersons were elated. "I thought, 'Wow, I really will be Matthew's father!' " he said. Connie immediately began filling out the paperwork.

At around 2:30 on October 7, Saracino telephoned Roberson. "Pastor Roberson," said Saracino, "I've got some bad news."

"What's that?" he queried.

"I was just contacted by Officer Bob Perez from the Wenatchee Police Department," she said. "I need to inform you that you can no longer have contact with any of the Everett children. And if you involve yourself in the future in any aspect of an investigation or in the hearings, Mr. Perez says that you'll be arrested," she said, according to Roberson.

Perez later testified that he didn't say this to Saracino. But the DSHS Service Episode Record of Connie Saracino's, dated October 7, 1994, reflects a telephone call from Bob Perez, who said, "There will be no contact with [Matthew] and Pastor Robbie. Caseworker is to notify F.P. [foster parent] and Pastor Robbie. Bob Perez said to tell the Pastor that if he tries to make contact with [Matthew] he will be arrested for tampering with a witness." According to her notes, Saracino then contacted Matthew's foster parents and Roberson.

Roberson was thunderstruck. "Why?" he demanded to know. "This doesn't make any sense. Here we are sitting there two days ago and everybody is supportive of Matthew being at my home, of my being involved in the family. And now you're telling me that I can't even see the family? What happened?"

"I can't give you any more information than that," she said. "We'll let you know."

"What am I supposed to do about this paperwork?" he asked. "I'm gonna try to get it down to you as soon as I can."

"Pastor," said Saracino, according to Roberson, "don't even worry about it. The Everett children will not be placed in your household, I can guarantee you. So don't even worry about bringing the paperwork back."

He was outraged. He called his wife and told her what had happened. Then the phone rang. It was Matthew. Perez had picked him up after school, then sat down with him outside the Gambill house and handed him his mother's graphic statement, he told Roberson.

"My mom didn't write this," he said, according to Roberson. "This isn't my mom."

"Well," said Perez, "yes, it is."

"No, it's not," Matthew repeated, according to Roberson. "You need to understand something. My mom and dad aren't smart. They're dumb. And my mom didn't tell you anything like this. She's lying anyway, because none of this stuff ever happened in our house."

According to Matthew, Perez told him he needed to "confess" to him and support the statement and say it was true and sign it. "Otherwise, I wasn't gonna be able to be put in your house."

"Well, Matthew," said Roberson, "I need to tell you something. I already got a call from Connie Saracino from CPS and they're telling me now that there's no way you're gonna be placed in my home anyway."

"What're we gonna do?"

"Matthew, whatever you do, don't lie," said Roberson. "Don't let them con you into saying something that is wrong. No matter what they tell you your mom said or your dad said or your brothers or sisters said or anything else, don't you let them make you lie. You tell them the truth."

The boy started to cry. "Please, Pastor Roby, you're the only person who's ever cared about us. And if you don't do something for us, nobody else is going to. Nobody else cares.''

"Matthew," said Roberson, crying himself, "I care. Believe me, I'm gonna do everything I can in my power to get to the bottom of this. I know your mom and dad are innocent. I know they didn't do anything and I don't know how I'm gonna get to the bottom of it or what I can do.

"You be faithful," he added. "You know what's right and you know what's wrong. And you just hang in there. I'll fight for you. Don't give in to them."

Roberson was good for his word. He helped Idella Everett make a written request for her children's DSHS and counseling records, and she gave him permission to copy, disseminate, and use the records as he saw fit. He copied court pleadings and police reports, and spoke to witnesses. "I began to do my own little investigation, you might say, from that point," he told me.

Yet he was mindful of Perez's warning and was afraid to be outspoken about his investigation. He was also afraid to go to court. He warned his congregation to be careful and told them he had to avoid contact with the Everett children.

"I was concerned for the welfare of our church and the well-being of the food bank," Roberson told me. "I mean, I worked hard to put all this together and I literally was scared. I didn't go to any of Idella's hearings or any of the hearings for Harold, either one. I mean, I stayed clear completely away from everything because I was afraid of jeopardizing the church and my family and the food bank."

Yet when he got a call from one of the Everetts' supporters asking him to attend Idella's sentencing on January 30, he threw caution to the wind.

As he entered the courthouse, a man met him at the

front door and handed him Matthew's psychological evaluation from Dr. Daut. "I think this will be of interest to you," said the man, who then walked away without identifying himself.

Roberson put the folded report in his pocket and went upstairs to Judge Small's courtroom. He listened closely to the statements of the attorneys. There was discussion that all five of the Everett children said Idella had molested them. Matthew's psychological evaluation was mentioned, but no one seemed to have a copy, and the report was important because it contradicted part of the information before the judge: Matthew denied that his parents had molested him. Roberson screwed up his courage and stepped forward, announcing that he had a copy of the evaluation. He handed it to Judge Small's clerk.

Rebecca Shaw argued in support of an exceptional sentence downward based on Idella's mental limitations and her history of being intimidated by Harold. Judge Small asked Perez for his opinion.

"Well," said Perez, "I agree with counsel on both sides here in this particular case. Mr. Everett probably carries the most weight in the family as far as what is or isn't done there. But on the other hand, Ms. Everett had opportunity, ample opportunity to disclose what was going on when Mr. Everett was not in the home. . . . But what I do know is that we have five children in four foster homes—one of her children resides with me and my wife—and I know how many nights I've sat up with that child, with the nightmares and the remembering what happened to her—a child that was so terrorized that she screamed until she did permanent damage to her vocal cords because of the things that happened, and other issues that I'm not at liberty to discuss. But what I will say is if I had known then what I know now—and I was in agreement with the prosecutor on this, that she receive a lesser sentence—that knowing what I know today, I couldn't in all good conscience recommend that now.''

Judge Small asked whether anyone wanted to speak up on Idella Everett's behalf, and Roberson stepped forward. He now says that ''I was shaking like a leaf because Bob Perez was standing behind me.''

According to the transcript, Roberson told Small he was speaking under ''literally, I must say, threat of law enforcement problems for myself.'' He explained he ran the East Wenatchee Food Bank and was very close to the Everett family. ''I'm here today basically to say that I continue to support Idella and Harold.'' He said that he didn't believe Everett was guilty, and he had been threatened about speaking up on her behalf at risk of charges.

''That very next day after the placement hearing I have continued to pull myself back. I have not had any contact with the family. . . . And it's been a heartbreak to sit back and say nothing. . . . And today, with Idella—I love her. And a lot of the things she's been charged for, I can tell you right now, did not take place in this family . . . the problem is with the rest of the sytem that is going on. . . . Anytime that anybody wants to talk with me, we were told, 'If you say a word, you're going to be in trouble.' . . . I can tell you, Your Honor, wherever they're coming up with this, it is not—I don't feel it's appropriate. I don't feel it's right. And that's about all I dare to really even say.''

By the time he finished speaking, Roberson was ''scared to death. I had my hands down and I kept waiting for Bob Perez to literally come up and handcuff me,'' he told me. He was afraid he would be arrested on some charge on the order of witness tampering or obstructing justice, as had happened with Paul Glassen. ''I knew that I was taking a gamble being there that day.''

After Judge Small accepted Shaw's argument that

Idella had committed the crime under the influence of her husband, and sentenced her to an exceptional reduced sentence of fifty-four months in prison, Roberson left the courtroom. On the way out the door, he passed by Perez. "We warned you, Roberson, we warned you," said Perez, according to Roberson.

Roberson went straight home and told Connie. "I think I might be in trouble," he said. "Bob Perez warned me more or less that he's after me. . . . I don't know what's gonna happen, but there's a possibility I'll be arrested for going up there and speaking up for Idella," he said. Shaken by the experience, Roberson kept a low profile for several months.

The day after her mother's sentencing on February 1, Ann came up to Bob and Luci Perez and expanded on her earlier words about Bob Devereaux. There is no way of knowing whether Perez made any notes, and his report doesn't reveal his questions or the information that he gave his foster daughter, but his report was written almost entirely in the form of direct quotations. According to the report, Ann contradicted her earlier statements to police and said Devereaux had sexual intercourse with her and others, including Kelly Allbee, daughter of Donna Rodriguez. Starting in kindergarten, Devereaux came to her house, often in the morning, and had sex with her with the permission of her parents, who joined in, she said.

"Before I was in foster care with Bob [Devereaux], we would all go to his house"—the Everetts, the Millers, the Knowleses, the Rodriguezes, and others. "Bob would rent gross movies at Videl Video by Value Pharmacy and we kids would have to watch them.[3] After about half a movie

---

[3] But note: According to defense investigations, Videl Video had no record that Devereaux rented any pornographic videos.

Bob would pause it and six kids had to go upstairs with the adults. One adult would stay downstairs with the other kids and watch the rest of the movie. My mom would usually stay with us while the other adults went upstairs first. When we got upstairs we went to the room that had three bunkbeds but they were down. . . . The kids had to get on the beds and the adults would line up and take turns with us. They did everything to us and would make us do it to each other while they watched.'' Then, according to Ann, they went downstairs while her mother went upstairs with more kids so the adults could take turns with them as well. These things usually happened on weekends, she said.

One of the adults was Paul Glassen. ''He came to my house with Bob Devereaux a few times when we were molested and they would touch us,'' said Ann. ''Sometimes he would just come over or Bob would call him and ask him to come over. . . . He did the same things as everyone else and sometimes he was there when everyone else was there and molesting me.''

Although it was far into Ann's disclosures and no doubt well past her bedtime, Perez decided to call Tim Abbey, who agreed to come over to the Perez house ''to avoid any conflict of interest.'' Perez was interested in Abbey's response to the goings-on of one of Abbey's former colleagues.

Ann told the assembled gathering that Devereaux had molested her many years before she came to live with him, starting when she was in kindergarten. It happened at the Everett home, and the homes of Linda Miller and Kerri Knowles. Glassen ''came over to my parents' house with Bob a few times and touched us the same way the other adults did.''

The interview ended about 10 P.M., after four and a half hours.

*   *   *

According to my investigation, the timing of Ann's words suggested something more than mere coincidence, as it came at a time when it appeared Glassen was about to slip out from under his prosecution. At his first hearing on the charges of obstruction in November, deputy prosecutors told the judge that Glassen was threatening to sue over the charges. They asked the judge to order a probable cause hearing, which would have put the court's sanction on their charges. The judge refused. "It's not the court's place to defend the arresting officer or the prosecutor or anyone else from liability," said the judge, according to Glassen. Instead he expressed skepticism about whether the prosecutors had a case against Glassen, and ordered prosecutors to produce a Bill of Particulars, a document that detailed the charges. In late January, Glassen's lawyer filed a motion to dismiss the criminal charges against Glassen, and on February 6, a judge pro tem indeed dismissed them.

When Glassen got word that he was named as a perpetrator, he made the decision to move to Canada with his Canadian-born wife and their five-year-old son. The state could contact him through his attorney.

"I knew what they could do to my son," he said to a reporter. "And I wasn't going to let Perez or anybody else start brainwashing him or God knows what."

15:

February–March 1995

═══════════

The Parade of Homes

═══════════

In the months to come, Ann often flew into rages, throwing things and generally disrupting the harmony of the Perez household. Sometimes the Perezes persuaded her to pull herself together by threatening to send her away. Other times, Perez called CPS and someone came and hustled her off to the short-term limbo known as "respite foster care," an alternative devised in recognition of the fact that foster parents sometimes need a breather . . . and a tool to enforce cooperation.

Because Perez kept no contemporaneous notes or recordings of his interviews and because Ann has been effectively contained, one cannot determine with accuracy that her behaviors were related to the process of interrogation or testimony. But in any case, when she returned, disclosures followed. These disclosures became too numerous to count; she disclosed to Bob and Luci Perez "about every night" on dozens of occasions, or at least "up to 48 times," Perez testified. "She talked and I listened," said Perez, adding that it was "great" therapy.

Over the weeks, Ann came a long way from January 20, when she made her first disclosure about sex orgies while huddled in a traumatized fetal curl under the Perezes' coffee table. "It got to the point because there were so many that she wanted to talk about as time went on, this was after ten months or eleven months in our home, that I would tell her, 'Look, if you want to tell me about something you tell me about one or two tonight, and then that's it for now,' " Perez told *Dateline NBC*.

In fact, the numbers of alleged victims and perpetrators at last became so great that Perez thought Ann might be exaggerating, he said at a defense interview, quickly adding the caveat that she was always truthful. His fleeting doubt was understandable: Over the months Ann named more than a hundred people who had abused her.[1] At last, he set up two days each week when Ann was allowed to make disclosures. In this way, he not only reduced household disruptions but satisfied himself that he had successfully separated his personal and professional lives.

Perez was increasingly mindful of the criticism of his dual relationship with his foster daughter, but felt any conflict was more illusory than real. In a defense interview, Perez said it was appropriate that he live with a key witness for the prosecution but the situation had its "logistical" problems.

"Well, let's separate it out," he told *Dateline*. "First from 8:00 to 4:00 usually I'm an investigator for the police department, and from 4:00 on I'm a citizen in my own home ... and I'm a foster parent." Ann was dis-

---

[1] Ann's medical examination by Dr. Douglas Eisert of Wenatchee Valley Clinic on March 3, 1992, was the sole medical "corroboration" for Ann's allegations. Although a medical examination of Ann by Dr. Ettinger a few days earlier (2/26/92) described Ann's genitals as "grossly normal," Dr. Eisert described the size of Ann's vaginal opening and relative absence of hymenal tissue as features "highly suspicious" for sexual abuse. He speculated that the possible causes of these features could include "digital penetration," but did not mention the possibility of penile penetration. Eisert observed no tears or scarring. Yet Ann came to allege she was a repeated victim of penile/vaginal intercourse by a large number of men (Progress Notes, Dr. Douglas A. Eisert, Wenatchee Valley Clinic, 3/3/92).

closing solely because she was at last secure, he said. "We're talking about a child who, for the first time in her *life,* felt safe, felt loved by someone." Still, according to his understanding with his chief and the Chelan County prosecutor, he needed corroboration. A confession would do.

Perez began to work his way down the list of names Ann and Mary had given him.

Donna Rodriguez and her daughter Kelly Allbee once lived on Cashmere Street, three blocks away from the Everett family, in a small, clean, but dispirited house. Kelly had been best friends with Ann Everett since kindergarten. To get together, the girls walked down the cracked and pitted sidewalk that bulged in places from the upheaval of tree roots, then hurried across the street.

Sometimes the girls played in Kelly's backyard, where you could see across the rooftops all the way to the brown hills east of the river. Other times they played on the upthrust hillock of sparse grass and straggly weeds in the shadow of the Everett home. Usually it was just Ann and Kelly, and sometimes Ann's sister Mary. Ann's mother, Idella Everett, was ponderous and childlike, but she was also sweet and kind. Kelly didn't much understand the nature of mental retardation, but she observed with wonder that Ann often bossed her mother around.

Not that it was surprising: According to Kelly, Ann insisted on doing things her way. She was stubbornly jealous of their friendship, rigidly demanding of Kelly's fidelity. If Kelly played with other girls, Ann stomped on home, storming, "I won't be your friend anymore." Mary, two years older but quiet and introverted, usually tagged after Ann. Then, abruptly, Ann was no longer living at home. When Kelly learned from the newspaper that this was because her parents had molested her, she was amazed.

On February 2, somewhere between 9 and 9:30, Kelly's school principal, Mrs. Perry, entered the classroom and bent down beside Kelly, who was then ten years old. Kelly looked at her, brushed her straight bangs back from her forehead with the palm of a pudgy hand, and smiled in perplexity. She was a large for her age, with chubby cheeks, straight brown hair, and an impish grin.

"Come with me," said Mrs. Perry, smiling in that enigmatic, authoritarian way.

Kelly looked at her uncertainly, her grin dropping away.

"Don't worry, you're not in trouble," Mrs. Perry reassured her, according to Kelly.

Perry took her to her office. Perez and Abbey sat like they owned the place at a table that sprawled before a bank of windows. Kelly looked at the men dubiously; neither introduced himself and she had never seen them before. The men stared at her in turn, their expressions inscrutable to a ten-year-old. Perez told her to sit on one of the chairs that was pulled up to the table. Mrs. Perry went away.

Perez, whom Kelly knew only as a big blond man with a full mustache and intense blue eyes, started to question her. The other man, the one with a beard and a composed face, regarded her raptly. Their attentions were mystifying to Kelly, accustomed as she was to the anonymity of childhood, and despite Mrs. Perry's words, she became convinced that she'd done something wrong. Still, the questions were innocuous, easy stuff: her phone number, her address. She answered politely, with a slight, shy smile.

"I know your friend Ann. She lives with me now," Perez announced.

"She *lives* with you now?" said Kelly in confusion.

Perez nodded. Then, Kelly told me, he asked a question

that caused her heart to flutter in alarm. "Ann told me that you've been molested by some adults. Is it true?"

"No way!" she gasped.

"Yes!" insisted Perez, according to Kelly. "I think it is!"

"What are you talking about?" she protested. "I ain't never been molested."

"Well, we *know* that's a lie!" snapped Perez, according to Kelly.

For a time, she stubbornly held her ground, repeatedly denying that she had been molested. Perez insisted she had. According to Kelly, he gave her names and frank sexual descriptions of events. "He said that a whole bunch of other girls told me you were there when it happened and everything," she told me later.

He told her that some of these things happened at a Bob Devereaux's house, a guy who had a foster home where he only accepted girls, she said. She knew Bob Devereaux slightly because she'd gone to visit Ann there two or three times when she was in his foster care. Kelly explained that her mom would drop her off but wouldn't go inside.

"My mom doesn't like me walking the streets and stuff," she explained, pushing back her brown bangs in consternation. "She keeps me home a lot unless she drives me over there."

"When she drives you over there, she goes to the door and she goes in, too, huh?" suggested Perez, according to Kelly.

"Nope," said Kelly, daring to look at Perez's darkening face.

"You've been molested at the Devereaux house. Ann told me she saw it happen," he said, according to Kelly. Ann had told him the day before, to be exact. Kelly chewed on her nails and denied it.

"Well, it was only two or three years ago, so you *gotta* remember," he said, according to Kelly.

Kids had gone out to the playground for morning recess. Outside the window they were laughing and running and throwing balls and flinging themselves at the equipment.

"Can I go play?" she begged.

"You're not going anywhere until we're through," he said, according to Kelly.

Because she wasn't cooperating, the interview dragged on for hours. At last, Perez drew a stick figure with a head and arms and legs. She looked at the crude drawing blankly.

"Circle your private area," he said.

Kelly took the pen and circled the place where the stick legs joined the stick body.

"And that's where you were touched, right?" She stared at the childish drawing, which was now imbued with so much meaning. "Right? Right? Right?" Perez persisted, according to Kelly.

"Yeah, *right*!" she said sarcastically.

Perez was apparently pleased. It had been a disclosure, by his standards.

Kelly was tired and she was hungry. She looked at the clock and saw it was past lunchtime. Kids had again drifted out to the playground. "Can I go eat lunch?" she asked. She was reminded that she wasn't going anywhere until they were through.

"I wanta go *home*!" Kelly sobbed. "I *need* to go home! I wanta go talk to my *mom*!"

Perez and Abbey were firm. "They just made me sit there and sit there and sit there and sit there and sit there," she said.

"Well, you're not leaving till this is over," said Perez, according to Kelly.

It was no use. The truth, as she knew it, must yield to the truth, as Perez perceived it. Kelly said she started agreeing with the things Perez said. "I was off in another world," she later recalled. But her answers didn't satisfy him.

At one point Perez got up and turned around and Kelly saw that he wore a gun and a badge. "You're a cop!" she exclaimed.

Abbey spoke up, for one of the few times during the interview. "You're safer now," he reassured her.

"This is enough fooling around," Perez snapped, according to Kelly, picking up the telephone that was sitting on the table. "If you don't start telling me the truth, you're never going to see your family again."

She stared at Perez, who was dialing the phone.

He explained that he was calling the police to arrest her mother, she said. "I'm calling my office now."

"No! No! No!" she cried.

He ignored her, speaking instead into the phone. "I've got a woman called Donna Rodriguez." According to Kelly, Perez gave out her address and said he wanted her mother to be taken to the jail. She began to cry.

Perez hung up the phone and looked at her. "Well," he said, according to Kelly, "you got ten minutes to speak now. Get it out and I'll stop that phone call." He added that the officers should be at her mother's home in five minutes. "They'll be there by two o'clock." He urged Kelly to hurry up or "your mom goes to jail and you'll never see her again."

"I don't want my mom to go to jail," she sobbed.

He bombarded her with questions. Kelly buried her face in her hands. "To every question I just said, 'Uh-huh,' you know, agreeing with him but not saying anything," she told me. Perez said, "There was a group of you," which included the Holts and Linda Miller and her kids, the Everetts, her mother. He said that a lot of adults molested a lot of kids.

"Uh-huh," she said, not bothering to wipe away her tears.

Perez started to type.

After a while he let her go to the bathroom. Kelly looked at her tear-stained, lying face in the mirror and thought about suicide. What am I doing? she asked herself, appalled at what she had said. "I oughta kill myself!"

By around 2:15 P.M., around five hours after the interview began, Perez had finished typing and Kelly was shaking and exhausted. She signed a two-page statement Perez thrust in front of her without knowing or caring what it said, simply because he told her she'd be able to go home if she did. Mrs. Perry came in and offered to bring her a salad, but by this time she had no appetite.

Perez and Abbey took Kelly to the CPS office and then on to a foster home.

At 2:30 P.M. on the same day, Donna Rodriguez, an attractive blond woman with a dimpled face and a matter-of-fact manner, had just arrived home from working at the Okanogan Senior Chore Services. She heard the crunch of tires on gravel and went to look out her window. Two marked and two unmarked police cars stood in front of her home. Rodriguez went boldly to meet them.

"What's going on?" she demanded of Perez and Abbey, who were first to approach her.

Perez took her arm. "We're going to the station," he said. After that, things happened so quickly that they took on the blur of unreality. She found herself forced into a police car, where someone spoke to her, but the words were swallowed up in the inhuman crackle of the police radio. Within minutes, she was hauled into Perez's office. She sat in a chair, surrounded by teddy bears and Perez's earnest animosity, for around two and a half hours. First he read the Miranda rights and asked if she understood them. "No!" she snapped. "I don't understand anything!" He read each sentence to her and had her initial them.

"Okay, your daughter saw you molest fourteen children," he said, according to Rodriguez. She gasped and asked for a lawyer, but Perez ignored her. "You did Kelly and then you let Bob [Devereaux] do her." Rodriguez said she didn't know Bob Devereaux. She reminded Perez that she wanted an attorney. "Oh, shut up!" he allegedly snapped. "You gave up your rights!" She began to cry. Perez scowled and hurled more accusations at her. Crying and shaking, she resisted. Perez confronted her with the statements of children, his convictions and theories, things that he said he *knew*.

According to Rodriguez, Perez said she'd go to prison for life. "You'll never see the light of day." He added that she'd never see her daughter again. All those things would change if she cooperated and told what she and Devereaux had done. In that case the system would go easy on her, he said.

Rodriguez stood up. Perez ordered her to sit down.

"Then I thought, 'Women raping little girls!' I mean, like, really!" Angrily, Rodriguez pounded on the desk. "If I ever saw a child sexually molested, I would report it!" As she recalls it, Perez's face reddened; his eyes bulged. He stood and drew his handcuffs from somewhere in the region of his back pocket, snapped the cuffs on her, and took her off to jail.

"We got another one," one of the jailers said, laughing. Jail officers fingerprinted Rodriguez and took her mug shots. She was refused a phone call and placed in the hole, a seven-by-seven-foot room with the sink and lidless toilet nudging a cot. She stared around her in disbelief and then jumped as the door to the cell closed with a heavy metallic clang.

Around 7 P.M., Abbey came to see her. "You got anything you want to say to Perez?" he asked, according to Rodriguez.

"No!" she snapped. Abbey told her he wanted her to sign some papers to voluntarily place Kelly in foster care. Rodriguez refused, although no one before her had dared.

After six days, Rodriguez was released so the charges could be further investigated.

The significance of her refusal to sign a contract for voluntary placement became clear in the days to come. Kelly was released to her father in Brewster, Washington, on February 3. He called Kelly's older sister, Janice Williams, and put Kelly on the phone. Kelly cried so hard she was incoherent. Later that day, Kelly's father brought her to Janice's home. As soon as she walked through the door, she burst into tears and Janice rushed to her.

Janice Williams was shocked by her sister's appearance. "She had red circles under her eyes. She had also bitten her fingernails halfway down her nail bed. She had not had a bath, she had not changed her clothes since the day before," she said. Kelly told Williams about the interview and the lies she told.

Based on what she said, the family decided that the girl had to be protected, hidden away from agents of the state. They made arrangements to have her interviewed on videotape by a representative of VOCAL. Time after time over the next few days, Kelly dissolved in tears and asked for her mother. She couldn't sleep, threw up, often burst into bitter recriminations, wailing that it was all her fault that her mother was in jail.

On February 21, Williams got in touch with Carol Billesbach. Knowing she was thrusting herself into the throes of bureaucracy, Williams carefully related her concerns about her sister and the way she was interviewed by Perez and Abbey, including the fact that Perez had threatened to arrest Kelly's mother if she didn't tell the things Perez wanted to hear.

"Well, that's how your sister perceived it," Billesbach said blandly.

Williams said Kelly had threatened to kill herself during the process and the state had a duty to protect her.

"Well, that's how your sister *perceived* it," Billesbach insisted. Although Billesbach said she didn't know anything about the claims but she would look into them, Williams had the feeling that she was well informed because she easily followed the complex story.

"Why should we give Kelly back to those people who abused her?" Williams asked.

"Well," Billesbach maddeningly repeated, according to Williams, "that's just how your sister *perceived* it."

"Yes," said Williams in frustration. "That's how she *perceived* it and she is telling us the truth." She told Billesbach she had Kelly's statement on videotape, and the family was hiring a lawyer to protect her. She demanded that the state do a colposcope exam to confirm or deny that Kelly was penetrated. She asked why nobody in the family was questioned about the abuse.

"Well, these things can take up to six to eight months," said Billesbach.

"Do you think it's *right,* what they did to Kelly?"

"That's how your sister *perceived* it," said Billesbach.

All in all, Donna Rodriguez was one of the lucky ones. Although she was rearrested on March 13, 1995, this time on 168 counts involving several "victims," a friend, Jean Wake, seventy-six, mortgaged her well-maintained home to post her bail and to help pay for Seattle attorney John Henry Browne. Months later, on August 20, 1995, two days before she was scheduled to go to trial, the prosecutor dismissed all charges against her.

Nearly a year after her arrest, Rodriguez said, "In the community's eyes, I'm still guilty." In her view, the Wenatchee government and its benign citizens had stripped away her reputation and the innocence of her daughter.

Perez and CPS caseworkers worked their way down the list of possible corroborating witnesses—the kinds of kids and adults whom they calculated would follow through with testimony. On February 7, the day after Paul Glassen's case was dismissed, Perez and Carrow went to the Chelan County Jail to again interview Idella Everett. Although Idella was assigned an attorney, her sentencing was over, she hadn't been transported to prison, and, in his mind, the woman was fair game. Based on what he had recently heard, many new charges could be leveled against Idella, a fact that might be just the lever he needed to urge her to disclose.

Idella was ungainly in her jail uniform and her composure collapsed in the face of her fear, but Perez was unmoved by her vulnerability. "Read the statements of these people. These people are *guilty* and I'm not gonna feel bad for them," he later said of Idella and the other criminal defendants to *Dateline NBC*.

Perez asked Idella to consent to a search of her home and outbuildings for evidence of the pornography connection. He read the consent-to-search form to her and Idella signed without being able to read or fully comprehend it. Because Perez also wanted to "discuss some new allegation of sexual abuse," he went on to advise her of her Constitutional rights, which she initialed and signed, again without being able to read them or, arguably, understand them.

Perez engaged himself in the effective and, no doubt,

satisfying process of interrogating the powerless. He told Idella that he knew she and others had abused several children, and questioned her about Devereaux, Glassen, Rodriguez, Steinborn, Kerri Knowles, Linda Miller, and an expansive list of others. For a long time, Idella gave only innocuous information. As the hours advanced, his interrogation intensified. According to Idella, he reminded her that there are consequences to lying and he had enough new information to charge her again. She wouldn't get lucky with an exceptional sentence downward next time just because of the sorry excuse of her retardation. In fact, she would neither see the light of day nor her children again. At last the woman came around and agreed to disclose and testify against others.

Perez extensively quoted Everett in his report, although, as always, he didn't record the interview: "I knew the adults were having sex with the kids, but I didn't organize it," he reported her to say. She allegedly said the adults made the kids undress, then undressed themselves, and Knowles told them how to pair up. "That's when we had sex with the kids. We didn't do it all night." She didn't switch around, she said, but "maybe the others did." She said she didn't know about anyone taking pictures or movies, but said Knowles was a *Star Trek* fan, a fact that Perez took as "corroboration" of the children's statements that Knowles had a lot of *Star Trek* movies.

Perez asked Everett about "the circle." "Our group got together on weekends," she said, and added that other adults, including Gary and Scharlann Filbeck, Linda Miller, and Dorris Green, were at Kerri Knowles's house "doing things to kids too." Said Idella: "To get into the circle, you had to have kids." Later she added, "You could pay money if you didn't have kids. Sometimes you paid at the door and sometimes, once inside you could pay. . . . Once per week we had sex with each other as a group.''

But Everett wasn't helpful when it came to implicating Devereaux. Sometimes the circle went to Devereaux's home, she said uncertainly, or . . . ''I guess I don't know for sure but they might have.'' She then recalled that Devereaux had been at her home one time. When Perez prodded, Everett remembered ''Papa Bob'' abused kids, but this wasn't the same Bob who was a foster parent. ''No this guy, Papa Bob drove a truck,'' and had a white beard and long white hair. Perez pressed on with single-minded determination, asking Idella more about Devereaux. But the woman was confused or slow or not fully cooperating. ''I don't think it (Devereaux) was the same Bob that abused the kids at my house.''

The interview began at 1:45 P.M. and ended at last call for dinner at the Chelan County Jail. Idella was shaking and in tears. Although she had implicated neither of them, the suspects on Perez's incident report reflecting this interview were Glassen, Devereaux, and Steinborn. In the case of Glassen and Devereaux, the reason for Perez's dogged determination appears obvious: Glassen was going public with his concerns, harshly criticizing the actions of local government agents, and much of this criticism centered on the Devereaux case. In light of Perez's intense emotions about the cases, their actions were highly suspect.

Perez later commented to *Dateline* about Idella and other Wenatchee suspects in a manner that reflected his outrage. ''They're not strangers. They're [the children's] own parents and then to make matters worse these parents shared their children with other adults. It was an everyday occurrence! It was a way of life.''

*   *   *

Next on Perez's list of potential corroborators was Bonnie Rogers, a girl frequently named as a victim by Ann and Mary, one of their circle of friends, and a former Devereaux foster child. On February 8, the day after he interviewed Idella, Perez met Bonnie and CPS caseworker Laurie Alexander at Alexander's office. A thirteen-year-old, Bonnie had blond hair, arched eyebrows, and a curve to her throat that promised she'd be pretty one day; she made good eye contact, which promised she'd be up to testifying.

Almost immediately, Bonnie told Perez and Alexander that she had lied about being abused by Larry Steinborn. She'd made up the story, she explained, because she didn't want to get in trouble for staying out late at her foster home. It wasn't the first time Bonnie had made a known false allegation. She also threatened or falsely accused her social worker, her teacher, her therapist, and her current foster parent. Still, she was the kind of kid who made a predictable witness: She was ever eager to please the authorities.

Perez asked her what homes she'd been inside. She said she spent a lot of time at Linda Miller's home because she was best friends with one of the Miller girls. Perez asked who came to the Devereaux home. At first she said "no one," and then, when corrected, fell into step and said people came while she watched television, and at these times Devereaux penetrated her with his finger.

At first Bonnie faltered and said Theresa Sanchez was gone when this happened. But again, after Perez persisted, the story changed. Bonnie was on lookout duty and when men came, she and Theresa raced upstairs and moved the bunk beds to barricade the bedroom door. The adults forced their way in, then took the girls downstairs to the living room, where Devereaux, Steinborn, and a guy "in his thirties or forties" made them "touch their things, did intercourse and touched our things,'' she said. ''People were on couches, all over the floor. Sometimes they would bring another friend.''

''Did anyone from CPS come to your home?'' he asked.

With a little prompting, Bonnie obliged: a CPS case-worker named Paul Glassen ''came over when the other people did. . . . They got him to join in and shut up some-how. He came about the same amount of times as the other guys.'' At first, she said, ''it was a shock and then it was 'oh well, here's another one of those creeps.' ''

Next up was Donna Hidalgo, known as ''Sissy'' according to the disclosures of Ann and Mary, her half-sisters. Hidalgo told me she had completed six years of college and was a licensed practical nurse. She had worked as a nurse, midwife, secretary, and housekeeper and was licensed as a translator in California. She was a mammoth and strong-minded woman and more intelligent than her appearance suggested to many Wenatchee officials who were prone to equate obesity with a variety of human inadequacies.

In early February, Idella Everett called Hidalgo from jail to say that Perez had come to see her and threatened her. From Idella's halting words, Hidalgo feared her step-mother had somehow implicated her. Idella told her that Saracino was coming to the Everett home to pick up the children's things. Hidalgo, who was staying at the Everett home at the time, negotiated for dates with Saracino and finally agreed she could come over on February 13, at 11 A.M. Saracino said her supervisor and maybe a foster parent or two would be with her. Fine, said Hidalgo.

Instead, Saracino brought Perez. ''He started jerking boxes down from the cabinets and going through every-thing. He trashed the house,'' Hidalgo said. He gathered up pictures of her sister and her husband, her father, other members of her family, her friends . . . none of them nude or otherwise pornographic.

Then Saracino went outside and Perez launched into a series of questions and accusations, she said. She denied everything. He said he had a written statement from Idella: Harold Everett had molested Hidalgo from the time she was eleven until she was fourteen. Hidalgo protested that not only was her father unable to write, but she didn't even know her stepmother until she was nearly eighteen. "Just shut the fuck up!" snapped Perez, according to Hidalgo.

When she denied molesting children, Perez retorted, "This came from the mouths of *children*. Are you calling these children *liars*? Children don't lie!" He revealed the anguish of his dual relationship. "I'm the one who has to sit up all night with these children and hold them and rock them and tell them that you sick perverted people will never hurt them again." Perez promised her the court would go easier on her if she admitted what he knew.

Hidalgo begged to go to the bathroom, but Perez said no, she said. She writhed and pleaded and actually threatened to urinate on him. She told me that when Saracino came back, Perez ordered her to stand in the open door to the tiny bathroom and watch Hidalgo, while he sat plainly visible just outside. It was an altogether humiliating experience.

At around two in the afternoon, almost three hours after he arrived, Perez hauled Hidalgo to the Wenatchee police station, where he questioned her without a break until five. She told me he refused to let go of his theory that she was herself a victim, which would have explained everything. "It's funny. You can remember things from your childhood, but you can't remember what your father did to you," Perez said, according to Hidalgo.

"That's because it didn't happen," said Hidalgo dismally.

Perez's voice droned on, she said, but his eyes fixed on his computer as he started to type. "You can go home if you say these things happened," he reminded her. "Otherwise, as a newlywed you'll have to bust up your marriage because you won't admit to being a sick pervert." Hidalgo refused to confess or to testify against anyone.

She was booked into jail on 614 counts. She remained in jail for a month before she saw her attorney, a public defender. At her original court hearing on February 14, she was asked to enter a plea, without benefit of an attorney. She entered a plea of not guilty and Judge Bridges gave her the phone number of the Barker and Howard law firm, which holds the Chelan/Douglas County public defender contract.

In the days and weeks that followed, Hidalgo put in over forty-two kites (penciled notes on jail memo pads) requesting an attorney, according to one of the jail guards. She was formally arraigned on March 6 and for the first time spoke briefly with her attorney, Phil Safar, a few minutes before the hearing. Then guards took her up to court from the jail on the basement floor of the courthouse. She was confused by the proceedings and didn't receive any paperwork describing the formal charges against her, just a form telling her the dates of her next hearing and trial.

While she was in jail awaiting trial, Safar communicated to Hidalgo the prosecutor's offer to reduce the charges to a single count of child molestation with a total sentence of six months in jail and community-based treatment if she would name and testify against Bob Devereaux, Pastor Roberson, or VOCAL spokesman Bob Kinkade. She refused. After all, Hidalgo didn't know Kinkade or Devereaux, and didn't go to Roberson's church or know Pastor Roby very well.

The next offer was three to four years without treatment if she would name and testify against others: this time Larry Steinborn and Linda Miller, a woman she had never met, she said. Again she refused.

"You know you'll look at life," said Safar about her potential sentence, according to Hidalgo. "That's a long time." He advised her that she would have to weigh her options. Hidalgo was adamant. She was not going to plea-bargain. Even if they agreed to release her the next day, she wouldn't agree to testify to lies against other people, including ones she'd never met.

At a court hearing, she complained about her attorney to Judge Wardell. Wardell "yelled at me to get in gear and get my own [lawyer]," she said. How she could accomplish that from the jail, she couldn't imagine.

In a letter dated April 27, 1995, Safar advised Hidalgo of the evidence against her and, in the light of that evidence, recommended that she accept a plea bargain. Most recently, the prosecutor offered to dismiss all counts in exchange for a plea to a single count of incest. "The prosecutor honestly believes that you are yourself a victim of sexual abuse," Safar said. He advised her that he understood she had rejected all plea offers and "further rejected any desire to provide testimony or information in exchange for prosecutorial immunity."

Safar told her that, in light of her ill-advised decision, he would be moving the court for release of state funds to pay for a psychiatric expert to testify about the suggestibility of child witnesses, a polygraph examination, and an independent investigator to assist in interviewing and obtaining background information on the children as well as the production of CPS and other documentation. Safar reminded her of the obvious: that she had agreed to waive her right to a speedy trial so that he could belatedly accomplish these things.

The judge later denied the defense motion for funds for expert services.

Hidalgo wrote a letter to Judges Bridges, Small, and Wardell on April 28, 1995.

"Please all that I am asking for is a fair and impartial judge, jury and trial because this is my life and reputation we are dealing with and I feel it is my legal right to obtain full and fair legal advice and legal representation in all court actions," she wrote.

Months later, in part because the judge had denied a defense motion for an expert witness, the jury split eleven to one for Hidalgo's conviction and couldn't arrive at a unanimous verdict. Two months later, discouraged and aware of a recent massive sentence, she finally agreed to enter into an Alford plea to a greatly reduced charge of incest in the first degree, a crime with a standard range sentence of twelve to fourteen months in prison, for which she received credit for the seven months she had stayed in jail pending trial.

"I never did anything and I'm maintaining my innocence, but the system is very biased," Hidalgo told the *Wenatchee World* after court. "It's almost impossible to get a fair trial here now. No matter where you go, someone is always pointing."

Next on Perez's list was Theresa Sanchez, a girl recently named by Ann and her corroborators and a reluctant key to the Devereaux and Glassen cases.

On a Tuesday night in late February, foster parent Janet Rutherford got a call from Carrow. "We need some information and we'd like Theresa to help out," said Carrow. She said her department and the police had concerns about someone "in the office," which, Rutherford learned, was Paul Glassen.

Rutherford agreed, but she was wary. Theresa, her foster daughter, had told her of the terrifying process Perez had put her through, as well as the fact that she had lied under pressure about Bob Devereaux. The Rutherfords were worried about Theresa, just as Glassen had been, because of her mental limitations.

But they had looked into the law and they were prepared. They'd also talked to the Foster Parents' Association based in Olympia. "Have you talked to Tim Abbey?" was the response. "He can help you." The Rutherfords knew enough by now to doubt it.

Rutherford told Carrow that she and her husband agreed to bring Theresa in for questioning as long as they could stay in the room with her. Carrow refused. Perhaps they could observe from behind one-way glass, Carrow suggested cautiously.

"I might as well be straightforward with you," she said, according to Rutherford. "Perez doesn't really like someone to be here."

"Can my lawyer be there?" asked Rutherford.

There was a long silence on the line. At last Carrow spoke. "It sounds like you have something to hide," she said, according to Rutherford. "Should we be investigating *you*?"

The Rutherfords brought Theresa in for her appointment, but they were prepared. As soon as Perez greeted them, they handed him a copy of a Washington state law that read in part: "Prior to commencing the interview the department or law enforcement agency shall determine whether the child wishes a third party to be present for the interview and, if so, shall make reasonable efforts to accommodate the child's wishes."

Perez ignored the papers and snatched Theresa away from them.

Inside his office, Perez asked her why she was being questioned. According to his report, she said, "To help you guys lock Bob Devereaux up."

He told Theresa what he claimed he knew: that already children had confirmed that Devereaux had molested her. He wanted her to give Paul Glassen's name, and said a couple of girls said Glassen had molested them and Theresa, she told me. Although she later said she was scared and intimidated by Perez, she stood up to him.

After around two hours, Theresa screwed up her courage and said to Perez, "My foster parents told me that you are not supposed to talk to me without anyone present for me. You should have had someone with you when you talked to me in juvie." According to Perez's report, he responded that "her foster parents had given her some misleading information" and said what they had told her "is not a requirement of the law." Yet at a defense interview, Perez said that he was aware of the state law that allows a child to have someone present during an interview.

He told her that if she had lied to him in August about Devereaux molesting her, he would send a report to the prosecutor so that he might charge her with false reporting. Theresa looked down and after a moment said, "I was lying."

Theresa described it differently when I talked to her: Perez picked up his phone and threatened to put her in "juvie" unless she adopted her earlier statement that Devereaux had molested her. Despite her fear, she resolved not to break down as she had before. She was tormented with guilt for months about what her words had cost Devereaux. After more than two hours, knowing the Rutherfords were just outside and inclined to make trouble, Perez gave up in defeat.

Later, he said he'd excluded the Rutherfords from the interview because they were "suspects," as Carrow had threatened they might become. In fact, at a defense interview in June 1995, Perez said that the Rutherfords were currently under investigation for child sexual abuse. Yet charges have never been filed and they were permitted to continue as foster parents at and beyond the time of Perez's interview.

Because of her failure to cooperate, state authorities sent Theresa to a juvenile facility for children with behavioral problems in Medical Lake, Washington. The Rutherfords were told that the placement was to be "permanent." But the girl's guardian ad litem intervened. After talking to Theresa's counselor, he learned that because she was not a child with significant behavioral problems she didn't belong at the facility. She was returned to the Rutherford home, but never again would the Rutherfords have faith in the social service system or in Wenatchee law enforcement.

"If you see a police car or a car you don't know," Janet Rutherford told her kids, "come in the house."

With resistance from Hidalgo, Rodriguez, Theresa Sanchez, and Kelly Allbee, it was time for Perez to expand his list of potential corroborating witnesses. On March 13 at 10:15 A.M., Perez, Alexander, Carrow, and Ann Everett set out on an adventure that would alter the course of many lives in the city of Wenatchee. Perez was at the wheel, but Ann directed the way. The names and descriptions that the girl was disclosing on a daily basis to Bob and Luci Perez had become confusing to a man who took few notes. Now was the time to pin things down.

Ann took them on an excursion through squalid neighborhoods of tiny cottages and moldering two-story wood-framed houses. As the drive progressed, the neighborhoods became increasingly upscale to reflect improved circumstances or expanded theories. The trip wound around her old neighborhood all the way to the northern part of town. And then across the bridge that crossed the roaring confluence of the Columbia and Wenatchee rivers to the diminutive but sprawling community of East Wenatchee. Ann got to miss a Monday at school and there was no mistaking her importance to this crowd, some of whom were scribbling down notes of things she said.

Now and then she pressed her stubby finger against the glass. "There's one," she said, pointing at the Ferry Street Market. It was second on the list after Donna Rodriguez's old residence. Every time she pointed, the car stopped and Perez queried her. Sometimes Ann recognized the home and one or two of the kids that lived there. Sometimes she remembered even the adults. Sometimes it was easy because they were relatives or longtime friends. All of the homes were places where Ann said she was raped, repeatedly and often, in orgies comprised of numerous adults and children, between January 1988 and March 23, 1994 (the day she came to live with Perez).

Ann pointed to houses, and the adults in the car jotted down addresses because, now and then, it pays to keep notes. The residences included those of Barbara Garaas, Karen Lopez, Devereaux, Linda Miller, Rodriguez, Kerri Knowles, Honnah Sims, and Pam Kimble. Later Perez, Carrow and Alexander reconstructed and filled in the gaps in Ann's memory. All in all, Ann pointed out sixteen homes in Wenatchee, with enough time to sandwich in a lunch stop.

Then it was across the bridge to East Wenatchee. This time the list was smaller, but at least as dramatic. Among the six locations Ann identified as sites of her molestation were the home of her grandparents, and the church and residence of Pastor Roby and Connie Roberson. The "unknown address" of a woman known as "Kathy" was the "last location that Ann Everett could remember and this ended the day's activities." Ann's activities then became those of a different sort—the activities recently typical of the Perez household, a household straining with therapeutic disclosures.

At 9:30 the next morning, Perez again dispensed with school and brought Ann to the CPS office, where he, Carrow, and Alexander interviewed her about the people who raped her over the last several years. "Ann had said she wanted to get it all out so she could forget about it," reads Perez's report.

Over the course of six hours she told stories that filled sixteen pages of Perez's report. The stories began with her grandfather, who repeatedly raped her when she was between the ages of two and eight, and went on to her grandmother, her parents, her brothers and sisters, their friends, neighbors, and relatives. For the most part, everybody did the "wild thing," which, Ann explained, was sexual intercourse or, in the case of women with girls, digital penetration. Adults swapped kids, "then they would change kids and start over. . . . When we were in the bedroom, we had to lay down and wait our turn.

"Bob Devereaux came over in the mornings and a man named Paul Glassen who worked at CPS," Ann said. Glassen and Devereaux, who brought foster kids Theresa and Bonnie in lieu of kids of his own, did all manner of sexual things to kids, including the "wild thing," she said. When she learned Glassen worked at the CPS office, "it gave me a not good, icky feeling."

Pastor Roberson touched her privates and did the "wild thing" at her house lots of times, maybe six times a week, when others were around, said Ann. Sometimes he brought Bill Davis, the church van driver.

Perez directed Ann's attention to the locations she had pointed out the day before. She described incidents at each of them with the same crowd as at the Everett home. "There were twelve kids, not counting Bob's kids." Some of the most exhausting events took place at the Devereaux home.

"When we got there, they took four kids upstairs; the parents took them. The rest of them, the kids, had to stay downstairs and watch a sick movie . . . it was a sex movie. . . . They were touching each other and doing the 'wild thing.' " Then Ann corrected herself: "Whoops, six kids actually went upstairs. They would go to a bedroom that had six beds. They were bunkbeds taken apart. There were three beds on one side of the room and three on the other sides. All the adults except one went upstairs. The adult downstairs stayed with the kids downstairs to be sure we watched the movie. There were more adults in the room than kids. We had to undress and lay on the bed; a kid on each bed. The adults undressed and got in a line and took turns with everybody. It was the touching thing, the 'wild thing' and we had to touch them, too."

The kids who were waiting downstairs went upstairs after the first group was done, said Ann. "We would keep on going upstairs and back downstairs. . . . This happened during the day and at night." All of the adults did it to each of the kids.

Ann was raped in orgies at the Miller residence, the Knowles residence, and Donna Rodriguez's apartment, she said. The East Wenatchee Pentecostal House of Prayer and the Roberson home were both hotbeds of activity. Connie Roberson touched the Everett children after they swam in the Roberson pool, she said. Pastor Roberson made the kids take off their clothes and did the "wild thing'' with the girls except for Roberta who, like the boys, he merely fondled. Connie put her fingers inside the girls and did the ''wild thing'' with the boys.

''That's all I can remember right now,'' said Ann at 3:30 P.M., ending the interview . . . or so it seemed. As Perez drove Ann to their home from the station, she pointed to a man walking on the sidewalk. ''That's Frank. He abused us too.'' Perez reported flatly: ''The interview did end with this final disclosure.''

Later, Perez reflected on his growing sense of commitment. ''Child molesters are the lowest form of life,'' he said to *Dateline*. ''They prey on little children who cannot defend themselves. I'm not the best investigator in the world but I will take up the cause of these kids and I will *believe* them and I will *defend* them. . . . I'll never be able to arrest every child molester. I'll never find out who every child molester in Wenatchee is, I don't have any illusions about that. But what I will do for the time I'm at this desk, I will do my best to see they're all rounded up, the ones that I'm made aware of.''

16:

February–March 1995

═══════════

Corroboration

═══════════

After VOCAL member George Wemberly videotaped
Kelly Allbee's recantation, VOCAL representatives
launched a local campaign against Perez and CPS. Some
uncharged Wenatchee residents came to accept the ger-
minal notion that something was amiss with the investigations. A few found it increasing difficult to look away
merely because these things were happening to someone
else. But thoughts became mired in ambivalence: After
all, weren't there checks and balances? Shouldn't matters
of justice be left to the experts, as local officials so often
reminded everyone through the local media?

A tiny minority of Wenatchee residents were immediately outraged, among them those who'd learned the hard
way what it is to be on the receiving end of a false allegation. Bob Kinkade, a former East Wenatchee police officer, was tried twice the previous year for allegedly
molesting his teenage daughter. Kinkade claimed the girl
was trying to get back at him for breaking off her lesbian
relationship. In two separate trials, he was acquitted on
some counts, but the jury failed to reach a verdict on
others. The ordeal left him enraged at the system and in-

evitably led to his affiliation with VOCAL. But Kinkade had a history and an attitude and the Wenatchee government shrugged him off.

In mid-February 1995, the Wenatchee chapter of VOCAL filed a complaint against Perez with the Wenatchee Police Department and submitted their videotape of Kelly Allbee. On the tape, an undeniably amateurish production, she sat on a couch and squirmed in childish discomfort while Wemberly asked her a series of questions about her interview with Perez. At times the girl was halting and, at times Wemberly asked leading questions. But, for many, the videotape was a searing indictment of coercive and suggestive police tactics:

Kelly: He [Perez] told me that I was there because he said that I'd been molested or something, kinda like.

Wemberly: And what did you say when he said that?

Kelly: I kinda said, ''What are you talking about?'' and stuff . . . ''I ain't never been molested.''

Wemberly: You told him that, honey, that you'd never been molested?

Kelly: Yeah.

Wemberly: Okay, and then what did he say?

Kelly: He said, ''Well, we know that's a lie,'' and something kinda like that.

Wemberly: How did he say he knew that to be a lie?

Kelly: He said that ''a whole bunch of other girls told me you were there when it happened'' and everything.

The dialogue continued:

Wemberly: You mean they interviewed you from 9 o'clock in the morning until 2 o'clock, honey?

Kelly:	Something like that. Like 1:30 or some-where around 2:00 'cause I remember he said, ''Well, like, we've gotta get around to the truth,'' and stuff. And ''I'll stop that phone call,'' after he called the police to, uh, take my mom.
Wemberly:	Is that what he told you, honey? Did he tell you that he was calling the police to have your mother arrested?
Kelly:	Uh-huh. He just said, ''This is enough fool-ing around.'' I assume he was calling the police, you know. Otherwise he was kinda warning me.
Wemberly:	What did he say, honey? This is what I have to get on record.
Kelly:	. . . Well, I knew that he was calling the po-lice. I think he said the police or, ''I'm call-ing the office now,'' or something kinda like that. And I was going, like, ''No, no, no!''
Wemberly:	And you said, ''No, no, no''?
Kelly:	Yeah.
Wemberly:	And then what did he say after you said, ''No, no, no?''
Kelly:	He just kept on calling. And then he said, on the telephone he said, ''I have a woman called Donna Rodriguez at 1006 8th Street and I want, something . . . to go to jail,'' or something like that.
Wemberly:	And then what did you say when you heard that, honey?
Kelly:	Um, then, um, then he said, ''Well, you got ten minutes to speak now. Get it out and I'll stop that phone call. 'Cause they'll be there in about five seconds . . . five minutes,'' or something like that. ''They'll be there by two.''

Wemberly: So he was trying to rush you into talking?

Kelly: Uh-huh.

Wemberly: Did you know what he wanted? Did . . . then what did you say when you heard that?

Kelly: Um, I was just crying and everything because I didn't want my mom to go to jail and stuff. And then he kept on asking me a bunch of questions. . . .

Wemberly: So were you basically agreeing with what he was saying?

Kelly: Kind of.

Wemberly: You were agreeing with him? Yes or no, honey.

Kelly: Yeah.

Wemberly: The camera can't pick up your head shakes. Okay, so you were agreeing with what he was saying regarding your mother?

Kelly: Yeah.

Wemberly: Okay, were you telling the truth or were you just agreeing with him?

Kelly: I was just agreeing with him.

Wenatchee police reacted defensively: Kelly's recantation was coerced, they said. Since she had disappeared with her father under suspicious circumstances, they wanted to find her to put her in "protective custody."

On February 16, Brewster, Washington, police interviewed Rob Dezellum, boyfriend of Kelly's older sister. The officers explained that Perez had ordered them to pick up Kelly. Dezellum said he didn't know where she was.

That evening, he got a call from Tim Abbey. Dezellem told him that in his opinion Kelly was emotionally traumatized and abused by Perez's interrogation. Abbey stuck up for Perez, who, he said, "had the biggest heart [I've] ever known for children.'' However, Perez had secured a warrant for Kelly's arrest, he said.

''Are you going to come after *me* now?'' asked Dezellem.

''I don't know,'' said Abbey mildly, according to Dezellem. ''I just met you.''

On February 27 a small group of picketers marched outside the Wenatchee DCFS office demanding an investigation of Perez and Abbey. Among them was Bob Devereaux, who had learned Kelly had named him and had since recanted. Wenatchee Police Chief Ken Badgley assured the *Wenatchee World* that an investigation was under way based on the complaint by VOCAL, but that Perez would be allowed to work as usual. ''We decide when people are pulled off cases, not complainants. If we feel the complaints are justified, we do it. Otherwise we don't.''

The next day, a half dozen foster parents picketed in freezing temperatures in support of Perez and Abbey. Many of their signs were the same: THE FOSTER PARENT ASSOCIATION SUPPORTS CPS AND THE WPD; others read simply, STOP THE ABUSE OF CHILDREN.

''We believe in them,'' foster parent Mickie Reyes-Vogam said of Perez and Abbey to a *Wenatchee World* reporter who covered the protests. ''They're just doing their job. The kids are afraid naturally, but they're afraid of the perpetrators. The kids are the victims, and these people [VOCAL] are putting them into too much turmoil. The community needs to support the people who are trying to protect our kids. Tim Abbey is doing a great job, and Bob Perez comes across like he's hard, but he's got feelings too.''

Foster parent Debi Cawdery admitted to some frustration with CPS. ''But they do a good job. They support the foster parents and we always know they care.''

March 6 was a morning of dueling rallies. Ten supporters of Perez and CPS wore purple ribbons and waved signs in front of the CPS office. The group of mostly foster parents, who called themselves the ''Purple Ribbon Brigade,'' for Perez's favorite color, included Luci Perez. Luci held a sign that was so long it trailed on the ground, with the names and sentences of fifteen people convicted in connection with the sex cases.

''We don't want to compete with them [the other demonstrators],'' she said to a *Wenatchee World* reporter. ''This is the only demonstration we're going to do, that and ask people to show their support by wearing purple ribbons. My husband will take care of the rest.''

A larger group of thirty critics organized by VOCAL lined up along Chelan Street wearing yellow ribbons and waving signs critical of Perez and CPS. In response to these demonstrators, Wenatchee Police Sergeant Mike Magnotti said he wanted to interview Kelly and her questioner George Wemberly. Perez's accusers hadn't given him enough information to properly check out their claims, he said.

''Frankly, if you saw the tape you'd have concerns about what was done to this young lady. . . . I couldn't get a case accepted by the prosecutor with an interview technique like that,'' he said. He didn't contemplate the irony of his words: If true, this fact implied much about Perez's unimpeded practice of not recording interviews.

By March 10, the Wenatchee Police Department completed its ''investigation'' and decided to take no action. ''The allegations were not sustained,'' said Chief Badgley to the *Wenatchee World*. ''In this instance, we have no supporting documentation or any witnesses available to make any other decision at this time.'' As to the videotape of Kelly's interview, Badgley said, "We didn't find the interview to be proper, and we haven't been able to talk to the girl or the man who did it. We suggested he come up and talk with us, but he never did."

In fact, he said, "Bob Perez, to this point, has my total support. He's doing a great job, and I have no concerns. I haven't seen anything that would dissuade me from that position at this time. It's just really unfortunate that instead of considering the victims in this case, certain people in the community have resorted to personal attacks on a detective who was assigned to this job by circumstance."

State DCFS official Roy Harrington told the reporter that nothing that had come to his attention would justify removing Abbey from his job with CPS. Harrington, who had likewise been provided with a copy of the Allbee videotape, said that he'd yank Abbey from his job "in a heartbeat," if the allegations of wrongdoing were sustainable, but from what he had seen they were not.

State and city officials came under fire from another direction. On the last week in March, aggressive Wenatchee attorney Steve Lacy filed claims against the Washington State Department of Social and Health Services, certain Wenatchee caseworkers, and Wenatchee Police Detective Perez on behalf of three former Wenatchee DCFS caseworkers—Juan Garcia, Paul Glassen, and Glassen's former supervisor, Juana Vasquez—for wrongful and retaliatory prosecution and employment practices.

Of these plaintiffs, the most troublesome was Glassen, who was proving to be not only slippery but a media draw. He announced he'd filed a grievance against DSHS through the State Employees Union. In fact, according to state DSHS officials who spoke to the *Wenatchee World,* this was the first time within the state of Washington that a caseworker was accused of hampering an investigation involving allegations of child abuse. Glassen had eluded prosecution, become increasingly verbal and confrontive, and now, perhaps not by coincidence, his name was appearing with alarming frequency in Perez's police reports.

VOCAL members decided to take their cause to the public. They scheduled a public meeting for March 15 at Eastmont High School and announced they would play the Wemberly interview of Kelly Allbee. The meeting had to be rescheduled after the school board became alarmed about holding the controversial public forum on school grounds.

On March 21, Kinkade and another VOCAL member, Bob Stewart, went to a meeting of Wenatchee city commissioners. The men handed the commissioners the Allbee tape and a bundle of papers—among them Perez's mug shots from a former arrest, and other documents that supported VOCAL's contention that Perez was dishonest and had a conflict of interest arising from his relationship with his foster daughter. They demanded that the detective be forced to step down from the Wenatchee Police Department.

Wenatchee Mayor Earl Tilly said that he was willing to set up a meeting between Badgley and Perez's critics, but only if the critics gave him a list of specific allegations. "They just gave me a pile of materials that's pretty disjointed and started reeling off allegations. I'm just asking them to put it in simple writing, point by point, and then we can talk about it." The materials Tilly received included the Allbee videotape.

Badgley agreed. "A lot of it is innuendo. Like the mayor, I want to see some specifics, something they can support with documentation. It's a little premature to make any comments about anything this group is talking about," Badgley told a *Wenatchee World* reporter with barely concealed scorn. "It's obvious what their motives are, so we're just going to go ahead and let them speak their piece."

Thus, Badgley relegated the complaints to the Constitutional dustbin where, by his apparent perception, such tired protest tactics belonged. None of the local officials showed the slightest empathy for Kelly. Whereas they had been quick to believe her before, the officials now refused to listen.

Instead, according to my review of police reports, they stepped up their investigation, which had recently foundered in the face of recalcitrant kids and suspects who refused to confess. The "parade of homes" gave the authorities some new direction and an excuse to go back and reinterview proven witnesses.

On March 3, Perez, Carrow, and Child Welfare Services caseworker Russ Haugen drove to the Integra facility for mentally impaired and sexually abused adolescents in Medical Lake, Washington, to meet with Jeff Town whose home was described as a hotbed of sex ring activity. Jeff was standing at the window when they arrived and he opened the door and awkwardly introduced Perez, Carrow, and Haugen to the staff attendant; then he and the attendant took them on a tour of the home. Perez toughed it out for fifteen minutes, then relegated Haugen to the den with the staff attendant, "to allow us some privacy," and sat down with Carrow and Jeff at the kitchen table.

Jeff was both eager to please and aware of their purpose. "I haven't really talked about my abuse too much to anyone. I'm glad you're here and I've been waiting to talk to someone," reads Perez's report. Jeff rattled on about the comings and goings and abuses in his neighborhood. Perez wrote that he was "speaking so fast that it was difficult to keep up. Occasionally I would direct him back to a specific question, but on the whole, once he began, he told his story uninterrupted.'' Although, as always, the interview was not recorded and Perez kept no notes or destroyed them, Jeff's rapid words were no match for Perez's memory. Nearly all of his incident report, typed seven days later, was in the form of direct quotations from Jeff Town.

In crude terms, Jeff described sex between the Holts and their kids; the Towns and their friends and relatives; and kids and adults at the Roberson church, where ''we were always talked to by Pastor Roby about God,'' and everyone went downstairs to the ''big area'' for feasts. He talked of sleepovers at the church which happened when ''if a sermon ran over late at night, the pastor called the parents and asked for the kids to spend the night.'' Thirteen boys and thirteen girls paired up, based on the ''heating system'' of body warmth, which, Pastor Roby explained, was more thermodynamically effective for boys than for girls.

There were probably thirty children downstairs and usually the parents didn't come with them, he said. ''Kids from the neighborhood would walk to the church by themselves and spend the night.'' He said Pastor Roby told the kids to undress and put their clothes against the wall or at the heads of their ''sleeping places,'' then played country music to calm them down, while they had sex.

''Usually what happened is that everyone fell into a trance,'' he said. ''I looked at the ceiling and it was weird. It was decorated for Halloween.'' Perez tried to direct him out of the weirdness by urging him to draw the church basement, but Jeff ''became somewhat frustrated with the effort,'' and Perez gave it up.

The massing of children was staggering. ''Sometimes kids had to triple up and sleep together. If there was an overflow, kids had to sleep upstairs. . . . We had to switch partners from night to night." Kids came back night after night and got into groups for sex, but "some people thought what the pastor did was wrong. . . . We didn't want to be forced to do it. If the top group didn't do it they would get yelled at really bad. He'd say, 'You will not come back to my church.' "

Jeff said the church van driver molested him. But before that information led to anything productive, he "went offtrack again." Perez sent Haugen and the attendant to get lunch, then asked Jeff to tell him more about the church. "Everyone did it to everyone. Roby whispered to the kids about where to switch to and what to do." The sleepovers were "every other Friday at the church."

Jeff said the van driver didn't want anyone to know his name. He came over for slumber parties, which lasted three days. "Somehow he got permission to keep us out of school on Mondays." Perez didn't bother to verify this fact and had he done so, his query would have contradicted Jeff's claim. Jeff "began to slow down and started to show signs of fatigue." It was now 2:40 and he had been talking for four hours.

Although timely reporting of allegations of sexual abuse is a requirement of Washington law, and although Jeff identified several victims and many other identifiable children were at risk, Perez didn't complete his report until March 10, a week after he interviewed Jeff.

In mid-March, Bob Kinkade called Linda Miller and told her Kelly Allbee had named her as a molester. Kinkade suggested that one or more of her children be videotaped by someone from VOCAL to preserve their statement. Linda was immediately alarmed. She had already had some dealings with Perez.

Miller had moved to Wenatchee in 1989 after her divorce, along with her four children: Charlene (twelve), Aubrey (ten), Mark (nine), and Allen (six); the family lived at the Quad apartments with Kerri Knowles and Knowles's three children. Twice in the past Aubrey had said she was molested: first years before in another state, most recently by Linda's ex-husband, Larry Steinborn. Aubrey said Steinborn had molested her, Ann Everett, and Bonnie Rogers in his truck. Miller reported it. Perez investigated and learned that the truck was returned to the dealer before the alleged incident. It was inescapable that the girls were lying.

At that point, Perez went to the Miller home to talk to Aubrey about Steinborn. He questioned Aubrey in front of Miller. ''You tell me the truth that I already know, or I'll lock you up and your mother has nothing to say about it,'' he stormed, according to Miller. Aubrey cried and said she had lied and nothing had happened. Miller was left with a dim view of Perez's methods.

Aubrey seemed the more likely of her children to be questioned, thought Miller. Now she watched Aubrey's interview by Michelle Holland of VOCAL and heard Aubrey deny that her mother had molested her. On March 22, a VOCAL representative leaked the existence of Aubrey's videotape.

At 9:45 A.M. on March 23, Perez and Laurie Alexander went to Sterling Middle School in East Wenatchee to interview twelve-year-old Charlene Miller. Her counselor told Perez that Charlene was in the ''borderline'' category in terms of needing special education classes, but she hadn't shown any behavioral problems. She was brought to a small interview room.

Mindful of some of the recent criticism, Perez was quick to point out in his report that ''Ms. Alexander took notes of the interview as I spoke to Charlene.'' The notes were destroyed or, at least, not made available to the defense, and the interview wasn't recorded.

Charlene rambled about people she knew and episodes of kissing and hugging and stories she'd heard from other children. Bob Devereaux was not allowed in their home, she said, "because of what he did to Theresa" and because "he played with himself." One time Devereaux came to her house looking for Theresa and he "played with himself" and "gagged them [the children] with his finger."

An hour and a half later, in light of recent criticism, Perez had lunch with Charlene and Alexander at the school cafeteria (and duly noted this fact in his report). When the interview resumed, Charlene listed the kids who stayed at the Devereaux house, but then she drifted away. "It appeared that Charlene could only stay focused on a particular event or series of events for so long before she would remember another person or event and begin talking about that."

Perez didn't equate her attention span to the length of the interview, but instead seized the reins, which is a function of a well-choreographed interrogation. First he steered her to the church. "We don't go to church now," she said. "My mom's trying to find a church where Larry's [Steinborn's] name won't be mentioned." Perez asked her if Steinborn had distinguishing marks or tatoos, and she responded, "He doesn't have any tattoos but he has a big herking penis."

Perez diverted her to the Devereaux house. "We went upstairs when his friends came. . . . The men all wore sunglasses. . . . The guys would come at around 9 at night; like three guys at a time would come until about six guys were there. They would hurt us."

Charlene drifted away. She said that her mother "made me feel safe; she gave me hugs around my neck and kissed my cheek. . . . I love Kerri too.'' She corroborated that Kerri Knowles liked *Star Trek* and also *I Dream of Jeannie*.

Perez directed her attention to the church. ''I remember Pastor Roby hid a molester there at the church once.'' He asked about sleepovers. ''I saw Pastor Roby touch my sister, Bonnie and Ann in a meeting downstairs. The church had a sleep-over and invited all the kids at church. Some adults came. . . . I saw lots of people doing it. There were maybe twenty kids.'' Among the children was a girl named Kelly whose mother named Donna had blond hair. Charlene's words confirmed Perez's theory that Kelly's ''recantation'' was coerced.

Perhaps misunderstanding Perez's question about ''the circle,'' Charlene said Pastor Roby made kids get in a circle and then he paired them up ''boy/girl, boy/girl. . . . If there was an extra, he would have them go to another room. . . . It would last about an hour. . . . At summer break, we stayed a week. On weekends, we would stay all weekend.''

Roberson threatened to punish anyone who didn't co-operate and have sex with each other, she said. ''One kid told me that Pastor Roby threatened to kill him.''

Perez terminated the interview at 1:25 P.M., almost four hours after it began. Laurie Alexander told Charlene that they would be back to pick her up after school.

Perez got hold of Douglas County Sheriff's Deputy Ed Allen, then drove to the Miller residence. Linda Miller was nowhere to be found. Back at Alexander's office, Perez listened as Alexander placed several calls to Miller's residence, trying to locate her. At 4:18 P.M., Gary Hill, Linda's friend, said she was on her way to CPS. By 4:55, it was clear to Perez that she wasn't going to show up. He began to search for her.

When Miller got home that afternoon, her friends told

her what happened, including the fact that most of her children had been picked up at school or at the bus stop and placed in state custody. She was outraged and terrified; she had a history of emotional problems, and she reacted badly to stress.

"No way in hell can they take my kids!" she stormed to her friends. She and her girlfriend Rickie Powell and Rickie's two kids went to pick up Aubrey, who had not gone to school but spent the day with a friend because Miller had been afraid Perez would question her. Instead of going on to CPS, at Rickie's suggestion they drove to the Canadian border. Rickie had a friend in Canada who might know what to do. Miller had nothing but the merest half-baked notion of what she should do.

At 7 P.M. on March 23, the same day that Miller headed to Canada, VOCAL staged a public meeting at the Douglas County Public Utilities District auditorium in East Wenatchee. The organizers showed the videotapes of Kelly Allbee and Aubrey Miller. Pastor Roberson was there after months of lying low. He brought along his folder of documentation. The meeting was later televised by KREM 2 television, a CBS affiliate out of Spokane.

"I finally was so concerned," Roberson said of his decision. "Donna Rodriguez had been arrested. I'd known Donna—she would help us at the food bank," he told me. "This new VOCAL group was kind of angry, stirring up the pot and doing protests and things like that. And I finally just said that I needed to *say* something."

At a prayer meeting, Roberson said he was going to the meeting to clear the air. He had refused to join VOCAL or participate in their activities, but the time for inaction was past, he said.

"It was obvious that everybody was making a lot of noise, but nobody was doing anything," said Roberson.

"And I thought maybe . . . the evidence I was able to put together, some of the documentation, might be helpful. And so I went to the meeting that night and stood up in the meeting and kind of expressed my concern for the Everett family, my findings, what I felt."

Soon after he started to speak, he noticed that two of a group of Wenatchee cops got up and left. Sergeant Magnotti stayed behind, watching him attentively, a fact that made him apprehensive. After the meeting, Magnotti approached him.

"I want to see that file," said Magnotti, according to Roberson.

"You're not seeing anything."

Roberson walked away and went up to KREM 2 reporter Tom Grant, who had interviewed him, Glassen, and Honnah Sims for his broadcast. Roberson showed Grant his documentation and emotionally set out his concerns. Grant and his cameraman, Dwayne Regehr, spent a long time going over the documentation that Roberson had accumulated over the months.

"I don't believe this," said Grant, according to Roberson. "This totally refutes everything that we've been hearing about what's going on in Wenatchee with the sex rings."

"It doesn't exist, Mr. Grant," said Roberson. "There *is* no sex ring in Wenatchee."

Roberson was heartened by Grant's response, but he had worries of his own. When he got home, he told Connie about the two cops who'd left the meeting as he started to speak. "Maybe we're getting closer to being arrested now." But he added optimistically, "Maybe with this information now finally getting out and going public . . . we won't have to worry about it too much."

Ignorant of the allegations that had already been leveled against him, Roberson was afraid that, like Paul Glassen, he was going to be arrested on some charge related to interfering with a police investigation.

It was nearly midnight when Miller and Powell arrived at the Canadian border, but to their disappointment the border officials wouldn't allow them to cross. Defeated, Miller, Powell, and the children spent a sleepless night near the border town of Tonaskat. The next day, March 24, Powell decided to return to Wenatchee. Confused and frightened, Miller stayed behind. Powell dropped her and Aubrey off near a friend's house, but Miller didn't know Powell's friends and stood hesitantly in the street and then took Aubrey into the barn that stood adjacent to the old farmhouse.

The dank, cavernous space terrified Aubrey and she immediately started to scream. Miller quickly was caught up in the contagion of fear. What if they were discovered and she was arrested for breaking and entering? "Let's go into town," she said to Aubrey, who wiped her eyes and agreed.

They hadn't walked far when a "gentleman" picked them up, said Miller. She asked him to take her to the police station. Maybe the police would help her find a place to stay. At the station, she gave the officers her name and showed them her identification.

Immediately her name came up on a computer, purportedly because she was wanted on an outstanding charge of defrauding an innkeeper for failure to return a rented violin. Caseworkers from the larger neighboring community of Omak, Washington, took Aubrey into protective custody. Tonasket Police Chief Don Schneider read Miller her rights at 4:15 P.M. and placed her in a four-by-eight-foot holding cell: a bare room with a single chair surrounded by wire mesh, which she accurately described as a "cage." She was monitored by a clerk, offered water and the opportunity to use the bathroom, but was not given a meal. The Tonasket police placed a call to the Wenatchee Police Department.

Wenatchee Police Sergeant Terry Pippin was with Officer Steve Crown of the Wenatchee Street Crimes Unit when the dispatch call came in from Tonasket at about 7:15 P.M. Pippin confirmed that Miller was indeed wanted for defrauding an innkeeper. But he also knew, and told the dispatcher, that Perez was looking for her so that he could question her about allegations of sexual abuse. Pippin placed a call to Perez, then he and Crown agreed to go to Tonasket to pick up Miller. They were on their way by 7:30 and arrived at Tonasket between 9:45 and 10 P.M. The officers loaded Miller's personal items in their car, advised her of her rights, and drove her back to Wenatchee.

She was unfailingly cordial. She said she was glad to see them but added, "sorry it's under these circumstances." Beyond that, Pippin said, "it was a quiet ride." On the way, somewhere near the brightly lit facade of the Rocky Reach Dam, Pippin called Perez at his home. Knowing it was going to be a late day, Perez was trying to catch a few hours of sleep. Pippin told him where they were and the time they should arrive at the Wenatchee police station.

The trio arrived in Wenatchee sometime between 12:30 and 12:40 A.M. on March 25. Pippin and Crown walked Miller to Perez's office. Pippin recalls that Perez was advising the woman of her Constitutional rights as he walked from the room to end his shift, although he wasn't able to hear anything of their conversation. Crown stayed in the room for a time until he, too, went off duty, at 1 A.M; he later testified that during the ten or fifteen minutes he was there he saw nothing unusual.

In fact, Crown testified at a hearing, Miller appeared

"almost jovial." On cross-examination, Crown qualified the term to mean neither "happy" nor "cheerful," but merely "friendly." Miller didn't appear tired, he said, although she claims she didn't sleep the night before and had had nothing to eat that day. In contrast to Perez, who "appeared fatigued" with reddened, bloodshot eyes, she appeared "refreshed." None of the officers admitted to concerns that the late hour affected the voluntariness of her statement. Yet Pippin testified that he saw no more than three or four interviews that began as late as midnight in his eighteen years on the force.

Miller told me that during her interrogation she was nearly always alone in the room that Perez shared with other policemen. Other officers remained at their desks for five or ten minutes, and Perez, under fire because of his interrogation methods, made desperate attempts to have them stay, saying he had to have witnesses.

According to Miller, for six hours the interrogation proceeded in Perez's typical fashion, with the usual stern warnings that unless she cooperated she wouldn't see daylight—or her children—again. She said Perez launched into a dialogue about what he *knew* had happened, including things children had told him, and of course children don't lie. He described the layout of the Devereaux house and said adults stood in line waiting to have sex with kids who were brought upstairs in shifts while others stayed downstairs to watch television. It was the version of events that his foster daughter Ann had given the month before.

Perez urged her to name the Robersons, Devereaux, Glassen, and VOCAL members Stewart and Kinkade, who by now were picketing and courting the press and only four days before had formally complained about Perez's tactics to local city commissioners. Exhausted, shaking, and crying, and in the throes of a migraine headache, at last Miller came around and named the names that she claims Perez had been flinging in her face.

She resisted confessing to her own actions. Perez told her she was sick and had buried the memories away, but he would help her get treatment, she said. The persuasion was so effective that Miller came to believe that although she couldn't remember anything, she indeed might be guilty. When Perez forcefully informed her ''You won't make it through the week'' because other prisoners would kill her if they found out what she was charged with, she at last ''confessed.''

The confession was entirely in conformity with the information Miller said Perez gave her: adults standing in line to have sex with shifts of children in the Devereaux home; children picked up by the church van every Friday night and driven to the Roberson church, where adults paired them up for ''organized sex orgies'' in the multi-purpose room in the basement and then plied them with such treats as donuts, chocolate milk, and cupcakes.

''My life is over,'' Miller told Perez before she signed the statement he typed.

''Your life is just beginning,'' he said, according to Miller. ''Go ahead and sign and you'll feel better.''

Perez felt better. The confession was a badly needed adult corroboration at a time when critics were poking around, suspects and victims were balking, and the credibility of his key child witnesses had come under fire. Miller's statement also addressed a couple of thorny issues for Perez. Glassen threatened Idella Everett that he would take her kids away if she told ''and kinda made sure the rest of us kept our mouths shut.'' Kinkade told her that Juana Vasquez somehow sneaked DSHS files to him. Even more ominously, Miller heard Kinkade and Bob Stewart met behind closed doors and plotted to videotape kids and get them to say Perez and not Devereaux had molested them.

Miller was booked into the Chelan County jail on 3,200 counts. Within the day she recanted her statement. ''It was the worst day in my life,'' Miller later recounted to *Dateline NBC*. She tearfully added that she was sorry and described what she had said as ''a pack of lies. It's vicious, *horrible* to be accused!'' Apologies, Miller learned, were inadequate in the face of the havoc her words created.

17:

March 1995

The Roberson Arrest

Perez and Carrow first briefed Douglas County Deputy Sheriff Robbin Wagg on the suspicious sexual goings-on at the Pentecostal church in early February 1995. Perez claimed several kids had made disclosures and based on these disclosures "the Pastor of this church and his wife were suspected of sexually abusing children at the church." The evidence was startling, it was corroborated, and it fell solely within Douglas County's jurisdiction and not that of the Wenatchee Police Department in Chelan County. Yet Wagg and his department sat back and did nothing: They didn't talk to potential witnesses, take action to protect the kids, or question or arrest the Robersons. Instead, according to Douglas County police reports, the Douglas County law enforcement community agreed to go along with Perez's plan that Perez "would compile the information" and forward it to the Douglas County Sheriff's Department when he got around to it.

On Thursday, March 23, Wagg learned that Perez and Carrow had met with Douglas County Sheriff Dan La-Roche and provided him with a packet of Perez's police reports pertaining to allegations of sex abuse at the Pentecostal church. Perez had already briefed LaRoche. Wagg and his partner Doug Helvey studied the reports.

The Robersons were clearly identified through the statements of victims; LaRoche, Wagg, and Helvey learned that the acts were numerous, ongoing, and profoundly serious; the allegations included many identified and identifiable child victims and adult perpetrators; church activities were ongoing and Sunday services were only a couple of days away. Yet Wagg and Helvey sat back and did nothing.

Instead they waited until Monday, March 27, to go to the Wenatchee Police Department to speak with Perez. Perez was pleased to inform the men that Miller had been arrested after confessing and verifying, in astonishingly similar terms, what the children had said. Despite the sheer volume of evidence, Wagg and Helvey did not want it to be said that the Douglas County Sheriff's Office failed to do its own investigation.

Wagg and CPS caseworker Laurie Alexander went to Newberry Elementary School to interview Ann Everett. "We told Ann that we knew what she had told Detective Perez about the touching that took place by Pastor Roby at his house." Roberson did "the wild thing" with all the girls except for Roberta, who he merely touched, responded Ann. Connie touched all the girls "inside their privates."

That evening, KREM 2 television of Spokane broadcast the VOCAL meeting in which Roberson condemned the investigation. The next day, March 28, Wagg prepared an affidavit for a search warrant for the East Wenatchee Pentecostal House of Prayer and also for the Roberson residence. Judge Wardell signed the search warrant. Later she told a convention of DCFS caseworkers that reading the affidavits in support of search warrants in these cases often made her physically ill.

While the delay heightened the risk of repetition of dangerous acts against children, it also enhanced the preparation of law enforcement. At approximately 11 A.M., Deputies Wagg and Helvey held a briefing with the Washington State Patrol Total Station Team—which included a patrol sergeant, a patrol detective sergeant, a detective, and two serologists from the crime lab—and with Sheriff LaRoche, the undersheriff, and seven deputies. Helvey assigned the officers and technologists to their responsibilities and they were on their way.

At 11:57 A.M., Pastor Roberson was sitting on a bench with one of the volunteers from the food bank when eleven cars and vans from the Douglas County Sheriff's Office, the East Wenatchee Police Department, the Washington State Patrol, and the Washington State Patrol Crime Lab pulled up on the sidewalk and broad driveway in front of the church with a great, visceral, orchestrated screech of brakes and crunch of gravel. Car doors opened and slammed shut and a throng of uniformed and plainclothes police personnel descended on the Pentecostal church.

Roberson rose to greet two of the officers who were striding toward him in a purposeful way. He identified himself and was immediately rewarded by having his hands forced painfully behind his back. Wagg handcuffed him, placed him under arrest, advised him of his rights to counsel and to remain silent, and placed him in a police vehicle. Around twenty volunteers and hundreds of people who were lined up for the food bank turned around and then gathered, their jaws dropping in amazement.

Wagg asked where Connie was, and Roberson told him she was at the Wenatchee Valley College. Then Wagg asked him where his daughter Roberta was, but Roberson refused to answer. In his report, Wagg noted that the pastor was failing to cooperate with the investigation and that

"Roberson did not appear to be surprised and showed no emotion when I advised him that he was under arrest and was going to be taken into custody." Both inactions, no doubt, signaled guilt to Wagg.

While deputies transported Roberson to the station, Wagg, a deputy, and a CPS caseworker drove to the Wenatchee Valley College to "attempt to arrest Mrs. Roberson." Wagg waited around the halls near what he had learned was Connie's classroom and then spotted her by her name tag. Once he confirmed her identity, Wagg took her to an empty room for arrest and questioning. At first Wagg told her they merely wanted to learn the whereabouts of Roberta. She said that she'd tell him if he'd give her the opportunity to talk to a lawyer. Stymied, Wagg saw to it that the woman was handcuffed, trooped in front of teachers and students, and brought to the Douglas County Sheriff's Office.

At the sheriff's office, Wagg advised Connie of her rights and she agreed to submit to a recorded statement. First, she said, he showed her a stack of five or six files. He told her that she and her husband had been accused of molesting children.

"All of these people say you've raped children. You're looking at life sentences. You might as well confess," said Wagg, according to Connie. After she firmly denied it, he turned on the recorder.

He asked her several questions about membership and activities at the Pentecostal church. She said nothing unusual happened. The one sleepover at the church that she could recall was around six years ago, she said. She agreed to supply him with a list of the members of the church.

"Where was Roberta?" he asked.

"Well, see, I don't know, ah, the realms of the law," she said, according to the transcript of her taped interview.

"I don't really know what's going on so I want to speak with my legal counsel before, you know, I say something. Because all you see in the papers are children being taken from the home all the time."

Wagg commented on the fact that Pastor Roberson spoke out at Idella's sentencing. "Isn't it true that he went over and testified on their behalf on sentencing on some of these people?"

"I know he went to court, but he doesn't tell me a lot of . . . what goes on."

"Even after they had been convicted of those kind of crimes?" persisted Wagg. "You don't think that [it] would be hard for him to go and testify on their behalf after what had happened to the kids . . . ?"

"I don't know," Connie said. "I couldn't say. I'm not him."

Wagg asked Connie if it would bother her to testify on behalf of accused people like the Everetts so that they might get reduced sentences.

"If I felt they were not guilty, I definitely would," she said.

"Ah," said Wagg. He hesitated for a moment and then asked Connie what she felt should happen to people who sexually abuse children.

"Well, they should be punished by law," said Connie. "Children are precious," she added.

Wagg described two kinds of sex offenders. In the first category was the offender that stalks children and molests them in a predatory way. The second category was "the person that's like a parent that loves their kid, but they let the touching get out of control," said Wagg. "If you had to categorize yourself in one of those two categories," he asked pointedly, "which one would you . . . categorize yourself in?"

"I'm in neither category," said Connie.

"Which do you think should get the more . . . severe penalty?"

"To me they're both the same."

"So you think they both should be punished equally?"

"Uh-huh."

Still Wagg pushed on. "Okay . . . so you don't . . . see a distinction between people that just, ah, I guess accidentally abuse their kids or people that purposely do it?"

"How do you mean accidentally?"

"I mean people that . . . touch their kids and then after it's done wish they hadn't . . . or the person that purposely goes out and tries to do that and solicit kids to touch?"

"Well," she said, "that's not accidental if you touch your kids."

Wagg persisted. He asked her whether counseling might be a better alternative than prison for a sex offender.

"You can always say or you can always pray that they're going to take counseling and that . . . things are going to change," she said thoughtfully, "but then that's an individual choice too."

Wagg tried yet another approach. "Do you think that kids are capable of lying about those kinds of allegation?"

"Oh, yeah. Yeah."

"What do you personally think?" asked Wagg, querying Connie, who had named her husband, about the children.

"I say that it is not true."

"So the children were lying?"

"Yes, because I do not believe that my husband would do that."

But, said Wagg, what about the fact that young children of relative sexual unsophistication were describing "intercourse and penetration and penises and vaginas? Do you think a normal child would have that kind of information that they could tell?''

No, said Connie with that maddening logic, not unless they saw it on television or in a movie or somebody had talked to them about it.

At last he gave up and had her booked into the Chelan County Regional Jail on ten counts of rape of a child in the first degree. The Douglas County Sheriff's Office did not utilize the Wenatchee Police Department's simple mathematical formula of computing counts based on the frequency of sex acts against multiple victims.

In his report, Wagg avoided discussing Connie's reasoned denials but pointed out that she had confirmed a number of things in the children's statements, notably that children identified as victims had attended church activities when they said they had, and had been to her home.

A deputy then brought Pastor Roberson to Wagg's office. After being advised of his rights, Roberson said he was willing to talk and didn't want an attorney present, but he didn't want his statement to be tape-recorded. He said he hadn't seen or taken part in any wrongdoing at his church. Wagg told him that the sheriff's department was in the process of searching his residence and the church as they spoke. Wagg explained that the technicians would be looking for semen and bodily fluid stains, among other things. Roberson said he didn't believe they'd find anything.

Wagg asked him about the troublesome fact that he had testified at the sentencing of an already convicted child molester, Idella Everett. According to Wagg's report, Roberson explained that ''he believed that Detective Bob Perez was lying and so was the Chelan County Prosecutor.'' In fact, ''Pastor Roberson stated that he believed that his arrest was a result of him being critical of Detective Perez and the Chelan County Prosecutor.'' He said he was innocent and yet ''he was expecting to be charged because he had testified at the Everetts' sentencing hearing contrary to Detective Perez and the Chelan County Prosecutor.''

When Roberson refused to reveal Roberta's whereabouts, Deputy Bolz transported him to the Chelan County Regional Jail and booked him in.

Meanwhile, Washington State Patrol Crime Lab technicians began the laborious process of searching the church, first visually surveying the premises for stains or sex objects or other items of tangible evidence. The technicians, assisted by members of the Washington State Patrol and Douglas County Sheriff's Office, took swabs of stains and removed and seized carpet swatches, cushions, items of cloth, clothing, towels, blankets, toys, portions of the wall, cassettes, two old computers, notebooks, papers including much of the CPS records and other documentation which Roberson had compiled, books, a ''Stim-u-lax Junior'' massager, photographs, a knife, letters, a calendar—in all, over fifty-five items, none of them overtly sexual in nature. The property inventory took up nine pages of Wagg's incident report.

When Wagg finished interviewing Roberson, he learned that the officers and technicians were still at work and that the crime lab technicians ''had recovered several stains that they advised to be body fluids.'' He rushed over to help out.

The search and other related police activities took around thirteen hours; officers carefully sifted through papers, boxes, and personal belongings at the house and church; made a computer map of the church building; confiscated records, phone lists, and other records; and scanned the church with infrared lights and laser equipment designed to detect the presence of organic stains. It was a spectacular, efficient, and thorough investigatory team effort, something that, according to all expectations, would do them proud.

A little over a month later, on April 6, Wagg received a phone call from Washington State Patrol serologist Kevin Jones. Jones said he had tested all of the submitted evidence for the presence of semen, but all of the test results were negative. No incriminating tapes, documents, computer programs, or sex objects were ever recovered. Yet law enforcement did not reveal the fact of the negative lab tests to the defense for several months, until just before the trial of Honnah Sims in July.

The Douglas County sheriff's limited investigation of the Robersons and their church was just beginning, yet Sheriff LaRoche justified his department's hurried arrest of the Robersons. "We had information these people are starting to hide. We're just afraid we're going to lose some people." LaRoche did not explain his statement.

On Wednesday, March 29, a judge found probable cause against the Robersons on ten counts each and set their individual bail at $1 million, in part "because of the flight risk." The judge issued an order forbidding them to talk to anyone except their attorney or the church's district superintendent, according to Roberson.

The Robersons spent several months in jail. The first day, guards shoved Pastor Roberson against the walls and bounced his head against the concrete, he said. Before his preliminary appearance a guard announced in front of him and several prisoners, "As long as the rapist preacher is with you guys, nobody is getting to use a telephone." The inmates put two and two together. That night, after he fell asleep, someone threw a blanket over his head, and several prisoners repeatedly punched him in the ribs, face, and abdomen. He claimed he was regularly beaten until he learned to buy his physical safety with candy bars.

Douglas County Deputy Prosecutor Steve Clem told the

Wenatchee World that at the point of the Robersons' arrest the Douglas County Sheriff's Office had independently interviewed persons other than those interviewed by Perez. No documentation supports this allegation.

At any rate, with the Robersons safely ensconced in jail, the Douglas County Sheriff's Office launched into its own investigation. On March 29, after Wagg and Helvey exhausted a number of unproductive leads in an effort to locate Roberta Roberson, Douglas County Prosecutor Steve Clem prepared an affidavit for a material witness arrest warrant for four-year-old Roberta Roberson.

The next day, March 30, Helvey, Wagg, and Carrow interviewed Mary Everett at the Wenatchee CPS office. The interview wasn't recorded. Ann was allowed to be present "for Mary's support," although she was warned not to chime in. Wagg asked Mary a number of rapport-building questions about her school and classes and then went right to the goings-on at the church.

Mary's demeanor abruptly changed. She didn't answer; instead she buried her head in her hands and as Wagg's report aptly put it, made "crying sounds." Still, Wagg persisted. "After about a minute Mary pulled her sweater up over her face." Wagg waited a minute, then asked her if other kids had touching problems at the church and she said, "Uh-huh." She said she saw Roberson touch kids. Then he asked her if she had touching problems. Mary hid her head and said, "Yes." He asked her to name the kids who were touched at the church and she buried her head and wouldn't answer.

Wagg tried another approach, one that might be criticized as suggestive or even leading except, of course, by local standards. "I asked [Mary] if she could answer yes or no if I gave her the names she previously [had] given to us and she nodded her [head] yes." Wagg went on to list the names of people he thought might have molested her and Mary nodded her head yes to each. In this manner, Mary "said" that the kids at the church had touching problems with Pastor Roby, Connie, van driver Bill Davis, Honnah Sims, and others. Then she became more expansive, picking up the rhythm, her words dancing forward, her statement gathering momentum.

Adults and twenty to twenty-five kids started upstairs in the church and sang songs about God. Then, after the singing, they went downstairs to the "big room," where the touching happened, she said. Usually this was on Friday, after kids' night, but sometimes it was Sunday.

Mary started to talk about a safer subject, the kids who went to the Robersons' house, but it was yielding nothing productive, so Wagg steered her back to the events at the church. Again, Mary "buried her face in her hands" and dropped her head to the table and "began to [make] crying sounds." After a bit, Wagg concluded that Mary "was becoming very soft spoken and I was having trouble hearing how she was answering my questions." Again, he complained, "she continued to keep her head buried in her hands and make crying sounds." When she refused to answer altogether, Wagg terminated the interview.

Mary was permitted to leave the room while her sister remained for her interview. "Ann Everett was much more open . . . about the touching at the church than her sister was," said Wagg. Not surprisingly, Ann parroted what her sister had just said. Ann was especially helpful when it came to describing details, including the "wild thing" between men and girls and women and boys, which happened in the "Big Room" (the name having been elevated to capitalization status with repetition in Wagg's report). There were only four Fridays when she was not touched at the church, and one slumber party lasted from Monday until Sunday, she said.

Both Pastor Roberson and Connie said they'd stab her

in the back if she leaked a word. She explained that Pastor Roby borrowed her dad's army knife. By a complicated maneuver in which Wagg overlapped and then extended two pencils, he concluded that Ann said the knife was ten inches long and very sharp, which she knew because she touched it while Roberson was holding it.

18:

April–May 1995

Ultimate Conclusions—
Orgies and Satanism

"It looks like the circle is growing larger," Chelan County Deputy Prosecutor Roy Fore told a reporter for the *Seattle Post-Intelligencer* in early April. "We believe at this point there are 16 young victims and possibly 51 suspects in what the children dubbed 'The Circle,'" Fore told the *Seattle Times* the next day. "We probably will wind up charging maybe only two dozen of the suspects." The reason for this selective charging decision was unstated.

Government officials, speaking with increasing confidence and a growing disregard for the concerns of their critics, cited the graphic confessions, the conviction rate, the corroborating statements of children. Most of the defendants had limited incomes, were even on public assistance, and were represented by public defenders. Yet personal computers had been found in several homes, a fact that Fore considered "odd." Unspoken but ever-present was the official concern about affiliations and the dissemination of information, the makings of a conspiracy of child abusers—a ring, maybe a cult, maybe something on a national scale.

Sheriff LaRoche announced that many more arrests were pending, and Wenatchee Police Sergeant Sherie Smith confirmed that her department was looking at a possible fifty suspects. "We've only reached the tip of the iceberg," she told the *Post-Intelligencer*. "Stay tuned."

But, as the *Post-Intelligencer* pointed out, the critics wanted the press to stay tuned as well, particularly the members of the national organization VOCAL, "who allege that law enforcement has run amok." The reporter pointed to the "weird turns" the investigation had taken, including the fact that so many of the defendants were women.

Psychiatrist Dr. Roland Summit, who had frequently acted as consultant to prosecutors in high-profile sex abuse cases across the country, told the *Post-Intelligencer* that child molestation by women is rare, but rarer still are cases of parents swapping children for sexual purposes. "This is very, very strange to have this amount of lascivious and uninhibited traffic in one's own children."

The sex ring cases were more confusing than strange to local prosecutors. And, in any case, "strange" was not a label they wished to associate with their community.

"Maybe some of these players were the same in different houses," Chelan County Deputy Prosecutor Doug Shae told the *Wenatchee World*. "But were they all the same big ring? That's hard to define. I know a sex ring makes for a flashy story, but I hate to speculate on this because the public is already perceiving this as a really weird town where 12-year-olds shoot people and weird sex stuff is going on, and that's not true at all. We're just like anyplace else."

The need to balance controversial prosecutions with public relations designed to soothe conservative apple magnates and ensure tourist dollars continued to plague Chelan and Douglas County officials in the months to come. But local authorities decided to look to their more immediate needs. Douglas County commissioners and Chelan and Douglas County prosecutors asked Washington Governor Mike Lowry for state funds to pay for counseling, foster care, additional prosecutors and police, expert witnesses, and sex abuse training.

Lowry allocated $141,098 to Chelan and Douglas Counties for the "extraordinary prosecution costs" of the cases. The money was allotted to the prosecutors and law enforcement bodies, but no matching funds were provided for the costs of defense. Wenatchee Police Chief Ken Badgley expressed his relief and made an admission of cross-county investigation that he and Douglas County would later disown. "Between the cases we've been working and the help we've given to Douglas County, we've really eaten into our overtime," said Badgley to the *Wenatchee World.*

With their enhanced budgets, the two counties expanded their investigations.

On April 3, Deputy Doug Helvey got a call from Linda Woods of Child Welfare Services (CWS.) Roberta Roberson was located at the home of her paternal grandparents in Everett, Washington. Helvey faxed a copy of Roberta's arrest warrant to the Everett CPS office and told the caseworker to roust up the local lawmen to arrest the four-year-old and take her into custody. Officials arrested the child at once and placed her with Wenatchee foster mother Mickie Reyes-Vogam.

Roberta's grandmother, Virginia Smith, told Wagg she took Roberta to the Providence Hospital emergency room for a physical examination, and the doctor said there was no sign of sexual abuse. Upon hearing this news, which to his way of thinking was far from definitive, Wagg called the Central Washington Hospital in Wenatchee and scheduled Roberta for a colposcope examination with Dr. Cici Asplund the next day.

Although described in some literature as physically noninvasive, a colposcope examination is a procedure so personally intrusive as to strain the limits of dispassionate medical inventiveness. The procedure was designed to detect certain types of cancer, but it isn't difficult to understand its attractiveness in diagnosing sexual abuse. A child is positioned with her legs spread or her knees flexed against her chest before a magnifying instrument with a 35-millimeter camera attachment. In this way it is possible to view enlarged images and take photographs of the genital and anal areas. For a young child, the procedure is often distressing and uncomfortable, according to experts, sometimes eclipsing the alleged event that preceded it.

The practice of using colposcopic evidence in child sexual abuse examinations was popularized by Dr. Bruce Woodling, a family physician from California. Woodling also popularized the practice of looking for subtle, almost microscopic irregularities that might be consistent with penetration or other childhood traumas. The fact that the colposcope is able to produce magnified photographs of subtle anatomical features that are often invisible to the naked eye may exaggerate these features and create the appearance that they are enormously significant. Minuscule bumps, tears, notches, scars, or absence of hymenal tissue may, in magnified slides, be identified as "irregularities," yet fall within the normal range of anatomical variation for a nonabused child.[1] Although colposcope

---

[1] Diagnostic findings of vaginal and anal penetration are often highly controversial and, according to medical experts, may be overinterpreted and thus highly misleading. For example, in studies by Dr. John McCann, such findings as notches, scarring, tears, or absence of hymenal tissues occurred with such frequency in nonabused children that they could not be said to result from sexual abuse. (McCann, Joan Voris, M. Simon, Robert Wells, 1989, "Perianal Findings in Prepubertal Children Selected for Nonabuse: A Descriptive Study, *Child Abuse and*

slides often find their way into the courtroom, where they work their technicolor magic on jurors as comparatively solid evidence, Woodling's methods have been widely criticized as misleading and unreliable.

According to his report, Wagg watched the examination from an adjacent room, then took possession of the films. Dr. Asplund told him the examination "was suggestive not conclusive for penetration." He dropped the film off at the photo lab to be made into slides, and later placed a copy of the slides into evidence.[2]

Then he called Douglas County Prosecutor's Office child interview specialist Jeanne Dierickx to set up an interview of Roberta. Minimally trained and newly hired, Dierickx was Douglas County's response to criticism of Chelan County's investigation. Wagg learned that she was already in the process of interviewing potential child victims.

The problem was, Dierickx's interviews for the most part garnered nothing, perhaps because they accorded with minimal standards of professionalism and humanity. She questioned several children, who said they went to the Robersons' church and talked about commonplace sermons and activities. Nothing seemed to stand in the way of these kids' disclosing: They named their body parts; sorted out good and bad and private part touches; distinguished between "on top of," "underneath," "outside of," and "inside of." They knew how to protect themselves by telling their parents or another adult if some-

---

Neglect, vol. 13, no. 2, 179–193; McCann Robert Wells, M. Simon, Joan Voris al., 1990, "Genital Findings in Prepubertal Girls Selected for Nonabuse: A Descriptive Study, *Pediatrics,* vol. 86, no. 3, 428–439.) Also see, Dr. Lee Coleman, 1996, "Manipulated Medicine: Understanding Sexual Abuse Examinations," *The Advocate,* Kentucky Department of Public Advocacy, vol. 18, no. 3.

[2] A later review of the colposcope slides by an independent doctor did not support a finding of vaginal penetration.

thing happened. Yet none of them, including Roberta, admitted to touching problems.

Dierickx took special pains with Roberta's interview on April 20, 1995, even inviting foster parent Mickie Reyes-Vogam and caseworker Susan Moore to attend. Roberta sat on Mickie's lap and colored in a coloring book.

"I had brought a stuffed bear with me to give to Roberta after our meeting," wrote Dierickx. She used the bear to instruct the child on the concepts of good touch, bad touch and private touch, which Roberta logically concluded, after some questioning, took place on "your private." Dierickx asked her to identify the body parts on a diagram and Roberta rattled through them: hair, eye, nose, mouth, stomach, arm, belly, knee, private. Then Dierickx asked her if she remembered about good, bad, and private or secret touches. She remembered. Dierickx was ready for the big question.

"I asked Roberta if she ever saw anyone who [had] bad touching problems, and she stated no," wrote Dierickx in her report. Roberta said she liked everything about the church; no one asked her to keep secrets; if someone did something, she'd tell; no one had touched her privates.

Undeterred, Chelan and Douglas County authorities worked their way through the list of names given by Linda and Charlene Miller, Jeff Town, and the Everett girls.

On April 4, Perez arrested and then questioned Kerri Knowles at the Wenatchee police station, but soon he had to leave and asked Detective Kruse to take over. Knowles said she didn't molest anyone or see anyone else molesting kids. Kruse pressed her, but she wouldn't back down. At last she said she had severe physical problems and a history of spousal abuse that left her with emotional scars; sometimes under major stress she blacked out. This statement left Knowles in the precarious position of making less than a total denial, in the minds of officials.

Kruse asked her about Bob Devereaux and Paul Glassen. She didn't know them, she said. What about Bob Kinkade? Yes, said Knowles, in fact she'd talked to him just minutes before her arrest. That was of interest to Kruse, who wrote in his report, "I am personally aware that Mr. Kinkade is the chapter president of an organization known as VOCAL and that Mr. Kinkade has publicly expressed complaints regarding the investigation of child sexual abuse by the Wenatchee Police Department." Kruse concluded, "It should be noted that despite her insistence that she didn't molest any children, she did admit it was possible [during a blackout] that the suspects listed above did sexually abuse children in her residences." The listed suspects included Kinkade, Devereaux, and Glassen.

On the same day as Kerri Knowles's arrest, VOCAL indeed publicly complained. Advocating on behalf of people accused in the sex ring and other Wenatchee sex crimes, VOCAL representatives filed a lawsuit in U.S. District Court in Spokane accusing state, city, and county officials, local investigators, prosecutors, jail officials, and even judges of civil rights violations. Bob Stewart went around town serving copies of the lawsuit on various defendants, including the Wenatchee Police Department, Douglas County Sheriff's Office, and the Wenatchee branch of Washington State CPS. The suit accused the defendants of "discrimination, sexual discrimination, selective prosecution, baby-selling, blackmail, forgery, retaliation, violation of civil rights, false arrests, and kidnapping of both adults and children."[3]

---

[3] The U.S. District Court in Spokane later dismissed this action, although several lawsuits were later filed against state, county, and city officials on behalf of several of the accused, through their attorneys.

In the face of the persistent local criticism, the Douglas County Prosecutor's Office was driven to make its cases stick. It was time to go back to proven witnesses, although in some cases the approach may have been inadvertent. Dierickx interviewed thirteen-year-old Bonnie Rogers on April 5; her foster mother, Debi Cawdery, stayed to help out. Bonnie said that ten kids lived in the Cawdery foster home, although none of the kids in the house counted among her friends.

Dierickx directed her through the good touch, bad touch, and private or secret touch routine, and had her name her body parts on the standard diagram. "I then asked Bonnie if she had any touching problems." She named two of the usual suspects: Bob Devereaux and Larry Steinborn. Then she displayed her foresight and that of her foster mother.

Bonnie "pulled a list from her notebook" and said "with these people." The list was artfully constructed and was edited and embellished by Cawdery. On a column on the left-hand side of the page were ten "guys," including Bob Devereaux, Larry "Sightborn," Duke, "a guy in his mid 30's," Tigger (nineteen or twenty), David (fifteen or sixteen), Jon (forties), and Bob Devereaux's son. Beneath this column was a column entitled "ladies or girls," which included: Linda Miller, Kerri Knowles, Kelly's mother, Bobbie (a former foster parent), Terri Hockett, and "a black lady, I think it's Duke's wife." On a column to the right entitled, "us," Bonnie listed herself with the last name of "Cawdery," Theresa Sanchez, Ann and Mary Everett, Charlene and Aubrey Miller, and Ruby Nelson (daughter of Kerri Knowles.) The ages of the the children were neatly lined up in a column beside the names. At the bottom of the page were the words, "Some Mexicans cross the street tried to kiss Theresa and me. Then tried to make us kiss them."

Dierickx obligingly went through the list with Bonnie in order to "clarify who the people were." Then, perhaps recognizing some of the pitfalls of the list, Dierickx steered her to safer ground. "I then asked Bonnie if anyone else had touched her that she hadn't already talked about with anyone else and Bonnie stated, 'Pastor Roby, Bill and Honna.' "

Bonnie said five or ten times Roberson, who was wearing "kind of a tux," pulled down his pants, raped her for five minutes, then told her she could leave. She said he told her, "If anybody here at the church touches you I will hurt or kill you or come after your family if you were to tell." She told Dierickx that she had never seen "other touching problems with other kids." But she had experienced many more problems of her own. Bill Davis, the church van driver, had intercourse with her for "five or seven minutes" inside a tent she and Davis had constructed of logs and blankets.

She went on to describe several separate occasions when a child would summon her to the tiny church bathroom and there the child's mother would pull down her pants, get on top of her, and penetrate her with a pen or pencil or other writing object for five minutes. One time it was Idella Everett, another time Honnah Sims, yet another time Linda Miller.

Bonnie's list got a further workout on April 26, when Debi Cawdery called CPS caseworker Laurie Alexander and said Bonnie "appeared to be ready to disclose additional information" about goings-on while she lived at the Devereaux home. Wenatchee Police Sergeant Mike Magnotti and Alexander met with Bonnie her foster home after school. Stung by public criticism, Perez was lying low.

Bonnie "got her journal and gave me a list of names

she had recorded as people who had been involved in the sexual abuse at Devereaux's house,'' wrote Magnotti in his report. It was the same list she produced for Dierickx. The ''black handwriting'' on the page, Magnotti explained in his report, was Cawdery's. Cawdery had ''discussed the list with Andrea and made clarifying additions when Bonnie had problems with names.''

Magnotti went through the list one person at a time, trying to clarify for himself who some of the more ambiguous might be. She, Ann Everett, Theresa Sanchez, and Charlene Miller were hurt, said Bonnie. The words ''hurt'' or ''hurting,'' Magnotti determined, meant that ''objects had been inserted into the girls' vagina's usually writing instruments and/or men's penises.''

The information was intriguing to Magnotti, particularly the possibility that yet another foster parent, Bobbie, might be a molester. Laurie Alexander drove Magnotti to the Wenatchee police station; on the way, Bonnie pointed out the location of a schoolmate who came up to her and said, ''Me and my group will beat you up if you testify or tell.''

At the station, Magnotti phoned Bobbie Smith. Yes, said the woman, for two years she'd been Bonnie's foster parent. Bobbie said that although she'd known Devereaux and his ex-wife Maxine, she'd never been inside their house. Magnotti asked Bobbie to hand the phone to her husband. Curiously, her husband told Magnotti he wouldn't allow him to come to his home unless he first provided him with personal references by Christians who attended the Methodist church. Magnotti backed off.

Instead, in the days to come, he questioned the ''Jon'' referred to on Bonnie's list. Jon Campbell said he knew Bob Devereaux because he worked at a local convenience store and Devereaux came in almost every day. Once he saw Bonnie, a ''blond child who was a diabetic,'' steal a piece of chocolate donut from his store. He had never been to the Devereaux home.

Magnotti was troubled by his investigations. And Bonnie had lied about being a sex abuse victim before. "Detective Ron Matney and I then contacted Bonnie at her foster home and I told her that I suspected she had not been truthful to me about some of her disclosures." According to Magnotti's report, Bonnie quickly admitted she "made up" the black lady and lied about Jon, whom she had never seen in Devereaux's house, "due to the pressure of the case." Bonnie said the rest of what she had said was true, but the person she saw could have been Bobbie or "her twin sister."

Chelan County continued on its single-minded pursuit of "corroboration," which, given problems with the children, called for adult testimony.

Larry Steinborn was arrested on a warrant on April 7, then brought to the station and interviewed by Perez and Detective John Kruse. Perhaps to get around the complaints about Perez, Kruse typed the report when it was complete.

For the first forty-five minutes, Perez "outlined the charges Steinborn was facing." They were staggering and Steinborn, we can assume, was sweating. Then, according to Kruse's report, Perez said he "had spoken to the prosecutor who had agreed to offer him a *deal*." Unlike nearly all of those who were accused, Steinborn was a convicted child molester undergoing community-based therapy under the conditions of a suspended sentence. Even an allegation not rising to the level of a conviction would be reason enough to yank his suspended sentence and impose prison time. As he was now abundantly aware, he had been named by numerous children. If convicted of these crimes, he faced cumulative life sentences. A deal has particular appeal to a man in Steinborn's circumstances.

According to Kruse's report, Perez told Steinborn that if he "was completely truthful about his own actions and the actions of others he had witnessed regarding child sexual abuse, no new charges of child abuse would be filed against him." The deal, Perez stressed, was contingent not only upon his truthfulness but his "willingness to testify in court" about what he saw.

Steinborn said he "understood this arrangement," but added that he hadn't seen or done anything. He wasn't getting it.

"At this point I took over the interview," said Kruse. "I made it clear . . . how important it was that he be truthful with me." The conversation continued for three hours, and if Kruse's report is to be believed, Perez merely watched.

After a time, dimly, Steinborn saw the light. He launched into a description of the times he had seen his wife, Linda Miller, have sex with children in 1993. Miller and Steinborn, at the time of the interview, had been on the outs for a long time.

Sometimes Miller's children crawled into their bed and she had sex with them, while he went off to sleep on the couch in the other room, he said. At other times, Bonnie Rogers and Mary Everett came over for slumber parties with Miller's daughters. When they fondled Miller, Steinborn walked away in disgust. Another time, Ann and Mary Everett and Kelly Allbee came to a slumber party with Miller's daughters. This time Kerri Knowles joined Miller in mutually fondling the children. The women asked him to join them, but Steinborn discreetly walked away.

He continued that children were all the time telling him they were molested by Devereaux and Miller and Knowles and Donna Rodriguez at the Devereaux home. Coming from Steinborn, the girls' confidences were nothing more than hearsay, insufficient for corroboration purposes. He was urged to tell what he saw at the Devereaux home.

Mindful of the "deal" or, as Kruse more delicately put it, the "arrangement," Steinborn complied, perhaps drawing on the store of information he had gained during the forty-five-minute period when Perez "outlined the charges he was facing." Steinborn said lots of kids, including Bonnie Rogers, Ann and Mary Everett, Theresa Sanchez, Charlene and Aubrey Miller, and Kelly Allbee were there, along with several adults besides Devereaux, including Linda Miller, Kerri Knowles, Donna Rodriguez, Donna Hidalgo, and, once, "a white man with a bald head and glasses" who worked for CPS.

He said he was relegated to the downstairs, where he watched pornographic movies and helped to contain the children. Everyone else went upstairs and then came back at various times. All of the adults and children told him they were having sex upstairs. For his part, Steinborn wasn't invited, although he would doubtless have refused in any case.

Steinborn had every reason to believe he had performed according to the terms of the contract. But, to his chagrin, he found this was not the case. "Both Detective Perez and I told Steinborn that if this was his statement, it would be unacceptable and that any deal with the prosecutor would be void, since it was our belief that he was not being truthful about his own actions," reads Kruse's report. The officers urged him to sign a statement but cautioned, "We further told him that by signing the statement we were not making any promises or threats to him and that he would be charged with the crimes outlined in the warrant filed by the prosecutor's office."

Steinborn was understandably confused, grasping only that he was caught in a contractual squeeze. He went ahead and signed the statement, and indicated to the officers' satisfaction that he understood what he was getting himself into. Perez then sprang the bitter news. Steinborn was about to be booked into the Chelan County Jail under all of the charges described in the arrest warrant—and they were legion.

As an officer came to take him to the jail, he had a sudden burst of memory.

"Steinborn then began disclosing sexual acts he was involved in," as well as details of the acts he'd witnessed, wrote Kruse in his report. Perez and Kruse took down a five-page statement: Steinborn admitted to sex with fifteen children at slumber parties at Miller's home and at the Devereaux home, where he went every week. According to Steinborn, children were told to have sex with each other in a bedroom while the adults watched. Then the adults lined up and took turns having intercourse with the children in an upstairs bedroom. Kruse said Steinborn relaxed and even giggled while he told the story.

Perez and Kruse asked him about the Robersons. Steinborn said he went to the food bank, but he didn't know what went on in the church, and neither of the Robersons came to the Devereaux home. Of course, the church was a Douglas County matter, so the detectives let it go. Statement complete, police booked Steinborn into the Chelan County Jail for multiple counts of child rape.

At this point, Steinborn was highly perplexed about what, if anything, the "deal" was. But months later, on September 25, 1995, Judge Bridges dismissed all eight counts of child rape upon the recommendation of Deputy Prosecutor Roy Fore.

On Monday, April 10, Bob Devereaux went to court to hear a motion on his case, argued by his attorney, Steve Lacy. To his consternation, he learned the prosecutor planned to slam him with additional charges. Devereaux was outraged and called the allegations "ridiculous. The story is impossible, totally impossible."

Although Chelan County Deputy Prosecutor Doug Shae acknowledged the troublesome facts that Miller had recanted her statement and there was a videotape of Kelly Allbee's "coerced" recantation, it turned out that Larry Steinborn, who was arrested the previous Friday, had corroborated the children's stories. He wouldn't yet file a formal complaint, Shae added, because he was looking at statements from two additional children. But beware, for the new charges were on their way.

By now, the children's stories were taking on a sinister, satanic twist that perhaps reflected the evolution of official expectations. On April 10, Jeanne Dierickx interviewed twelve-year-old Charlene Miller at her foster home in Pasco, Washington, over cocoa, coffee, and zucchini bread. In accordance with sound procedure and in response to recent criticism, Dierickx tape-recorded the interview, although this practice would never be pursued with a child witness in neighboring Chelan County, and apparently was never repeated in Douglas County.

Dierickx ran through the usual questions to establish rapport. She asked Charlene if she knew her numbers and colors and the differences between truth or lies. Then Charlene volunteered that Bonnie Rogers used to steal and to "tell lies a lot."

"She used to steal?" queried Dierickx, choosing the safer of the two subjects.

"Yeah."

"Oh."

"She probably still does."

Dierickx moved to safer territory, asking Charlene about her understanding of the concepts of over and under and inside and outside, the difference between good, bad, and private or secret touches, the parts of the body.

"Now," said Dierickx, "has anyone ever talked to you before about touching problems?"

Charlene said her kindergarten teacher discussed the concept with the class.

"So am I the only one who sat down with you and talked to you about touching problems or has there been other people?"

"Not really," said Charlene, who by then had been interviewed several times by Chelan County authorities.

"Not really, okay," said Dierickx, without pursuing Charlene's response. "Well, have you ever had any problems with touching?"

Charlene said she "got molested a couple times," once in Phoenix, Arizona, a long time ago, the other at Bonnie's house on Ramona Street, the foster home of Bob Devereaux, in 1993 or 1994. Devereaux invited some of his friends to the house and "most of them were skinny," except for the fat one she recognized as Larry Steinborn because he'd been married to her mother, she said.

The adults who came to the Devereaux house were "mostly male," and there were "a lot" of them. The touching happened during spring break. Charlene said she and Bonnie and Ann Everett went to the Devereaux house to play and do homework and friends of Devereaux came over around 9 o'clock at night. "They molested me and my friends," she said.

Devereaux's friends got on top of Bonnie and Ann. Once they were on top of them, then "I couldn't see no more 'cause they were wearing black." Their pants were down, but Bonnie usually wore clothes when they were on top of her.

Bonnie was dressed? "That you could see?" asked Dierickx.

"That I could see," Charlene obliged.

"That you could see," Dierickx said, satisfied.

Charlene said she saw this happen about nine times. Nobody said anything. But they did it to all of the girls in the presence of each other. She said she couldn't identify anyone, except Steinborn and then only through his bulk, because everyone was dressed in black and wearing sunglasses.

Dierickx had some difficulty grasping this concept.

"They . . . always wore sunglasses," said Charlene.

"They wore *sunglasses*," responded Dierickx.

"Uh-huh."

"Okay. And then what happened after the person with the sunglasses told you to take off your clothes?" It was easier to swallow if the sunglass-wearer was singular.

Charlene corrected her.

"Okay, so who was the person who had sunglasses on?" persisted Dierickx.

"They *all* had sunglasses on," Charlene insisted.

"They *all* had sunglasses on," Dierickx repeated. "Okay, who was the person who was on top of you, then?"

Charlene didn't know because the room was dark, her eyes were closed, and everyone was unidentifiable in their black clothes and sunglasses.

In fact, she provided few details of what she had experienced except that she had been molested "sexually." In response to Dierickx's strikingly leading question "was there something inside of you? Okay, what do you think that was?" Charlene said, "Andrea calls it a dick." She couldn't remember what it felt like after they were done. They were inside of her in this manner for a "couple minutes."

No one said anything and after they were finished they just left. Despite their black garb and sunglasses and the darkness of the room, she "could see the bulge of their bodies.'' Besides happening on spring break, the incidents happened on weekends. She and the others hadn't told because she heard somebody tell Devereaux, ''Tell those kids if . . . they tell we will kill 'em.'' When she heard her molesters talk among themselves, she concluded, ''It could have been females dressed up as males.''

Charlene said that she and Theresa Sanchez, Ann Everett, and Bonnie Rogers sometimes stayed the night watching movies, mostly not with ''sex scenes'' but with ''funerals.''

Then, she said, ''from what I know from my mom's confession, she was watching.'' From the language of the transcript, one can discern Dierickx's consternation that someone had provided Charlene with Miller's statement before they questioned her. Dierickx asked Charlene how she knew that Linda Miller had confessed. She said that social worker Laurie Alexander told her. ''She said that everything I said was true.''

''Well,'' said Dierickx, ''everything you do tell me is true, I know that. Because I believe you.''

''No,'' said Charlene, ''she said my mom confessed to everything I said.''

Not only had Alexander told her the things her mother had confessed to, she explained, but so had Bob, a ''police officer,'' who was also Ann's foster father. She knew Bob from last year, she said, '' 'cause I got in trouble for lying.'' She explained that, at that time, Bonnie and her sister Aubrey ''wanted to make up a lie'' that Larry Steinborn ''hurt'' them. ''I had to be a part of the lie even though I didn't want to be involved.''

Dierickx clearly became uncomfortable with the interview, which, putting aside the question of credibility, was going over previously trammeled ground. After all, this was to have been an independent investigation. And then there was the fact that providing children with information about what others had said was considered highly suggestive according to the conventional wisdom of sound interview procedures. "What kind of questions did they ask you?" she asked, and then explained, "I don't want to have you talk about the same things that you already talked to them about, because I know that's kind of upsetting."

"So far it's been everything I talked about," said Charlene, not apparently upset.

"Everything you talked about. Okay, well is there anything that . . . you didn't talk about with them that you want to tell me?"

"I don't think there was."

Charlene said the last time she talked to Alexander was "a couple Fridays ago" and Bob the police officer was there, too. Perez and Alexander's interview apparently never rated a police report.

Stung by public criticism, Perez hung back for a time. The investigation continued in a style reminiscent of his own. On April 19, Detective Mike Magnotti and Katie Carrow brought Aubrey Miller to the CPS office and interviewed her for four hours, with "numerous breaks." It is clear from Magnotti's report that Aubrey—despite persistent reminders that other children and adults had named her as a victim—insisted she didn't remember abuse by anyone but Larry Steinborn and Alan Hughes. In fact, Aubrey was "visibly agitated and hesitant to talk."

Magnotti excused himself to go to the bathroom. When he got back, Carrow told him Aubrey had decided she would be more comfortable if he listened in on the intercom and watched behind one-way glass from the adjacent room. The room was fitted for the use of audiovisual equipment, although it was apparently never used for videotaping interviews and CPS supervisor Abbey later told me that the DCFS office contained nothing so much as a tape recorder. In any case, it was a good place to observe an interview.

According to Magnotti's report, Carrow asked "a great many clarifying questions," while "Aubrey frequently took deep breaths, [and] made discouraging noises." To reassure her, "Carrow and I both told Aubrey that we had talked to other children and adults who had mentioned her and now we needed to hear her side of the story." At last, with the help of a line drawing by Carrow, Aubrey said Devereaux, Steinborn, and others had fondled her, Theresa, Bonnie, and Ann, and Devereaux had had intercourse with her.

After Carrow asked what she admitted was a leading question, Aubrey said, "I read in the paper about the sex ring," adding that the paper said people in the church had sex with kids. When Carrow pushed on, "Aubrey again began to exhale strongly, make discouraging noises and again said that she didn't want to talk, that it was hard." After some more encouragement, Aubrey went on to describe things that "mostly I saw."

Connie and Roby Roberson touched her, Kelly, and Roberta, she said. Roberson said if she told, he would kill her.

Go on, urged Carrow.

Aubrey squirmed and wrapped her arms across her chest. People could get in trouble if she said they did something they didn't do, she said.

"He didn't do anything?"

"He touched me," Aubrey said, according to Magnotti's report. While she was lying in bed trying to put her pants on, Roberson came in, pulled down his pants, and "stuck his penis in my private." He told her if she told, she'd go to hell.

"In addition, prior to the main disclosure," Magnotti's

report reads, "Aubrey told us the details of being video-taped at Bob Kinkade's house in East Wenatchee."

Some clue to the depth of official animosity toward Kinkade and VOCAL and its impact on the Miller children lies in Charlene's medical records. On May 2, officials took Charlene to Dr. David Cook of Central Washington Hospital. She had been his patient in the past, along with other family members, and Dr. Cook last saw her two or three years before. "There have been no concerns in the past brought to my attention of possible child abuse and/or child sexual abuse," Cook wrote in his report.

Dr. Cook asked Charlene, who was playing with a "Nintendo-type of device," why she was in his office and involved with CPS. She said they were giving her "in home protection" because "Laurie Alexander doesn't want people to hurt me anymore. . . . There is a mob of people who want to hurt me." Dr. Cook, no doubt assuming Charlene would describe the sex ring, asked about the mob. Charlene said that the people were involved in a group called "VOCAL."

In Charlene's mind or the minds of her protectors, the VOCAL "mob" had supplanted the transgressions of her ongoing molesters. Or perhaps it was put to her that they were her molesters. Charlene, after all, was molested by people wearing sunglasses and black clothes.

As the criticism escalated, officials and child advocates across the state aligned in support of the Chelan and Douglas County prosecutions—politically charged cases of massive embarrassment potential. The official, if unstated, position was that the critics were resorting to dirty tricks like interviewing children, digging up records, and speaking out for guilty people—even those whose guilt had been established in a court of law—because they were in it themselves. The complaints were nothing more than noise, and the noise was merely an audible smokescreen. After all, legal checks and balances were in place.

At the cusp of a brief but potent media frenzy, Wenatchee residents were invited to a taping of a Seattle television show, *Town Meeting,* on April 24 at the Wenatchee Center. Kinkade was there, as outspoken as usual, and identified as always as a formerly accused offender. So was Luci Perez. Purple and yellow ribbons were in abundance.

Panel members Lucy Berliner, a social worker and research director for Harborview Medical Center's Sexual Assault Center in Seattle who has advised and testified for prosecutors across the country in child sex abuse cases, and Rebecca Roe, a Seattle deputy prosecutor specializing in child rape cases, said that they were impressed by the Wenatchee investigations but troubled by the willingness of some community members to believe that authorities and children were lying. Neither explained how they had come by their information.

"To what gain would they make these stories up?" asked Roe. "It's preposterous to think law enforcement gets some sort of charge out of falsely accusing people."

Berliner said that while it would be wrong to question children in a coercive or threatening way, "professionals don't *do* that and to assume that professionals do is what's disheartening . . . that people in this community are divided over their confidence in their own government and the authorities." Berliner later told me she hadn't read the police reports.

Among the critics who were televised was Pentecostal Sunday School teacher and Albertson's bakery shop employee Honnah Sims, a friendly, pleasantly articulate young woman who, everyone agreed, didn't look the part of an abuser. According to Sims, Luci Perez approached her at the conclusion of the meeting and uttered the chilling words, "You're next."

It was very close to the truth. In fact, May 22 marked the date of Sims's arrest. After the initial shock wore off, Honnah and her husband Jonathan used their credit cards to retain Robert Van Siclen, an experienced attorney from the Seattle area.

But Sims wasn't "next." Instead, on May 2, came the arrests of Gary and Scharlann Filbeck. Gary Filbeck, who is totally illiterate, was previously convicted for molesting the couple's daughter. Gary, like Steinborn before him, was offered (and ultimately received) a "deal." Ironically, the cases the Chelan and Douglas County prosecutors were zealously pursuing involved suspects with no previous felony history.

At the end of lengthy and aggressive interrogations by Perez, both confessed. Ever mindful of the critics' concerns, Magnotti sat in on Perez's interviews, took notes that apparently were later destroyed, and then typed the Filbecks' statements.

Although Scharlann's statements were of interest, Gary's elevated the allegations to the realm of Satanic ritual. They started out typically, by Wenatchee standards: episodes of mutual fondling by Harold and Idella Everett, Donna Hidalgo and her husband Manuel Hidalgo-Rodriguez, the Robersons, church van driver Bill Davis, and the Filbecks, at the Everett home. Harold made him do it. Roberson came to the home a few times, and Gary saw Roberson put his hand "up inside" Mary Everett and have intercourse with Mary and Ann. Filbeck himself had sex with the girls and fondled Roberta. Roberson made him do it.

He heard Scharlann talk to Bob Devereaux on the phone, said Filbeck. After she hung up, Scharlann said he was going to come over with some friends and beat them up to stop them from telling what they knew: Devereaux came to the Everetts' and had sex with an older woman and "played with the little ones."

By Wenatchee standards the definition of *played with* was clear and didn't require further elucidation. *Doing it* was another matter. "He did it to them; little Ann and Mary." *Did it,* Filbeck explained, meant "they took their penises and put it in their vaginas." Devereaux brought some other kids and "everybody there would do it to them." The Everett boys were there and Harold did it to them but not Matthew, who had to do it instead to his sisters. Filbeck knew it was wrong, but, "I'm afraid of all of them that came there."

There was a guy who came over, "about your height. He had a beard. He was Tim Abbey." After a response we can but imagine, Filbeck quickly clarified, "He came to talk to Everett, he never had sex with the kids." It was another guy: "This guy worked with Tim Abbey, he had an office in another place. . . . I don't know his name."

There was "a girl with big tits" who got fondled, naturally enough, on the "big tits," and "a little Hispanic boy," with a mother named Pam. Filbeck described orgiastic acts of oral sex while the television was turned up loud, so people wouldn't hear the kids who "would stand there and cry and . . . screamed alot."

After a time the talk turned to the Robersons' church, which, Filbeck explained, he had quit the year before because "I wasn't getting nothing out of the Bible. We also quit," he hastened to add, "because of all the stuff that was happening." There were a bunch of kids downstairs and "everybody took their clothes off and fondled everybody."

Of the events at the church, the most interesting happened during Sunday services. "We used to go in there, in the pews on the main floor and Roby'd get the Bible out and tell everybody to start praying and Roby'd call some little girl up and do it to her.''

Pastor Roberson was ''kneeling with his hands up like the Pentecostals do and he'd take the girls' clothes off and lay them down and do it to them right on the stage. He said that was the way to get the devil out of them. Everybody got excited and they'd start doing it, taking kids up and doing it.'' Personally Filbeck exercised more restraint than the rest. ''I just fondled them, the ones he just got done doing it to.''

''Roby would say, 'Hallelujah, there goes the devil!' He'd pull it out and come all over their vagina. 'That's to wash the devil away.' ''

By this time the results were in from the state patrol crime lab: no semen had been detected at the Pentecostal church. But the discrepency was of little moment because by the time the matter went to trial, Filbeck's story had changed.

19:

Summer–Autumn 1995

═══════

Resolutions

═══════

By the time I settled into Wenatchee life in June 1995, the problem of witness recantations was epidemic. Nearly every adult and the few children who weren't tightly contained by state agents recanted their statements within days of making them. Nothing induced most adults to testify, not even coercive state laws.

Several years back, Washington State enacted the Special Sexual Offender Sentencing Alternative (SSOSA), which offers qualified criminal defendants the opportunity of a suspended sentence and community-based sexual deviancy therapy in lieu of most or all of their prison sentences. To qualify, a defendant has to admit he's an offender. Clearly the price of denial is high: Many Wenatchee defendants who received sentences between twenty and forty years could have avoided prison altogether. In Wenatchee another option to prison was to turn on friends, neighbors, and relatives and agree to testify. Again, there were almost no takers.

Among them was previously convicted child molester Gary Filbeck. In late May, Filbeck took advantage of his "deal" by pleading to a single count of second-degree assault. In exchange for his promise to testify against several defendants, prosecutor Gary Riesen recommended an exceptionally low sentence of twelve months, less credit for time served. Filbeck, unable to work, could spend the time in the comparative freedom of work release. Riesen justified the sentence to Judge Carol Wardell: The man was at risk in prison if he rolled over on others; his "conduct, although serious, has been less serious than the others involved."

The argument wasn't very convincing, but after all, nobody who was familiar with the workings of the judicial system was convinced that a "deal" became an approximation of truth merely because it was sanctioned by the court. Judge Wardell grimaced but put aside her concerns for community safety and gamely accepted the plea and Riesen's recommendation that Filbeck be released pending his testimony and eventual sentencing. In Wenatchee, one had to go the extra mile when it came to adult corroborating witnesses.

"I just know that now that Mr. Filbeck has pleaded guilty, he's in a position where he won't invoke the Fifth Amendment," said Riesen. "That means he's available by subpoena of the state to testify on other cases, but I don't know how that will affect those cases."

Riesen had high hopes. Already Filbeck was subpoenaed to testify at the upcoming trials of Donna Hidalgo and her husband Manuel Hidalgo-Rodriguez. And then there would be the Miller trial, and the Knowles trial, and the Devereaux trial, and the Sims trial, and the Davis trial, and the Roberson trial. Douglas County didn't plan to charge Filbeck for his crimes in their county, as long as he came through as a witness.

Scharlann Filbeck pleaded guilty and was released to the community under a similar arrangement. But, in her case, Riesen's plan failed.

In late June, Cherie Greenfield called me. Greenfield was a former rape counselor and current chair of the Concerned Citizens for Legal Accountability (CCLA), a Wenatchee grassroots group critical of the prosecutions, and she considered herself a friend of Tim Abbey but also of Paul Glassen. I had met her once: She had a fall of shiny brown hair and a distraught manner that, she admitted to me, came from her highly conflicted affiliations. This time, she was barely able to contain the excitement in her voice: Scharlann Filbeck was released from jail pending testimony and sentencing. She wanted to talk to someone. Would I be interested?

Sure, I said, although I was not at all certain what I was getting into. Greenfield offered to lend me her camcorder and to give me enough information to set up an interview. There was one string attached: She wanted a copy of the videotape to store for safekeeping. She wouldn't come along because she might get charged with something, she said.

Scharlann was staying at the home of her parents in a suburb of Yakima—an hour away from Wenatchee and out of harm's way in the minds of Wenatchee officials. We sat in a tiny living room: The chairs and couches were draped with spreads; a clock intricately housed in needlepoint stood in the place of honor under the room's largest window. ''Scharlann made that,'' said her mother proudly. In another room, a dog yapped incessantly.

Scharlann looked sixty but she was thirty-nine, toothless, gaunt, and stringy-haired from poverty or desolation or the loss of forty pounds in jail. She said she'd been in special education classes for most of her school years and when she dropped out in her teens she was able to read at the third- or fourth-grade level. She was taking a course of antipsychotic medication for depression, and prescription drugs for recurring migraine headaches. Yet all in all she was better off than Gary: a dyslexic who couldn't read or write, had been a special education student all through school, and now was working out problems as a sex offender. She and Gary were desperately poor.

Years before, Gary Filbeck was convicted of molesting their daughter Caroline Hunter, who was now twenty; after that Caroline lived for years as a foster child in the Devereaux home. Now Detective Bob Perez was "harassing" her to accuse Devereaux of molesting her, Caroline told her mother. Perez and CPS caseworkers, "kept coming to her house day and night, waking them up in the middle of the night," said Scharlann. Caroline said that over the course of the last year when she and other Devereaux foster children were walking, Perez sometimes followed in his car and hounded them to turn on their foster father. At last she appeared on KREM 2 television, where she described Perez's actions and said she hadn't seen anything unusual in Devereaux's home.

Scharlann watched the television clip with Caroline at her daughter's home one day in April of 1995. Caroline, who had herself been in special education all her life, seemed very afraid of Perez and warned her mother that the detective might come after her next. "She figured that if they couldn't get to her, then they could get to me and her dad," Scharlann told me.

On May 2, Scharlann had just returned from the pharmacy with her migraine medication when she heard vehicles pull up in the driveway of a neighbor's home. Detectives Perez and Magnotti and a Douglas County deputy sheriff strolled toward her house. Before she had time to take her pills, police forced her and Gary into separate police cars and then drove them to the Wenatchee police station. By the time she arrived at 11:45 A.M., Scharlann was rocked by a migraine, in tears and desperately confused. An hour into his interrogation, Perez made arrangements for her to get her medicine, but after she took it she was "groggy and. . . . out of it."

Perez sat on her right and Magnotti on her left at another desk; yet Perez asked nearly all the questions, she said. She told me Perez had a red book sitting on his desk and he lifted up pages and named adults and children on the pages who had said she'd had sex with kids. When she denied it, Perez said she was a liar. Perez said he knew these things were true and she'd better admit it or she would get "a hundred to a hundred fifty years," said Scharlann. He told her she'd be killed if she went to prison, she said. "It was like a beast standing there over me, frightening me."

Perez promised to go easy on her if she confessed, otherwise "he would go ahead and put me in a jury trial and . . . I would be hung," she said. Scharlann, whose IQ is in the mid-70s, believed she could indeed get the death penalty for child rape. Because she was confused and not responsive, Perez became increasingly angry and called her "stupid," "retarded," and "mentally ill," she said. When he said this, "Mike Magnotti asked him to get out of the room and take a coffee break." When he left the room, Magnotti told Scharlann that "he was apologizing for Perez. And I said, 'I don't want no apology by you. I want an apology . . . from Perez.' "

It didn't come. When he returned, the harsh interrogation resumed. Nearly seven hours after the interview began, Scharlann broke down and signed a confession.

I interviewed her on June 23 and returned four days later when I finally got my hands on copies of the police reports. By my second interview it was clear I was immersed in a highly volatile situation: Scharlann Filbeck was a key adult corroborating witness to the high-profile cases of Devereaux and the Robersons—and she had already pleaded guilty and was awaiting sentencing tied in to her agreement to testify.

She recanted to me her signed statements about child abuse almost in their entirety. According to her confession, she said Harold Everett made her put her hands inside Ann, and forced her, Devereaux, Paul from CPS, and others to have group sex with kids two or three times a week for around four years. Everett told everybody what to do, except "Harold didn't force this Paul guy 'cause he could take care of himself."

Perez urged her to respond to the question of critics: Why had everyone kept silent for so long? People had threatened her, she said. Donna Hidalgo "told me to lie for her in court. . . . Kerri Knowles also, before she was arrested, told me that if I said anything, she'd kill me." Bob Devereaux "threatened me on the phone about a couple of months before he was arrested. He told me that if I told he'd see me put away for years."

Strangely, only Magnotti later signed her statement as a witness.

Scharlann also recanted to me most of what she had said to Douglas County Sheriff's Detectives Doug Helvey and Tom Couey on May 11 about activities at the Roberson church: that Roberson had called two or three children to the front of the church to sing during services, and then fondled them.

A couple of subpoenas stared at me from the coffee table: Filbeck was a critical government witness in trials that stretched interminably over the weeks to come. She couldn't go through with the "deal" she'd worked out with the prosecutor because she had to testify to "lies," she said, mopping at her eyes with shaking hands. If she didn't, her plea agreement would be yanked away. The prospect of turning on others to save her skin was untenable, but so was the prospect of prison. The events unfolded in a bewildering way and now she was trapped in the kind of moral dilemma we like to believe we left behind in Salem in 1692. "They're just throwing me away," she said.

What was I to do with this critical witness recantation at the heart of ongoing, high-profile prosecutions? There was no attorney-client privilege; I made it clear that I was not, nor would I ever be, Scharlann's lawyer. But if I wrote about it or even told anyone, wasn't I hanging her out to dry? In the end, I decided the decision to publicly recant had to be hers alone.

Who knew about the interviews? I wondered. If the Wenatchee government found out about her recantation, tried to shut me up, charge me with a crime like witness tampering, and seize my records, Scharlann and her plea bargain were at risk. So was I. I took very seriously what I saw to be stunning evidence of retaliation against people like me: people who spoke out (like Kinkade), investigated (like Roberson), or merely did their job (like Glassen). I decided to store the tapes with someone who might give them, me, and my source some measure of political protection.

When I first arrived in Wenatchee, someone had given me the card of Washington State Representative Val Stevens, a Republican from Snohomish County who had been outspokenly concerned about the government's activities in Wenatchee. Now I called Stevens and she agreed to store copies of the tapes and not disseminate them.

I had also agreed to store a copy of the first tape with Cherie Greenfield as a condition of the interview. I was uneasy, but Greenfield promised she wouldn't show it to anyone. Instead, within hours she and CCLA members copied and passed out videotapes to several Wenatchee residents—a fact that immediately came to the attention of Devereaux's attorney and prosecutors. By the time I heard about it, the tape was propagating at an alarming rate. I called Scharlann's father, who said a cop and a prosecutor had dropped in on Scharlann after our interview; they were angry and Scharlann was scared. I called Greenfield, who first denied she'd passed out the tape and then explained her dangerous logic: Devereaux, Glassen, and the Robersons were more deserving than Scharlann Filbeck.

In July I was subpoenaed by defense attorney Steve Lacy to appear at a motion to dismiss the Devereaux case, and ordered to bring the Scharlann Filbeck videotapes. Sitting on the witness hotseat beneath Judge Small, who showed no sign of warming to me, before a couple of prosecutors who beamed me hostile stares, across the courtroom from Perez and Tim Abbey, I knew I had well and truly run afoul of the Wenatchee government.

I testified that Scharlann understood the videotapes would remain confidential except for journalistic purposes. I said the videotapes were privileged by something "akin to a journalistic privilege." My words sounded unconvincing, even to me, because I hadn't reconciled myself to the need to hire an attorney and had only the vaguest notion of the body of privilege law which, as it applies to journalists, isn't even defined by statute in Washington.

Chelan County prosecutors Doug Shae and Roy Fore made it clear that my meddlesome behaviors were reprehensible. Wasn't I an officer of the court? The truth was, I wasn't sure. Was I an officer of the court for all intents and purposes even when I wasn't acting as a lawyer but as a journalist? What were the implications anyway—that lawyers aren't supposed to criticize the sometimes dubious functionings of the legal system under any circumstances? That lawyers are too ethical to be journalists?

Judge Small resolved the matter. If he'd known I was also a lawyer, he wouldn't have sworn me in because "you are an officer of the court until such point as you are disbarred."

The room tilted. Small ordered me to hand over the tapes and I quickly complied. At the time, in an emotionally charged Wenatchee courtroom, under the malevolent glares of the judge and two angry prosecutors, it never occurred to me to risk contempt of court in defense of Scharlann Filbeck, a fact for which I take no pride.

The worst of my fears were never realized: Scharlann wasn't called upon to testify, although she was subpoenaed at the Roberson and other trials. Douglas County sheriffs did not pursue charges against her and Chelan County recommended, and Scharlann received, a reduced sentence and community-based treatment. After a time, she was allowed to live in a community outside Wenatchee with Gary Filbeck, her husband of twenty-one years, who by then had received the benefit of his plea bargain. I wasn't arrested, although Chelan County prosecutors knocked around the idea of charging me.

With the release of the Scharlann Filbeck tapes, the case against Robert Devereaux began to collapse. The charges against Devereaux were amended after the Filbecks' arrest, to reflect the statements of a growing number of children and adults. Devereaux was rearrested on 335 counts of child rape, 335 counts of child molestation, and charges of intimidating a witness (the Filbecks). But in July, faced with the Scharlann Filbeck tapes, growing witness recantations, former foster kids who came forward voluntarily to say nothing had happened, and Devereaux's feisty lawyer, Chelan County prosecutors dismissed all felony counts against Devereaux in exchange for his guilty plea to misdemeanor assault (for spanking a child in his care) and misdemeanor obstructing justice (for warning someone that he might be arrested).

Devereaux talked to me before court at a time when he was torn with feelings of relief and guilt. He was afraid that a guilty plea, even to nominal offenses, would have a ripple effect on pending prosecutions and that he had sold out. Not according to my dim view of the legal system in Wenatchee. With the best of defenses, a trial is a gamble; in this case the stakes pitted a potential life sentence against the prosecutor's recommendation of no jail time. Up to now no defendant who went to trial on the sex cases had been acquitted; judges typically ruled adversely to the defense in trial and pretrial motions, and many community members were expressing dissatisfaction with the minimal checks and balances at the trial level. The plea bargain ensured Devereaux's freedom—which, however, was small consolation to him. "I've lost everything anyway, my house, my retirement, my livelihood, my reputation," he said. Devereaux settled for a measure of freedom, moved into a tiny house outside of Wenatchee, got a job in a gas station/convenience store, and made a new start at the age of fifty-eight.

Also in July, Judge Bridges permitted Douglas County prosecutors to amend the charges against Pentecostal Sunday School teacher Honnah Sims on the very eve of trial—extending the time frame when the crimes were said to take place by a matter of months because otherwise she had an alibi. Her attorney, Robert Van Siclen, described the ploy as trial by ambush. But Sim's pretrial hearing revealed much about the state's witnesses.

Bonnie Rogers testified at the pretrial hearing that Perez interviewed her two or three times and her caseworker talked to her "more times than I can count" about what Devereaux did to her over the five and a half years that she lived as his foster child. She said her "mother" (foster mother Debi Cawdery) started taking notes and then encouraged her to keep a journal "about being raped." She admitted that she'd told lies that people had sexually abused her, including a threat to accuse Pete Cawdery, her current foster father, because she was "angry." Bonnie admitted "it's very possible" that she had made other false allegations. She said that she "has a tendency" to make false allegations. "Sometimes I say things I don't mean."

Also at the pretrial hearing Ann Everett said her sister Mary, also a key state witness, now lived with her at the Perez home. The Perezes had a swimming pool and lots of pets, including a dog, cats, chickens, and turkeys, said Ann. She, Mary, and Bob and Luci Perez had just come back from Disneyland, where they went on "Splash Mountain" and "lots of rides."

Thirty miles from Wenatchee, the courthouse is probably the only three-story structure in Waterville, county seat of Douglas County. The building stands proudly—a prim white-painted stone edifice—on a side street blocks from the tiny business district. On July 26, the first day of Honnah Sims's trial, Sims's supporters crammed the polished wooden benches and spoke in low voices before the trial began. I sat in the no-man's-land populated by prosecutors and police and caseworkers and Perez supporters, and watched Sims.

She was huddled with her lawyer, smiling at her well-wishers in a way that almost convinced them she was okay. That Sims could feel okay was hard to imagine: She faced one count of first-degree child rape, one count of first-degree child molestation, two counts of second-degree child rape, and two counts of second-degree child molestation, crimes carrying a standard range sentence which, at its high end, was well over twenty years, and even the possibility of a life sentence, should she receive an exceptional sentence.

After the opening statements, thirteen-year-old Bonnie Rogers testified that Sims had raped her in the small church bathroom during services by sticking an object inside her that "hurt really, really bad." Afterward Sims told her she or her foster family would be hurt or even killed if she told anyone what happened.

On cross-examination, Van Siclen questioned Bonnie about her journal, which Bonnie called her "rape book." She said that her therapist had recommended that she keep the journal. The book didn't mention Honnah Sims.

"I didn't keep it for that," she said. "I kept it for Devereaux."

Bonnie added that sometimes the book included things that weren't true. "I lied," she said. "People were pressuring me." She said that she didn't know why she hadn't told Perez about Sims when he questioned her about Devereaux.

The next day, Ann Everett took the stand. She hugged her large gray and purple "Flying Purple Kid Saver" teddy bear to her face and sat with her back to the judge and her face concealed from Sims and her attorney. She spoke softly into a microphone held by Jeannie Dierickx, who stood at her side.

Sometimes after church services Pastor Roberson had told the adults and children to go downstairs to the basement for sex, she said. Roberson made everyone take their clothes off and put them in the corner. "Then they would touch us." Ann said up to sixty adults and fifty children went to the church on Fridays, although the sexual activities usually involved about twenty adults and twenty children. The women penetrated her with their fingers and the men "put their private inside my private," and then moved up and down on her. On cross-examination she said she couldn't remember what a man's "private" looked like.

When called to the stand, Mary Everett refused to testify.

Douglas County Sheriff's Detective Doug Helvey said he had only investigated between five and fifteen child abuse cases, none as complex as the alleged sex ring. He said he allowed one alleged child victim to be present while he interviewed another (Ann and Mary Everett), but this happened before his training. In hindsight, he said, it had been a mistake, not in accordance with proper interview techniques.

Van Siclen held up a book that Helvey had received as part of a forty-hour training program in sex abuse investigations. The spine was barely creased.

"Did you even read this?

"I skimmed through the books," said Helvey, "but I haven't read through the whole thing."

Was it strange that Ann Everett was interviewed so many times, usually by her foster father? "I thought it was unusual," said Helvey. "But nothing has been shown to me . . . that would lead me to think he [Perez] did anything unusual. . . . I have not investigated Detective Perez at all."

After Helvey stepped down, deputy prosecutor Frank Jenny called Linda Miller to the stand, although she had long since recanted her statements. Tearfully, she told the jury that she lied because she was coerced by Perez to make and then sign a false statement. Jenny called several cops to the witness stand in an effort to impeach her. Van Siclen objected and accused the deputy prosecutor of trying to "poison the jury's mind" by impeaching his own witness. Bridges overruled the objection, allowing the officers to testify about the confession and Miller's demeanor, and to read the contents of her long, detailed, and graphic statement, which implicated Sims.

The following week, after the prosecution rested its

case, Van Siclen paraded in nine Pentecostal church members, who all said that they'd seen nothing unusual at the church. Among them was Bill Davis, who himself was arrested in April for raping and molesting Ann Everett and Bonnie Rogers. Davis said he went to the Robersons' church every week on Wednesdays, Fridays, and twice on Sundays from the summer of 1991 until the Robersons' arrest, and never saw any sexual activity. "The doors to the church are always open. If something like that was going on, it would have been pretty obvious."

A woman said the church had strict rules about modesty and little girls had to wear dresses with high necklines. A man said he'd invited a specialist from Deaconess Hospital in Spokane to interview his children about their involvement with the church; the hospital submitted a report to the Douglas County Sheriff's Office.

Roberson talked about his church and the food bank in its basement and his practice of giving food to local church camps and youth groups. In tears, he said he didn't know why the children of his congregation had made accusations against him. Connie was similarly mystified. Honnah's husband John Sims had no better explanation. "We felt the work going on at the church was really important. . . . The pastor seemed to be somebody that was like us . . . a hardworking person that we could relate to," said John Sims.

Robert Devereaux testified about his observations of Bonnie Rogers, who was his foster child for four and a half years, and Ann Everett, who was his foster child for about six months. Bonnie was very aggressive toward the other children in his home, he said. Ann was emotionally disturbed: She screamed so much that she permanently damaged her vocal cords. Both girls wanted to attend the Pentecostal church. Ann sometimes became violent when he occasionally restricted her from going. "Once she bit

me,'' said Devereaux. Bonnie often threatened to leave
the Devereaux home and have the church van pick her up
at someone else's home.

Bonnie's counselor, Lynn Madsen, testified that Bonnie
was a diabetic who had been sexually abused as a very
young child and then abandoned by her family. She had
been bribed with candy by her abusers. This history taught
her to be manipulative and to use tricks to get what she
wanted, he said. ''When she was under a great deal of
stress, she would often make sexual threats,'' he said. As
a matter of fact, said Madsen, Bonnie sometimes threatened to accuse him of sexually abusing her, especially at
times when he wouldn't let her use markers or sit beside
him during counseling sessions. One time she asked if the
kids he counseled would get the toys in his office if he
got fired, then implied she could get him fired by falsely
accusing him of sexually abusing her, he said.

Dr. Philip Esplin, an Arizona psychologist who spe-
cializes in international research on child witnesses, testifed that an investigation in which a foster parent probed
crimes involving his or her foster child would be ''fun-
damentally flawed, unwise, and dangerous.'' People with
an emotional investment in an investigation ''are not neutral and not emotionally detached. It's very important for
an investigator to have a neutral position,'' said Esplin.

He criticized the concept of multiple child interviews.
Repeated interviews send a message to a child that what
he or she said in the past is insufficient or incorrect, he
said. Children may then add false or misleading information to please the interviewer. Esplin said that interviewers should guard against preconceived notions that
the crimes occurred. Even the use of words like ''I know
this is hard for you to talk about'' might lead children to
think the questioner believes something bad had happened.

A witness should never be questioned in the presence of another witness, he said. Whenever possible, interviews with children should be recorded, so that investigators might analyze a child's statements over time to see if they have changed, he said. Special care should be taken when dealing with children suffering from physical and emotional problems.

Honnah Sims was the last witness. In a floral dress and a lacy sweater, her brown hair swept back in waves around her face, Sims looked like a Sunday School teacher. She looked at the jury as she denied her guilt, then her mouth crumpled.

On Friday, July 28, the case went to the jury. Within three hours the jury was back. As they filed past Sims on their way to the jury box, some smiled at her. She began sobbing as the verdicts were read. At the end of the fifth verdict of "not guilty," John Sims vaulted from his front row bench and yelled, "Yes!" Honnah Sims stood, turned, and clung to John as the sixth and final verdict of "not guilty" was read. Supporters sprang to their feet, yelled "Yes," and applauded.

John Sims told the *Wenatchee World* after the verdict, "It's a tragedy [the girls] had to get on the stand and say this stuff that's not true." He spoke bitterly of the trial. "When we got up this morning, we didn't think about tomorrow. It was an interesting trial. Too bad we were involved in it."

In contrast to John Sims's restraint, the jury appeared outraged. "I'm really insulted as a citizen of Douglas County to have this thing brought to trial and to spend the taxpayers' money with the kind of evidence that was brought to court to prosecute these people," said Karl Ohler, foreman of the Honnah Sims jury to the Associated Press. Juror Danny McGregor described the police investigation as a "witch hunt." Said McGregor, "It's like somebody spit out some names, and they went out arresting people. I can't believe it went to trial because when the prosecution ended, we were sitting there and I didn't see [anything] yet.''

In fact, some of the jurors called for an outside investigation of the prosecutions. Ohler told the *Wenatchee World,* ''I feel the citizens of the Greater Wenatchee area are not safe with the sort of police actions involved in this particular situation. It makes me wonder how many other people are sitting in jail or have to spend a lot of money and time to defend themselves who haven't done anything wrong.''

When I interviewed him a few days later, Ohler, an electronics technician who formerly worked for the Spokane School District, said, ''The whole thing reeks. I felt sorry for the kids. It's not good for their psychological well-being. How can they live a normal life after this investigation?'' He said he was also concerned about the people who had pleaded guilty or been convicted at trial as a result of Perez's investigations, people who, according to Ohler, were treated as ''disposable people.''

Ohler said the jurors were very concerned about Ann residing in the Perez home. ''It's obviously a conflict of interest.'' Because of the conflict and because of Bonnie's admitted past false accusations the children had little or no credibility, he said. In his opinion, ''videotapes should be standard procedure.'' He was astonished about other things that spoke to the absence of evidence, such as the extensive testimony and graphics concerning the investigation and testing by the Washington State Patrol Crime Lab, which revealed no semen or other evidence.

Yet, said Ohler, some of the jurors had reservations about making a finding of ''not guilty'' on all counts. One of the jurors said, ''She's done something or she wouldn't be here." He admitted that "it's hard to not feel that way in a child abuse case."

Ohler was pleased the jury overcame this bias but feared there would be consequences for his speaking out after the verdict. He said he often finds himself "looking for cops," and that he "feels it's a possibility" that he might find himself charged with something or "end up in some kind of accident."

In the days that followed, Chelan and Douglas County prosecutors tried to reassure area residents that their remaining cases were on solid ground. Clem was philosophical because the jurors had, after all, merely found reasonable doubt. "Just because you have a weak case [that] doesn't mean you don't charge."

Perhaps the solution was a change of players: Douglas County deputy prosecuting attorney Frank Jenny left his position with the prosecutor's office and moved out of town immediately after the Sims trial.

"It's kind of a red flag to the community that not everything is exactly as we've been told it was," said Cherie Greenfield of the Sims trial. Greenfield was among CCLA members who, on July 24, presented a petition with approximately two thousand signatures to the three Chelan County commissioners—Tom Green, John Wall, and Earl Marcellus—calling for an outside investigation. The commissioners agreed to support the request, but emphasized that they weren't themselves accusing any investigators of wrongdoing or criticizing their investigative procedure. "But when you have a petition with 2,000 signatures, that indicates a lot of people are concerned," said Wall to the *Wenatchee World*. "And if it takes an investigation to either justify or dispel those concerns, I think that would be appropriate."

The commissioners sent a one-paragraph letter to Washington State Attorney General Christine Gregoire, the Chelan County Superior Court judges, and prosecutor Gary Riesen, requesting review of the petitions, "so that you may give serious concern to the request of the petitioners." Among the requests of the petitioners was consideration of convening a twelve-member state grand jury to investigate evidence of possible criminal activity or corruption by Wenatchee and Chelan County officials.

Douglas County commissioners refused to support an inquiry. Confronted with the CCLA petition, Commissioners Brian Maydole and Jay Weber said that the most they could do was apply political pressure for an investigation, and they refused this remedy. "I'm not saying the request is illegitimate," said Weber, but added that it was improper for his office to push for an independent investigation. "It will not serve justice," Weber said. "It should go to the people whose job it is to handle that."

Maydole said that the "independently elected officials," such as the Superior Court judges, the prosecutors, and the sheriffs, should be the ones to determine the need for an independent investigation. "That's how we view the process," said Maydole, illogically. He added that the commissioners decided that to pass on the petitions "to the powers to investigate would be giving tacit approval that an investigation is warranted. None of them have given any facts or reasons why an investigation is warranted."

"They said I did a good job of tampering [with] the jury pool," said Greenfield of her meeting with the Douglas County commissioners. "I don't understand why they refuse an investigation. It has the air of hiding something."

To no one's surprise, the efforts to launch an investigation at either local county level became lost in the political process of buck-passing, avoidance, and good intentions, and nothing came of them.

Among those who were disappointed was Chelan County Commissioner Earl Marcellus. Marcellus was sensitive to the plight of some of the defendants because he knew firsthand the vulnerability associated with mental retardation. His daughter Jennifer, twenty-two, has Down's syndrome and is highly susceptible to pressure, he said. "She will say anything you want her to admit to."

But it was Marcellus's mostly business acquaintance with Roberson that led him to doubt the propriety of the investigations. "Roby contacted me late in January or early February," and then "numerous times" after the Everetts and other members of his congregation had been charged. "He wanted me to do something," said Marcellus. "But I turned a deaf ear for a couple of reasons. I was brand new on a challenging job [as County Commissioner] and I was buried. And if there were that many people and that many charges, there had to be some truth to it."

Yet he told me he had lingering worries that multiplied after he met with Representative Val Stevens and Spokane television reporter Tom Grant on separate occasions. The issues were real, and "they were issues no one would touch." Immediately he perceived that it was a political "no-win situation." The crime of child molestation "is so heinous and repulsive to society that if you give the appearance of coming out on the side of alleged abusers you're looking at immediate political suicide."

Marcellus considered himself tough on crime. "Molestation is a deplorable crime, but for innocent people to go to jail is equally deplorable." He decided he needed to act on his concerns as a matter of professional ethics. "I don't view myself as a politician but a representative of the people," he said. "When I was sworn into office I was sworn to protect individual rights. According to the

Washington State Constitution, all political power is inherent in the people.''

But he was careful, preferring to work behind the scenes. ''I tried to keep my head down.'' It wasn't easy. For one thing, there was what he perceived as an absence of governmental accountability. ''I was appalled at the lack of objectivity and the entrenched power base within the Wenatchee government,'' he said.

Marcellus became increasingly critical of Wenatchee officials, even speaking out to the media. At the same time he became proportionately worried about official reprisals, loss of business relationships—even the possibility of someone running him off the road.

The Concerned Citizens for Legal Accountability worried about Manuel Hidalgo-Rodriguez's upcoming trial. After all, in every Chelan County case in which a defendant was convicted of a felony, he or she was represented by a public defender, and every trial in Chelan County had led to a conviction. As the trial began, it became evident that there was cause for concern: The judge permitted the prosecutor to amend the information on the eve of trial. A new alleged victim, Ann Everett, was added; the defense attorney had no additional time to prepare for the new evidence.

Hidalgo-Rodriguez, thirty-six, a bulky farm laborer with a bushy mustache, spoke only broken English. The first day of trial, he responded angrily to the proceedings, calling the arguments lies or gesturing angrily at Perez or Magnotti. After Judge Carol Wardell threatened to throw him out, the man sat sullenly, his eyes shifting between his attorney, Edward Stevensen, and his interpreter. ''Pardon my client if he shows a little anger and frustration,'' said Stevensen to the jury during his opening statement. ''You'll notice Mr. Hidalgo is an angry man. He's been sitting in jail for a while and he feels falsely charged. . . . Please wait to hear both sides before you decide whether to convict.''

Riesen set the jury straight on the fact that they had nothing in common with Hidalgo-Rodriguez. ''The house on Cashmere Street [the Everett home where many of the alleged rapes took place] was a little white house, but it was not a little white house where things were nice and life was good.''

Perez testified that Mary Everett, also a witness in the case, came to live with him and his wife in June. The relationship was approved by his boss, Wenatchee Police Chief Ken Badgley, said Perez. ''I was the only [sex crimes] investigator in the department, so I was assigned to the case,'' he said. ''My chief told me to continue my work but keep in regular contact with him and CPS.''

''I have no questions,'' responded Stevensen when it came time to cross-examine Perez.

Bob and Luci Perez sat in the courtroom, watching their foster children testify, on the second day of the two-and-a-half-day trial. Unabashedly, Perez encouraged the girls as they testified, sometimes giving them the thumbs-up sign. His wasn't their only encouragement: Katie Carrow stood close beside the girls as they testified, sometimes holding their hands. Stevensen conducted only limited cross-examination, revealing that the girls' statements had been inconsistent and lacking in detail.

Harold Everett had forced him to molest the children, Gary Filbeck said in a monotone when he took the stand. Gary said he and his wife Scharlann returned frequently to the Everett home despite Harold's threats to them and that he saw Hidalgo-Rodriguez molest children. Although he said that he entered into a guilty plea and agreed to testify in exchange for a lighter sentence, he answered no when Riesen asked him, "You're not telling a lie to get a better deal for yourself?"

In midtrial, alarmed by what they perceived as inadequate defense representation, CCLA representatives shopped around and presented Judge Wardell with a letter from an attorney who said that he would represent Hidalgo-Rodriguez if the matter were continued for two weeks. CCLA members Connie and Mario Fry told Judge Wardell they would put up $10,000 of their own money to pay for the legal representation.

"Where is this attorney?" snapped Wardell. "I don't see him in this courtroom." She said that she saw no basis to continue the trial and no need for a change of attorney, and ordered that the trial resume.

The next day, the jury convicted Hidalgo-Rodriguez of a single count of child molestation. The count was the one involving Ann Everett, that was added by amended information immediately before trial. Although jurors had trouble with the credibility of the child witnesses, the deciding factor was the testimony of Gary Filbeck, they said.

Despite his volatility at the beginning of the trial, Hidalgo-Rodriguez sat impassively with his arms folded across his chest as the jury read the verdict. The man had cause for despair: His attorney discouraged him from taking the stand, did limited cross-examination, and called few witnesses, none of them experts. Within a couple of days of the conclusion of the trial, Hidalgo-Rodriguez's attorney, Ed Stevensen, went to work for the Chelan County Prosecutor's Office.

At his sentencing, Hidalgo-Rodriguez said, through an interpreter, "They think I'm guilty of something I didn't do. . . . The only problem was I lived there. If I hadn't lived there this wouldn't have happened." Judge Carol

Wardell sentenced him to approximately five years in prison.[1]

After the sentencing, I stood in the hallway not ten feet from Perez and a cluster of social workers. Chuckling, Perez loudly remarked, "There's nothing I like more than watching perverts get sentenced."

Perez, no doubt, was highly pleased when Linda Miller went to trial in mid-September, with her detailed confession admissible against her. Miller was found guilty on all eight counts of first-degree child molestation. Caseworkers, cops, and critics gathered in the courtroom to hear the verdict, and reacted with unrestrained joy when it came. The cops and caseworkers were even more jubilant when Miller received an exceptional sentence of thirty-three years.[2] As with every victory, the verdict was perceived by Wenatchee officials as a total vindication.

---

[1] The conviction of Manuel Hidalgo-Rodriguez was upheld by the Washington State Court of Appeals in the spring of 1997. His appellate attorney, a former partner of Hidalgo-Rodriguez's trial attorney, did not raise such critical issues as the eleventh-hour amended information, Perez's relationship with his foster daughter, or ineffective assistance of counsel.

[2] In June 1997, Linda Miller's conviction was overturned and the case was remanded for a new trial by the Washington State Court of Appeals, based on abuse of judicial discretion in refusing to provide state funding for an expert witness on coerced confessions [Dr. Richard Ofshe], and refusing to permit the testimony of rebuttal witnesses.

20:

Autumn–Winter 1995

The Outsiders

In the fall, Ann Everett's behavior became the barometer for the rise and fall of the state's trial successes. In September, on the Friday before she was expected to testify against her half-sister Donna Hidalgo, she had another tantrum—one of those emotional firestorms in which she screamed and yelled and heaved things around the house. Perez had the eleven-year-old arrested for malicious mischief, the Chelan County prosecutor filed criminal charges, and Ann did a stint in juvenile detention. When she was released, she was hauled off to a respite foster home. Immediately after she testified against Hidalgo, she was returned to the Perez home and the only things that promised her any stability in her chaotic world: her sister, her room full of toys, and two adults who doted on her words.

Next up was Kerri Knowles. "The allegations have come out of Perez's warped mind," Knowles said to *Wenatchee World.* But she was philosophical. "I'm a survivor. I'll never say I'm guilty because I'm not and if the jury doesn't believe me I'll go to jail. I'm ready because God has a purpose for me. I know that."

On the eve of Knowles's trial, Ann had another tantrum, just as she had before she testified against Hidalgo. The case was delayed and the prosecutor recommended that Knowles be released from jail. Although this time Ann wasn't arrested, deputy prosecutor Roy Fore said he was worried the trials were taking their toll on the girl.

Fore wasn't worried about her testimony. "She's not recanted—recantation is not a concern for us—and the last word I heard is that she wants to testify," said Fore. "But I asked to delay the trial to basically find out if we're asking this child to do more than she's able to do. We want to get together—the prosecutors, CPS, police— and ask, 'Is it worth it?' In some ways calling a kid as a witness is just victimizing them all over again . . . and it's not worth harming her any more."

Perez agreed. "People never think about the kids in these cases or how all this has affected them. This investigation at the police end is closed—I have no more suspects to interview—but this will never be over for these kids, and if it means we consider a child's welfare over sending people away, I say let them go and dismiss the case."

Chelan County prosecutors had their first opportunity to put Perez's statement to the test with the trial of Susan Everett, niece of Harold Everett. Susan's was one of the most recent Wenatchee arrests. On September 5 at the Chelan County Jail shortly after her arrest, she retracted her confession to me for the first time. She said that Perez came to the house in Grandview, Washington, where she was staying with her sister Karen Lopez. Perez and the Grandview police officer who was with him were looking for Lopez, but Susan was handy and cousin to Perez's foster daughters, so he took her in as well.

Susan Everett (who has only a ninth-grade education, was on medication and under psychiatric care, and was recently hospitalized because of the death of her infant daughter) said that Perez then questioned her for four hours. He listed children and said she molested them; when she denied it, Perez called her a liar and yelled at her, she said. He said that he would personally help her if she confessed, and see that she got over thirty years if she didn't, she said. He took no notes, but started to type during the course of the interview. When at last she "confessed" and Perez finished typing her statement, Everett read through it quickly. "None of it was true," she said. "It was disgusting."

In mid-October, at a pretrial hearing that promised some spectacular testimony because a relative of Susan hired prominent Seattle attorney John Henry Browne, reporters and onlookers milled around in the hallway or converged for brief sound bites. After a while prosecutors announced that Ann couldn't testify because she was undergoing psychological testing. Sources said she was in a locked mental facility.

The *Wenatchee World* reported that "the evaluation came after a third incident where the girl lost control at her home, screaming, running away and at one time, causing enough damage to her bedroom to warrant a malicious mischief citation." The *World* added that "prosecutors say they're concerned because the incidents seem to occur around the same time the girl is scheduled to testify in a trial."

One of the upcoming cases now in jeopardy given the girl's fragile emotional state was that of Karen Lopez, who told her story to me shortly after her arrest. According to Lopez, Perez said he would go to the prosecutor and "get a deal" if she would talk. She said she wanted a lawyer, but Perez ignored her. He warned her she would get thirty-five to forty years and never see her kids again unless she made a deal. He had gotten a deal for the Filbecks, he said—less than a year in jail. He urged Lopez to agree, as they had, to testify against others. "Let me tell the prosecutor we got a deal," said Perez. When she refused, Perez shrugged. "Well, we'll go for thirty-five to forty years."

Chelan and Douglas County prosecutors refused to be defeated by the shrinking band of child witnesses, or the glare of public scrutiny, even if it meant sticking to marginal witnesses and excluding others. Much of the high profile criticism came from outsiders, among them Tom Grant, who by now was providing daily hard-hitting television coverage of the prosecutions. Grant was struck, as I was, by the fact that most of the identified or easily identifiable people named by children as victims, perpetrators, and witnesses to events at the Roberson church (including church members) and the Devereaux home (including foster children) were not even interviewed by the police. With core child and adult witnesses available, intensive investigation only threatened to muddy the waters of the prosecutions.

Police interviews that failed to yield confessions or corroboration often didn't merit a report. When deposed in May 1996 as part of a civil action, Perez said that he didn't recall ever generating a report or even taking notes in those situations where a child did not disclose abuse. On the other hand, said Perez, he could recall only one situation where a child, referred to him as a possible abuse victim, denied abuse.

Sue Farell was among the potential Roberson witnesses who was interviewed by the authorities. She told Douglas County Victim Witness Coordinator Jeanne Dierickx that nothing unusual happened at the church. Much later, in August 1995, Perez interviewed her, but if he reported it, the report was never made available to the defense.

Referring to the interview with Perez, Sue, then about

to enter the seventh grade, told Grant that she was at home with her eleven-year-old brother Tony and one of his friends when they got a crank call from some kids. Tony called 911. To their surprise, a little while later Magnotti and Perez came to the door and asked to come in and talk to them about the crank call.

At first Magnotti asked them about their birth dates and other details and scribbled the information in his note-book. Then Magnotti followed up on the crank call by calling the kids Tony said were the callers and telling them to stop. In the meantime, Perez tucked a thumb in the belt of his trousers, rested his palm on the butt of his revolver, threw out his chest, and made an unauthorized search of the place, according to the children. He didn't have a search warrant and didn't bother to ask permission: After all, these were kids.

Perez searched the kids' rooms, the kitchen, riffled through a pile of folded laundry lying on the couch, poked around in the closet. After this, said Sue, "They questioned us about the sex rings." Tony and Sue both said their mother didn't want them to be questioned unless she was there. Perez and Magnotti ignored them, they told Grant.

First Magnotti took Tony and his friend outside, closing the door and leaving Sue alone with Perez. Perez named several adults and asked her if they had touched her. Each time she denied it, she said, "He said thirty other kids had told him I'd been touched." When she denied it, Perez said she was lying. Quite naturally, Sue felt pressured by Perez, "because he asked me if I'd been touched and I told him no, and he kept on calling me a liar. . . . It made me feel bad inside," she said. "I was telling him the truth."

After about twenty minutes, Perez went outside to talk to Magnotti and Sue trailed behind. When she got outside, she saw that Tony was over in the neighbor's yard talking to Magnotti, and Tony's friend was sitting on the porch.

Tony knew Ann Everett from school. She was "kinda mean," he told Grant in a videotaped interview. One time he didn't feel like talking to her and Ann said, "If you don't talk I'll tell my dad [Perez] and you'll get arrested. I'll try to make up some stuff." Tony said she made the same kind of threats around three times a month.

Standing in the neighbor's yard, Magnotti questioned him about the church. "I'll make a deal," said Magnotti, according to Tony. "If you tell me something, if you tell what happened there, then you won't get in trouble." Tony said he didn't know what he might get in trouble for. Nothing had happened. Magnotti wasn't buying it, he said.

"Well, that means you're scared."

"Why are you questioning me like this?" asked Tony.

"You don't have to be afraid. Police are supposed to help little kids, you know."

In fact, Tony *was* scared. Magnotti had "a mad voice," he told Grant. He was also scared of being misinterpreted, having heard some stories about the investigation. "Sometimes people ask trick questions. . . . If I answer it wrong or something my mom will get thrown in jail or something like that," he said of the interview. "I was afraid that Perez, he was gonna ask me a trick question . . . 'cause some people did." Kids at school were afraid all the time that they'd be yanked from their homes and their parents arrested. When it happened, often the kids just seemed to disappear.

After a time, Perez strode away across the lawn. After Magnotti chatted with Perez for a few minutes, Perez walked back to Tony and announced, "I might come back." The words haunted Tony.

The words also haunted Brenda Farell, mother of Sue

and Tony. She got the news that police were at her home when she heard her name on the police scanner while she was driving home from a visit to the hospital. "I thought maybe he was here to take the kids away because I go to that church," she said. "I was scared . . . in shock!"

She called and left a message with a sergeant of the Wenatchee Police Department, but he never got back to her. A friend talked to one of the Wenatchee police officers, who said that what had happened was "standard procedure" because she "could have been a suspect."

The first day, Farell hid. After that she decided, "I'm not gonna hide. I'm not gonna let him [Perez] chase me out of my home. My daughter told the truth that day and I'm gonna believe her. I'm not gonna look out of my window every time I see a car. . . . I'm gonna let her be a kid."

Farell's concern was something more than paranoia, especially after she and her children talked to Grant. He discovered that his interviews were followed by a wake of arrests: At least five people he talked to were arrested shortly after talking to him and many others were named as suspects in police reports. "It would seem to me that I'd talk to people and interview them and suddenly they'd get arrested," he said. "I felt obligated to tell people that if they talked to me they might draw attention to themselves. It just made sense. This was the way this investigation went. As soon as you criticize them [the government] then you get arrested. How could I in good conscience talk to people without warning them?"

In the midst of his investigation, Grant learned he'd been labeled a "pervert" by foster parents at a meeting of the Wenatchee Foster Parents' Association. He discovered that the allegations were repeated from the highest annals of Washington State's Department of Social and Health Services and might have been the subject of an official investigation. The claim shocked outside media sources because it smelled strongly of vindictiveness, but it was merely unsettling to Grant. Over the months, he had become used to this odor: Even an investigator for attorney Robert Van Siclen was barred from a courtroom because police said he was under investigation as a molester. The personal attack was the kind of thing Grant came to expect from Wenatchee—so obvious that it was almost funny, except that such an allegation defies humor.

It certainly was no laughing matter to me, because at any time I could be next and I didn't have a television network to stand behind me. Not only was I hanging out there, but I was outraged. By now I had interviewed scores of people myself, some of them children, many of them facing charges. I'd watched hopeless trials and reviewed troublesome documents until my mind screamed for a solution—something more closely approximating justice than the sorry process of criminal procedure in Wenatchee.

I sat at my kitchen table, my eyes on the tidy rows of East Wenatchee houses, and felt desperately alone. Although my husband was entirely supportive (and my sons mildly tolerant), I had no money, no powerful ties, no experience with activism or even with politics, no strategic brilliance adequate to the magnitude of this mess. I couldn't even talk Seattle-area newspapers into assigning a reporter to write about the cases. But I was here, I'd seen the problem, and I felt it had become my responsibility to draw attention to the significance of the cases in light of my legal experience. I extended my leave of absence and my loan, securing it with our mortgage. The decision was simple: Do the right thing or live with the ultimate cowardice of doing nothing at all.

But how to do it? I picked the brains of my lawyer colleagues, sat in grim huddles with representatives of professional organizations and with politicians who, from their expressions, wished I would simply go away. One of these was Washington State House Speaker Clyde Ballard, himself from the Wenatchee area. "It's a minefield. If you go out on a limb, they'll cut you down," said Ballard of his political colleagues and the voting public when I talked to him over the phone.

The next day I sat on a soft leather chair in Ballard's gracious office in the state capitol building in Olympia, across from Ballard and two nervous lawyers. Ballard appeared genuinely troubled by the prosecutions. But it was a political can of worms, he told me honestly. Coming down on the wrong side of the question would be certain "political suicide," he said. "Keep me in the loop," said Ballard as I was leaving. "But don't give me any facts."

To my mind, Ballard's response was exactly the wrong solution. Facts were what these people needed. I decided to put together an investigative report—solid, documented, annotated, researched, and technically accurate in the manner of a long legal brief—something that would give those with power the ammunition to do something. We lawyers tell ourselves that our legal writing is an irresistible combination of documented facts, subtle persuasion, and implacable logic. In reality, our writing is sometimes dry, boring, rendered blandly unoriginal by reference to endless sources. But as a tool, it's hard to beat.

I got up before five every morning to outline the sections I wrote each day, hunched over records and interview notes, and typed until I was exhausted; watched the tail end of the night owl movie with my son, who was a night owl himself; crawled into bed, then got up three or four hours later, when another burst of adrenaline—or desperation—kicked in. The result, titled *"The Wenatchee Report,"* was a substantial, heavily documented chronicle of apparent civil rights violations by state and Wenatchee-area officials, especially as they affected the investigation and prosecution of alleged sex offenders. It took me around four months to research and five grueling near-all-nighters to complete the two-hundred-page report.

It was late September. I bundled up the report, stuffed it in my car, and sped across the mountains to Wenatchee. I had somehow fixated on the importance of getting the report out to coincide with an upcoming article by Dorothy Rabinowitz in the *Wall Street Journal,* and this very weekend Rabinowitz was in Wenatchee. On the stretch into town a siren wailed. Not here, I prayed. Not now. After months of living with the fear of official reprisal, I was genuinely, and foolishly, terrified. But the state patrolman gave me a ticket for driving more than eighty miles an hour in a fifty-five-mile-per-hour zone, flashed me a bland smile, and let me go on my way.

Over the next few days I spent many hours and hundreds of dollars at copy and mailing centers. The women at the mailing center didn't raise an eyebrow at my report (embarrassingly named after their hometown), or at its lofty destinations. First was the U.S. Department of Justice, then the U.S. Attorney's Office for the Eastern Division of Washington State in Spokane, which had already alerted the Justice Department of my concerns. I sent the report to several legislators, including Speaker Ballard and Washington Governor Mike Lowry, as well as to a large number of humanitarian agencies, public interest groups, and the media.

''The Wenatchee Report'' and its convergence with media coverage of the events seemed to get almost immediate results. *Time* magazine political writer Margaret Carlson read it and came to Wenatchee. She told me she used the hard edge of my report to scrape the ice off the windshield of her rented car on the frosty Halloween morning when she interviewed several Wenatchee residents. The CNN camera crew used my report to prop up their camera for an interview. And, on October 3, within days of receiving *"The Wenatchee Report,"* and reviewing the first of a series of biting articles in the *Wall Street Journal,* Governor Lowry and Speaker Ballard wrote to U.S. Attorney General Janet Reno requesting review. The letter read, in a curiously ambiguous fashion:

> *As you may be aware, actions and allegations related to reports of sexual abuse of children in Chelan and Douglas counties here in Washington state have led increasingly over time to great concern by many state residents and officials.*
>
> *We have concluded and trust you will agree that review by your office offers the best means to respond to this situation. A review as you deem appropriate, of underlying allegations and the actions of officials with respect to those allegations would be of great value to the communities involved in this matter.*

What did it mean? The letter was clearly written by someone of a legal bent who was hedging. Yet, whatever a "review" was, many Wenatchee citizens were elated. The white knight was charging through town, its lance tilted and ready. The letter was less than reassuring to those like me who were aware of Reno's track record as a zealous prosecutor intent on obtaining confessions in some of the nation's most troubling and notorious child abuse cases.

In the controversial 1980's "Country Walk" prosecution, Reno, as Florida prosecutor, concluded on the basis of ambiguous statements that Frank Fuster had molested a young child his sixteen-year-old Honduran-born wife

Ileana was baby-sitting. Reno, then running for state attorney general, set up a special unit in the prosecutor's office; at its core was a couple who represented themselves to Reno as experts at interviewing children. The couple used highly coercive and suggestive methods to extract children's statements—a fact that was clearly evident in transcripts of the interviews. Because these methods left prosecutors with spotty results, Reno decided to focus on Frank Fuster and offer Ileana a reduced sentence if she would plead guilty and testify against Frank. Ileana refused.

Reno had her placed in "protective custody," where she was isolated and often forced to remain naked under suicide watch. According to Ileana's sworn statement, which was made a part of the court record, she was drugged most of the time she was in jail and spent most of the time in solitary confinement. The investigator hired by the Fusters described her as looking like a fifty-year-old, with "sores and infections" on her skin. He said that Ileana told him she was often forced to remain nude in her cell and was occasionally hosed down by officials.

Ileana's attorney hired two psychologists who visited the teenager day and night to help her "retrieve" memories of abuse. After eleven months, the methods were at last successful and Ileana testified against her husband, while Reno sat beside her, holding her hand. She claimed Frank had fondled and kissed children and also that he had put snakes in her vagina and hung her by the wrists in the garage while a child was suspended by his feet beside her. Ileana pleaded guilty, served three years of a ten-year sentence, and was deported. Frank Fuster was convicted and sentenced to six life terms plus 165 years.

Another case prosecuted by Reno, in 1989, was that of fourteen-year-old Bobby Fijnje, who was accused of sexually assaulting several children at a church. Reno successfully moved to have the boy tried as an adult; he faced a mandatory life sentence. Although Fijnje was acquitted, he suffered greatly throughout the process of the investigation. The case bore similarities to the Fuster case, based on Reno's singular zeal to obtain confessions.

Fijnje, a diabetic, was placed in custody, deprived of food, and suffered insulin shock before he agreed with prosecutors that he had touched a child. Once he was released from custody, he immediately retracted his confession. Reno then directed an aggressive process of interrogation toward a growing group of children, whose stories became increasingly bizarre. Reno ordered Fijnje to be isolated from his family and placed in a juvenile facility for his own safety because Reno said (without any proof) that his parents were likely satanist pornographers, which was the reason he was reluctant to talk about his own abuse.

Reno's heavy-handed methods toward child abuse prosecutions weren't discussed at Senate hearings to confirm Reno's nomination as attorney general under the Clinton administration, although supporters cited her commitment to child welfare. Yet Reno's approach to such cases as this is markedly similar to her conduct in ordering the FBI to storm the Branch Davidian compound in Waco, Texas. After a three-week standoff, Reno ordered an armed assault of the compound with tanks and chemicals, which resulted in mass suicides and the deaths of many families by fire and bullets. Reno justified her actions with the claim that she had "the clear impression that since the FBI had assumed command of the situation, they had learned that the Branch Davidians had been beating babies." This claim was never supported by proof of any kind, the FBI later admitted the claim was false, and Reno wasn't later able to recall who gave her this information. Reno's portrayal of the Branch Davidians as monsters that must be destroyed began an act of war that instead destroyed children in the name of protecting them. It was the ultimate manifestation of child abuse hysteria gone awry.

Despite the risks an investigation headed by Reno might entail, Lowry's and Ballard's letter meant they recognized the enormity of the injustice—or so one would think.

The Wenatchee government was outraged. After all, hadn't Lowry given them a financial windfall in recognition of the enormity of *their* problem? In the minds of government officials, *"The Wenatchee Report"* and the governor's and speaker's letter to Reno were viewed as part of a larger conspiracy of outsiders and they set out to prove it through the friendly medium of the *Wenatchee World*.

"We don't know what their agenda is," said Wenatchee Police Chief Ken Badgley. "Are they going after a state agency, local people, or is it just an honest inquiry? . . . It concerns me if they're making decisions based solely on one source of information [*"The Wenatchee Report"*].

"I don't see any balance at all," said CPS Supervisor Tim Abbey, referring to *"The Wenatchee Report."* "Most of these issues have been addressed in court and readdressed. Are they now questioning every rape in the area? It just makes me sick. Where is the truth anymore?"

Chelan County Prosecutor Gary Riesen was forced by the bad news to return home from a meeting of county officials. "In June the governor's office called us and asked us, 'Do you want any help to deal with the child abuse in the community?' They asked me, we didn't ask them . . . and they sent $19,000 to my office for extraordinary prosecution expenses in connection with these cases. And now the governor wants to investigate me for using the money he sent me? I am astounded by that, shocked,'' said Riesen.

But Riesen's outrage went further. ''And beyond the governor's deal, which is completely amazing to me, is that Clyde Ballard, who is my representative, got his information about this situation from a reporter from New York City [Dorothy Rabinowitz of the *Wall Street Journal*] who spent three days in Wenatchee. But neither he nor the governor asked me one question about what was going on here or about cases where we had convictions, including cases where juries composed of the citizens of Chelan County found these people guilty beyond a reasonable doubt. Again, I am shocked that my representative would not ask me to find out what are the facts.''

The first of Dorothy Rabinowitz's several brittlely ironic articles appeared in the *Wall Street Journal* on September 29, 1995, and drew considerable national attention. The editorial was immediately labeled ''tabloid journalism'' by Wenatchee officials.

Once the Rabinowitz article hit the stands, the serious outside media barreled into Wenatchee. All of the national coverage by the *Washington Post,* the *Wall Street Journal,* CNN, the London *Independent, Time* magazine, *Dateline NBC,* and others presented the serious controversies concerning the cases: bizarre allegations, claims of coercion, retaliation, the targeting of a vulnerable population. Beleaguered local government officials bristled, then adopted defensive strategies that were often filtered through the friendly pages of the *Wenatchee World,* which, with a circulation of thirty-eight thousand, virtually captured the market in Chelan and Douglas Counties. After a time the *Wenatchee World* appeared to many outsiders to be little more than a political pawn.

World editors made the apparent decision to shock and

inflame their readers through graphic and sexualized language, and detailed and sometimes slanted coverage of events, confessions, and children's statements. Steve Lachowicz, *World* assistant managing editor, apologized in November for some of the sexual terminology used in the coverage of the sex cases. "But," he wrote, "the time for delicacy seems long gone. . . . Our readers, and those elsewhere around the country who have had to rely on shameless pretensions at journalism need to have the necessary ammunition to refute claims that no children have been sexually abused."

Lachowicz quoted Rabinowitz as saying, "Twenty-eight innocent people are sitting in prison. . . . It's terrorizing." Said Lachowicz, "What is really terrorizing is that so many national journalists (and I am forced to use the term loosely) have failed to get so many of their facts straight, ignoring credible evidence of abuse presented in numerous trials. . . . The stream of twisted, one-sided reports might have our newsroom laughing every morning were we not so busy shaking our heads in depressed dismay at the conduct of some of our peers."

Some local journalists advocated for local accountability, even acknowledged what some of us suspected—that the Wenatchee Valley was curiously contained in a geographic, political, and social time warp. *Wenatchee World* columnist Kel Groseclose wrote, "Our consciousness has been unceremoniously dragged from circa 1955 to the harsh realities of 1995 in a matter of months." Groseclose conceded that one of these "realities" was "latent racism. . . . We haven't had to deal with it directly because we've either found subtle ways to keep persons of other ethnic backgrounds totally out or we've managed to keep them economically deprived and geographically isolated. . . . The time is now coming, if it's not already upon us, when we shall have to change our narrow attitudes and work hard at creating justice and equality in our institutions. . . . It's good for us finally to realize, for better or worse that we're an integral part of the world.''

Groseclose's view was by no means universal. Dave Jenkins, owner of the Four Seasons Inn in East Wenatchee, suggested at a chamber of commerce meeting that maybe the chamber could convince a news program such as *60 Minutes* to do a report on the national media's ''bad journalism.'' Alas, said Wenatchee Chamber of Commerce president Melanie Shaw philosophically, such a thing would be unlikely, since journalists don't like to report on each other. Certain journalists have a ''set of principles they believe in and they believe Wenatchee fits these principles,'' said Shaw, lamenting that the national journalists were unfairly trying to compare the Wenatchee cases with such notorious cases as McMartin. Shaw later told reporters, including one from *Newsweek,* that Wenatchee's offenders and critics might be part of a child abuse underground with national affiliates and the ability to organize, network, and seduce the media into accepting the concept of a ''witch hunt.''

Beyond the persistent claims that outside journalists were sloppy, sensation-seeking, opportunistic, or enemies of children, it was difficult for local officials and the supportive local media to precisely articulate the nature of their concerns. At their core was a profound resistance to criticism from outsiders. Chelan County prosecutor Gary Riesen told a Spokane reporter, ''We like the stories where we don't get dumped on. Those East Coast reporters can make you look like a complete goober.''

Upon release of *''The Wenatchee Report,''* the governor's and speaker's letter to Reno, and the response of high-profile national media, the local police and prosecutors couldn't even expect support of their former allies by silence, apathy, or politics: the Seattle and Tacoma newspapers, television, and radio stations. Local officials resented the state press as well, a sign that the communities had become significantly insular. "What possible reason on earth does the Seattle media have trying these cases on their airwaves?" said Wenatchee radio talk show host Kelly Hart of a panel discussion headed by a Seattle radio talk show host. "They think we are pawns in a big game, small-town hicks who don't know anything."

"We got defensive," *Wenatchee World* editorial page editor Tracy Warner told me. "People react like we're stupid, small-town people." Warner described this as the "Ma and Pa Kettle syndrome. It's easy to convince people in the cities that people in small towns are stupid and corrupt." And, of course, there was the fact that these suddenly maligned government people weren't abstract strangers. "We know these people, we've watched them work over the years."

Some of the official defensiveness might have spilled over into the prosecutions, theorized Warner. "You asked me why Badgley kept Perez on. I think he kept him on because he thought, 'I'm not gonna let these criminals tell me how to run my department.'" Some of the critics had been charged; others were suspects who didn't know when to let well enough alone. Kinkade, for example, had been "getting organized . . . pounding on everyone," said Warner.

The three local judges angrily reacted to the media coverage and the complaints about their rulings. In sentencing Susan Everett, who entered an Alford plea to the gross misdemeanor of communicating with a minor for immoral purposes, Judge Bridges said, "In this case, I hope to convey some concern for you because there are a number of people, as well as members of the media, who argue these charges are so outlandish and bizarre that they could not have happened. . . . I'm encouraging you to have counseling so the cycle of abuse can stop with you.''

When Leo Catcheway entered a guilty plea to a greatly reduced charge of molestation, Judge Carol Wardell said she wished members of the media who were critical of the sex ring cases had heard Catcheway's statement in support of his guilty plea. In her chambers after the sentencing, Wardell told a *Wenatchee World* reporter, ''Here we have a man who stands by his conviction. He was arrested by Bob Perez, investigated by Child Protective Services and the Wenatchee Police Department. Yet there were no critics here to hear his statements, to watch his sentencing. It's bothersome to me that they aren't hearing this side of the story, that they don't want to hear this side of the story.'' (Of course, Catcheway had entered into a plea agreement and his story was far different than the one the witnesses had told: His statement described one-on-one molestation of a single victim and not as, as children had said, that he was the camera-toting henchman at the heart of a pornographic sex ring.)

In justifying his eleventh-hour decision to pull the plug on television coverage of the upcoming Roberson trial by ten television crews including CBS, NBC, ABC, Fox Broadcasting, and *Courtroom Television,* Judge Small said, ''This court must assure all victims of child sexual abuse and their parents and guardians . . . that the process is not one that will subject them to such an inordinate amount of media attention that they stop coming forward . . . and allow this silent epidemic to continue.''

The judges became increasingly intolerant of critics, instructing deputies who were assigned to the courtroom to keep a watchful eye on the onlookers. Viewers were booted for coughing or grimacing—all of them known troublemakers. My meddling was by now well-documented; under the forthright glares of deputies who stood facing us down, their hands resting beside their gun belts, I willed myself into total immobility.

Cherie Greenfield was one of two people evicted from a court by a Wenatchee judge because of a facial expression. Greenfield was also investigated by Wenatchee police for allegedly sending a bouquet of dead flowers to prosecutor Roy Fore during a trial, an act police took as a "death threat." Terrified by this allegation, she fled the Wenatchee area. She called me at my home and tearfully explained that she'd do whatever was necessary to protect her family. When she returned, Greenfield apologized to Perez and other government officials for her role in the CCLA, which she now forcefully disowned.

Fear of retaliation is a powerful thing. Dorothy Rabinowitz said to me that her editors wondered if she needed the services of a bodyguard while in Wenatchee. Like the mother of the Farell children vowed not to do, I found myself peeking at passing cars from behind my curtains whenever I stayed in Wenatchee. The first phone number in my address book was that of a bail bondsman.

But government officials, through the local media, devised a peaceful solution. By November the Wenatchee Chamber of Commerce created a task force and invited police, DSHS, prosecutors, and the *Wenatchee World* to weekly meetings. Every week, speakers briefed local citizens on the government's perspective toward the investigations, and discussed strategies "to present Wenatchee in the most accurate light in response to this media barrage of misinformation," said board chairman Gil Sparks.

Chamber president Melanie Shaw wrote that the chamber had been working "diligently and proactively" to portray Wenatchee to the media as a city that comes down on the side of children. "Wenatchee is a community that is willing to deal head-on with tough issues," said Shaw. "We are confident that our judicial system was carefully designed by our forefathers to ensure that such widespread corruption could not exist. . . . Yes Chambers of the 90s do more than stand on the sidelines and cheer, no matter what is happening to the players on the field. We are there in the game, side by side, with you.''

Chamber meetings on Thursdays were reported in the *Wenatchee World* on Fridays. Speakers presented medical evidence, prosecutors proudly strutted their statistical success ratio, police and DSHS officials described their abiding concern for children and the impenetrable system of checks and balances bounding their investigations.

''I've never seen anything like it,'' said Robert Van Siclen, attorney for Roberson, who was now bearing the brunt of the *Wenatchee World*'s articles. ''Wenatchee became a little community defining itself. The *World* was the only act in town. They openly pressed for public opinion that would sway the community and the prosecution of these people.''

But the single-minded governmental insistence on maintenance of the status quo received yet another setback from another troublesome outsider: Paul-Noel Chretien, an attorney with the U.S. Department of Justice, most recently in the department's Office of Information and Privacy. By the time he heard about the events in Wenatchee, Chretien had given considerable thought to the interests of justice that should be, after all, every prosecutor's concern.

In an article that appeared in the November 29, 1995, *Wall Street Journal,* Chretien wrote, ''There are good reasons most of the mass child sex abuse convictions of the 1980s have been reversed. But this news apparently hasn't reached Wenatchee, Washington, where dozens of men and women are accused of child sex abuse in a series of bizarre prosecutions.''

The next day, in an article in the *Washington Post,*

Chretien said he offered to sit at counsel table *pro bono* to assist the Robersons because he believed they were wrongly indicted. "I think the cases in Wenatchee are outrageous, and a lot of attorneys here feel the same way," he said, and added that when "obviously innocent people have been convicted you have to step in and do something."

Chretien had already been working to provide *pro bono*, posttrial assistance to the defense in another criminal matter, that of then-sixty-one-year-old day-care center operator Violet Amirault, her daughter, and her son in Fells Acre, Massachusetts, a case that had much in common with other notorious day-care center cases that arose in the 1980s.[1] Due to his outspoken comments about the Wenatchee cases, Chretien was forced by his bosses to withdraw his services from the Amirault case after Douglas County Sheriff Dan LaRoche and Wenatchee Police

---

[1]Violet Amirault, her son Gerald, and her daughter, Cheryl Amirault LeFave, had run a day-care center for twenty years when accused of raping a new pupil, age five. Police called approximately eighty parents and encouraged them to question their children about abuse by the Amiraults and to inject questions about items that had come up in other notorious cases—secret rooms, magic rooms, clowns—a fact that implied the authorities' belief in a national conspiracy. The children were sent to a pediatric nurse, an advocate of recovered memory therapy, who researched and wrote about satanic abuse and the existence of nationwide satanic conspiracies.

Children came to allege that the Amiraults and other teachers had raped and tortured them and hung them naked from trees. Violet Amirault became a robot that looked like R2D2 and bit them and flashed warning lights at them if they didn't cooperate with sexual torture. Although the Amiraults were alleged to have raped children with knives and "magic wands" in a "magic room" and a "bad clown" was said to throw fire around the room, no physical evidence corroborated the charges. Violet Amirault and her daughter were convicted and sentenced to eight to twenty years; her son was sentenced to thirty to forty years.

After five failed appeals, a Massachusetts Superior Court judge overturned the cases against Violet and Cheryl based on the violation of their rights to face their accusers. On March 24, 1997, the Massachusetts Supreme Court overruled this decision and reinstated the conviction of the women and denied a motion for a new trial by Gerald. The cases of Violet Amirault and Cheryl Amirault LeFave were remanded for a new trial but Violet died of cancer in the late summer of 1997.

Chief Ken Badgley wrote jointly to U.S. Attorney General Janet Reno complaining about him.

"My involvement in the Amirault and Wenatchee cases have been the best and most gratifying things I've done as a lawyer," Chretien told me. He explained that this had much to do with his perception that poor investigations are destructive to the goals of criminal prosecution. "Ironically, these abysmally trained investigators who have an incentive to 'discover' abuse not only abused children and ruined innocent adults, they also set back the fight against real abuse," said Chretien. "These 'children's advocates' have been revealed to be so biased and unprofessional that few will believe real cases of abuse."

21:

Winter 1995

═══════

The Roberson Trial

═══════

By November the case against the Robersons had fallen into such an evident state of disarray that many believed the matter wouldn't proceed to trial. For much of the month Ann Everett remained in a mental hospital, too ill—or too fiercely conflicted—to testify. Bonnie Rogers was largely discredited by her admitted habit of making up false allegations that implicated such untouchable sources as her therapist and foster father. These witnesses—and a convicted sex offender testifying under a promise of no Douglas County charges—were the crux of the case against the Robersons. Permeating everything was the controversy surrounding Perez's investigation that had been outlined in the national media accounts of the event. Common sense said the case would go away. But by now it was clear that common sense had little to do with the strategies of the local governments.

Douglas County authorities struggled to distance themselves from the Chelan County investigations, and from Perez. But this ploy had its share of problems. Douglas County Victim/Witness Coordinator Jeanne Dierickx did most of the child interviews, but few bore fruit and none led to uncontaminated information. Douglas County Sheriff Dan LaRoche told me Dierickx used "blind interview techniques," which meant she was given little or no information before she talked to kids. Although the Washington State Training Commission offers a forty-hour class in child interviewing once a year in the spring, "we couldn't get her in," said LaRoche, who assured me Dierickx stuck to the commission's standards.

Douglas County Prosecutor Steve Clem also praised Douglas County's interview techniques. "They're as blind as can be," he said, and then told me his cases in no way relied on Perez's investigation. "I can tell you that he may have referred cases to us," said Clem, but added that Douglas County's investigation was wholly independent. Since I had studied the police reports, I found this claim was wildly incongruent with the fact that Douglas County sheriff's officers held off their investigations for weeks after agreeing to let Perez check out matters on their side of the river. Had Clem *read* the reports? I asked.

Clem brushed me off. He was unconcerned that kids' statements were contaminated by the onslaught of interviews, including several by Perez, "because the kids were straight" throughout their interviews with Douglas County officials. The statements of children were backed up by adults, he said, referring no doubt to Linda Miller and Scharlann Filbeck (both of whom had long ago recanted), and Gary Filbeck (who had made a "deal").

And there was another strategy—downsizing and downplaying the more sensational claims of the witnesses as creations of the media. Again the ploy was amazingly inconsistent with the official documentation. "We don't view this as a sex ring," said Clem.

"Well, group sex, then," I said, unimpressed with his use of semantics.

"I'm not aware of any group sex. It's not in any reports

I've seen." The comment was a near-echo of the words of Harborview Medical Center research director Lucy Berliner, who had advised prosecutors in Chelan and Douglas Counties and who told me in an interview that Wenatchee-area officals made a mistake in labeling the cases "sex rings" and that she found the concept of group sex with multiple children "highly unlikely," something she would "scrutinize really carefully."

Of course, absence of group sex was among the facts that could be manipulated by a prosecutor's charging decision. By charging a case as one-on-one incest, prosecutors avoided all the fuss and complexity of proving improbable scenarios. This had been the prosecutors' strategy in both counties all along, one of the reasons why there had been so many convictions in Chelan County.

When I recovered myself enough to press him, Clem admitted that sex was alleged to take place between kids and adults "in the presence of each other." He added that nobody much went to the church anyway, so it was of little moment.

LaRoche agreed. "This is not a sex ring," he said. "It's an abuse case."

Apparently no one got the word to Perez. By now, Perez believed himself to be a crusader, recently martyred by the outside press and the critics. "The perception is, I'm out cruisin' the streets snatching up people," said Perez to the *Seattle Times*, "but this is what I'm really doing." The reporter wrote that Perez slid open the drawers of a metal file cabinet, revealing a drawer crammed with CPS reports of suspected child abusers. On one of his walls was a bulletin board with neat rows of the driver's licenses bearing the bad photographs of people he had busted—even those whose cases had been dismissed or drastically reduced, such as Donna Rodriguez and Bob Devereaux. Each bore a colored sticker signaling the disposition of the case. Blue meant dismissal. Perez scoffed at the designation. "So far as he's concerned, everybody on the board is guilty," wrote the reporter.

"I don't have any trouble sleeping at night, if that's what you're asking," said Perez to the reporter, as he rocked in his beat-up office chair. "I know there are people who can't believe this whole thing but . . . first, I never said everybody was having sex with everybody at the same time," he said. "Or that every adult had full intercourse, and reached orgasm, fifteen times in a night. I never said that. No child ever said that.

"But look, there was a sex ring. I know there was a sex ring, OK? I did the work—my work is tight. I'm proud of the work."

The critics were biased, LaRoche told me, describing some of them as "ultra-right-wing conservatives who want to dismantle CPS," among them Washington House Speaker Clyde Ballard and Chelan County Commissioner Earl Marcellus. LaRoche dismissed Spokane newsman Tom Grant as naive because of his immediate belief in Roberson's innocence. And he described Bob Kinkade as a "convicted child molester," although in fact he was not. Still, the case gained LaRoche an invitation to go on the Oprah Winfrey show and some show by "a black talk show host," whose name he couldn't recall, but who offered to pay his way to New York.

LaRoche was concerned about a federal investigation, he told me. The Douglas County Sheriff's Office was once investigated "on some two-bit manslaughter case" in which "the guy was a ding-a-ling." The suspect was Hispanic or, as he put it, an "alien," who made a claim of civil rights violations. Douglas County had to send reports to the FBI, but LaRoche never heard the results. "The files stay open. They never clear you."

Would Douglas County proceed with the trial? "Let's

say you're a prosecutor," Clem put it to me. "You have
a choice: You close your eyes or you seek a determination
of has there been touching."

By all indications Clem was abdicating responsibility
to the jury. But first he agreed to defer part of the decision
making to an outside prosecutor. On recommendation of
Robert Van Siclen, he agreed to seek a second opinion.
But he apparently only sent reports from the state's perspective. "They never asked me for my side of the case,"
said Van Siclen, who by then had compiled considerable
investigative data of his own. Not surprisingly, based
solely on the language of the police reports and "confessions," the recommendation was that there was sufficient
basis to proceed to trial.

But the prosecutor's case was crumbling and Van Siclen was confident he could prove it. On the last weekend
in October, a week before trial, Van Siclen spent the
weekend on his boat. His efforts were exhausting and he
still had a long way to go. "I can always sleep on my
boat," he told me. He lent his home to Roby and Connie
Roberson so they could do a Seattle radio show and get
away from the explosive tensions of Wenatchee.

Over the weekend the other shoe fell. Faced with an
obviously flawed case, and no easy out via the outside
prosecutor, Clem arrived at yet another strategy—a way
to rehabilitate the case on the eve of trial. On Friday,
October 27, late in the afternoon, he filed ten new child
sex abuse charges against Robert Roberson and seven
against Connie. All involved new victims and charges. On
Saturday morning, the *Wenatchee World* called Van Siclen for comment. "That was the first I knew of it," said
Van Siclen, who told me he was deeply shocked. He read
about Clem's decision after a *World* staff member faxed
it to him.

Roberson thought the charges were filed in retaliation

for his appearing on the Friday radio broadcast. "This is just more of the improprieties and that's why we need a federal investigation to get to the bottom of this," he said to the *Seattle Times*. "They [the Douglas County Prosecutor's Office] even had an agreement made . . . with my attorney that they were going to drop some of the charges," he said, "and now all of a sudden they're throwing the kitchen sink in."

Van Siclen confirmed that he had been told by prosecutors that certain charges would be dismissed. " 'You can count on it,' they said." At the time the words were said, he had no idea that new charges would be filed.

Papers outside of Wenatchee picked up on the perceived unfairness of the eleventh-hour prosecutorial decision, as well as some of the almost ludicrous conflicts of interest that affected the integrity of all of the prosecutions. As stated in Spokane's *Spokesman Review,* "The lead detective, Bob Perez, is the foster father of the key child victim. Judge John Bridges, who has presided over several of the cases, is married to Susan Moore, a state child-welfare worker. Moore is the ex-wife of Douglas County Prosecutor Steve Clem. Clem is prosecuting the highest-profile suspects in the case. Bridges used to be Perez's personal attorney. Judge Pro-tem Kathleen Schmidt set bail at $1 million for one of the accused, Honnah Sims, and at the same time was the guardian ad litem for one of Sims's alleged victims."

In fact, by then Perez was foster parent to *two* of the state's key witnesses in Roberson's trial. Judge Small, the Roberson judge, had been involved in a business venture with Chelan County Prosecutor Gary Riesen. A Chelan County deputy prosecutor went on a camping trip with the Perez family, including Ann Everett, while the cases he would prosecute were pending. Judges who presided over the cases and other government officials paid social visits to Perez's home while the Everett children were his foster children and while trials were pending. Dave Bohr, one of the defense attorneys who represented sex-ring cases (notably that of Gary Filbeck, the only adult corroborating witness in the Roberson trial), was campaign manager for Chelan County Prosecutor Gary Riesen, and Riesen appointed him special deputy prosecuting attorney, an appointment valid at least until revoked by the prosecuting attorney (which had not happened by the conclusion of the Roberson trial.)[1] The attorney who was guardian ad litem for Perez's foster kids Ann and Mary Everett and other Wenatchee foster children was the first defense attorney for Bob Devereaux. And—as William Parker, attorney for Connie Roberson, later pointed out before Judge Small—Clem (who was assisting in trying the Roberson case) had once been guardian ad litem for Jeff Town, a fifteen-year-old boy who was now one of the witnesses against the Robersons.

"What's going on down there is criminal, a vicious attack," said Parker a day or two before the trial was slated to begin. "In my opinion, they shouldn't be going forward on anything and this is a waste of the taxpayers' money." It "reeks of mismanagement from the prosecutor's office," said Van Siclen.

Clem was unperturbed. "The defense attorneys are using what I'm sure . . . some day in the future will be called the 'O. J. defense,' where they sling mud, make wild accusations and see conspiracies all around them," he said to the *Wenatchee World*. He struggled to encourage the media to divorce their views of his case from those of

---

[1] The appointment was made by Certificate of Appointment signed by Chelan County Prosecutor Gary Riesen, and Oath of Office, signed by David M. Bohr on July 30, 1990, both notarized by Chelan County Deputy Prosecutor Douglas J. Shae.

Chelan County. "I think that the media which has contacted our office to discuss the trials . . . are coming from the perspective that it is an investigation by Detective Perez and is somehow subject to the same contents contained in *The Wenatchee Report* by Kathryn Lyon."

Clem and LaRoche were hopeful I'd back them up on this. When I interviewed them individually on October 17, both denied they'd heard of me or my work in Wenatchee. Yet within hours of the interviews I was contacted by a *Wenatchee World* reporter and a local radio talk show host, both aware of my interviews and anxious to confirm that Douglas County's investigations were distinct and superior to those in Chelan County. I was unable to oblige them. There were some improved procedures, to be sure: One child interview was taped; Douglas county hired a specialized, if untrained, interviewer; fruitless interviews merited police reports. But to the significant extent that Douglas County's investigation relied on that in Chelan County, it was hopelessly contaminated, I said. Neither the *Wenatchee World* nor the radio station bothered to quote me.

In the midst of the media hoopla about the Roberson trial, prosecutors battled to wrap up stray cases. All charges were dismissed against Karen Lopez and church van driver Bill Davis. Ralph Gausvik was convicted at trial in an open-and-shut case. Gausvik's public defender didn't cross-examine Perez, although the detective had spearheaded the investigation against his client and Gausvik and his common-law wife Barbara Garaas were first named by Perez's foster child; nor did he introduce medical or other expert testimony. The jury ignored the fact that one of the children testified that his mother had put her penis inside him. When Gausvik received a twenty-three-year sentence, Barbara Garaas took the advice of her attorney and entered a guilty plea to reduced charges.

What the exact charges against the Robersons would be was unclear until the first day scheduled for trial, Monday, November 6. The Douglas County Prosecutor's Office dropped all twenty-two of the original charges against the Robersons, leaving only the seventeen new charges, which were filed on October 27. The Robersons faced a clean slate of victims, including Mary Everett, Aubrey Miller, and the Roberson's own young daughter Roberta—new acts, new faces, new charging periods.

Judge Small denied motions for dismissal brought by Van Siclen and Parker, who claimed that the prosecutor's eleventh-hour filing and its failure to meet defense discovery demands met the "textbook definition of case mismanagement or misconduct." Small instead suggested that the defense had made a "substantial showing of the need to continue [the trial date]," a remedy which his client shouldn't be forced to elect, said Van Siclen. In the end the Robersons and their attorneys opted for only a few more days because they saw no percentage in allowing Douglas County prosecutors additional time to rehabilitate their case. Child hearsay motions and jury selection were scheduled for November 13.

"It's a case that ignored startling realities from the git-go," said William Parker in his opening statement on November 20 in the Waterville courthouse. The Robersons regarded him stoically. Connie sat erect and pensive; the pastor tented his fingers against his mouth. "You'll see gross inconsistencies from one interview to the next," said Parker. "There are too many disturbing facts, there are too many disturbing shadows that the advocates in this case don't want you to see."

Douglas County Deputy Prosecuting Attorney Eric Biggars shone a curious light on one of the shadows. He told the jury that the Washington State Patrol forensic analyst would testify that the crime lab found no semen on items seized from the church. There was a good reason for this, Biggars explained, one that tended to prove his newly constructed case. The fact that "the pastor at no time ejaculated" was consistent with "the type of abuse these children suffered."

Following the opening statements, Douglas County Sheriff's Detective Robbin Wagg testified that none of the child victim interviews was recorded on audio- or videotape. "That's not the way we do things," said Wagg. It was soon apparent that many of the ways Douglas County in fact *did* things were significantly flawed.

Washington State Patrol forensic experts described the complicated process of securing the church, searching and examining it over a period of thirteen hours with infrared lights and laser equipment, and extracting materials for laboratory analysis. "I can just tell you there is no semen in this church," said one of the state's experts.

Gary Filbeck was the state's sole adult eyewitness. Small denied the defense motion to bring in Filbeck's previous incredible statement that Roberson had stuffed a woman into a car and burned her alive. Filbeck testified that he saw Roberson call three children to the stage of the church and molest them. Five other adult participants waited their turn, sitting together on a small couch while Roberson preached, he said. Each act took between three and five seconds.

Not only was Filbeck's testimony inconsistent with his earlier statements, but it was often internally contradictory. On direct examination he couldn't say what a "lie" is and he described the last month of the year as March. He was confused and halting when describing his "deal" with prosecutors in exchange for testimony.

Pastor Roberson beamed with pride and Connie Roberson averted her face with emotion as five-year-old Roberta testified. Earlier, they had decided to spare their daughter the pain of confrontation at the child hearsay hearing by offering to be excused from the courtroom, or, alternatively, waiving objection to a hearing in chambers, where Small would examine Roberta's competency. But on that day, walking down the courtroom hallway, Connie and Roberta came face-to-face. After a moment of shocked silence, both wheeled around and ran in opposite directions: Roberta to the ''advocates'' that surrounded her and Connie to the lower level of the courthouse, where she stood, overcome with emotion.

Now, other than this incident, the Robersons were seeing their daughter for the first time since she had been detained by agents of the state. Roberta was composed and beautiful and in many ways unchanged. And if she had indeed made any statements that her parents had sexually molested her, she now firmly recanted them. When Biggars asked if her parents had touched her ''in a bad way,'' Roberta repeatedly answered, ''No.''

Biggars tried to discredit his witness. In a seeming attempt to impugn her memory, he asked Roberta what she got for Christmas last year. She said she got a telephone with a door on the side where candy was concealed. Roberta said that she could only count to forty. Then she sang her ABC's to the delight and astonishment of onlookers, who, like most of us, sometimes need a reminder that trials are about real people.

Thirteen-year-old Mary Everett said the Robersons had molested her many times at the church and their home, stripping her and other children, tying them up, and taping their mouths before molesting them. This was a version of the events that differed from police reports, incorporating Mary's abstract statements and events suggested to her in cross-examination by Van Siclen. Mary named other victims and twenty-three perpetrators. She said Roberson abused her and Ann with "his private," while Connie used "her fingers and her private." On most Wednesdays, Thursdays, Fridays, and Sundays, "bad stuff" happened, said Mary.

"Have you told us the whole truth here today?" asked Van Siclen.

"Yes," said Mary. "I don't lie much."

Other alleged child witnesses offered differing and more abstract versions of the events. Eleven-year-old Aubrey Miller briefly answered Biggars's questions, as she clutched a teddy bear. In response to his question, she told Biggars that a lie "is like I don't have my baby doll," but she assured him she knew the difference between a good and a bad touch. Biggars handed her an anatomical drawing and asked her to identify the areas of her "upper privates" and "lower privates," then to circle where she was touched in a "bad way." She complied and in this way indicated that Pastor Roberson had touched her genitals one time in the church bathroom. But she contradicted herself and said he touched her genitals through her clothes while she was in the kitchen. She also contradicted herself about whether Connie Roberson had been in the kitchen at the time. Aubrey denied that Connie had touched her.

Aubrey contradicted her sister Charlene's testimony. Aubrey said she never spent the night at the church, while Charlene testified that both had spent the night several times. Charlene admitted she and Aubrey had falsely accused their stepfather of sexual abuse three years earlier. Still, she insisted, Roberson had molested her. In language reminiscent of therapy, Charlene said she previously denied abuse to defense investigators because "I pushed it so far down inside of me I didn't remember it at the time." On cross-examination she said that therapy had helped to restore her memories. "I used to be closing doors,'' she said. ''Now I'm opening them.''

Fifteen-year-old Jeff Town, described as having the mental capacity of an eleven-year-old, became totally confused. When asked to point out his molester, Jeff pointed not to Pastor Roberson but to his attorney, Van Siclen. After Van Siclen magnanimously stood up and identified himself, Jeff belatedly pointed to Roberson. Biggars handed him an anatomical drawing and Jeff pointed to show that Roberson had touched his buttocks and genitals with his hands. What remained of his testimony was strongly undercut when incontrovertible evidence established he was in an institution 150 miles away at the time of the alleged molestations.

Out of the presence of the jury, Van Siclen argued that Jeff should be disqualified because he was apparently incompetent and was taking medication, including lithium. Among other apparent symptoms, the boy slurred his words. The motion was denied.

The defense case was distinguished by its adverse rulings. Van Siclen called for the admissibility of Dr. Lee Coleman, a psychiatrist who was expert at reviewing colposcopic and other genital medical evidence and drawing medical opinions based on this evidence. In an offer of proof outside of the presence of the jury, Dr. Coleman testified that he had reviewed colposcope photographs and other medical evidence and concluded that Wenatchee doctors had misinterpreted the results of the genital examinations of the alleged victims in the Roberson case; in each case there was no medical evidence of abnormalities beyond the normal range of variation for nonabused children.

Van Siclen said that previous medical testimony was inaccurate and misleading and lent credibility to otherwise unreliable child statements in several earlier cases. ''I think it (the basis of Dr. Coleman's proposed testimony) is significantly important . . . it sends a message not only to this court and case, but to the entire community."

But Clem successfully argued that the psychiatrist was experienced not in examining children but in examining colposcopic findings. Judge Small agreed. "His experience is essentially vicarious," said the judge, describing Dr. Coleman as "an armchair quarterback. Granted, a well-read armchair quarterback." Armchair quarterbacks were not appreciated locally.

Later, Dr. Coleman told me Judge Small's rulings were "thinly veiled attempts to appear neutral." Although he has testified about colposcope findings in many court proceedings throughout the nation, in this case "it was very obvious that [Small's ruling] was strictly political. . . . If they were interested in justice, they would invite people like me." Instead, the judge was afraid to confront controversy that was raised by the medical evidence, he said. "There is no moderation in Wenatchee."

The defense then called Dr. Deborah Harper of Spokane, who, after review of the colposcope photographs, testified that she disputed many of the findings of doctors employed by the state to examine Ann and Melinda Everett but agreed that Aubrey Miller had an abnormal absence of hymenal tissue and a larger than normal vaginal opening, which might be consistent with abuse.

Small greatly restricted the testimony of another defense expert, forensic psychologist Dr. John Yuille, professor at the University of British Columbia. Dr. Yuille was not permitted to testify even in a general way about such issues as suggestibility, memory, the concepts of "repressed" or "recovered" memory, the value of videotaping child interviews, or the cross-contamination of children who were interviewed in the presence of each other. Such testimony would "invade the province of the jury," according to Small.

"It was the strangest thing," Dr. Yuille later told me. He said he has testified extensively in Canada (primarily for the police and prosecutors) and the United States (primarily for the defense) and that some few times his testimony had been ruled inadmissible altogether, but "I never encountered this before." He was surprised that Small greatly restricted his testimony, for example not allowing him to use the word "suggestibility" or talk about the concept. "Surely educating the trier of fact is a good thing?" he mused.

His testimony might have been particularly instructive. Although he was prepared to testify to interviewer errors, repressed memories, and the importance of recording interviews, he also hoped to testify to a theory that he describes as "latticed" allegations, which result from poor investigative techniques.

The common features of a "latticed" allegation are: (1) There are several, sometimes many, alleged victims; (2) there are several, sometimes many, perpetrators; (3) the allegations are not one-to-one but multiple and overlapping; (4) the children and suspect may "share a common context" (for example, a day-care center); (5) most children undergo multiple, poor-quality interviews; (6) as the case progresses, allegations tend to increase in seriousness, sometimes becoming more fantastic; (7) the case often attracts much media attention; (8) there is no clear resolution to the investigation of the cases.

John Yuille and coauthors Monica Tymofievich and David Marxsen, in a paper entitled "The Nature of Allegations of Child Sexual Abuse," *Allegations of Child Sexual Abuse: Assessment and Case Management*, (Brunner and Mazel, New York, New York, 1995) wrote:

> If a child is subjected to a series of poorly done interviews, a dynamic might be established between the inter-

viewer and the child whereby the interviewer, with the best intentions, subtly shapes the allegations of the child. . . . The interviewer is trying to find out if anything else has happened to the child, and eventually gets the child to agree to a more serious allegation. As there are other alleged victims in the case, every time one of the children makes a new allegation, a new round of interviews is conducted to reverify whether the newly "discovered" form of abuse occurred with any of the children. This could result in the charges' increasing seriousness until they verge on the fantastic. It becomes impossible to tell whether or not the children were in fact abused.[2]

In an offer of proof outside the presence of the jury, former Wenatchee CPS caseworker Juan Garcia testified that he saw Perez coercively question Cherie Town at the Town residence. After Jeff was removed by CPS following his parents' arrest, he was sent to Pine Crest Hospital in Coeur d'Alene, Idaho for psychiatric treatment, where he remained during the time he said the Robersons had molested him, Garcia said. Garcia testified that he had complained to his supervisor, Tim Abbey, about the methods of foster parent Micki Reyes-Vogam, who was "reprimanded" for questioning her foster children about sexual abuse. Although Garcia made these reports multiple times, Abbey, "was not that concerned," he said. Judge Small refused to permit any of Garcia's testimony to go before the jury.

---

[2] Yuille cautions that this dynamic is "purely conjectural, but says that it offers a possible explanation for such cases and their confusing, inconsistent, and often fantastic patterns. Cross-contamination between children or families might further serve to explain these allegations. Knowledge of each other's allegations could be disastrous if an interviewer were to attempt to ascertain whether the children could confirm each other's story, and doubly so if the interviewer were to use inappropriate techniques." (Yuille, Tymofievich, and Marxsen, "The Nature of Allegations of Child Sexual Abuse.")

The judge refused to permit testimony by children to show the pattern of Perez's coercive interrogation techniques. In another offer of proof outside of the presence of the jury, Kelly Allbee testified that Perez came to her school and interrogated her between 9 A.M. and 2:15 P.M. and refused to let her eat lunch. Perez said, "You were at Bob Devereaux's house and a whole bunch of people molested you," she testified. "And he kept at it and at it and at it." Kelly said that she had been scared and "freaked out," she "wanted to get out of there," and she felt suicidal.

She testified that Perez had said, "You better start telling the truth or your mom's gonna go to jail and you'll never see her again. . . . Then I started agreeing with him. . . . Later on he picked up the phone and said 'Your mom's gonna be arrested.' . . . Then he says 'You'd better start zooming. Talk real fast and tell what I want to hear or your mother's going to jail. . . . You got ten minutes. I can stop the cops from arresting your mom.' "

Judge Small ruled that Kelly and other children were not permitted to testify as part of the trial because the defense hadn't made a sufficient showing that Perez's acts were habitual. For this reason the relevance of the children's testimony was outweighed by its prejudicial effect, especially given Perez's "limited relationship" to the case.

Some clue to Small's rulings could be discerned by his statement to *Newsweek* reporter Mark Miller, who asked him during the trial whether he would be available for an interview. According to Miller, Small replied that he would be granting no interviews until after the Robersons' *sentencing*.

In spite of the rulings, the defense was clearly making progress. Many teenage witnesses testified they went to the church on the same nights and days Mary testified she and others were molested while bound and gagged. They saw nothing amiss and people were constantly coming and going to the food bank, which was never locked and was connected to the church. Adult defense witnesses verified the children's statements.

On Wednesday, December 6, Van Siclen at last had had enough of the court's routine use of unrecorded sidebars. Repeatedly Van Siclen asked that the court reporter be allowed to record the arguments of counsel and the judge's responses, which were made at the bench out of the hearing, if not the view, of the jury. Each time Judge Small cajoled him out of it.

Fed up at last, Van Siclen argued that the judge was depriving his client of a record for appeal. Small refused to ask the court reporter to move her equipment a few inches closer to the bench so that she could record the proceeding. Instead he ordered the jury to troop out of the courtroom each time Van Siclen wanted to make a record of the responses to objections. One time when Van Siclen requested a sidebar, Small looked at the jury, rolled his eyes, and asked the jury to recess. Van Siclen was incensed.

"When you send the jury out, you're mocking me," he said to Small after the jury had filed out. "You're making facial expressions. You're making me look like the bad guy."

The disruptions while the jury trooped out of the courtroom continued throughout the day as defense attorneys called state and county employees to the stand. Katie Carrow, CPS caseworker, testified that when she interviewed one of the children, "I told her we'd already talked to other children and adults who said things and now I wanted to hear her side of the story."

"And at some point as she was verbalizing what was going on did you reach a point where you weren't getting

any more information and you told her you thought there
was more for her to tell?'' asked Van Siclen.

"Yes, among others,'' said Carrow.

"Would that be a suggestive question?''

". . . I would not call it a suggestive question. I would
call it a conversational question,'' said Carrow.

Carrow said when she interviewed Jeff Town and found
evidence of abuse she didn't follow up with a written
report, although Van Siclen cited Revised Code of Washington 26.44.030, which mandates written reports of ''non
emergent'' abuse allegations within seventy-two hours.
Although she had interviewed Jeff on March 3, Carrow
didn't make a written report, and Perez completed what
Carrow called a ''joint report'' on March 11.

Donna Anderson, therapist for Children's Home Society, testified about Roberta's therapy, which she had escalated once she learned the girl might be placed with
relatives. Anderson had showed Roberta a book with
graphic, cartoonish illustrations of adults, naked and in
sexual situations. She explained she had introduced the
book as a therapy device with Roberta because she believed she was molested by her father.

Perez took the stand wearing a navy shirt and one of
his many ties with a pattern of the moon and stars. It had
been a battle getting him there because his attorney, Patrick McMahon, and Douglas County prosecutors argued
he played no role in the Douglas County prosecutions.
Judge Small permitted him to testify, under tight parameters, because his foster children were named as victims—but only as his testimony pertained to them. Perez
appeared nervous, but he adjusted his tie, thrust out his
chin, and calmly faced the dapper Van Siclen. What were
some of do's and don'ts of interviewing children? asked
Van Siclen.

Perez said that among the main list of don'ts in child

interviews was "not to ask leading questions." Questions, he said, should be "open-ended"—ones that don't suggest the answer to a child. "It's important not to tell a child the specifics of what another victim or suspect said," he said. He added that an interviewer should "get down to the level of a child and not violate his personal space . . . not stand and hover over" the child. A child might want to hug or hold him during the interview, said Perez, but that would not be appropriate. "Boundaries must be established in the interview."

Perez said he hadn't bought or read any policy protocols, training manuals, or psychological or social treatises about interviewing children. He threw away Katie Carrow's notes of their interview with Jeff Town and, after all, no policy barred such an action. He admitted he didn't report to authorities in writing Jeff's disclosure of abuse within a seventy-two-hour period as the law required, although he verbally informed another police officer of the boy's statement. "All of the children named [by Jeff] were already in foster care," said Perez, although this in fact was inaccurate. At any rate it would be "difficult to take action" regarding the unnamed children "because I don't know where they are."

At the end of the morning of December 6, Small mysteriously announced the court was adjourned. The reason wouldn't become generally known until the next day: Defense investigator Larry Daly told Judge Small he had taped an interview with a girl who was a classmate of Mary Everett late the night before. The girl said Mary was badly bruised by Perez the morning she was supposed to testify. Mary told her this kind of thing had happened before and just a few days earlier Perez threw her to the ground and kicked her. Van Siclen argued that Perez's actions were violations of criminal assault statutes and

Washington administrative codes, and immediate action should be taken to report Perez's conduct to the proper authorities. He called for a joint interview of the child and a ruling that if Mary confirmed the allegation, he could question Perez on the subject in front of the jury.

Over the prosecutor's strenuous relevancy objections, Judge Small agreed to set up a joint interview of Mary involving representatives of DCFS, law enforcement, the prosecutor's office, and the defense. Detective Perez was not to be advised of the meeting, cautioned Small, to protect Mary and the integrity of her statements.

At the interview, attended by eight adults from these various agencies, Mary said Perez had forcefully grabbed her arm. She showed them a large purple bruise. He had bruised her because she was "acting like a butt" by playing up and refusing to go to her room, she said. She added that at some recent but indefinite time Perez had painfully twisted her arm behind her back, threw her to the floor, and straddled and sat on her.

On December 7, Perez took the stand and tersely acknowledged he had bruised his foster daughter's arm the morning before she testified against the Robersons. "On November 30, did you have a situation arise in your home with Mary in which you grasped her by the arm and put a large bruise on the triceps of her right arm?" asked Van Siclen.

"I did," said Perez, explaining he had grasped her by the arm and led her to her room.

"Within the last three to four weeks was there another occasion when you grasped your foster daughter, twisted her arm behind her back, forced her to the ground, and straddled her?" asked Van Siclen.

"No, I did not."

"Has anything like that happened in the last five

weeks?'' asked Van Siclen, rocking on his heels and looking at the floor of the hushed courtroom.

"Yes, it has.''

"As a foster parent, are you aware of foster parents' requirement for corporal punishment?''

"Yes, I am,'' testified Perez.

Although the defense wasn't permitted to explore Perez's motives or whether he had been disciplining Mary, the prosecutor was allowed to establish that he had been merely ''restraining'' her.

"Within the past four weeks has there been any discussion between yourself and perhaps Luci regarding Mary and her moving from your home?'' asked Van Siclen.

"No,'' said Perez flatly.

"Was it under consideration?''

"No.''

"Within the past five weeks did you discuss such a subject?''

"We have had meetings with the guardian ad litem, the caseworker, and counsel.''

Van Siclen asked if during those meetings the subject had come up that Mary was having difficulties in his home.

"In my opinion,'' said Perez, ''she was not happy. The purpose of the staffing was that Mary indicated on occasions that she wants to move.''

After the excitement of the Perez testimony, it was almost anticlimactic when the Robersons took the stand, also on December 7. Pastor Roberson explained that he was not an ordained minister but he took on the responsibilities of the East Wenatchee Pentecostal Church at the request of church elders in 1989.

"My training was the school of hard knocks,'' he said. He said he'd opened the food bank when approached in April 1991 by an organization in Wenatchee, after they'd lost the food bank at the Catholic church. The food bank served around 110 people on the days it was open, which added up to thousands a month, he said. "I did all the work except on Sunday morning."

Roberson testified that he came to know the Everett and Miller children because of their participation in church activities. Ann and Mary Everett and Aubrey and Charlene Miller "ran around a lot together," he said. Roberson said that be became concerned because of the arrest of Harold and Idella Everett, and at that time he started to conduct his own investigation, gathering documentation, watching court proceedings, talking to other concerned people. He said that he attended Idella Everett's sentencing hearing and testified on her behalf and when he left the courtroom, Perez, who was standing behind him, said "We warned you Roberson, we warned you!"

But prosecutors called Chelan County Prosecutor Roy Fore as a rebuttal witness. Fore testified that he sat near Roberson and Perez at Idella Everett's sentencing hearing and followed Roberson when he left the room, yet he didn't hear the exchange.

Roberson said in January he was warned, "If you have any further contact with the Everett children or go to hearings, you will be arrested for witness tampering." Nevertheless, he said he became "a little vocal" when he spoke out in a public forum about "what was going on." He was arrested within days of the forum.

Roberson firmly denied he had molested any children.

And, firmly and biting back tears, so did Connie Roberson. She described herself as "a typical minister's wife." She said she cleaned the church, ordered books and Sunday School literature, cleaned and organized the food bank, played the piano and sang at church, taught Sunday School and "took care of Roby and Roberta."

The jury listened intently.

But many of the media had long since scurried to their telephones and laptops with the news about Perez. By the end of the day, the state and local responses were both astonishing and predictable. Although Chelan County Deputy Prosecutor Roy Fore said it would be inappropriate of him to say whether any further action would be taken against Perez, Perez's attorney, City Attorney Patrick McMahon, muttered, "There's nothing to it," moments after he and Perez left the courtroom. Before a bank of cameras, McMahon accused the defense of trying to shift focus from the abuse of children to an attack on his client. "They want to point the finger at a detective who had nothing to do with the case."

By the next day, the official word was in: The Department of Social and Health Services found the Perez home was safe. Washington state DSHS spokesman Kathy Spears said, "After investigating, we find that the defense team's allegation of abuse, which was not made by the foster child, is unfounded, and we believe the children are safe in their foster home." Spears was splitting hairs, because the word "abuse" came from Daly and not from Mary, but there was no disputing the child's words, which Perez had validated. Spears's conclusion is hard to reconcile with the language of the Washington Administrative Code governing foster care, which bars such "physical restraints" as "a large adult sitting on or straddling a small child."[3] In referring to "investigating,"

---

[3] WAC 388-73-048(1) prohibits corporal punishment. However, under section (2), "The use of such amounts of physical restraint as may be necessary to: (a) Protect persons on the premises from physical injury, (b) Obtain possession of a weapon or other dangerous object, (c) Protect property from serious damage, shall not be construed to constitute corporal punishment."

Section (4) provides: "*Physical restraints which could be injurious are not to be used. These include but are not limited to: A large adult sitting on or straddling a small child*, sleeper holds, arm twisting, hair holds, and throwing children and youths against walls, furniture, or other large immobile objects." (italics added)

Spears meant only that state officials had reviewed the transcript of the interview with Mary ordered by Judge Small, and spoken to some of those present.

Wenatchee Child Welfare Services Supervisor Steve Warman was among eight adults who took part in the interview. He told the *Wenatchee World* that Perez's actions were reasonable. ''She told them she was behaving like a butt and that he had asked her to do something and she refused and she was calling him names and he'd asked her to go to her room and she wouldn't go, so he grabbed her around the arm and put her in the room and that's where she got the bruise from,'' said Warman. ''We don't consider a little bruise from grabbing her arm and putting her in her room abuse. That's not abuse, and we don't consider restraining a child when they're out of control abuse either.''

Douglas County Sheriff's Detective Doug Helvey and school counselor Nick Holstrom, who were also present for the interview, said they believed the events Mary had described represented reasonable restraint.

Larry Daly, also present, strongly disagreed. ''She said it hurt, it hurt, it was painful, and I've got to tell you something, that's abuse,'' he said. ''I intend to see the governor about this,'' said Daly. ''I can't believe anyone with a reasonable mind, sitting in that room, listening to what the child said, would try to minimize it. You know if it was anybody else, if that child went to a teacher and told the teacher what she told us, she would be removed from the home and there would be a police investigation.''

Not so, said Helvey. ''If I were to go out as a patrol deputy and I found this exact same situation in a home in Douglas County I would not arrest either parent,'' he said. Regarding the Everett children, ''because of what they've been through, they don't know how to be mildly upset. They just throw a tantrum, and the only way to keep them from hurting themselves or things in the home is for them to be restrained." In fact, he said, "I've got kids, and in my opinion Bob and Luci show amazing patience. . . . It just upsets me, because I think the children have been through way more than they deserve, and to some degree Bob has also."

Holstrom agreed. "I've been through so many of these and I wouldn't have even reported this one. I just feel really ticked off, that Mary had to go through this whole scenario."

"All this stuff they came up with was just done to make Bob look bad," said Helvey.

On Friday, the attorneys made their closing statements. "It takes a sex offender to catch a sex offender," said prosecutor Eric Biggars of the deal his office had struck with Gary Filbeck. The comment had an ironic twist, wrote Dorothy Rabinowitz in an editorial in the *Wall Street Journal*. Wrote Rabinowitz, the comment "inspired mordant reflections on the part of some spectators about the Wenatchee police, and child care workers."

Clem got in a final, petulant dig as he commented on the absence of semen in the church. Some of the stains on the church floor were suggestive of organic matter, he said, maybe even bodily fluids. Maybe the congregation urinated on the stage, Clem speculated, shrugging. Who could say what these people would do?

The case went to the jury at 7:30 Friday night. Small gave the jury a set of twenty-nine instructions to wade through. The Robersons, their lawyers, their supporters, and the media headed to the Waterville restaurant where they had convened for lunch and conversation nearly every day since the trial began. Some sat at tables pulled together in the brightly lit dining area. Others headed to the gloomy booths in the adjacent bar area. Back at the courthouse, sketch artists sold off their used courtroom drawings for fifty dollars a sketch.

Pastor Roberson, who had hoped against hope for an immediate acquittal, was obviously feeling the strain. Connie blinked back tears and hugged her friends. The Robersons gave their attorneys amateurish paintings done by friends, and someone gave Van Siclen one of the court-room artists' sketches. For those of us who slumped on chairs or benches in the restuarant, it was a long ninety minutes.

At around 9:00 P.M., word came back that the jury was recessing for the weekend. The Robersons' faces were etched with a mixture of relief and dread at the long hours stretching in front of them.

But the weekend was eventful. First, at a gathering of the Wenatchee Foster Parents' Association, sponsored by the Policemans' Guild, Perez was awarded a plaque for his exemplary service as a foster parent.

The Robersons went to their church as usual, although Roberson had stepped down as official pastor when he was charged. Instead, James Layne, Yakima-based district superintendent for fifty-four Pentecostal Churches of God in Washington, northern Idaho, and Alaska, led the serv-ice. "This morning we know that one of the most impor-tant things to pray for is this jury," Layne said. "We pray that the truth will prevail. . . . We pray for an acquittal." As he listened, Roberson sat with his arm draped around one of the children of his congregation and watched two six-year-old twins and their eight-year-old sister who were coloring Bible illustrations.

"We know it's all in the hands of the Lord," said Con-nie Roberson, clutching her Bible after the service. "If I go to prison, it's because there's someone there who needs the Lord. If I don't go to prison, it's because the Lord needs me out here," she said.

On Sunday afternoon, I was talking by telephone to Pastor Roberson when a call came in over his police scanner.

"Hold on," he said. "It's Perez's code number . . . calling for backup in detaining an eleven-year-old in a parking lot!" Our minds raced to the same question: Could it be Ann Everett?

It was. Ann was arrested after Perez reported she was out of control in a Payless parking lot in Wenatchee. Luci Perez said Ann had climbed on top of the car, caused a small dent, and kicked her sister Mary. Ann was hauled off to juvenile court and cited for malicious mischief in the third degree and assault in the fourth degree. Ann spent the night in juvenile detention and was released pending trial to the Perez home at a hearing in juvenile court on Monday, December 11: the day of the Roberson verdict.

That morning, the usual procession of the charged, the concerned, the media, and the merely curious wound its way up the sage-covered hills, past the high pastures where brown stubble thrust itself through the snow, to the Waterville courthouse, then on to the usual Waterville restaurant. Shortly after noon, word came that the verdict was in. Connie and Roby Roberson huddled with their lawyers then trooped back to court.

When the jury walked into the courtroom, they dropped their eyes, avoiding eye contact with the Robersons or their attorneys—usually not a good sign for the defense. First Connie stood, clutching her husband's hand in the hushed courtroom. As the eight-man, four-woman jury looked on, Judge Small read the verdicts. After each reading of "not guilty," Connie forcefully squeezed Roby's hand and sobbed. In the end, she was acquitted of two counts of first-degree child rape and three counts of first-degree child molestation. A suppressed moan erupted

from the spectators, most of them Roberson supporters—
who had been warned to avoid such displays.

Then it was Pastor Roberson's turn. He stood, his chin
quivering with emotion as he learned that the jury found
him not guilty of four counts of first-degree child rape,
four counts of first-degree child molestation, and one
count of third-degree child molestation. As Judge Small
read the final count of "not guilty," the Robersons' supporters and many of the jury members were crying, and
their friends and relatives rushed forward to embrace
them.

Said Connie Roberson after the verdict, "If you ever
have that dream where you're falling off a cliff and you
either hit bottom or wake up—that's exactly the way it
was. Falling and falling and finally coming to an end."

Within days the Robersons were given physical custody
of Roberta, who would be subject to such limited CPS
restrictions as counseling for a period of six months. A
couple days after she came home, I called the Robersons'
residence to ask about her.

"Just a minute," said Pastor Roberson.

"Hello," said a tiny child's voice. For all my attempts
at professional detachment and dispassion, I was entirely
undone.

In the days to come, jury members talked to the press.
Some of them commented that the trial had degenerated
into ugly and offensive name-calling. Worse, it was an
evidentiary vacuum. Jury foreman David Fruit, a Douglas
County orchardist, told the *Wenatchee World,* "There
were some of us on the jury that were very concerned and
disturbed that neither the Douglas County sheriff nor the
Douglas County prosecutors had invested any time or effort on determining the truth or falsity of the charges."
Fruit added that the jury was offended by the prosecutor's
"insulting" closing remarks and by his failure to inves-

tigate responsibly. "He said in court it's his responsibility to find the truth that would exonerate the innocent as well as convict the guilty. It seems he didn't do that."

The jury may have achieved some insight into what it is to be wrongly accused. Said juror Wes Olinger, "when they were standing up and reading the charges, being not guilty, I really felt sorry for those people, for what they had to go through." Pastor Roberson, Olinger said, "looked broken. I almost felt like reaching in my pocket to give him money."

But some didn't share these sentiments. Months later, Judge Small told Siegesmund Von Ilsemann, Washington, D.C., bureau chief for *Der Spiegel,* a German weekly newsmagazine, that the three acquittals in Douglas County didn't signal innocence. "You must understand. A jury verdict means only there's a reasonable doubt of their guilt," said Small, according to Von Ilsemann, meaning the Robersons and Honnah Sims might indeed have committed the crimes.

22:

Winter 1995–Spring 1996

═══════════

Happy Ending

═══════════

The end of the Roberson trial brought with it the artifice of closure, the ironic sense of justice done yet unresolved. In a country hungry for happy endings, how could we resist being lulled into complacency by the stunning acquittal of the minister and his charming wife, their emotional reunion with their adorable five-year-old daughter?

Wrote John Carlin, reporter for London's *Independent,* "It is a perfect Hollywood script. The leading characters are a crusading church minister, a rogue detective and a dashing defense lawyer. The setting is small-town America. The story is about one man's battle for justice and a father's love for his child. There is a witch hunt, there are false accusations of illicit sex and a nail-biting courtroom climax. And, yes, there is a happy ending."

Therein lay the danger. By December 12, the journalists and photographers and film crews had folded up their notebooks and tripods and rushed out of town to new assignments and holidays with their families. A long doldrum settled over Wenatchee: a sense of waiting, of bitter unease. Part of the unrest began at the offices of U.S. Attorney General Janet Reno, who was known to have made an undisclosed decision about the allegations of civil rights violations in Wenatchee.

In the wake of the Roberson trial, Wenatchee city officials moved toward ''community healing'' and the Robersons, their lawyers, and the journalists got in their final licks. A reporter for the *New York Times* said the Roberson verdict was a ''stunning rebuke to Detective Perez.'' But in the myopic world of local government there was a solution to this public perception. Chelan County Prosecutor Gary Riesen announced that the investigation was ''officially closed'' and Perez would be rotating in January from his exciting position as sex crimes investigator, into the mundane world of the street crimes division.[1] It was strictly a routine rotation. As they always had, Wenatchee-area bureaucrats defended the police and prosecutors and pointed out the official statistics that passed for legal checks and balances in Wenatchee, and the fact that the bad press was nothing more than media sensationalism.

Writing of the politically charged atmosphere surrounding the Roberson decision, John Carlin perhaps summed it up best in the *Independent*. ''The local chamber of commerce, the mayor, the editors of *The Wenatchee World* bristled. Their town was being portrayed as darkly insular, weird. So they hit back, accusing *The Wall Street Journal,* in particular, of engaging in tabloid journalism, and the media, in general, of being engaged in a disinformation conspiracy with a network of child molesters.''

In the eyes of Wenatchee officials, I was part of this

---

[1] In fact, according to a statement by Wenatchee Police Chief Ken Badgley to the *Wenatchee World,* Robert Perez is on active duty with the Wenatchee Police Department, but his primary duty is assisting city attorneys on the multimillion-dollar lawsuit against Perez, the city of Wenatchee and various state, city, and county officials. (''Teacher Backs Girl's Sexual Claims,'' The *Wenatchee World,* by Jeanette Marantos, January 27, 1997).

conspiracy, as I had worked to keep the public focused on the need for an outside investigation. I had experienced that behind each official statistic there dwelt a human being.

On Christmas Day, 1995, I talked to most of the convicted Wenatchee women who were imprisoned at the Washington State Correctional Center for Women, a seemingly innocuous cluster of low-slung buildings surrounded by coils of razor wire. It was clear these women were pinning their hopes on an outside investigation, but their thoughts were preoccupied with their children.

The prison Christmas was bare-bones, according to Carol Doggett: Inmates got a bag of candy and a cafeteria-style holiday meal. "Last Christmas, Mark and I sat in the bedroom and listened to the children laugh," she said. "Even then we knew we wouldn't have them forever." Doggett said that she hadn't seen her children in nearly a year.

"If I could have one wish for the new year," said Linda Miller, whose children had testified against the Robersons, "it is that they listen to the children when they say nothing happened. When a little girl says, 'Don't make me go home to him [Perez],' why don't they listen to her? . . . I just want the kids to be safe."

The previous Christmas, Jeanie Bendt was in the Chelan County Jail. A guard threw a bag of candy at her and said, "You don't deserve this." Months later the state terminated her parental rights. "I wanted to die," she said. But she was powerless in her legal efforts to fight the actions, just as she'd been powerless months earlier to resist the methods of Perez, or her lawyer's persistent advice to plead guilty. Now Bendt was struggling to vacate her plea.

Laura Holt's last Christmas with her family was in 1993. Christmas 1995 was just another day. She worked

all day for thirty cents an hour. Holt said that she shared
a unit with Doggett, Dorris Green, Connie Cunningham,
Bendt, and Cherie Town. Along with Idella Everett and
Linda Miller, the women have lost a total of twenty-seven
children. The loss of the children is all that matters, said
Holt. "The rest can be replaced."

Dorris Green agreed. "I think about my kids twenty-
four hours a day," she said. "I get in no trouble here,
have no infractions, mind my own business. But I feel sad
all the time. I know my kids need me." Green said that
within the next month she was expected to go to dependency court, where the state would try to terminate her
parental rights.

"I wish people could get to know the women who are
here, the people who've been wrongly accused," said
Connie Cunningham, who received a sentence of over
forty years for complicity to her husband's abuse of their
children. "Our foremost thoughts are for the children. We
worry about their mental damage because of these investigations. We worry about their damaged relationships.

"These investigations make a mockery of a very real
thing," she said. "The pain of being abused is very real."
Cunningham said she was worried that children in Wenatchee, like her own children, are being asked to assim-
ilate false but painful memories. "We're caught in the
grip of a system that we're barely beginning to understand. We're not asking for pity, but only for fair play."

Among those who agreed with this sentiment was
Washington State Representative Val Stevens. In late December, Stevens wrote to a representative of the state Department of Social and Health Services, calling for a probe
of Perez's credentials as foster parent and requesting that
the Everett children be removed from the Perez home because of his admissions of bruising and sitting on Mary
Everett. Stevens and Washington State Senator Pam

Roach were among those who proposed legislation designed to prevent some of the pitfalls of the Wenatchee
investigation, including videotaping of child interviews.

The Robersons came to legislative hearings along with
Roberta. "There are too many innocent people being destroyed. . . . We're here today because too many people
are saying the system works fine. It's broken. It's trashed,
it's absolutely trashed," testified Pastor Roberson in
Olympia, in support of a house bill.

Child protection advocates reacted predictably. Mary
Ann Murphy of Spokane's Regional Center for Child
Abuse and Neglect also objected to Roberson's statements. "It incenses me that anybody would trivialize the
injuries that we see in children," she said. But as fired
CPS worker Paul Glassen testified to the legislators, "You
have an agency that will not tolerate any internal criticism
or criticism from the community."

All of the bills to require videotaping of child interviews in sex abuse cases or to adopt child abuse investigators standards bills were later defeated, at the strong and
concerted urging of Washington state prosecutors.[2] Yet
prosecutors, unanimously and in another show of force,
successfully supported a "two strikes and you're out" bill
that mandates life in prison without possibility of parole

---

[2] A proposed bill drafted by John H. Hill, director of the Pierce County Department
of Assigned Counsel, would have created a pilot project involving a multisystem
child abuse interview team with such goals as reducing the number and frequency
of interviews of children, training interviewers according to established protocols,
and reliably recording child interviews. The bill, in drastically altered form, formed
the basis for legislative adoption of a review of child sexual abuse interview protocols and training standards through the Washington State Institute for Public
Policy. The institute's report, released in January 1997, proposed the adoption of
a pilot study such as that introduced in the 1996 legislature, to assist the state in
"evaluating the merits of videotaping." The institute's proposal included creating
an advisory group made up of prosecutors, defense lawyers, police, and victim
advocates to oversee the project, a state-of-the-art videotaping interview room, and
a reliable means of collecting data. The pilot project was reintroduced, and defeated, at the 1997 Washington legislature.

for certain defendants who have been convicted a second time for a sex offense, and other bills that enhanced consequences for child sex offenders. The paradox—draconian penalties for people who might be convicted as a result of unreliable interview methods—troubled prosecutors not at all and rated not a word in state newspapers.

By the end of January, editorials in the *Washington Post,* the *Wall Street Journal,* the *Washington Times,* the *Seattle Times,* and the *Seattle Post-Intelligencer* called for a federal investigation.

The *Washington Post* compared the circumstances in Wenatchee with the case of Elisa Izquierdo, a Brooklyn six-year-old who was allegedly beaten to death by her crack-addicted mother. According to the *Post,* the Izquierdo case "raised issues about the failure of the social service system in New York to protect a child in spite of requests from various quarters that she be removed from home for her own protection. . . . Such failure to act on evidence is one large part of the problem in dealing with cases of abuse of small children. Another large and entirely different part arises from circumstances such as those in the East Wenatchee, Wash., case, in which young children are pressed into testifying under circumstances suggesting that their testimony may be manipulated. Both parts of the problem have to do with the same thing: the fact that the society is dealing here with helpless, immature kids who, in the first instance, are incapable of defending themselves and, in the second, may be unreliable, overly influenced testifiers."

The *Washington Post* recognized that both extremes are part of a greater whole, a dysfunctional system irresponsibly dealing with vulnerable children. It suggested a solution responsive to critical fears that the pendulum might swing to the detriment of children: "It's time now for the Justice Department to look further into the Washington cases and to encourage a national consensus on standards for all similar prosecutions.''

It was just after 10 A.M. on February 2 when I received a call from the Public Affairs Office of the Department of Justice. The caller asked for my fax number because, he said, the department had made a decision regarding the Wenatchee sex-ring investigations. He couldn't hang up quickly enough.

In this way I was amazed to find myself among the privileged soon-to-be-faxed recipients of the letter written by U.S. Attorney General Janet Reno to Washington Governor Mike Lowry. I was sandwiched on the media list somewhere between the *Seattle Times* and the *Washington Post* and I was surprised to be there because up to now the Justice Department had patently ignored me.

The faxes arrived hours later, by coincidence or design at nearly the close of the business day in Washington, D.C. They arrived with hardly a whimper, were totally eclipsed by the threatened Seattle Seahawks transfer, and were all but incomprehensible. But the bottom line was clear: Attorney General Reno had declined to conduct an investigation of the practices of the Chelan and Douglas County governments.

''Based on a thorough review of the available materials, both the Civil Rights Division and The United States Attorney have concluded that these complaints do not present evidence of prosecutable violations of federal civil rights law,'' wrote Reno.

''Though I recognize that the charges in this matter raise serious issues and are certainly of deep concern to the community, the department's law-enforcement mandate is limited to investigations of possible violations of federal criminal laws,'' she went on.

In fact, Reno's decision was superficial and didn't pretend to determine the existence or nonexistence of civil rights violations, but only that these violations, if any, were not "prosecutable" according to practices of the current administration.[3] Why wouldn't the law apply to the many allegations of coercion, denial of requests for counsel, unjustified separation of children from Hispanic parents, and other serious allegations detailed in *"The Wenatchee Report"*? Because, according to Reno, the statute is "most often applied" in cases involving the illegal use of physical force as opposed to psychological coercion. Although this application is *usual,* it is not a requirement of the law, which is deliberately general, as is the Constitution to which it refers.[4]

What was the "thorough review"? A *Seattle Times* reporter had checked it out. "During a four-month review, Reno's office did not contact . . . Perez, his supervisors, either of two county prosecutors who filed charges, or several of the most vocal critics of the child-sex abuse prosecutions."

I checked among many of the key players and reminded myself that I'd offered several times to make myself and my documents available to the federal government. To the best of my knowledge, there hadn't been the semblance of an investigation. If the key government figures such as those in the prosecutor's office weren't contacted, it was unlikely that even police reports or legal proceedings were considered.

---

[3] United States Code Section 242 provides for penalties to "whoever, under color of any law, statute, ordinance, regulation, or custom, willfully subjects any person in any State protected by the constitution or laws of the United States, or to different punishments, pains, or penalties, on account of such person being an alien, or by reason of his color, or race, than are prescribed for the punishment of citizens . . ." According to this body of federal law, "prosecutable" violations are those where state or local government officials are shown to engage in misconduct which is both "official" and "willful."

[4] The law has been applied, for example, where a public defender allegedly extracted money from a client under a threat of inadequate legal representation.

Instead, by all indications, including the statements of Wenatchee government officials, the Justice Department relied for the most part on my investigative report, *"The Wenatchee Report,"* at least as the evidence of the concerns. Because the idea of a federal investigation was originally my own, and because it looked like I was the source of the "available materials," I was forced to ask myself if I had somehow dropped the ball.

The *Washington Post* said my report first raised major doubts about the cases. If so, that was as much as I had intended, as much as I had the power to accomplish, as much as I had represented in my report. State officials in Olympia had canceled my appointments and ignored my letters, phone calls, and requests for statistics; many Wenatchee-area officials had snubbed me; the key child witnesses were tightly contained by local authorities, far from the reach of someone like me. I was one person with no money, political backing, or subpoena powers, yet my report and the doubts it raised were *it*? There was a lesson there, but I didn't know what it was.

In the end, Reno's decision probably represented nothing more than the vagaries of the political winds. As a Justice Department source put it to me, the Wenatchee-area cases did not have the right measure of political appeal. A Spokane newspaper quoted an anonymous Department of Justice source as saying, "These victims were not blacks or gays. These are not people this administration is particularly sensitive to." Even less politically attractive was the very magnitude of the cases. According to an article in the *Washington Post,* Department of Justice sources claimed that federal intervention in Washington State's judicial proceedings would be "highly unusual" because the Department of Justice "would, in effect, be alleging that local prosecutors and judges were involved in misfeasance."

Washington's governor expressed disappointment in Reno's decision. Governor Lowry's deputy press secretary, Martin Mungia, said the governor hoped Reno would do a more thorough review. ''We were optimistic the Justice Department would get involved,'' said Mungia to the *Washington Post,* ''so now we have to digest this and see where we stand. . . . This was the best avenue to offer a good impartial review of the situation.'' To me, this appeared true: The obvious state remedies were such vehicles as a state grand jury (a virtually untried remedy in Washington State, which must be triggered by the request of such local government officials as a county judge or prosecutor), an investigation by the Washington State Patrol (whose officers are trained in traffic and drug matters), or the Washington State Attorney General's Office (the agency representing the DCFS employees who are now named as defendants in massive civil lawsuits).

''I just can't believe it,'' Bob Devereaux said to me, his voice rising in consternation. ''I was so sure they'd step in. How can they just ignore us? What happens to the people in this little town when there's injustice? How can we have faith in the system?''

''Look at what Janet Reno did at Ruby Ridge, look at what she did at Waco. This is what happens when justice resides in the shadow of politics,'' said Connie Roberson's attorney William Parker.

''Reno did not give Wenatchee a clean bill of health,'' lamented *Wenatchee World*'s editorial page editor Tracy Warner. Yet Reno had done the right thing, in his opinion. ''The federal government and the Justice Department have no business intervening in state and local court matters. Reno really has no authority to dive in with criminal investigations of police departments simply because noisy people are upset with local verdicts.''

Washington State House Speaker Clyde Ballard, himself from Wenatchee, said the Reno decision left many questions unanswered. With customary caution, Ballard told the *Wenatchee World*, "I'm not going to make judgment calls until I know what happened, but it's endless the reports I get. My phone never stops. I don't know if I'll hold a town hall meeting, but whatever I do will be designed to find a solution to the problem because I can guarantee you a lot of people on both sides are unhappy." Ballard did little or nothing.

Most Wenatchee officials were jubilant about the Reno decision and publicly announced they'd been vindicated. "I'd say I have felt all along our office had followed the proper procedures and used the state court in the proper way," said Chelan County Prosecutor Gary Riesen. "The fact that they decline to investigate confirms that."

"We couldn't have written it better ourselves," said Perez's attorney, City Attorney Patrick McMahon, in an interview with the *Seattle Post-Intelligencer*. But McMahon took on a tone of arrogance and menace when he spoke to the *Wenatchee World*. "Probably the most negative things ever written about the Wenatchee Police Department were in Lyon's report, and although we think it's totally false and incorrect the Justice Department looked at that, presumably at face value, and made a determination there was nothing there. It should put anyone on notice who plans on suing the Wenatchee Police or Detective Perez that we will seek every redress for sanctions from frivolous, unfounded lawsuits."

In February, I met with Kent Caputo, attorney for then-Governor Lowry. The governor wouldn't meet with me, said Caputo, because "that would be taking sides." I had an "agenda," he said, because I had authored *"The Wenatchee Report,"* which called for a governmental investigation. Yet Lowry *had* met with a delegation of prosecutors purported to represent the position of all of the prosecutor's offices throughout the state, said Caputo. Their position was simple: The governor should stay out of it—we'll police our own.

Caputo spoke in savvy political platitudes: "They're circling the wagons," he said, "the line has been drawn in the sand." If Governor Lowry decided to support a state investigation, "the battle lines will be drawn." Wenatchee-area officials, prosecutors across the state, and state officials were enraged that the governor went over their heads, not consulting them before sending the letter to Reno, he said.

Through it all, he wove the thread of the governor's abiding "concern" about the situation. The word *concern* took on the kind of abstract quality bespeaking political edginess that it had when I'd met months earlier with Washington State House Speaker Clyde Ballard, who said the Wenatchee cases were "troubling" to him but potential "political suicide." Of course I could only gauge the depth of the governor's concern by way of his emissary, who was, at least, visibly nervous. Caputo said the letter Lowry sent to Reno's office didn't so much signal the governor's concern about the investigation as his concern about the nightmare of dealing with it himself. The letter was written in deliberately vague language in an intent to convey maximum neutrality and minimum input on a course of action, said Caputo, who played a role in its construction.

Now the issue had dropped squarely into the governor's lap and he clearly had no idea what to do with it. The governor would be happy to direct the responsibility elsewhere, said Caputo, while reminding me that I had made it difficult to divert responsibility to the more obvious state investigative body—the state attorney general's office. Months earlier, I had sent the governor and Reno letters that underscored the fact that the state attorney general is legal counsel for DCFS caseworkers who were entwined in the criminal prosecutions and in pending civil suits.[5]

I proposed alternatives, but didn't walk away with the expectation that anything would come of them, and indeed apparently Governor Lowry did nothing. In any event, I wasn't going to be part of the equation. "I'm gonna take a whole lot of flak for just talking to you," said Caputo.

Before I left, Caputo gave me a copy of a letter on City of Wenatchee letterhead that was hand-delivered to the governor's office on February 8. The letter, dated a day earlier, was directed to the governor and to House Speaker Clyde Ballard, and signed by Wenatchee Mayor Earl Tilly and two Wenatchee city commissioners. The governor had considered the letter with some relief.

The letter began by expressing satisfaction that Reno "found no improprieties" in the investigation. "The Attorney General's investigation is not the only independent investigation that came to the conclusion that the investigation was proper and legal. The City's insurance pool had the former police chief of Bellevue, Don Van Blaricom, complete an independent investigation of the Wenatchee Police Department's involvement in the cases. It is Mr. Van Blaricom's finding that the Police Department acted properly and legally. He even went so far as to comment that it was the worst case of 'media frenzy' he had ever seen. . . . We are confident that the City of Wenatchee acted appropriately at all times in these matters and we have always felt that these matters should be handled through proper channels and not in the press. Time

---

[5] State Attorney General Christine Gregoire had demonstrated the effects of a similar conflict of interest when she investigated allegations of abuse involving DSHS employees at the Okay Boys Ranch, a state-licensed juvenile home, and the results had been released in a recent report.

has shown that this was the proper course of action to take.''

D. P. ''Don'' Van Blaricom is a retired police chief from Bellevue, Washington, who for the last eleven years has made a substantial living as an expert witness-consultant on the propriety of police activities. Wenatchee's insurance carrier through the Association of Washington Cities hired Van Blaricom at the rate of $1,850 per day. But the city didn't have to fork out major bucks, because he worked with lightning speed. The entire investigation took only a day, which he spent interviewing four Wenatchee police officers (Perez; his chief, Ken Badgley; and two other officers) and reading the two-hundred-page *''Wenatchee Report.''* He didn't talk to any witnesses, attorneys, children, or defendants, nor did he review any police reports, legal paperwork, transcripts, or other documentation.

Instead, he assessed the relative credibility of the police and the critics whose concerns, he claimed, were all neatly set out in *''The Wenatchee Report.''* At a press conference at Wenatchee City Hall, Van Blaricom said the report had ''no credibility in it'' because it relied on ''disgruntled employees'' and ''people who pled guilty or were found guilty in court after all the protections of the criminal justice system.'' (In fact, many of the witness statements on which *''The Wenatchee Report''* relied were from people who were neither convicted nor accused, including children, and the report was based in large part on Wenatchee police reports, court pleadings, transcripts, and other official documentation. Unlike Van Blaricom's investigation, *''The Wenatchee Report''* took four months to complete.)

Perez and his colleagues, on the other hand, were entirely credible, said Van Blaricom. He didn't try to verify the statements the officers made to him by cross-checking

them with police reports or transcripts, in part because the
officers had "testified under oath and juries believed
them." As a result, people were charged and convicted
under courts of law, which "seems to be sufficient" to
prove they are truthful. He said that police are frequently
called upon to lie and use ruse to extract confessions—
indeed, cops have "a duty to lie" because such is a badge
of good police work. Yet cops can't lie convincingly
about themselves because they can only lie when it is "for
good of God and country," he said.

Leading questions, psychological coercion of adults,
and destruction of notes are similarly appropriate, even
desirable police techniques if they get results, said Van
Blaricom. "I have no problem with an aggressive police
investigation," he said. In his opinion, such aggressive
techniques weren't improperly used against people of
mental limitations or this fact would have been successfully raised as a defense. Although he said that the use of
leading questions with children isn't a good idea and children can be suggestible, he added that in this case leading
questions weren't at issue because there was corroboration.

Nor did he feel it was a problem that Perez, in his dual
role of chief investigative officer and foster parent, lived
with key complaining witnesses. They weren't his real
children, after all. He claimed, inaccurately, that Perez's
foster child only once made statements to Perez and his
wife while they were alone, and then the circumstances
were unavoidable.

Van Blaricom said the only problems with the investigation were the result of a media "feeding frenzy,"
which led public criticism to get "out of hand." The media were naive or misguided about the dynamics of group
sex abuse, he said. "It's probably happened in their own
community as well but it's not been discovered by them."

Van Blaricom said the Wenatchee Police Department "should be credited" for its ability to recognize and aggressively investigate this problem and that "it's a terrible irony" that the Wenatchee Police Department was criticized after it did such a uniquely good job.[6]

Van Blaricom admitted to a reporter from the *Wenatchee World* that he isn't an expert on child sex abuse investigations and he has handled few of such cases during his twenty-nine years in law enforcement. City Attorney McMahon, who introduced Van Blaricom at the press conference, said that there would be no written report of his findings and that the press release had been a police obligation in the face of the possible civil lawsuits. Van Blaricom added that if the results had been unfavorable to the Wenatchee Police Department, they wouldn't have been released to the general public.

By the end of February, many of these lawsuits became a reality. Six former sex ring defendants filed claims through their attorney Robert Van Siclen: the Robersons, Honnah Sims, Donna Rodriguez, Karen Lopez, and Susan Everett. The claims, preliminary to lawsuits, named state child welfare agencies, local police, and prosecutors. Attorney Steve Lacy filed claims against Perez and state welfare agencies on behalf of Bob Devereaux and three former Wenatchee DCFS caseworkers, Paul Glassen, Juana Vasquez, and Juan Garcia. In all, state and city officials and agencies faced claims approaching a hundred million dollars. Perez, as promised, filed counterclaims for malicious prosecution against the civil plaintiffs, through his attorney Patrick McMahon.

---

[6] In another ironic twist, reported by the Associated Press on February 22, 1997, Van Blaricom was accused of sexual abuse in a civil lawsuit filed on June 27, 1996, by a woman claiming to be his daughter who said that Van Blaricom had sexually molested her in the 1970s. Van Blaricom has countersued for defamation and denies the allegations and his paternity of the woman.

In the face of the lawsuits and relentless public criticism, McMahon went on an aggressive campaign to silence the critics. On February 2, 1996, hours after the Reno decision was faxed to Wenatchee city officials, I was served at my home with a faxed copy of a subpoena *duces tecum,* which ordered me to appear at a deposition and produce documents, notes, tapes, and letters that I had gained in the course of my investigations. The subpoena was from Perez, through McMahon, and purported to be in response to civil actions by three of the plaintiffs in lawsuits against Perez, the Washington Department of Social and Health Services, and certain named caseworkers and other government officials. Also subpoenaed on that day were Spokane television reporter Tom Grant and VOCAL representative Bob Kinkade. Working individually, the three of us had been responsible for much of the national awareness of the Wenatchee cases.

I set out on the difficult mission of finding an attorney. It was tough because most lawyers have better sense than to willingly represent another lawyer, and because I was the worst kind of lawyer: one with next to no money. I had a difficult case: There is no statutory journalist privilege in Washington State and the body of Washington common law on journalistic privilege has never been applied to book writers. The ACLU wouldn't take my case; nor would the Authors' Guild, because I wasn't expected to win. I announced my intention up front: I would go to jail before I handed over confidential information or names and facts about my sources to the government they feared.

But I wasn't the only problem. Lawyers are expensive; lawyers are controlling; lawyers vary hugely in matters of competence. I got lucky with Steve Hemmet, formerly an attorney for the U.S. Department of Justice, and Thomas Nast, great-great-grandnephew of the political cartoonist by the same name, who wrote the kind of brief that appeared destined to carve new territory at the appellate court level.

Tom Grant's subpoena was quashed as overly broad: Not only had Perez's subpoena called for his broadcast tapes and documents, but the ebb and flow of his sources, interviewers, and conversations. Kinkade had no out. He submitted and McMahon asked him to name the members of the Concerned Citizens for Legal Accountability, and to reveal his own use and dissemination of information via the computer. Perez, it seemed, wanted to find out which Wenatchee citizens were exercising their First Amendment rights to assemble freely and exchange ideas.

In his brief in my case, McMahon made his animosity toward such practices perfectly clear. I was not acting as a journalist, but as an "attorney/advocate," or, as he more colorfully put it, "a chameleon of significant proportion" because I had stepped outside of my more usual lawyer role. McMahon described my writings as "materials advocating against the government."

"Contrary to Lyon's assertion that the First Amendment does not allow journalists to be used as post-facto private investigators for Perez, the same is certainly true that it does not allow Lyon to hide behind its protections while using it as a tool to espouse her dislike for police, governments and the Attorney General of the United States," wrote McMahon. "Ultimately, the question becomes one of whether her reporting is truthful and whether Lyon is acting in conspiracy with these Plaintiffs and others involved in these sex cases. . . . A conspiracy between Lyon and the Plaintiffs as well as Lyon being the tool of the attorneys suing Perez and the Wenatchee Police Department by publishing prejudicial information in a negative pretrial media blitz needs to be explored under oath."

And, of course, there was the bottom line. "Lyon has attacked Perez and the Wenatchee Police Department and proclaimed police impropriety of the greatest magnitude, despite the constitutional safeguards and checks and balances of our criminal justice system. The record of successful criminal prosecutions of child sex abuse offenders in Chelan county speaks for itself," wrote McMahon.

My attorneys warned that McMahon's brief signaled possible criminal conspiracy charges. *Reader's Digest* senior staff editor Trevor Armbrister, who was in Wenatchee researching an upcoming article, called to say he'd spent some time with McMahon and other government officials and he felt that they were on the verge of arresting me.

Also on my mind was the possibility of civil contempt for failing to submit to deposition. I was afraid for myself and afraid for my sources. Why would they come forward to journalists if they couldn't speak out without fear of reprisal? What hope was there for justice in Wenatchee then?

In an abstract way, I thought about jail most of my waking moments. Would they give me an extra blanket? Would they let me wear my underwear? Would somebody beat me up, like they had some of the alleged molesters, because I was one of the "critics"?

When I spoke of my circumstances, I found a curious catch in my throat. I was profoundly embarrassed to ask for help, and I yearned for a professional distance that, in my circumstances, was no longer available to me. I felt, in a sense, like a victim. The feeling was debilitating and altogether unpleasant and minuscule compared to the experiences of those I considered to be true victims—the wrongly accused and the children who were regularly reminded that they'd been betrayed.

Writers wrote affidavits on my behalf, among them

Armbrister, who wrote: "I believe that attempts to compel Ms. Lyon to submit to a deposition and to provide documentation . . . constitutes an outrage. The parties requesting this deposition know what has been happening in Wenatchee; it is their silence and refusal to face unpleasant truths which has compelled courageous journalists . . . to proceed with their work."

In the end, Thurston County Judge Thomas McPhee ruled that my work was privileged and had only been waived as to the videotape of Scharlann Filbeck, which Judge Small had already ordered me to produce. I was saved and my sources were intact and I was privileged to glimpse the humanity at the noble but maligned heart of journalism.

Similar repressive rumblings came out of Wenatchee in the months to come. Wenatchee police officials forced the closure of an America Online Wenatchee Web site run by the CCLA because it contained *"The Wenatchee Report"* and legal and other documents unfavorable to Perez. The site remained shut down for a few days and then reopened on the condition that certain offensive documents were deleted. A CCLA member who wrote letters to the editor of the *Wenatchee World* critical of the local police investigations told me he was warned by a police department employee that Wenatchee police were keeping dossiers on people like him.

CCLA heads Mario and Connie Fry were deposed: The questions were intensely personal and explored issues of their pasts, the pasts of acquaintances and friends who were critical of the government's practices, their religious affiliations, their contribution to the contagion of information. McMahon asked them to disclose the membership, organization, and practices of the Mormon church to which they belonged. The Frys were badly shaken and other Wenatchee residents who had once dared to speak out became notably restrained.

Wenatchee officials successfully blocked efforts by several U.S. congressmen to hold federal congressional hearings on the Wenatchee cases as well as similar cases across the nation. In a letter dated June 24, 1996, directed to Washington State Congressman "Doc" Hastings through his legislative aide, Todd Ungerecht, Chelan County Prosecutor Gary Riesen wrote that the media reporting of the events "has been largely inaccurate. These cases have been characterized as all arising from allegations made by two foster children in the care of a detective for the Wenatchee Police Department. Only a small portion of the cases which our office prosecuted during this time frame were related in any way to the statements made by these children."

In addition to this grossly inaccurate statement, Riesen's letter attempted to downplay the cases as simple incest, and to remind Congressman Hastings that checks and balances were at work in Wenatchee's legal system at all times. Riesen inaccurately wrote that the "bulk" of "The *Wenatchee Report*," which had formed the basis for federal review, concerned the Doggett case, which "was not related in any way to the other sex abuse cases" investigated by his department and by Perez.

Riesen reminded Hastings that all defendants were represented by counsel and have a mandatory right to appeal or file a personal restraint petition "if they feel that their constitutional rights were somehow violated in connection with these proceedings." Further, the Justice Department had reviewed the "complaint filed by Kathleen Lyon a Public Defender that persons civil rights had been violated in these cases and found there was no basis to proceed with any sort of investigation." Not only had Riesen got my name wrong, but he wrongly claimed I had filed a complaint with the Justice Department, and greatly over-simplified Reno's findings.

Riesen's letter revealed that Riesen had met with Ungerecht on June 19, 1996. Following this interchange and communications with other Wenatchee officials, Congressman Hastings forcefully discouraged the proposed federal congressional hearings because they would include the Wenatchee matters. Hastings was a Washington state representative, and within the convoluted protocal of politics, his opinion prevailed.

Outside of Wenatchee, some journalists were applauded for their coverage of the Wenatchee sex cases. Television reporter Tom Grant won the George Polk Award for local television reporting. The *Wall Street Journal's* Dorothy Rabinowitz was one vote shy of winning the Pulitzer Prize for her coverage of the Wenatchee and Amirault cases.

And on March 26, 1996, Perez was made first recipient of an award—Wenatchee's City Employee of the Month—for such achievements as his "12 years of outstanding service to the City of Wenatchee," the two years he "served as detective" during his rotation in the sex crimes unit, and the fact that he "devotes numerous hours to the youths of Wenatchee by stopping by schools, and parks. . . . He says he does this as he likes to 'romp with the kids.' "

No doubt the city's award confirmed Perez's own sense of his accomplishments. As Perez said to the London *Independent* in November 1995, "I'm very satisfied. I've made a major impact on the lives of these children."

According to reports out of Wenatchee, the impact on some of the kids tightly contained in state care was profound. An investigation by the *Seattle Post-Intelligencer* uncovered that at least one-third of the children involved in the cases were given psychotropic drugs by state officials after they entered foster care. Nine-year-old Steven

Everett who, according to medical records was "in denial" and "non compliant," tried to hang himself after his parents were sentenced. By March 1995, his therapist reported that Steven often threatened suicide and scratched, bit, and otherwise mutilated himself. According to DCFS records, when he ran away from foster care in April 1995, doctors upped his dose of Zoloft and Steven "tried to stick [a] metal object through his chest." Steven was confined to a Seattle psychiatric hospital and placed on the antidepressent amitriptyline, a drug that is so powerful that it necessitates an electrocardiogram every three months for the first three years, and every six months thereafter.

Developmentally delayed Jeff Town attempted suicide while on psychotropic drugs. Twelve-year-old Donald Holt was transferred from Pine Crest to a mental institution in King County. On a course of the antidepressant Zoloft, Donald jumped off a milk crate with a rope around his neck, after hearing voices telling him to hang himself. He survived, but his mental state remains unstable.

23:

Summer 1996–Winter 1997

Recantation

The sky had passed that point between dusk and darkness by the time Mary Everett found her way to the boxy, wood-frame home of her grandparents, Earl and Ella Spoonemore, in East Wenatchee. It was June 2, 1996, and she had just run away from her foster home. As Mary sat in the kitchen, she fiddled with the salt and pepper shakers and shot her grandmother shy, sideways looks . . . like a stranger, like someone who wasn't sure she was welcome. Her parents were in prison, Pastor Roby and Sister Connie were probably mad at her, and, she saw, her grandma Ella Spoonemore looked her age. Mary perhaps believed she had caused all of these things. A large oxygen tank leaned on its stand behind the old woman's shoulders; as Ella sat heavily, the wooden chair creaked in protest.

"Grandma, do you still love me?"

"Honey, I never stopped loving you," said the old woman, patting Mary's arm with a cool and leathery hand.

"I lied, Grandma, I lied," said Mary, crying softly. "Bob Perez told me what to say. He gave me ideas about what to say and then told me to put them in my own words."

It was a wonder her grandmother was forgiving. After months and years; after an eternity of therapy during which Mary cried and no one cared; after regular reminders that her sadness and homesickness and loneliness were part of a distant memory of hideous betrayal; after endless rounds of questioning by police, caseworkers, and therapists; after a painful process of resignation, Mary had turned on her relatives, friends, and neighbors.

It was all lies, Mary said now—all those things about adults doing what she came to call the "wild thing": adults having sex with kids and kids having sex with each other, group sex in the "big room" of the church—all of it. In court she went even further: *They tied us up, bound and gagged.* To her ears, her words were so weird and improbable that surely no one would believe her. But the authorities had believed her so quickly and so absolutely that clearly they wanted it to be true. After all, for those many months when she denied it, they'd called her a liar, she said. She had cried and cried, buried her face in her hands, pulled her sweater over her head, and they just pushed harder.

"I know you're lying," Perez had said, according to Mary. "Now I'll tell you what I know." When she finally said what he wanted, state officials placed her in his home.

"Bob Perez told me what to say," she told her grandmother. "He gave me ideas about what to say and then told me to put them in my own words."

After they talked awhile, she and her grandmother decided to call now-ordained Pastor Roberson. When Roberson answered, Ella Spoonemore explained what happened, then handed the phone to Mary. Mary begged Roberson for his forgiveness and then went on to explain what had happened. Roberson recognized the significance of her words: This was the first time someone had actually testified, then retracted her statement. He taped the conversation.

"I had to make it all up," said Mary. "Bob Perez was there and he pressured me to say it." She said Perez "got some information and told us to use it and, like, he told us to use our own words. First I said it didn't happen, and then he forced me to make up a lie." Mary said everything she had said or testified to about people hurting her was false. She made up fantastic stories in the hopes that nobody would believe her, she said.

Perez had hurt her, she said. He and Luci had hit her several times, and time after time Perez had twisted her arm behind her back, forced her to the ground, and sat on her with all his weight, she said. They often locked her and Ann in their rooms. Some CPS caseworkers also pressured her to lie, said Mary.

She talked to Roberson for over an hour. Then Roberson called his attorney, Robert Van Siclen. Finally he called Chelan County Commissioner Earl Marcellus. Marcellus picked up the phone at around 10:45 that night. Roberson's voice was tense with excitement. Could Mary spend the night with Marcellus and his family? Marcellus was taken aback.

"Hey, you're really putting me in an awkward position," he said. Roberson tried to reassure him, then set up a conference call with his attorney, Robert Van Siclen.

"I was reluctant mostly based on legal concerns," Marcellus told me later. Was it legal to take in a child who had run away? "I was convinced by Bob Van Siclen that I should have nothing to worry about," he said.

Marcellus had another worry—retaliation. He worried that the *Wenatchee World* would "use this as an attempt to discredit me and convince its readers that I am biased." After all, he was an elected public official and he wanted his concerns about the investigation to remain objective and credible. And he worried about retaliation "by the system"—the tense jangle of nerves that was the Wenatchee government, caught up in a national scandal and a massive lawsuit.

In the end, "the child's well-being was more important than any retaliation that might occur. I wanted to do the right thing. The right thing was making sure the safety and well-being of Mary Everett was first and foremost," he said.

He agreed to meet Mary at a restaurant midway between East Wenatchee and his home in Leavenworth, a Bavarian-inspired community in the foothills of the Cascades. When he arrived, Marcellus saw a girl with long brown hair and glasses standing with a woman; a man waited in the shadows.

"I'd never seen Mary before," he said. "I'd never talked to her. I was surprised at how relaxed and normal she appeared." He said she smiled at him and his wife, Linda, and was very polite. "I had thought I'd meet up with a young lady who was very introverted," said Marcellus, "someone who was shy, an emotional basket case. . . . With all that she'd been through, I thought she might be whimpering and cowering."

Instead, Mary was composed and friendly. Once they were in the car, Marcellus assured her she didn't need to talk about what happened. "I just want you to know you don't have to talk about anything," he said to her.

Mary said little. "She said to us that she didn't want to be back in the foster care system," said Marcellus. "She said she wanted to be with her family. Her fear of the police and CPS was obvious."

They arrived at the Marcelluses' home around 1 A.M. Mary slept on the couch in the living room. In the morning, Marcellus went to work. Later, he called home and talked to Linda, who told him she and Mary were having a "wonderful conversation" and making cookies. After a time, Marcellus told the other commissioners he had a "personal crisis" and rushed home to watch an interview with Mary by reporter Tom Grant.

In the Marcelluses' living room, Mary struggled through a one-and-a-half-hour recorded interview. She insisted she'd never been molested, yet Perez had pressured her to make up false allegations about several adults, including her parents. She said Ann told her she'd lied when she said several adults molested her. "I thought she seemed truthful," said Marcellus, who watched the taping.

Mary said she had told Perez before he interviewed her that she hadn't been abused. He said, "Well, we'll see if you're lying." He got in her face, she said, and accused her of lying, threatened and intimidated her, and told her what he believed had happened, and told her to repeat what he wanted her to say. Eventually she broke down.

Mary said Perez hit her "hard" on the back and shoulders. She said the Perezes often locked her in a room, where the door lock was reversed so that it could only be locked from the outside. Her sister Ann told her Perez had broken her arm, she said.[1] "It was obvious she was fearful of the law officers, government entities and CPS," said Marcellus.

After the interview, "we all went to Neil Fuller's office," he said. Fuller, an attorney, was Mary's guardian ad litem, a court-appointed special advocate for the child. Although Marcellus felt the lawyer was "in an awkward position," Fuller agreed that Mary should go back to her grandparent's home. According to Marcellus, "While we were in his office, Fuller suggested that he would try to do everything he could to avoid her arrest as a runaway."

---

[1] DSHS officials claim the injury occurred in a sledding accident.

That night Spokane television station KREM 2 broadcast a portion of Grant's interview with Mary. The broadcast included a shot in which Marcellus was in the room. Later, he received a call from Tracy Warner of the *Wenatchee World*. "I was dumbfounded," said Marcellus. "My blood pressure kind of went off the chart because of the way Tracy Warner was portraying things in his articles, and supporting the hatchet job of [*World* reporter] Jeanette Marantos."

The next morning, June 4, a reporter from the Associated Press interviewed Mary over the phone at her grandparents' home in East Wenatchee. "I was, like . . . I was pressured to . . . When Bob first came to talk to me about my parents, I said it never happened," said Mary. "He said, 'Mary, I know you're lying,' " she said. "I don't like being called a liar."

In the middle of the conversation, a Douglas County sheriff's deputy arrived at the Spoonemore home. Mary moved away from the phone but left it lying on the chair. Reporter Aviva Brandt heard much of what happened after the officer arrived. She heard Mary crying. "She was hysterical," Brandt told me. Brandt heard Ella Spoonemore ask the deputy if he had a warrant. The deputy answered, "I'm not here to take her away now. I just want to talk to her."

According to Brandt, Ella said, "I was told I could have her," adding that the girl's guardian had approved this arrangement. The officer reassured her that he didn't intend to remove Mary. But moments later the deputy said he was taking her to the CPS offices. Brandt heard the sounds of Mary sobbing, and Ella cried out, "You said you weren't gonna take her."

"I wanta stay with my grandma," shrieked Mary.

The deputy refused to allow Ella to go with her granddaughter to the CPS office. Mary wasn't allowed to return to her grandparents' home.

Like many people who had been following the cases, I assumed the development would represent a significant turnaround. As stated in a front-page article in the *Washington Post,* ''The recantation . . . has raised troubling questions about the men and women who are serving long prison terms for child sex abuse that the girl says never happened, and about the dozens of children who were taken from their homes and put in foster care during the investigation.'' In fact, her testimony had directly contributed to the convictions of her parents and of Manuel Hidalgo-Rodriguez, Donna Hidalgo, Linda Miller, and others, and she had named several others as her abusers. Children and adults had been confronted with Mary's words and encouraged to validate them, thus contributing to the contamination of the investigations, and to a string of guilty pleas.

To no one's surprise, Wenatchee officials said they didn't believe Mary's recantation was reliable. They announced that they wouldn't be reexamining past investigations or the convictions based on these investigations.

McMahon told the *Wenatchee World* that Roberson and the others had influenced Mary because they stood to gain. ''None of this is true,'' he said, ''but these allegations don't surprise me. Look at it. We have a bunch of civil lawyers who played criminal defense attorneys, and they did it for a big payday, and we've got some successes against them and they're going to have to respond. They got their butts kicked and now they're going for damage control.''

Chelan County prosecutors claimed to be unaffected by Mary's recantation, openly wondering if indeed there had even been one. Officially, it was only a rumor. ''We haven't seen a tape, we haven't received anything about a recantation," said Chelan County Deputy Prosecutor Doug Shae to the *Seattle Times*. "We've heard about it from the media, and other people we don't consider reliable. Everyone who has told us about it has given us a different version. . . . But sure, if it came to us, we'd be obligated to examine it." Shae went on to recite the corroboration, the confessions, the official statistics, the checks and balances.

Once again, Lucy Berliner seemed to be at the forefront of the Wenatchee official stance, although she was no more factually informed than before. "I can't imagine it [the recantation] came as a surprise to you," she said to me, her voice dripping with scorn. She described Mary as an emotionally troubled child who was saying things to get her way, or get attention, or confirm the bias of her questioners, who were themselves advocates or journalists who had sought her out. "It's extremely disturbing that adults would solicit the recantation of a vulnerable child to try to draw attention to their agendas," said Berliner.

DCFS regional administrator Roy Harrington told the *Washington Post* that a family court would ultimately determine where Mary stayed. He denied the existence of a conflict of interest arising from the fact that his department, accused in civil lawsuits of helping to coerce false sex-abuse allegations from children, had taken custody of Mary. Harrington told the *Post* that DSHS wasn't itself involved in "damage control."

"We've got a responsibility to supervise this child's dependency," he said. "If the child has run away, we have the responsibility to find a replacement home consistent with what the [family] court has ordered." He added that CPS caseworkers from Wenatchee who allegedly helped coerce Mary's recanted statements would continue to be able to gain access to the girl. But, Harrington conceded to the *Wall Street Journal*, Mary's recantation does "raise legitimate questions" about the cases.

These questions concerned Van Siclen and others who feared that Mary would be subject to manipulation by state agents, defendants in the pending lawsuits. "They will do anything to try to save their skins," said Van Siclen to the *Washington Post*. "There's no telling what they'll do with this girl."

"CPS is completely out of control," he said to me. "You can't trust these people, they've manipulated the system. . . . In my opinion, it's a conflict of interest." And, speaking of the state's control over Mary, he said, "I don't understand why they took her from her grandparents. Her grandparents were willing to take care of her. They were capable. And even Neil Fuller said she could stay with her grandparents."

Fuller was angry that the state had gone outside his authority, at least until there was a resolution of her circumstances. But he was also angry at Roberson and Van Siclen, who had set up the interview with him without telling him Mary's recantation would be televised.

"I feel like it was a setup," said Fuller to the *Wenatchee World*. "Here we were, sitting in my office playing this game about, 'How are we going to protect her and look out for her best interests?' which at the same time almost Tom Grant is playing this tape on television. I'm not going to confirm or deny whether this girl has recanted. There's so much going on here, I can't look at the surface and say, 'Yeah, this is the truth.' What's the truth? It depends on the side of the road you're standing on."

It was by no means clear which side Fuller himself stood on. He told the *World* that an assistant attorney general came to him and asked him to sign a stipulated order barring Mary from contact with the media. "I refused to sign it," said Fuller. "They're cloaking it in the guise of 'We don't want any more damage done to her.' But I told them, 'Aren't we trying to do the same thing as Roberson? Isn't this a form of damage control?' "

In a separate interview, Fuller told the *Wenatchee World* that he had warned Mary she had exposed herself to criticism and further trials by her recantations. Most of his conversation with the girl was confidential, he said, "But you can quote me on this. I think the child is confused about what the hell is going on in her life and she's not sure about anything. She's manipulating the system to the hilt. When she's on the stand testifying about abuse, the defense attorneys say she's [lying], and when she turns around and says, 'I lied and Perez hurt me,' she's the best thing since sliced bread. Think about what happened to this kid. She's so ingrained in the system she's learned how to manipulate."

"We're just trying to protect the child," Wenatchee CWS head Steve Warman told the *Wenatchee World*. "We're basically the parents of the child, and when someone who has no authority comes in and parades her in front of the media, no matter what she says, it's just not right. It's not in her best interests. We didn't parade her in front of the media when she was saying the other."

He said Mary had been placed in three foster homes since her parents were jailed. She was temporarily staying at a fourth foster home and ran away when she learned she was going to be moved to yet another home. Warman added that the girl was removed from the Perez home in December because she complained that her foster parents were too strict. Now she was said to be in a "secure" group home facility in a neighboring community, run under the auspices of DSHS. She wasn't permitted access to relatives or made available for interviews, and she remained totally in the control of state officials—defendants in the pending lawsuits, including therapist Cindy Andrews, who allegedly continued to press recovered memory therapy on Mary.

In the days and weeks to come, the city of Wenatchee was in a turmoil. According to *Washington Post* reporter William Claiborne, who again traveled to Wenatchee to investigate the developments, "There is no question . . . that the mood has changed here significantly as a result of M.E.'s recantation, dividing the community more than ever and turning the hunters, in effect, into the hunted." But the Wenatchee officials were not about to concede to any level of failure. While he was in Wenatchee, Claiborne told me that McMahon said prosecutors were considering charges, including witness tampering, against Marcellus, Roberson, and Van Siclen. "It's idiotic," he said.

But true. On June 18, the word was out that Chelan County prosecutors had submitted information to "an independent outside agency"—the Washington State Attorney General's Office—to investigate formal criminal charges against Marcellus. As Marcellus was an elected county official, he might not be a proper subject of an investigation by the county he served, said Chelan County Undersheriff Daryl Mathena.

LaRoche said the Douglas County Sheriff's Office was conducting its own investigation of Marcellus and other suspects. Douglas County had concurrent jurisdiction, because Mary ran away to Douglas County and was taken from there to the Marcellus home, he said. Chelan County Prosecutor Riesen asked the attorney general to investigate Mary's recantation. "I think it's only appropriate to treat this as a whole, since they happened together."

In July, state Attorney General Christine Gregoire wrote to Riesen, "We concluded that a violation of unlawful harboring of a minor may have occurred," read the letter. "We recommend that further criminal investigation be conducted." But state officials declined to assist with the investigation of possible crimes or of Mary's recantation.

Douglas and Chelan County officials put the word out to law enforcement bodies in the larger metropolitan areas west of the mountains, with no luck. In August they at last found a taker in nearby Grant County, which agreed to investigate for both counties. On August 19, J. R. Winn, head of detectives for the Chelan County Sheriff's Office, said Marcellus, Van Siclen, Tom Grant, and Robert Roberson were being investigated for possible criminal charges, including witness tampering and harboring a minor. The possible charges were later expanded to include the felony of unlawful imprisonment—a category of kidnapping. For a while, frightened for his family, Marcellus packed up his children and sent them to stay out of town.

Some of the suspects were questioned, others claimed privilege, in other cases the Grant County investigators simply backed away. In a report on his investigation, Grant County Sheriff's Detective Ken Kernan said that he had trouble getting information from Van Siclen, Roberson, and Mary's grandparents the Spoonemores.

Then, in October, word was leaked that Marcellus, Grant, the Robersons, and witnesses would be called to a special inquiry hearing before a Wenatchee judge. A special inquiry hearing is a judicial investigation procedure that has rarely been used in Washington State. Its purpose: to determine probable cause where the determination isn't possible through normal fact-finding by police and prosecutors. By law, the hearing is closed to the public and its results are confidential. Connie Roberson's subpoena for hearing on October 15, which was drawn up by Douglas County Prosecuting Attorney Steve Clem, commanded her to testify and to bring with her audio- and videotapes, notes, correspondence, and other records, papers, and documents that might be relevant to Mary's interviews.

After Mary recanted, the *Seattle Times* and the (Portland) *Oregonian* renewed their requests for a federal investigation, despite Reno's decision. On July 3, *Wenatchee World* editorial page editor Tracy Warner wrote an editorial somewhat bitterly calling for an outside investigation. The position was an almost complete turn-around from his position right after the Roberson trial, a little over six months earlier.

Wrote Warner:

> Calls continue to mount for an outside investigation of Wenatchee's so-called sex ring cases. Sources as lofty as *The Wall Street Journal* and the *Seattle Times* have called for a federal probe. State legislators call for grand jury investigations or legislative hearings. There even is talk of hearings before Congress. No one in Wenatchee should object. Send an army of investigators, grand jurors, special prosecutors, detectives, legislative aides, whatever it takes. If an outside probe will help shed light on these difficult and complex issues, then by all means, probe. No one should fear the truth. The question is, what is the best way to find the truth and tell it, fully and impartially? Anything less than full disclosure will not diminish the controversy that has tormented this community for two years.

A few days earlier, Warner told me he was considering calling for an outside investigation in his column, although he said he was "confident" that some of the convicted were guilty. "I've nothing against taking a closer look," he said. "I'm not saying the right thing was done." He admitted he was troubled by Mary's recantation. It could, after all, be the truth—a possibility that the authorities failed to consider.

Warner was exhausted by the attacks that had torn his community—and his newspaper—over the last several months. He said he suffered over the criticism from media he once respected. ''I'm part of one of the institutions that's been pounded on by the publicity campaign. It's like being in a psychological war,'' he said. ''The constant pressure is hard on the people in this town.'' Some of the pounding was intensely personal. Warner said that he was ''shadowed'' by a car with an anti-CPS bumper sticker, and he received phone calls slamming his published opinions. ''My wife asked me not to write about this.'' Worse, ''I have my integrity questioned. . . . Having your integrity questioned all the time is really difficult.''

''I anguished a lot,'' said staff writer Jeanette Marantos, who provided most of *Wenatchee World*'s coverage of the cases. She told me the past two years were among the most difficult of her life. The national response to her articles was ''surrealism,'' she said. ''Everything I did was wrong. I was dumbfounded.'' She said she didn't understand the reason for the criticism. ''I tried to be objective.'' She added that she tried to be thorough, while at the same time, ''I tried not to taint the trials.'' There was more information she could have included in her articles, she conceded, ''but that should come out in the trial.'' She unconditionally believed the government line about checks and balances. But she also admitted to certain pressures: When she printed facts Perez found unfavorable, sometimes ''Bob and Luci Perez berated me.''

She almost persuaded me she was unaware of what was obvious to many: Her articles were part of a local campaign of political propaganda. But the next day in a front-page article in the *Wenatchee World,* Marantos falsely reported that I believed the evidence proved that some of the Wenatchee accused were guilty and confessed that *"The Wenatchee Report"* was "full of holes." Although I was warned about Marantos, it was my turn to be dumbfounded.

Things moved along in a fashion that would be remarkable in most communities but that was almost banal in Wenatchee. At least seven legislators appealed to Governor Mike Lowry to open an inquiry into the CPS role in the prosecutions. Lawmakers proposed legislative hearings before the Washington State's House Law and Justice Committee. Carol Hopkins, executive director of the San Diego-based National Justice Committee, a group dedicated to combating problematic child abuse prosecutions, proposed congressional hearings on "the abuses of the child-abuse industry," to include the Wenatchee and other cases. None of these proposals flew.

Members of the CCLA started a petition drive to enlist support for a state grand jury, and again appealed to Reno to reconsider a federal investigation. One of their members, Stephen Hughes, who continually fired angry letters off to the *Wenatchee World* about the investigations, was arrested on a seventeen-year-old warrant for failing to pay $470 in court costs on a 1979 forgery charge—the day after he complained loudly of the investigations at a Wenatchee City Commission meeting.

The appeals process ground slowly forward for the people in prison, although those who had pleaded guilty had limited appellate rights. The Seattle branch of the American Civil Liberties Union agreed to take a look at the actions of the involved DCFS agents. The city of Wenatchee voted to indemnify Perez and other city employees in the lawsuits filed by Van Siclen and Lacy, which might cost Wenatchee residents as much as seventy-five cents per each one thousand dollars of the assessed val-uations of their property. Spokane County Superior Court Judge Michael Donahue consolidated two lawsuits brought by Van Siclen's clients; granted a motion for change of venue, moving the trial to Seattle's King County; and denied a motion by McMahon to place Roberson and the other plaintiffs under a media gag order.

For months no one heard from Mary Everett, except the agents of the state and their professional affiliates who were entrusted to protect her. Then, in November 1996, Mary's therapist Cindy Andrews wrote a declaration as part of a motion to have attorney Robert Van Siclen removed as attorney in pending multimillion-dollar lawsuits against her, Perez, and various city, county, and state employees and entities. She wrote that in her opinion, Mary's encounter with Marcellus, Roberson, Grant, and Van Siclen was "a devastating and destructive confrontation for [Mary] from a mental health perspective." Said Andrews, "I noticed that her emotional condition substantially deteriorated following the period of time she spent in the Marcellus home" and as a result of her interviews by Roberson and Grant.

Andrews reported that after the girl was returned to CPS she repeatedly ran away from foster care and crisis centers and appeared so disturbed that she was subjected to mental health evaluations for involuntary mental health commitment of up to six months. She cut herself with scissors, swore, ran away with a "male runaway," and tried to jump off a second-story balcony in an apparent suicide attempt. Later, she threatened to jump out of a third-floor window, got into trouble with the police, and sat in the middle of the street "waiting to be hit by cars."

Although more blatant attempts to draw attention to her plight are hard to imagine, Andrews laid all of Mary's remarkable behaviors at the feet of the people who had sheltered her or taken down her recantation when she ran away in June 1996. Andrews, herself a defendant in the upcoming lawsuits, said that in her opinion Mary's June 1996 interview by persons "with adverse interests to her" was a "cause in fact" of her deteriorating mental state and need for ongoing mental health intervention. She wrote that at the time of her report, Mary was an inpatient in a mental facility and that Andrews counseled her by telephone twice a week.

McMahon moved to have Van Siclen disqualified from the cases because he was a suspect in a criminal investigation and because McMahon claimed he would call Van Siclen as a witness in the coming lawsuits on the question of probable cause for the arrests of Roberson and Sims. The motion was denied. That the plaintiffs' lawyer would be a witness for defendant Perez was surprising and unlikely, but reminiscent of McMahon's announcement, when he tried to depose me, that he would call me as a material witness for Perez.

Kerrie Knowles's charges were dismissed on condition that she not join in the lawsuits. On February 14, 1997, Sam Doggett filed a Complaint for Damages and Equitable Relief against Perez, Abbey, Reiman, Boggess, Andrews, Dr. Franklin D. Walker, and their respective spouses, as well as the city of Wenatchee, Child Protective Services, and Pine Crest Hospital.[2]

But among all these extraordinary events one stood out as an example of the desperate measures taken by government agents to rehabilitate their causes and the equally desperate moves of civil plaintiffs to draw national attention to theirs. On December 17, 1996, Michelle Kimble walked into the DCFS office, flanked by CPS caseworker Katie Carrow, where she was greeted by Perez and Tim

---

[2] The action against Pine Crest Hospital was later withdrawn after the facility declared bankruptcy.

Abbey. Michelle was confronted with a previously prepared memorandum headed by the greeting "To: Michelle Kimble, From Det. Bob Perez, re: Interview." She read on: "Any statement you make today as it pertains to any and all Plaintiffs and/or witnesses involved in the Roberson, et.al. v. etc., will not be used to initiate any criminal investigation against you." Otherwise, the memorandum informed her, her statement was "voluntary" and not induced by threats or promises.

"It is also understood that you initiated the first contact with the Wenatchee office of Child Protective Services on December 12, 1996 and made disclosures of sexual abuse that were committed against you at the hands of Robert Roberson, also known as 'Pastor Roby,' and others and this interview is simply a follow-up to those initial statements that you made to CPS supervisor Tim Abbey and CPS Social Worker Kate Carrow," read the statement. Kimble signed on prepared signature lines along with Perez, Carrow, and Abbey.

In this strange way, Michelle retracted her recantation of a statement to Perez made more than a year earlier. Wenatchee Police Chief Ken Badgley defended Perez's action in connection with the memorandum. "I think it's important to remember we're not going out and hunting these people [potential defense witnesses in the pending lawsuits] down. But if they want to make a statement or clarification, fine, we'll take it," he said to the *Wenatchee World.* "It was a case where she came in and wanted to clarify what took place."

But Roberson's attorney Robert Van Siclen forcefully disagreed. In a motion filed on January 17, 1997, Van Siclen set out facts supporting his claim that Michelle was coerced this time as she had been before, and that she had again recanted, this time to him and Roberson.

According to Van Siclen's brief, in 1995 Michelle Kimble, then seventeen, lived with her young son and her parents in Wenatchee. During Perez's investigation of sex cases, "Michelle was branded as a sex-abuse victim and confined." It was a familiar scenario: Police arrested her mother, Pam Kimble, and state officials took all of the kids in the home into custody, including Michelle's small son. Perez questioned Michelle. At first she denied anyone had abused her. Then, according to Van Siclen, Perez "yelled at her, called her a liar, and refused to accept that she was not abused and that she did not witness any sexual abuse at the church or by Pastor Roberson. Finally, to stop Detective Perez's verbal abuse, his coercion, and his intimidation, Michelle gave up and agreed to make a statement according to what Detective Perez wanted her to say."

Also in 1995, when Douglas County Sheriff's Detective Helvey followed up on Perez's interview of Michelle, she said her statement to Perez was a lie. According to Helvey's statement, attached as an exhibit to Van Siclen's motion, she told him Perez had yelled at her, refused to listen, and called her a liar. Under the circumstances, she was never called upon to testify, charges against her mother were dismissed, Michelle's son was returned to her, and the family was reunited.

More than a year later, on December 12, 1996, Michelle went to the Wenatchee DCFS offices to talk to a caseworker about the welfare of her son and *not* to talk about Roberson, she said. According to Van Siclen's recorded interview of Michelle and her declaration attached to the lawyer's motion, Abbey saw her and beckoned her into his office. He told her CPS had made "mistakes" before, and she reiterated that Perez had forced her to say Roberson had molested her, said Michelle.

On December 17, five days later, Carrow drove out to Michelle's home and told her she had to go to the CPS

office to talk to Perez, wrote Van Siclen. Carrow drove
Michelle to the DCFS offices, where Perez was waiting
with Abbey. Perez started to question her about Roberson.
At first she denied abuse, but said that Perez again refused
to listen. Only after what Van Siclen described as "considerable pressure" did Michelle sign the memorandum.
She told Van Siclen she was afraid her son would be taken
away in a "criminal investigation" if she didn't do what
Perez wanted. According to Michelle, Perez told her to
read her original statement and tape-recorded it as she
read aloud. He told her she might be expected to testify
in the upcoming civil suits, she said.

"Their outrageous conduct obstructs justice to the point
of jeopardizing or destroying plaintiff's right to have a
fair trial," wrote Van Siclen. He moved for restraining
orders to stop the defendants in the civil case from contacting witnesses, and sought sanctions against them.
Among these defendants was Andrews, under contract
with the state DSHS, because he said she was maintaining
regular contact with Mary and applying "false memory
therapy" while she was in a mental hospital. Van Siclen
said Andrews was "brainwashing" the girl and creating
a conflict of interest because Andrews was both a therapist
who had the ability to affect her memory, and a defendant
in his lawsuit.

The *Wenatchee World* related the gist of Van Siclen's
motion, and also the fact that Roberson and Michelle were
in Los Angeles taping for the *Leeza* television talk show,
which was set to air on January 30, the day before Van
Siclen's hearing. CCLA head Connie Fry told me she sat
with Michelle during most of the trip by bus and plane to
Los Angeles for the *Leeza* taping. Michelle appeared natural, spontaneous, and unafraid around Roberson, said
Fry. As she had many times in the past, she hoped that

now Michelle's story would be told the girl and her child would be safe, said Fry.

At the taping, Michelle cried and chillingly described the day in 1995 when Perez and caseworkers came to her home, arrested her mother, seized her son, and interrogated her while her brother huddled in handcuffs beside her. After she said what Perez wanted, she, her son, and her siblings were placed in separate foster homes. Now her mother was again terrified her children would be taken away, she sobbed. It could happen to her own son, she cried.

She told host Leeza Gibbons that Roberson had never molested her.

By the time the show aired, Leeza Gibbons learned that officials approached Michelle immediately after she returned to Wenatchee and that now she said Roberson had coerced her to lie, talk to his attorney, and appear on the *Leeza* show. State officials escorted her and her mother to the courthouse and Michelle signed an anti-harassment order against Roberson. Gibbons explained the situation to her audience at the beginning of the show. "You decide," she said.

Chelan County Sheriff's Inspector Mike Harum explained to the *Wenatchee World* that Michelle, Katie Carrow, and Pam Kimble came into his office after Michelle taped the *Leeza* show. "She said she'd been raped [in past years] by Roby, and she was tired of him forcing her to lie," he said.

The events left Judge Michael Donahue in a quandary at the hearing on January 31. "There is something about this that has a strong aroma," he said of Perez's December interview of Kimble. "Why didn't a different investigator take the statement?"

On the other hand, "I'm equally concerned by the action of Mr. Roberson," in response to claims that he had contacted Michelle Kimble and dragged her to the *Leeza* show. "It's awfully hard to draw conclusions as a judicial officer, what really happened," said Donahue. He agreed to restrict Perez's contact with witnesses but allowed Ann and Mary Everett to remain in state custody and in therapy with Andrews, although Van Siclen had argued that the state's conduct in the case of Michelle Kimble implied improper influence in the case of *all* potential child witnesses in the state's control. "It shows some questionable judgment under the circumstances," said Donahue of Andrew's therapy. "It's not a problem that is to go away. It's jury bait in the extreme."

McMahon complained of the *Leeza* show and the fact that someone—allegedly a CCLA member—had passed out fliers at a local school. Perez got some angry phone calls, he said. "It's a form of mental intimidation, it's a form of mental rape," McMahon said of the abuses endured by Wenatchee Police Officer Bob Perez.

In all, some forty-five men and women were arrested during Perez's investigations. Twenty confessed; nearly thirty vulnerable men and women were convicted of felonies (many as a result of Alford pleas), and most of these remain in prison—some with sentences exceeding forty years. More than thirty children remain in the hellish limbo of Wenatchee therapy and foster care or in mental facilities, where they are often given mood-altering drugs to facilitate memories and disclosures, contained by agents of the state, subjected to continued interrogation guised as therapy, and isolated from all they hold dear.

24:

Epilogue

═══════

Reflection

═══════

On January 14, 1997 I traveled to Salem for the three hundredth anniversary of Salem's Day of Fast and Repentance in response to the 1692 witch trials. Clearly, modern Salem has cashed in on the many commercial possibilities of its history. Cartoonish witches careen across municipal trash cans, policemen's uniforms, and the shelves of museums and gift shops. At a time when we are no less vulnerable to the triumph of panic and prejudice over reason, it is difficult to escape the dismal reminder that Salem's past has merged with our nation's present.

The Robersons were in Salem for the event, and so were many of the former defendants from the most notorious child abuse prosecutions in our nation's history: Ray Buckey, Kelly Michaels, Bobby Fijnje, Scott and Brenda Kniffen, Violet Amirault, Cheryl Amirault Le-Fave, and many others. They listened, nodding, as Dr. Richard A. Gardner, clinical professor of child psychiatry at Columbia University, described what he called the three great waves of American social hysteria. The first was the Salem witch trials, the second the contagion of fear of communist infiltration that culminated in the McCarthy hearings in the 1950s. The third, said Gardner, is our response to allegations of child sexual abuse.

"I believe that more innocent people have suffered in its course than all of those who suffered in Salem and the McCarthy era combined," he said. Many in the audience wiped away tears. The suffering he referred to is profound, striking as it does at the heart of American families.

In recent decades, arbitrary interventions and overzealous prosecutions have become so commonplace and so blandly unchecked in cases of alleged child sexual abuse that the pattern appears immutable. But history tells us that, as with other inquisitions, political zeal will moderate, abstract fears and widespread panic will abate, public reason will reemerge, and humanity will prevail. One day, laws geared to protect children will do just that— through training and the adoption of standards for interviewing children and preserving their statements, and through procedures for dealing reasonably with their alleged offenders.

This episode, the most recent outbreak of massive social hysteria, will drift from our consciousness and when we speak of it decades from now it will be in a curious and remote way. By then, no doubt, powerful figures will have seized upon some new official monster as a political cause, reached out to us through the media, and convinced us to abandon our common sense and our humanity in response to the tug of our fears.

"If you think that we've gone beyond the Middle Ages regarding humanity, you're wrong," Gardner told me. "The percentage of people who will believe the incredible hasn't changed. Things are no better, we just have different kinds of bogeymen." He isn't convinced that the phenomenon at work in Wenatchee will abate anytime soon.

"The problem with false sex abuse accusations is that there will always be sexual abuse," said Gardner. "It's a wonderful delusion for hystericals and paranoids, because you can't say it doesn't exist," he said. "It's so ubiquitous. It's unique because there's no end in sight. It's the greatest hysteria on earth."

Indeed, there has been little relief for the wronged of Wenatchee in the more than three years since the sex ring prosecutions flourished—no official whisper of regret for the excess of zeal by Wenatchee authorities; no sparse acknowledgment of responsibility for the losses to families torn asunder by state interventions.

After all, there is a lot to answer to. "I've seen a lot, unspeakable mass murders, other things. And yet when I went to Wenatchee and saw what was going on I was still deeply shocked," said John Carlin of London's *Independent,* who has worked extensively as a foreign correspondent. He told me he was struck by the government's "willful blindness," which he described as "their almost deliberate refusal to see wide-eyed the real facts of the matter because they were swept up that they were doing the righteous thing." It has been a "monstrous injustice," he said, a national societal problem to which no one has claimed responsibility. "We've become self-involved. We lack ironic self-doubt."

Some of our acquiescence may be the result of our failure to recognize the significance of what we are seeing in a broader context. According to Siegesmund Von Ilsemann, Washington, D.C., bureau chief for *Der Spiegel,* a German-language weekly newsmagazine, "There's always kind of a weird singularity about it." Cases such as the one unfolding in Wenatchee "are treated more as a curiosity than a social phenomenon with its roots much deeper in society."

It is tempting to view the events in Wenatchee as a

curiosity—some aberrant manifestation of small-town life. Certainly, elements of insularity born of geography and distance—factors of isolation and stubborn autonomy and defensiveness—were part of the Wenatchee inquisition. But just as clearly, the pattern of social hysteria that fueled the investigations and prosecutions is rooted in the heart of American history, and bounded neither by time nor place.

The problem of how to do a child abuse investigation has tormented communities across the nation since the 1970s, when the horror of pedophiles touched the imaginations and political heartstrings of opportunistic government leaders and caused them to greatly restructure our laws. The existing legal framework had germinated unremarkably from the disparate tangle of emotion, power, politics, greed, and conformity that made up American society; some of these laws indifferently reflected a lengthy period when some American jurists, politicians, and journalists ignored abuses toward women and children. Matters of child sexual abuse, usually incest, were deeply shrouded in a cloak of embarrassment and shame.

In the early decades of the twentieth century, private charitable organizations were entrusted with matters of abuses to children. Statistically, incest cases were reported to these agencies with about the same frequency as they are reported today, according to John E. B. Myers, professor at McGeorge School of Law, University of the Pacific, in Sacramento, California, a notable and extensively published expert on the legal aspects of child abuse prosecutions.

Most Americans had no idea of the common occurrence of incest because to speak of it was taboo. Until as late as the end of the 1970s, child sexual abuse remained a ''hidden problem,'' said Myers. ''Nobody knew about it.'' Yet the problems of child abuse had been identified to the private charities that quietly dealt with the children. Despite what we are led to believe, the occurrence of child sexual abuse isn't actually on the rise, he said. ''The debate about sexual abuse has increased. The rate of child sexual abuse has not.''

This is contrary to public understanding, given a wealth of misinformation and misapplication of statistical data. Kenneth V. Lanning, supervisory special agent with the Behavioral Science Unit of the FBI, commented on inflated and false information in two publications distributed through the U.S. Department of Justice:

> Some professionals . . . in their zeal to make American society more aware of this victimization [of children], tend to exaggerate the problem. Presentations and literature with poorly documented or misleading claims about one in three children being sexually molested, the $5 billion child pornography industry, child slavery rings, and 50,000 stranger-abducted children are not uncommon. The problem is bad enough; it is not necessary to exaggerate it. Professionals should cite reputable and scientific studies and note the sources of information. If they do not, when the exaggerations and distortions are discovered, their credibility and the credibility of the issue will be lost.[1]

Lanning continued:

> The best data now available [the 1990 *National Incidence Studies on Missing, Abducted, Runaway, and Throwaway*

[1] Kenneth Lanning, ''Child Sex Rings: A Behavioral Analysis,'' for National Center for Missing and Exploited Children, U.S. Department of Justice, 1992, p. 1; Kenneth Lanning, ''Investigator's Guide to Allegations of 'Ritual' Child Abuse,'' for National Center for The Analysis of Violent Crime, U.S. Department of Justice, 1992, p. 1.

Children in America] estimate the number of stereotypical child abductions at between 200 and 300 a year and the number of stranger abduction homicides of children at between 43 and 147 a year. Approximately half of the abducted children are teenagers. Today's facts are significantly different from yesterday's perceptions.

Inflamed by frightening (if misleading) statistics and the real need to protect children, by the 1970s lawyers, feminists, and child advocates pressured legislators for reforms designed to protect children. These efforts led, in 1974, to the passage of the Child Abuse Prevention and Treatment Act—also known as the Mondale Act, for the bill's sponsor. The act created national unity in child abuse laws, but permitted enormous acts of discretion by child-care professionals such as Child Protective Services caseworkers. Cases were frequently overreported because of mandatory, coercive reporting requirements combined with huge financial incentives. Consequently, according to a recent United States government study, less than one-third of cases that were reported and then investigated in 1994 were found to be substantiated.[2]

A variety of agencies sprang up at state and local levels; the more innovative or cooperative of these tapped into state and matching federal contract and grant money. Many of these agencies, often therapy programs, played at least an ancillary role in investigating child abuse. After all, when a child disclosed sexual abuse, these professionals had to disclose this fact to authorities.

At the same time, legislators responded to the concerns of their inflamed constituents with laws designed to make

---

[2] U.S. Department of Health and Human Services, National Center on Child Abuse and Neglect, *Child Maltreatment 1994: Reports from the States to the National Center on Child Abuse and Neglect,* Washington, D.C.: U.S. Government Printing Office, 1996.

it easier for a child to testify and tougher for a criminal defendant to question him or her. Child hearsay laws eroded the ability of the defendant to confront and cross-examine the accuser, and allowed hearsay witnesses (who frequently were advocates for the child) to interpret the child's statements. Mandatory standard range sentences removed discretion from judges and placed it in the hands of prosecutors, thus creating a huge and unhealthy incentive for plea bargaining.

In Washington and many states, large periodic increases in criminal sentences in child abuse cases (for those who deny abuse or who otherwise don't qualify for treatment) are unmatched in other areas of criminal law. A single count of child rape in the first degree carries a potential life penalty (as does a single count of child molestation) and a standard range sentence approaching twenty years. Child rape includes oral sex and penetration, no matter how slight. Child molestation includes touching of the clothed or unclothed genital or anal areas, but also of the breasts (even of a child who is far from forming them) combined with the element of sexual gratification. Thus, a wide variety of behaviors can be punished without regard to their relative menace or intrusiveness. Washington was the first state to enact a statute that permits indefinite confinement for sex offenders after they have served prison time, and has mandated life in prison without possibility of parole for certain categories of sex offenders.

Yet, with all of these serious potential penalties, Washington and many states have deliberately avoided legal requirements for training child interviewers, or legal standards for interviewing children or recording their statements. Psychologist Dr. John Yuille believes these facts ''carry the potential for a very real risk of false convictions of alleged offenders, and of alienation of children from families.'' Washington laws permit investigators to pursue "opaque or hidden investigation procedures" by destroying notes, not taping interviews, and otherwise concealing the tracks of their investigations, he said. As the result of our system of laws, professionals within the system of criminal justice have become "less and less accountable.

"How many poorly constructed cases will it take before there is general skepticism?" he mused. It was a good question. Cases in many ways resembling those in Wenatchee have cropped up all over. Many of them are poorly investigated. When asked to investigate what he called "multidimensional" child sex rings (those involving multiple alleged perpetrators and victims), FBI agent Lanning was forced to the conclusion that there was no reliable evidence to support the allegations in any case brought to his attention. There was no physical evidence, corpses, or mutilated remains; statements of alleged victims had been contaminated by the investigation process or by erroneous public perceptions; these statements were often improbable and bizarre. Lanning said that children's accounts in such cases should be investigated thoroughly but with "skepticism":

Overzealous intervenors must accept the fact that some of their well-intentioned activity is contaminating and damaging the prosecutive potential of the cases where criminal acts did occur. We must all (i.e., the media, churches, therapists, victim advocates, law enforcement, and the general public) ask ourselves if we have created an environment where victims are rewarded, listened to, comforted, and forgiven in direct proportion to the seriousness of their abuse. Are we encouraging needy or traumatized individuals to tell more and more outrageous tales of their victimization? Are we making up for centuries of denial by now blindly accepting any allegation of child abuse no matter how absurd or unlikely? Are we increasing the likelihood that rebellious, antisocial, or attention-seeking individuals will gravitate toward "satanism" by publicizing it and overreacting to it? The overreaction to the problem can be worse than the problem.[3]

Much of our overreaction may stem from the fact that we "shroud everything sexual in a veil of secrecy and hypocrisy," particularly when it comes to children, said psychiatrist Dr. Roland Summit. "If we recognized child sexual abuse as part of human behavior, there would be more focus on prevention and less on punishment," he said. "People shudder and turn aside. Even people in the profession have this aversion. Every profession needs to be apprised of how it overlooks the problem," said Summit. "We all need to deal with it in a more reasonable and less reactive way."

Of course we react strongly when it comes to kids. We tend to sentimentalize children, to ascribe qualities of innocence and purity to them—qualities that reflect our love and the immense tug of our maternal and paternal instincts. Children have a symbolic quality, a quality of being untrammeled and yet a renewal of ourselves. They are our hope and our future. And, however we may sometimes try to ignore them, we are arrested by their words.

Children also reflect our own sense of security. As adults we have a tremendous need to believe our world is a safe place, said Summit. We believe in our institutions, such as marriage and children of the union, which ground us in a sometimes chaotic world. "When sex abuse happens and it's said people get by with it," our sense of

---

[3] Kenneth Lanning, "Investigator's Guide to Allegations of 'Ritual' Child Abuse," Behavioral Science Unit, National Center for the Analysis of Violent Crime, U.S. Department of Justice, January 1992, p. 39.

security is damaged, Summit said. "We begin to question who to trust. We begin to question whether our children are safe." We begin to give in to our fears, which are only just at bay at the best of times.

Many of our fears have their birth in "urban legends," such as the warning that began in 1970 that Halloween candy and apples might be laced with razor blades. In fact only a handful of such incidents were documented. Yet the warning is repeated by word of mouth and popular media and fliers and bulletin boards and has been entrenched in our collective national consciousness. Our expressions of these fears may reinforce our sense of community, and at the same time reinforce our attachment to deeply ingrained folk tales.

The atmosphere of sustained fear and its logical companion, the communal desire for vengeful prosecution, have sometimes engendered extreme and highly controversial investigatory practices such as "recovered memory" therapy. Yet Summit thinks that the criticism has gone too far. Because of therapeutic claims of ritual abuse and torture, claims which he finds "absolutely absurd," the reasonable concept that "sex abuse can be so terrible you can put it out of your mind" has been rejected. "Everything related to dissociation is now scorned as fraud," he said. But Summit admitted to some concern that the therapy technique was at times misused.

There is little dispute that the incorporation of a false memory by a child might cause him or her harm. But Lucy Berliner of the Harborview Sexual Assault Center denied that her clinic's approach would support such beliefs. "We have no interest whatsoever in treating children for problems they don't have. We have no interest in supporting a false belief." Nor does she believe that others in the mental health professions would deliberately contribute to a false memory. But the influence of a therapist or other authority figure need not be deliberate to have a profound effect on a child's memory and the reliability of his or her words.

Dr. Elizabeth Loftus, a cognitive psychologist and professor at the University of Washington and one of the nation's leading experts in the field of adult memory, told me that hundreds of studies show that any form of supplying information to people of any age during the interview process is a form of selective reinforcement that may decrease the reliability of subsequent statements. She has no doubt that professionals sometimes contribute to false memories in children.

"If you believe real child abuse has long-term deleterious consequences, then what happens when you create a false memory of child abuse? Are you creating a victim who is also likely to have long-term troubles?" asked Loftus. "Having a real and a pseudo memory are in many ways the same. If you create the memory, are you not creating child abuse?"

Child interviewers may fail to recognize the impact of their biases and expectations on their interview subjects. In 1991, while Dr. Douglas Bicklen, a teacher and autism researcher at Syracuse University, was on a trip to Australia, he saw a method of communication that had been devised to assist cerebral palsy patients—a method called "facilitated communication." An aide, or "facilitator," steadied the patient's wrist and guided his hand to a diagram that resembled a typewriter keyboard. In this way, patients were able to point to letters and spell out words.

Bicklen decided to put the method to use with autistic patients, with astonishing results. Soon, even young children were writing detailed and technically correct sentences, often far beyond their age level. As a result of these new methods of reaching their previously untapped thoughts, many of the patients were believed to be gifted.

Bicklen helped found the Facilitated Communication Institute at Syracuse and invited practitioners from across the nation to learn the technique. But, strangely, children didn't achieve spectacular results with all facilitators. A boy named Matt refused to spell out words with his mother and his aide found it strange.

One day the boy spelled out that his father had molested him. Matt's father was arrested that very day. Matt's parents began to investigate the Syracuse program and learned that aides had recently learned that the incidence of sexual abuse is high in a population of autistic children. In fact, autistic children with adult facilitators were accusing their parents all across the country, and most of these parents were denying the charges.

At last Syracuse designed a study in which a child and her aide sat at a table with a panel between them so that they could hold hands and touch the keyboard together, but they had entirely separate fields of vision. Each was shown a picture of an object and asked to type what he or she saw. When a girl saw a cup and an aide saw a hat, the girl typed "hat." The results were the same with every picture.

In similar tests throughout the country, the results were nearly identical. The aides were themselves controlling the words of the children. The findings devastated the professionals, who had been unconscious that their expectations had overcome any attempts at communication by the child.

Similarly, a child may be a conduit for the expectations of his interviewer who rejects contrary information. Dr. Stephen Ceci, professor of psychology at Cornell University and noted expert in child memory, and Maggie Bruck, associate professor of psychology and pediatrics at McGill University, reviewed the transcripts of interviews of children at the Wee Care Center as part of an amicus brief in

the case of Kelly Michaels. Ceci and Bruck concluded the
transcripts demonstrated biases that were revealed by the
interviewer ''persistently maintaining one line of inquiry''
even when the child consistently replied that nothing had
happened. For example:

Q: Pretend this is a big knife because we don't have a
  big knife.

A: This is a big one.

Q: Okay, what did you have to do with that? What did
  you have to . . .

A: No . . . take the peanut—put the peanut butter—

Q: You put what's that, what did you put there?

A: I put jelly right here.

Q: Jelly.

A: And I put jelly on her mouth and on the eyes.

Q: You put jelly on her eyes and her vagina and her
  mouth?

A: On her back, on her socks.

Q: And did you have to put anything else down there?

A: Right there, right here and right here and here.

Q: You put peanut butter all over? And where else did
  you put the peanut butter?

A: And jelly.

Q: And jelly.

A: And we squeezed orange juice on her.

Q: You had to squeeze an orange on her?

A: Put orange juice on her.

Q: And did anyone . . . how did everybody take it off?
  How did she make you take it off?

A: No. Lick her all up, eat her all up and lick her all
  up.

Q: You had to lick her all up?

A: And eat her all up.

Q: Yeah? What did it taste like?

A: Yucky.
Q: So she made you eat the peanut butter and jelly and orange juice off of the vagina too?
A: Yeah.
Q: Was that scary or funny?
Q: Funny, funny and scary.

When I interviewed him, Ceci said child sexual abuse investigations are very difficult for an interviewer to treat with neutrality. "After multiple interviews for weeks and months there is a tremendous amount at stake for the interviewer," he said. A heightened risk of suggestibility emerges from the "atmosphere of accusation," he said. Some children subjected to the process come to believe things that didn't happen.

Another unchecked process at work in Wenatchee is that of false confessions, which may have resulted when Perez and other officials pursued their expectations and biases against a vulnerable adult population. Professor Gisli H. Gudjonsson, psychologist with the Institute of Psychiatry in London, was formerly a police detective with the Reykjavik Criminal Investigative Police. He has pioneered empirical evidence regarding suggestibility that he used to analyze and testify about such notable confession cases as the Guildford Four and the Birmingham Six.

In his book entitled *The Psychology of Interrogations, Confessions and Testimony* (John Wiley and Sons, 1991), Professor Gudjonsson described theories of interviewing and the factors that impact the psychology of confessions. Some of the factors that bear on the reliability of adult confessions are similar to those that affect children's statements. For example, leading questions distort responses, as do questions containing strong expectations.

Police have the ability to control the immediate situation during an interrogation. They enter the interview with certain expectations, assumptions, and theories about the subject of their investigation. Information contrary to the officer's expectation may be falsely interpreted as lies, defensiveness, misunderstanding, or evasiveness, said Gudjonsson, citing a variety of studies.

One study concluded that, next to mistaken identifications, self-incriminating confessions were the most common cause of false imprisonment. In the study, a large number of people who falsely confessed were found to be mentally handicapped.[4] Others were psychologically vulnerable or disturbed in some way. What the groups of false confessors had in common was that they were abnormally susceptible to suggestion.

At the best of times, a suspect feels enormously intimidated, powerless, frightened, and debilitated in custodial interrogation, wrote Gudjonsson. He may give in to pressure for immediate gain just to get away from the intolerable stress of the interrogation. While, on some level, the suspect realizes the terrible consequences of confessing, the immediate need for relief prevails.

At other times a suspect may actually come to believe he committed the crime through the process of police investigation, wrote Gudjonsson. Sometimes the suspect comes to distrust his own memory because of subtle influences by the interrogator; the resulting doubt and confusion may cause an alteration of his perception of reality. Tactics that may create false memories include repeated confident statements of belief in the suspect's guilt, lengthy interrogation often of high emotional intensity, isolation, insistence that the suspect accept the officer's words, and the efforts to make the suspect afraid of the consequences of repeated denials, wrote Gudjonsson.

---

[4] R. Brandon and C. Davies, *Wrongful Imprisonment* (George, Allen and Unwin, London, 1973).

A study of 350 defendants wrongly convicted of capital and potentially capital cases in the United States showed that 139 were sentenced to death and 23 were executed before their innocence was established. The authors of the study showed that the largest number of errors (twenty-three percent) were the result of a police investigation, and of these, the largest source of error came from the process of a coerced confession.[5]

Although few child protection experts will debate that their past investigatory methods sometimes went too far, many professionals are stubbornly resistant to critical scrutiny, which is the logical prelude to change. Some of this resistance is part of the enormous, intensely emotional schism in lucrative professional communities surrounding child sexual abuse. "The problem of polarity is the lack of dialogue," said Dr. Yuille. "It tends to push people into positions so that they tend to defend the position rather than solve the problem."

Dr. Loftus agreed that the level of polarization among mental health professionals who work in the field of child abuse is a "challenge to the industry." In areas of the reliability of "repressed" memory, Loftus experiences extreme animosity from some laypersons and professionals, including certain of those within her field. Yet when she speaks, writes, or testifies in other areas of memory, "the arguments are so very civilized. . . . You can have intelligent, healthy controversy, argue about issues, but you can still accept and trust each other," she said. "That's what's missing from child abuse cases. There's no trust in the industry, no respect."

Many feel the blade that is splitting the professional

---

[5] Hugo A. Bedau and Michael Radelet, "Miscarriages of Justice in Potentially Capital Cases," *Stanford Law Review*, vol. 40, pp. 21–179, 1987.

communities in Washington State (and across the nation) is wielded by the Harborview Sexual Assault Center, of which Lucy Berliner is research director. In 1977, according to Berliner, the center was one of the first in the field to receive a federal grant to support funding of a demonstration project for child witnesses. The center was charged with "developing a community response that would encourage the child to seek medical treatment and to cooperate with the authorities," she said. The project was so successful that it received an award from the U.S. Department of Justice, was viewed as a "seminal" approach to child abuse cases, and has remained a model for national programs.

But experts claim the Harborview approach is heavily biased toward prosecution and state intervention with families, sometimes emphasizing legal strategy over neutral truth-seeking. Dr. Richard M. Soderstrom, a gynecologist associated with Children's Hospital in Seattle, is one of a very few American physicians who will dispute colposcopic findings in his testimony. In Washington most colposcopic findings originate with Harborview doctors or physicians trained in Harborview methodologies. In fact, Harborview's training program in specialized gynecology, which varies from a few days to several months, is given to doctors throughout the nation, many of whom will go on to testify for the government.

"The training from Harborview is not necessarily inadequate, but it is heavily biased," including information many experts consider false, unreliable, or highly controversial within the field, said Soderstrom. "They strongly believe they're protecting children and you're guilty until you're proven innocent," he said. The attacks by prosecutors on the professional findings and the character of any doctor who dares to question colposcopic findings has negatively impacted the integrity of his profession, he said. He has resigned himself that he will be forced to abandon the practice of testifying.

The "assumption of abuse" and the pursuit of theories open to distortion and erroneous findings are a disservice to the profession, agreed Dr. Lee Coleman, psychiatrist from the University of California. Although Coleman believes most doctors would agree that colposcopic results often lead to false conclusions in the case of normal childhood genital variations, doctors across the country refuse to testify to this because "they're afraid to be labeled as having helped a child molester." They have learned that should they dispute colposcope findings, they're "vilified," said Coleman. "They've been frightened. They don't want to be involved in controversy."

Because medical findings have a profound impact on jurors in cases otherwise devoid of tangible evidence, the imbalance in the area of medical testimony is highly significant.

Berliner and Summit, both pioneers in the field of child sexual abuse, admitted to me their past overzealousness, but spoke of mistakes in their field in an abstract way. "We were less aware than now of the potential to distort and influence [a child's statements]," said Berliner, speaking of past decades. "There has been a natural process of evolution. It started in a world where no one accepted that abuse happened. In the early eighties some people made errors that we would not now make, to encourage statements."

Dr. Summit, whose theories set much of the tone of relentless prosecutions in the latter part of this century, said that he has been criticized for failing to take false accusations into account, but "that's not what we were into at the time." Summit added, "There's an interesting cycle of discovery in child abuse on various occasions in the last century and a half," including a spell in the seventies and eighties that reflected "an epidemic of putting people in jail," he said.

Neither would accept responsibility for the logical results of flawed interview techniques. As to the possibility of the conviction of innocent persons, Berliner said, "I don't think it happens very often. I think we have a system that protects against that."

I considered the dangerous message of their words: Time passes; the learning curve is novel and abstract; we note our mistakes but forgive them as well-intended; we bear no responsibility for the results—as long as our legal system is intact.

Is the legal system a panacea to a flawed investigation? "The only tool we have right now to convince poor investigators to change their ways is criminal justice," said Professor Yuille. "I don't think the adversarial system is a very good one to use as a model for dealing with the maltreatment of children."

After all, the system pulses with laws reactive to the social and political climate—often wielded by impassioned prosecutors caught up in crusader zeal. The sometimes unhealthy alliance between laws and prosecutors who themselves helped to shape these laws affects the admissibility of otherwise helpful evidence. Child hearsay laws and laws governing the admissibility of expert testimony are among those that, in politically charged courtrooms, prosecutors often exercise to their advantage. Dr. Loftus found that strenuous efforts were made to restrict her testimony about the unreliability of "repressed" memories. "Obviously they're trying to suppress information all the time," she said of prosecutors, backed by various therapists and child advocates. "Why would you want to do that if you want all the information? They want a conviction, which to them is more important than the truth.''

"Once you take a system that is based on deceit and you withhold exculpatory evidence," there can be no justice, said Dr. Gardner. After thirty-six years of testifying in court, he called the concept of checks and balances "fantasyland. I can tell you that it has nothing to do with justice," he said. Justice belongs to those with money; or, conversely, "the more money you have, the more injustice you can buy," he said.

The correlation between money and an effective defense is often most pronounced where there is a bad investigation. But with the best of defenses, we are misguided if we blindly accept (as many officials, politicians, and self-serving lawyers would have us do) that judges and juries are invulnerable to political pressures or social paranoia, or that they possess an innate ability to sift the truth from the rubble of a badly flawed investigation.

All too often, where cases are overturned or prosecutions unsuccessful, prosecutors fail to apply what they have learned to enhance the truth-seeking process. "It's a very strange thing, frightening really in a democracy. At the time the McMartin interviews were done, we needed to learn how to do them," said Professor Yuille. "Instead, the lesson we learned was that when a problem is revealed in the record, we should stop keeping records. It was a surprise to me. I guess I'm an optimist about human nature. I thought that they'd take home the message so that it wouldn't happen the next time."

Former McMartin prosecutor Glenn Stevens agreed. "The lesson that should have been learned from McMartin was techniques to get believable, unimpeachable evidence from the mouths of children. Once things get surreal and improbable, let it go. You can't sort out what

to believe and it's unfair for the jury to have to do so."
Instead, said Stevens, too often "they've learned the
wrong lesson": to selectively charge and to try cases individually so as to sidestep the difficulty of proving complex and improbable events; to "destroy all notes and
everything that could impeach the officer's credibility";
to refuse to videotape or even to adopt legal standards for
interviewing children.

Prosecutors have the unique ability to control the investigation and the destiny of cases that come before
them. Instead, too often prosecution is about ruthless ambition—the misuse of power to control and manipulate
evidence in order to achieve courtroom victories for ultimate political gain. Children may become little more
than political pawns: visible proof that prosecutors, many
of them elected officials, are making our communities
safe. Other times, said Stevens, "prosecutors use kids as
a shield to deflect criticism from themselves. They tell
you, 'If you criticize me, you're criticizing what the kids
are saying. You're subjecting them to further abuse.' "
To judges, juries, journalists, and the rest of us, the arguments are all but irresistible.

Where prosecution is not in the interests of justice,
prosecutors are obligated to dismiss. "The problem is,
how do you explain that to the media?" said Stevens.

Our ability to access and resolve controversial information and to redress systemic failures through the media
is most restricted during those historic episodes most aptly
characterized as inquisitions. As was the case in the
McCarthy era, the official response to child sex abuse
prosecutions has two prongs: the law and public reprobation—typically meted out through the media. The media not only fuel the flames of community outrage but
subject the accused to the blows of public condemnation

and eventual social and economic ruin. The alternative—posing a balanced controversy—may expose the media to attacks of putting children at risk.

Faced with this dilemma, all too often journalists seek the high ground of political correctness by avoiding the controversy altogether. Seattle and Tacoma newspapers and radio and television stations resisted coverage of the Wenatchee cases for months out of a belief that they might be criticized for helping pedophiles and not protecting children. "There was so much social pressure," said John Gilly, who has been a reporter for over twenty years, much of it at the *Tacoma News Tribune.* "It was so politically incorrect."

Striking the right balance in the controversy is no easy task for journalists, especially at times of government repression. In South Africa, said reporter John Carlin, "the people who accused you of lacking objectivity were those who committed the atrocities. They demanded 'balanced' coverage as a means of obscuring the injustice. I would take the position that I detected echoes in Wenatchee of the sort of thing I saw in South Africa on the part of the government, in the sense that, in my mind, there's a sort of transparent attempt to keep journalists from coming out with the truth. If you treated the claims with equal validity, it would obscure the truth," he said.

Richard Wexler, a former journalist and assistant professor of journalism at Pennsylvania State University, and current president of the National Coalition of Child Protection Reform, believes that in terms of media coverage, Wenatchee is a turning point. "What is striking is that the media learned to be more skeptical in Wenatchee" at the early stages of the prosecution, he said. San Francisco Bay area writer and screenwriter George Paul Csicsery agreed. Wrote Csicsery in the March 1996 edition of *Heterodoxy,* "Wenatchee is important not so much for what has taken place there, bizarre though that may have been, but because it marked a milestone in the way these allegations and trials have been represented. After years of helping to spread the epidemic of false accusations, the news media turned a corner in Wenatchee. . . . By the end of 1995 it was safe for most (but not all) reporters to use expressions like 'false allegations' and 'leading questions' in reference to child abuse cases.''

If the media tide has indeed turned, this fact may provide relief to many professionals who have written in dispute of popular beliefs about child sexual abuse at the risk of personal vilification and financial loss. Even FBI Agent Lanning, who has spent much of his professional life training, researching, and consulting in matters of child sexual abuse and is strongly committed to his concerns about genuine child abuse, is not immune. After he wrote that according to his investigation there was little corroborating evidence of organized satanic cults or sex rings molesting and killing children, Lanning was labeled a ''satanist'' who had infiltrated the FBI in order to conceal the problem of sexual abuse.

The fact that state and national media unflinchingly presented the controversies of Wenatchee may signal the eventual demise of an era of social hysteria surrounding allegations of child sexual abuse, and the beginning of a more reasoned approach to this immensely subtle terrain.

But we remain vulnerable to our prejudices and the seductive need to reduce the enormous complexity of our society to stark black and white terms. Well-meaning Wenatchee citizens and professionals yielded to the familiar spectrum of paranoia, political mind control, and inquisition. Few of us cared to intervene. Instead we acquiesced to the targeting of an unfavored population, mentally stripping away the layers of their humanity, much as we dehumanize our enemies at times of war. The concept of justice became abstract, removed by the legal tribunal as something free from personal accountability. Our compassion failed us.

In the end it is up to us as individuals to confront our fears and biases, the false security of our politically created monsters, the dangerous illusion of a black-and-white world, and our failures of personal and professional accountability. We are all part of the community of man. When all is said and done, the assaults on Wenatchee citizens are assaults on our humanity.

Experience should teach us to be most on our guard to protect liberty when the government's purposes are beneficent. Men born to freedom are naturally apt to repel the invasion of their liberty by evil-minded rulers. The greatest dangers to liberty lurk in insidious encroachment by men of zeal, well-meant but without understanding. (Court Opinion, *Olmstead v. United States,* 1928, by Justice Lewis Brandeis.)